Citizen
Coke

Citizen Coke

The Making of Coca-Cola Capitalism

BARTOW J. ELMORE

W. W. NORTON & COMPANY

New York • London

For information about permission to reproduce selections from this
book, write to Permissions, W. W. Norton & Company, Inc.,
500 Fifth Avenue, New York, NY 10110

For information about special discounts for bulk purchases, please
contact W. W. Norton Special Sales at specialsales@wwnorton.com
or 800-233-4830

Manufacturing by RR Donnelley, Harrisonburg
Book design by Ellen Cipriano
Production manager: Devon Zahn

Library of Congress Cataloging-in-Publication Data

Elmore, Bartow J.
Citizen Coke : the making of Coca-Cola capitalism /
Bartow J. Elmore. — First Edition.
pages cm
Includes bibliographical references and index.
ISBN 978-0-393-24112-9 (hardcover)
1. Coca-Cola Company. 2. Soft drink industry—United States.
3. Sustainable development. 4. Social responsibility of business.
I. Title.
HD9349.S634C6323 2005
338.7'663620973—dc23

2014022329

W. W. Norton & Company, Inc.
500 Fifth Avenue, New York, N.Y. 10110
www.wwnorton.com

W. W. Norton & Company Ltd.
Castle House, 75/76 Wells Street, London W1T 3QT

1 2 3 4 5 6 7 8 9 0

TO MY FAMILY

Contents

Illustrations follow page 212.

Figures

Citizen
Coke

A Creation Myth of Citizen Coke

I drank a lot of Coca-Cola. Growing up in Atlanta, the homeland of this famous soft drink, it was hard not to. After all, this was the product that helped make my town what it was. Few other southern cities could claim a business enterprise as big and powerful as the Coca-Cola Company. As former Atlanta mayor Andrew Young stated on the occasion of Coke's hundredth birthday in 1986, "When we talk about Atlanta's boom and our billions of dollars of new investments, you really have to give Coca-Cola credit." The company helped nurture what Young called a "global, international perspective in this city when other cities appeared to be returning to the Dark Ages."[1]

I realized over time that I was a Coke man for the same reason Milwaukee citizens were Brewers fans and Green Bay loyalists were cheeseheads: Coke was the industry that made my world possible. Coca-Cola, in my mind, was a builder. The Atlanta company was an ambassador to the world that we were proud to claim as our own because it was a force for good, a company recognized for its ability to solve problems wherever it went. It was a public citizen whose success ultimately improved the lives of those around it. This was Citizen Coke.

Coke had spent a long time, and a lot of money, promoting this image of selfless service. When Georgian pharmacist John Stith Pemberton created Coca-Cola in an Atlanta pharmacy in 1886, he advertised it as a "brain tonic" that "Cures Morphine and Opium Habits and Desire for Intoxicants." Drink this, Pemberton bally-hooed, and all your mental and physical anxieties will vanish. This was magic in a bottle for a country that had just suffered long hard years of war and Reconstruction. Coke offered liquid serenity for a nation on edge.[2]

From the very beginning, then, the Coca-Cola Company said it was in the business of public betterment, and its message was not entirely unfounded. Many of Coke's leaders over the years were mag-nanimous men who used corporate profits to build a better world. Pemberton's successor, Asa Griggs Candler, who ran Coca-Cola from 1891 to 1916, gained widespread popularity in Atlanta for his char-itable works. He was credited with executing monumental "golden deeds," such as bailing out the Atlanta real estate market during the Panic of 1907 and offering million-dollar loan guaranties and direct aid to help Georgia cotton farmers during an agricultural depression in the 1910s. Candler was Atlanta's "first citizen," a man who used his wealth to improve the lives of others. Upon his death, the *Atlanta Journal* eulogized, "Service, a beautiful and a noble term despite its worn usage, was the master motive of his well-nigh four score years."[3]

Robert Winship Woodruff, the "Boss" of Coca-Cola who remained the undisputed leader of the company from 1923 up to his death in 1985, garnered similar praise for being a man of the people. Wood-ruff gave millions of dollars, often anonymously, to charitable foun-dations around the world, and his largess helped to build formidable institutions in Atlanta, such as the Woodruff Arts Center and Emory University. In 1979, Robert Woodruff, along with his brother George, gave a $105 million gift to Emory, which was in fact the largest single donation to an educational institution at the time. I had a personal connection to Woodruff's beneficence, passing an imposing statue of the cigar-wielding Boss on my way to class at Woodward Academy, formerly Georgia Military Academy, a school Woodruff had attended as a child and generously supported as an alum. Other Atlanta residents have similar stories about Woodruff's humanitarian presence in their lives.[4]

But charitable work, according to Woodruff, was just a small part of what made Coca-Cola good for the world. He believed that the

Georgia Military Academy (GMA) cadet officers in 1908. A grimacing Robert Woodruff, future president of Coca-Cola, is third from the left, back row. I attended this K–12 institution, now Woodward Academy; it was renamed after Colonel Woodward, seated third from the left. I owe Robert Woodruff a debt of gratitude, as he generously supported my school with financial aid. In a way, he helped pay for my education.

business of selling Coke was philanthropy in and of itself. After all, by patronizing independent bottlers, local ingredient providers, and a host of private retailers, Coca-Cola helped create jobs even in some of the poorest parts of the world. Coke acted as a "priming agent," as one company executive put it, stimulating "a widening variety of trade activities" wherever it went. The key was outsourcing. Coke did not integrate backward into ownership and management of suppliers, and because of this, Woodruff proclaimed, it helped bring economic prosperity to benighted parts of the world. Coke was not "selling the world short," the Boss said, it was "selling the world long." It was doing more by doing less.[5]

What made Coke so appealing economically was that it seemed to ask very little for the rewards it generated. *Time* magazine captured this image of Coke in 1950: "Coca-Cola is not what the non-American thinks of as a typical U.S. business, like steel or automobiles. It is not a product of the vast natural resources of the land, but of the American genius for business organization. It rests on such intangibles as market analysis, sales training, advertising and financial decentralization." According to *Time*, Coke placed few demands on the provider communities that supported it. The company could grow without consequence for centuries to come, and the world would be a better place because of it.[6]

This illusion of self-sustainment helped Coca-Cola justify its expansion into communities around the world. The company was an invited guest in many international polities because it was seen as a low-cost enterprise that would stimulate local economies. Few stopped to consider what the company asked of them, thinking only of what they could ask of the company.

But as Coke began to expand its commercial empire in the latter half of the twentieth century, it became clear that the promise of big profits for little cost was more fiction than fact. Coca-Cola and other similar mass-marketing companies were consumers as much as they were producers, and they required natural resources in order to survive. Over time, Coke placed heavy demands on ecologies around the world. It was an organic machine whose perpetual growth was contingent upon the extraction of abundant supplies of natural, fiscal, and social capital in the places where it operated.

Like many other people across the world, I benefited from what Coke's profits provided but had only a vague notion of how those profits were generated. This book was an attempt to understand the demands Coke placed on provider communities that served its needs for the last 128 years, an attempt to examine Citizen Coke as a consumer rather than as a producer. It was as much a historical quest as a journey to understand the economic and ecological reality behind all that Coke I drank growing up.

Introduction

Coca-Cola was the world's most valuable brand in 2012. That year, the company was all over the map, operating in over two hundred countries and selling more than 1.8 *billion* beverage servings per day (one serving for every four people on earth). It was the twenty-second-most-profitable company in the United States, with revenues topping $48 billion and net income over $9 billion, making it one of the greatest profit-generating businesses in world history. By the twenty-first century, Coke had conquered the globe, its market reach unmatched.[1]

How did this happen? How did a patent medicine created in a small southern pharmacy in 1886 become one of the most ubiquitous branded items in human history?[2]

The easy answer is marketing. Some have claimed that Coke was successful because it was a "want maker," adept at conjuring up magical, eye-catching advertisements that persuaded people to buy its nonessential products. As the story goes, Coke's genius lay in its ability to link its product to patriotic events, American family life, and even religious iconography. Coca-Cola's advertising and promotional campaigns transubstantiated the company's sugary beverage into "an old friend, a piece of everyday life, a talisman of America," and it was this iconic status that helped to explain its commercial success.[3]

Rosy-cheeked Santa Clauses and smiling GIs in Coke's advertisements surely helped create consumer loyalty for its beverages, but this was only the veneer of what Coke had to sell. Behind the advertisements, Coke vended a concoction of sugar, water, and caffeine, packaged in glass, plastic, or aluminum. To be successful Coke had to turn these products of the earth into a real, drinkable beverage that could be placed on retail shelves all around the world.

In short, Coca-Cola had to acquire copious quantities of natural resources in order to thrive. By the mid-twentieth century, Coke was the single largest buyer of sugar in the world, the largest global consumer of processed caffeine, the biggest commercial buyer of aluminum cans and plastic bottles in the nonalcoholic beverage industry, and a major water guzzler. Here was a company with an unmatched ecological appetite for an array of natural resources. It gorged on commodities in order to make profits.[4]

Yet this hefty diet did not make Coke fat. Even as the company consumed more and more, it maintained a lean corporate figure, investing little in the productive industries that supported its growth. For the vast majority of its history, Coke did not own sugar plantations in the Caribbean or decaffeination plants in the United States or coca farms in Peru. It remained a third-party buyer, letting others engage in the oft-unprofitable business of mining and processing resources from the natural world.[5]

Coke's success, in other words, was not manufactured in-house. The company depended on infrastructure built and managed by a host of public and private sector partners. Indeed, it would not be unfair to call Coca-Cola the Forrest Gump of the twentieth-century economy, a native son of the American South that seemed to find his way into a dizzying array of global trading networks. The company became connected to numerous supply chains through corporate intermediaries counted among the biggest commercial titans of their day, including the Sugar Trust, Monsanto Chemical Company, Cargill, General Foods, Kraft, McDonald's, the Hershey Chocolate Company, and Stepan Chemical Company. These businesses fed Coke's insatiable demand for cheap commodities, and by doing more—by building factories and distribution facilities, warehouses and processing plants—they enabled Coke to invest less.

Government played a large role, too. Federal agencies subsidized farmers to fuel the production of corn Coke needed to produce its sweeteners. Local governments also invested in infrastructure, such as public waterworks and municipal recycling systems, which helped reduce the price of raw materials. Throughout the twentieth century, Coke's growth always hinged on its ability to use government scaffolding, its sleekness in part a product of expanded government power.[6]

Ultimately, Coke's genius, its secret formula in many ways, was staying out of the business of making stuff. The company consistently proved adept at tapping into technological systems that were built, financed, and managed by others. It maintained a slender organizational structure compared to other similarly profitable multinationals and kept off its books the costs and risks associated with natural resource extraction and ingredient production. It was the ultimate outsourcer, long before the term "outsourcing" became popular. Success lay in partnerships, and Coke proved masterful at making friends.

But *Citizen Coke* is not just the history of one soft drink. Coca-Cola is the main character in this book precisely because its dependence on others offers windows into much bigger worlds. To be sure,

Coke figures prominently, but many supporting actors populate the stage. Some are rivals of Coke, others allies, still others something in between. Each has a discrete history to tell, but it is in their interactions that the real story unfolds.

At its heart, this book chronicles the making of "Coca-Cola capitalism," a shorthand term I will use to refer to an outsourcing strategy first developed by America's mass-marketing giants at the turn of the twentieth century. I call it "Coca-Cola" capitalism because Coke deployed it so effectively, but there were other firms—Pepsi, McDonald's, software firms, and many others—that followed similar strategies to huge profits in the twentieth century. These companies channeled natural resources through global production and distribution networks that they did not own or directly manage. Often, this meant relying on public infrastructure to extract raw materials and transport finished products. By minimizing front-end expenses and distribution costs, a company functioning in this fashion could make substantial profits as a kind of third-party distributor of wares produced by others. It was an opportunistic, in-and-out strategy for making money; with virtually no plantations and few factories to weigh it down in specific locales, the company could go in search of new sources of supply as well as new markets for distribution wherever they were to be found.[7]

For years, Coca-Cola capitalism has been largely ignored in classic tellings of the rise of big business in America. The historical canon of corporate capitalism treats Coca-Cola and other similar consumer goods firms as masters of marketing but gives short shrift to their deftness in coordinating the transfer of natural capital through commercial channels. This book looks beyond Coke's advertising to explore the soft drink firm's role as a kind of commodity broker, bringing together technologies and infrastructure it did not own to create broadband channels of ecological exchange essential to the making of modern America.[8]

Coca-Cola capitalism emerged in an era of excess, the Gilded Age of the late nineteenth century, when cheap commodities extracted from ecosystems all around the globe were available in unprecedented quantities for commercial consumption. This was the dawn of American corporate monopoly, when gigantic industrial titans—the Sugar Trust, U.S. Steel, and Standard Oil—began to build huge factories to turn nature's bounty into cheap commodities for a nation hungry for consumer products. Government aided this expansion, offering both direct and indirect subsidies to encourage the development of large-scale agribusinesses and modern manufacturing facilities. It was on the glut of this industrial and agricultural output that Coke built its empire.

Coke's key contribution to the economy was making abundance transportable. It did this by first condensing a surplus of mass-produced commodities into a concentrated syrup that could be easily shipped to independent distributors around the globe. This dense parcel of biota could then be unpacked, diluted with water, and resold to consumers in massive quantities. In this way, Coke became a commodity compressor that made the bounty of the modern industrial food system digestible for global consumers. It was an anticoagulant for a congested economy, allowing stockpiles of commodities to flood freely through commercial veins to retail outposts all around the world.

But as Coke's trade arteries stretched into distant markets in the twentieth century, the company had to find new sources of abundance in order to prevent its many satellite buyers from becoming anemic. Coke simply could not afford to let supply-side scarcity slow its syrup stream to a trickle. It made money by transacting exchanges between independent producers and distributors with profitability always contingent upon increasing the flow of natural resources through its system. To survive, the company needed more nutrients to keep its expanding commercial veins filled. How Coke managed to keep company commodity channels replete with ecological lifeblood for over 128 years is the story that follows.

The ingredient label on the back of a Coca-Cola container is our road map. In each chapter, I examine one of the critical ingredients in Coca-Cola: water, sugar, coca leaves, caffeine, and high-fructose corn syrup. Glass, aluminum, and plastic, critical raw materials needed for Coke's empire, are the subject of the penultimate chapter, since Coca-Cola would never have been able to sell its product without copious quantities of these packaging materials. I explore the private sector partnerships and supportive state policies that enabled Coke to acquire natural resources from global providers at dirt-cheap prices. The narrative arc is both a corporate chronology and a journey through a Coke's life cycle, beginning at the point of extraction and ending in a consumer's body. We follow Coca-Cola as it transitions from the Gilded Age into an increasingly globalized international economy, asking how it managed to bring all these raw materials to market at such low cost.[9]

In short, this book is an environmental history of Coca-Cola capitalism, one that restores the connection between the Real Thing and the real ecologies that supported it. This is the first corporate history of Coke to offer this perspective. When scholars have discussed Coke's natural resource demands, they have often privileged moments of crisis when the company faced dire shortages of supply. Besides these brief glimpses into the company's environmental dependencies, Coke's materiality has largely remained the stuff of magic. Overlooked in past narratives was this question: why were instances of scarcity indeed so rare for Coke? After all, examining the company's ascendancy over the long term, one is struck not by the temporary checks to Coke's growth but by the firm's remarkable prowess at securing access to excess for such long periods of time.[10]

Ultimately, *Citizen Coke* shows how Coca-Cola was a product of abundance; it took a great deal from the earth to produce profits.

It was an extractive industry, even if its systems of extraction were often hidden, operated by others. To be sure, it was no U.S. Steel, a company that directly mined ore from the ground, but Coca-Cola nevertheless stimulated the growth of many industries connected to the land. Dependent on the relentless expansion of agricultural surplus, it patronized bottlers that extracted billions of gallons of water from aquifers, and it partnered with massive chemical processing plants to transform nature's bounty into commercial goods for sale.

Coca-Cola's ecological appetite was insatiable—enough was never enough. Year after year, the company demanded more of its suppliers, even when it appeared the push for growth was having unhealthy consequences—both for the environment and for consumers. By the end of the twentieth century, excess began to show at the back end of the business as millions of empty beverage containers formed mountains in municipal landfills and as human stomachs stuffed with high-fructose corn syrup began to bulge over belt buckles. Coke's commercial arteries were becoming clogged at their terminus, yet a constant flood of commodities continued to pour into the system.

Problems also emerged farther up the corporate bloodstream. Coke's bottling franchisees in arid regions of the world found that they had to dig deeper and deeper to access water resources from overstressed groundwater sources. Farmers in America's Midwest that supplied the corn to produce Coke's sweeteners became utterly dependent on tremendous quantities of fertilizers and pesticides to keep their monocrop farms afloat. Much the same was true overseas, where Coca-Cola's sugar and coffee suppliers placed heavy demands on local water resources and soil nutrients. All around the world and all along Coke's supply chain, nature was showing signs that there was nothing natural about Coke's perpetual growth.

It became clear by the twenty-first century that Coca-Cola demanded much of the world, and it was not at all clear that what it offered in return was worth the cost. Could this economic system of making money by scavenging on other industries' excess—in short, Coca-Cola capitalism—be sustained, both economically and environmentally, in the future? More importantly, should it? Turning to the past offers a starting point to answer these questions. So it is that we first go back to a time long before the problems of Coca-Cola capitalism manifested themselves, to tell the story of the birth of Citizen Coke.

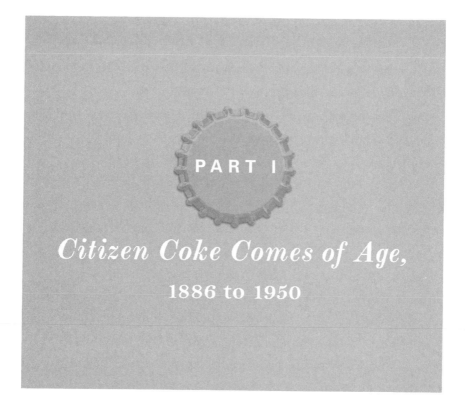

PART I

Citizen Coke Comes of Age,

1886 to 1950

LOOKING FORWARD FROM THE YEAR of Coke's genesis in
1886, it would have seemed improbable—indeed, downright fantastical—that Coca-Cola would become the most-
recognized brand in human history. As one Coke executive
would later put it, "The Atlanta venture needed only to be
described to be disproved." Here was a company whose founder
was a cash-strapped morphine addict operating out of a small
pharmaceutical shop in a southern city that had just begun
to implement the first Jim Crow segregation laws. No doubt,
Atlanta had made huge strides in attracting business and commercial development since Reconstruction, but many businessmen in the New South still lacked the financial resources to
launch a national—much less global—enterprise. Pemberton
was no exception, and early prospects for generating capital

from outside investors looked bleak. No wealthy magnates—no Carnegies, Vanderbilts, or Morgans—had signed on to the Coke project, and few investors were willing to risk money on the business as late as 1892.[1]

So how did Coke survive? How did it acquire the resources it needed—both natural and fiscal—in its early years to become such a successful enterprise by the 1950s?

What follows in Part I is the story of a corporation coming of age. We begin at a time when Coke's leaders were fortuneless, when, out of necessity, they forged partnerships and alliances with a host of private and public sector partners that helped them acquire the raw materials they needed at low cost. The company became a patron of some of the biggest industrial monopolies of the day, businesses such as Henry Havemeyer's Sugar Trust, which marshaled heavy machinery and industrial laborers to bring an unprecedented superfluity of cheap commodities to US buyers. Coke was a scavenger that capitalized on overproduction. It made money in the margins, selling a mixture of cheap commodities at markup prices. Glut was the prerequisite for profits.

Coke had been born in a world of excess, and its continued growth in the twentieth century would forever be contingent upon the perpetuation of abundance. As it grew, it demanded more—more sugar, more caffeine, more water. Coke's survival depended upon a political economy that encouraged cheap commodity production. As a result, Coke looked to government to help it get what it needed, to keep overstressed markets from crashing, to keep the bubble growing bigger and bigger.

1

Tap Water

Packaging Public Water for Private Profit

Just add a few squirts of carbonated water. Those were the instructions John Stith Pemberton gave his salesmen to pass along to Atlanta's soda fountain operators when they peddled the first batches of Coca-Cola syrup in the spring of 1886. This was a pilot run to see if Coke had the stuff of a best-selling patent medicine. Vendors were likely skeptical. After all, this was not the first time smooth-talking syrup salesmen had come calling, claiming to have an elixir that would change the world. Nevertheless, they gave it a go, dripping a sample of the thick brown syrup into a glass and filling it with about five ounces of bubbly water.

Neither Pemberton nor his first clients envisioned the flood those first few drops would unleash. By the end of the twentieth century, Coca-Cola bottlers and retailers would use over 79 billion gallons of water annually to dilute Coke syrup. But water added as an ingredient at bottling plants represented less than 1 percent of Coca-Cola's total

water footprint. The company consumed even more in the production of the bottles and agricultural commodities that went into Coke's
beverages—an estimated 8 trillion gallons per year. Considering the
whole supply chain, Coke's water consumption in 2012 exceeded that of
Sweden, Denmark, and Norway combined, enough to meet the annual
cooking, cleaning, and drinking needs of over 2 billion people, or close
to a quarter of the world's population.[1]

GAINING ACCESS TO ALL this water required making friends,
something Coke's founder realized early on when he first reached
out to Atlanta's soda fountain operators. In 1886, John Pemberton,
fifty-five, simply did not have the money, wagons, or staff to ship
finished beverages to retailers. He was a man who was struggling
financially with very little capital to spend on developing distribution infrastructure or setting up soda fountains. Though he had
established a successful drug business in Columbus, Georgia, prior
to the Civil War and opened a booming pharmaceutical operation
in the swanky Kimball House in Atlanta during Reconstruction, by
the 1870s his business fortunes began to sour. He, like many other
entrepreneurial pharmacists of the time, had tried to make it rich in
the patent medicine industry, a trade that was booming by the late
nineteenth century. Entrepreneurs nationwide were concocting various tinctures and nostrums, using the power of print media to market their potions to a nation seeking cures for headaches and pains
attendant to life in crowded and bustling Gilded Age cities. Most
of these medicines contained few or no real curative properties, but
this did not matter. Americans were eager to find relief for ailments
licensed doctors could not effectively treat. Pemberton believed he
could exploit this market and package a product that would attract
the weary and downtrodden. So he designed his own patent medicines, including Triplex Liver Pills, Globe Flower Cough Syrup, and

Lemon and Orange Elixir, advertising these products as panaceas for pain and digestive troubles.[2]

But success would not come in the first go-around. By the 1880s, the patent medicine industry featured "breezy competition," as the *Atlanta Constitution* put it, with hundreds of entrepreneurs looking to strike it rich with bizarre "snake oils" and "brain tonics." Pemberton was up against popular potions such as Pond's Extract, a "Vegetable Pain Destroyer," and Samartin Nervine, "the Great Nerve Conqueror," whose advertisements cluttered the hometown paper. The curative properties claimed for these medicines knew no bounds. Samaritan Nervine supposedly treated everything from "epilepsy" to "ugly blood diseases" and even "brain worry." Others, such as Wilbor's Compound of Pure Cod Liver Oil and Lime, promised to tackle deadly diseases such as "Consumption, Asthma, Diphtheria, and all diseases of the Throat and Lungs"— claims as difficult to swallow as the product must have been. For Atlanta's ladies, the list of medicines "specific for woman's diseases" was voluminous, including Bradfield's Female Regulator, which, "if taken during the CHANGE OF LIFE," would prevent "great suffering and danger."[3]

Thus Pemberton was up against sizable competition, and though he had short-term success in the trade, ultimately he was unable to produce a patent medicine that gained widespread popularity. As a result, in 1872, he filed for bankruptcy. Like many other Americans, Pemberton was hit hard by the Panic of 1873, and he would spend the rest of the 1870s paying off debts.[4]

In light of his financial hardships, Pemberton knew that he had to be judicious in choosing his next business venture. The smart strategy, from his perspective, was to hitch his future enterprise to a rising star in the industry, rather than to risk investing in an untested patent medicine. He knew, in other words, that piggybacking on the success of others was a smart business plan.

Pemberton found such an apt prospect for imitation in a French nostrum called Vin Mariani. Created by Corsican pharmacist Angelo Mariani in 1863, this patent medicine had achieved global success by the 1870s. People loved the drink the world over, and why not? At base, Mariani's concoction was a Bordeaux wine mixed with cocaine, enough cocaine to produce a noticeable buzz for habitual users. This was a beverage that offered quite a potent punch, but Vin Mariani's physiological appeal only partially explained its success. Angelo Mariani's great asset was his connection to a global pharmaceutical network that allowed him to get his product into the hands of cultural and political elites around the world. Famous figures such as Queen Victoria, President Ulysses S. Grant, and even Pope Leo XIII provided testimonials lauding Mariani's products that were later used in promotional advertisements. Though no evidence suggests that the pope ever approved the use of cocaine wine for communion (imagine the sales!), his advocacy of the beverage carried particular weight the world over. Mariani was able to tap into such social clout because of his cosmopolitan status. He came from a family of famous French chemists and doctors. An aristocrat with a home in Paris, the cultural epicenter of late-nineteenth-century Europe, Mariani was known as a "noted entertainer," often hosting "visiting strangers and local celebrities of the highest rank, his guests sometimes exceeding 400 in a single evening." He could milk social, fiscal, and political capital that few patent medicine competitors could rival.[5]

Pemberton certainly did not enjoy the same advantages as Mariani. He was cash-strapped and living in a Deep South city that many still considered behind the times. Hardly an international socialite, he suffered from debilitating stomachaches that kept him bedridden for weeks at a time. To numb his pain, he frequently indulged in morphine, a drug many suspected he first began using after being both shot and slashed with a sword while defending Columbus from invading Union troops on April 16, 1865, just days after Lee and Grant met to negotiate surrender at Appomattox Court House. Doped up and with little money in the bank, Pemberton was down and out. The best plan of action for someone like him was not to compete head-on with Vin Mariani but to capture a portion of the successful brand's market share through imitation. This was a strategy the Coca-Cola Company would later lambast in the twentieth century, but it was one that its capital-poor creator recognized as the only path to success in the 1880s.[6]

So Pemberton produced his own "French Wine Coca" in 1884 and began to sell it in Atlanta. He added some special ingredients to distinguish his product from Vin Mariani, most notably powder from the West African kola nut, but for all intents and purposes, his product was a complete knock-off of the French brand. Pemberton's wine became quite popular in the South almost immediately, thanks, no doubt, to the buzz Vin Mariani's advertisements had already produced about the benefits of coca wine. But success was short-lived. The South had become a hotbed for puritanical temperance agitators, and Pemberton feared that those believing alcohol to be a devilish vice would attack his beverage. The citizens of Atlanta approved a referendum banning alcohol sales in city saloons in November of 1885, and, in response, Pemberton believed it was prudent to create a temperance drink containing carbonated water rather than wine.[7]

So Pemberton got to work, mixing various essential fruit extracts and oils with sugar to create a new flavor profile for an alcohol-free soda beverage. Ingredients included nutmeg and Chinese cinnamon oil, lemon and orange flavoring, and vanilla. In all there were roughly a dozen flavor components, including kola nut powder and coca leaf extract. Kola nut contributed some caffeine to the beverage, although Pemberton also added caffeine from other sources, while the coca leaf extract imbued the drink with trace quantities of cocaine. All this was sweetened with lots of sugar, over 5 pounds per gallon of syrup, and cut with citric acid. Pemberton added so much sugar because he

knew that sweetness sold. After all, people loved French Wine Coca
not just because it contained cocaine and alcohol but also because it
was imbued with the sweet juices of Bordeaux grapes. On the suggestion of his new business partner, Frank Robinson, Pemberton called
the new drink Coca-Cola, changing the *k* in "kola" to a *c* to create a
catchy alliterative name.[8]

Pemberton's decision to make water (not wine) Coca-Cola's foun-
dational ingredient was more than just an expedient solution to temperance agitation: it was a way to save on costs. Water, unlike wine,
was cheap and in abundant supply in the South. Angelo Mariani, his
Italian competitor, was just a short jaunt away from the finest vine-
yards in the world, but Pemberton was thousands of miles removed
from the best Bordeaux producers. Eliminating wine as an ingredient
allowed Pemberton to develop an inexpensive product. To make the
beverage cheaper still, Pemberton minimized shipping expenses by
distributing concentrated Coca-Cola syrup, rather than finished beverages, to soda fountain operators in Atlanta and surrounding towns;
independently owned vendors added water to Pemberton's syrup.[9]

By this time, Pemberton had created the Pemberton Chemical
Company, partnering with Atlanta businessman Ed Holland and
two new arrivals to the city, Frank Robinson and David Doe from
Maine, both entrepreneurs who had been in the newspaper and printing business. Robinson and Doe did not come with much cash, but
they did offer Pemberton the use of a printing equipment they had
brought with them. Ed Holland, scion of an Atlanta banking mag-
nate, allowed Pemberton to rent out a new workspace in a redbrick
building owned by his father at 107 Marietta Street, a major commercial artery in the downtown corridor.[10]

Working out of his new office, Pemberton ran a sleek business.
His simple distribution system allowed him to exploit not only soda
fountain operators' infrastructural resources but also their marketing power. Pemberton chose respected establishments to peddle his

product, confident that customers would trust retailers they knew and liked.

Joe Jacobs's pharmacy represented the ideal. Located off Peachtree Street in the middle of Atlanta's commercial district, the shop was frequently packed with well-dressed men and women, the city's elite. Jacobs himself was a member of this high society, having earned a tidy fortune as a pharmacist in Athens, Georgia. When he came to Atlanta in 1884, he spared no expense bejeweling his business with elegant accoutrements. The soda fountain on the first floor, operated by Willis Venable, featured a polished marble countertop that stretched over twenty-five feet and floor-to-ceiling windows that invited customers to come inside. This was a place to see and be seen, and Pemberton wanted in.[11]

With the help of men like Jacobs, Pemberton sold approximately 600 gallons of syrup (over 76,000 servings) during the first spring of operation in 1887. There was a market for cheap drinks sold in glasses at soda fountains at a price point attractive to poor customers in the South. Rather than pay $1 for a bottle of French Wine Coca, consumers could purchase Coca-Cola for just 5 cents. With his new product, Pemberton had found a convenient way to mass-market cheap syrup through established fountain businesses.[12]

Early sales of Coca-Cola, however, did not allow Pemberton to dig himself out of his financial hole. In order to make money on a low-cost soda drink, Pemberton had to sell a lot of syrup, and though 600 gallons was a good start, it was not enough to recoup investment costs. By the end of 1887, Pemberton was out of money, and his original business partners—Ed Holland, Frank Robinson, and David Doe—were not much help in alleviating financial strains. Frank Robinson had sunk everything he had to help incorporate the Pemberton Chemical Company in January of 1886. David Doe left the company in 1887, and Holland remained detached from company affairs. Willis Venable, Joe Jacobs's soda fountain operator, who also invested early in Pemberton's enterprise, had little capital to offer the company, having spent a great deal of money on a recent real estate project. Throughout 1887, the future of Coca-Cola was uncertain, as feuding factions competed for ownership of the Coca-Cola formula.[13]

The title battle was a complete mess. It included original investors, as well as new stakeholders, such as Pemberton's son Charley and Atlanta businessmen George Lowndes and Woolfolk Walker. The dispute was not completely resolved until 1891, when prominent Atlanta pharmacist Asa Candler became sole owner of the enterprise by buying out competing investors claiming ownership of the Coca-Cola formula. A year later, Candler officially incorporated The Coca-Cola Company (with a capital *T*), offering one thousand shares at $100 to investment brokers in the Northeast. Determined to maintain control of the company, Candler held on to five hundred shares himself. By this point, Pemberton had passed away, having lost an extended battle with his gastrointestinal problems. He would never see what Coca-Cola was to become.[14]

COMPANY LORE AND MOST historical accounts portray Asa Candler as the savior of the Coca-Cola brand. Robert Stephens, a family friend of the Pembertons, described Candler's influence thus: "Coca-Cola became a go because it was pushed and pushed by an energetic man. . . . He paid them [Pemberton and associates] for something of no use . . . and he made it a go by his own efforts." As the story goes, Candler had grown up in rural Villa Rica, Georgia, a town some thirty-odd miles east of Atlanta founded by his gold-prospecting father. At the young age of nineteen, he left home to apprentice as a pharmacist in Cartersville, Georgia, with aspirations of becoming a doctor someday. In Cartersville he discovered there was money to be made in the pharmacist business, and he decided not to pursue medical school. In 1873, he came to Atlanta with plans to start his own business. With just a chunk of change in his pocket, he quickly worked his way up the ranks at an Atlanta pharmacy owned by George J. Howards, and by 1886 he had made enough money to go out on his own, establishing Asa G. Candler & Company, with headquarters right in the heart of the city on Peachtree Street. He was a self-described workhorse, a stoic man whose Methodist beliefs in discipline and personal sacrifice governed his business decisions. Having established a successful pharmaceutical operation of his own through thrift and hard work, he was looking to purchase patents for popular drugs. After tasting Coca-Cola in a soda fountain in Atlanta, he became keenly interested in becoming its promoter. He approached Pemberton in 1888 about buying the formula for Coca-Cola, and Pemberton agreed to the sale. Nevertheless, it would take Candler three more years to officially resolve competing claims to the title of the formula.[15]

After the purchase, Candler immediately developed an aggressive and organized marketing campaign designed to spread Coca-Cola quickly and efficiently throughout the South. He had a knack for creating widespread distribution networks. As a child, for example, he had started a mink-skin trading business that extended from his family's hunting grounds in Villa Rica to Atlanta—no small feat for a young teenager. Capturing the audacity of his adolescent undertaking, Candler later wrote: "Atlanta was thirty-six miles away and there was no railroad, but that seemed to be the best possible market, so I sent the skin in to town by wagon, and I said to myself, 'Maybe I'll get twenty-five cents!' I got a dollar—the first I had ever made."[16]

Candler would be equally courageous with Coca-Cola. He believed the key to the beverage's success was getting it into the hands of customers that had a track record of indulging in patent medicines, so he offered soda fountain operators in Atlanta and surrounding towns free samples of Coca-Cola, requesting distribution to their loyal customer base. He employed a small but loyal sales team, some, such as his son Howard Candler and nephew Sam Dobbs, with direct family ties. These "drummers," as they were colloquially known at the time, took Atlanta's rail lines out of town, heading in every direction to preach to soda operators the promise of economic prosperity that came with selling Coca-Cola. They enrolled the support of major grocers and retailers who in turn became local pushers, distributing syrup to smaller businesses in the community. Coca-Cola's drummers traveled far and wide, often working dawn to dusk, and their hard work paid off. By 1890, Coke could be found throughout the South, with less than half of sales that year coming from Atlanta. Five years later, Candler said that Coca-Cola was "now sold and drunk in every state in the Union," with annual sales of syrup reaching 76,000 gallons. Considering the fact that there were just fifteen drummers receiving salaries from Coke in 1899, this national conquest was remarkable.[17]

For many, Candler became the American dream's poster child, a self-made man who took a few thousand bucks and turned an obscure drink into a respected brand known around the country. As his son put it on the occasion of his father's death in 1929, it was Asa Candler "who discovered the potentialities of Coca-Cola and it was he who risked all to put it on the market and nurse it along until it was able to finance itself." Candler was a fitting figurehead for the Coke brand, certainly more appealing than the morphine addict Pemberton. Candler was to be the father figure, a man who sacrificed everything to nurture Coke to maturity.[18]

But Candler's success was less self-created than legend might have it. Candler could only risk meager funds on Coca-Cola because when he first signed on to the venture, he was reportedly $50,000 in debt and hoping to find a way out. Just like Pemberton, he had little money to invest in expensive distribution and production facilities. In fact, his decision to incorporate the Coca-Cola Company in 1892 was driven by his desperate need to raise capital, but he was unable to unload shares, drawing in just $7,500 from the initial offering. At that time, the Coca-Cola Company employed around thirty employees, including Pemberton's original business partner Frank Robinson, who would spend the next two decades designing Coca-Cola's advertising campaigns. But Robinson, while a master of print promotion, was no wealthy financier. If Coca-Cola was going to grow, Candler was going to need help.[19]

So Candler continued Pemberton's established business model of utilizing small independent vendors to help spread Coca-Cola far and wide—and the distribution system worked. Coca-Cola was able to expand rapidly into distant markets at low cost because it did not have to pay for shipping finished beverages; it just sold syrup. Candler could put barrels of syrup on one of the many trains heading out of Atlanta and expect soda fountain operators to add water—roughly 80 percent by volume of the finished product—at the point of sale. The shipping savings were incalculable. Coca-Cola would have gone bankrupt if it had not relied on soda fountains to supply its water. Instead, the company began accumulating cash, over $50,000 after expenses in 1896.[20]

Still, Coca-Cola faced competition from a number of well-established soft drink companies, some of which had been around a lot longer than Coke. Philadelphia's Hires Root Beer, for example, first emerged in 1876, the brainchild of pharmacist Charles Elmer Hires. By the 1890s, this root beer had gained national popularity, with Hires plastering promotional pitches in national print media, including the *Atlanta Constitution*, claiming that his beverage was "The Purest and Best Drink in the World." The concoction, made from a variety of wild root and berry extracts, was prominently featured in Joe Jacobs's weekly advertisements to the Atlanta community.[21]

Other drinks caused a similar stir. Moxie Nerve Food, conceived by Dr. Augustin Thompson in the mill town of Lowell, Massachusetts, made it to stores in Candler's hometown by the 1880s, and in

Waco, Texas, a pharmacist named Charles Alderton was slowly gaining a following for a new drink he had created in 1885 called Dr
Pepper—named, some contend, after a doctor whose daughter Alderton had once hoped to court. Though only regionally popular at first,
Dr Pepper would become a well-known national brand in the early
twentieth century.[22]

If Coke was going to beat out these competitors, it was going to
have to consider bottling its product in order to capture new customers in largely untapped nonurban markets. Candler, however, was initially opposed to this idea. He believed that developing an extensive
network of bottling enterprises would cost too much money. "I don't
think we want to have it bottled," he recalled saying to those who
proposed the idea back in the late nineteenth century, adding that
Coke had "neither the money, nor time, nor brains, to embark in the
bottling business." Candler also shunned the idea of partnering with
independent bottlers, fearful that these novice entrepreneurs, "who
care nothing about the reputation of what they put up," would ruin
the company's good name. Unlike the popular soda fountain shops
of the Gilded Age, which had become centers of cultural exchange
in the late nineteenth century, beverage bottling companies were
still very rudimentary in the 1890s, and there were reports that all
sorts of unwanted items—including dead animals, spiders, and other
insects—would end up in the bottles. Candler did not want to be
associated with shoddily run businesses.[23]

By now, however, the number of soda fountain operators selling
Coca-Cola had risen from just five shops in Atlanta to dozens more in
cities like Columbus, Birmingham, and Memphis, and some of these
independent businesses had decided to become Coca-Cola bottlers on
their own.

The first of these enterprising distributors was Joseph August
Biedenharn of Vicksburg, Mississippi, head of the family-owned
Biedenharn Candy Company. "Uncle Joe," as he was affectionately

known in the business, was just the kind of guy Candler wanted in the Coke family. He had grown up in Vicksburg in the years after the Civil War, the eldest son among fourteen children, and had worked his way up in the grocery business under the tutelage of his father, Herman Henry Biedenharn. Over the years, he and his family built a booming business and established quite a rapport with Vicksburgians. Biedenharn was a man people respected and admired. Thus, in 1890, when drummer Sam Dobbs came to town to sell Coke, he naturally called on Uncle Joe. Biedenharn, for his part, was already interested in expanding his soft drink business. He heard constant requests for soda water from his clients, so Coke looked like an attractive addition to Biedenharn's bottled beverage portfolio. He accepted Dobbs's 5-gallon keg of syrup and quickly sold all of it.[24]

Initially, Biedenharn acted as a kind of regional wholesaler, redistributing syrup received from Atlanta to other retailers in towns around Vicksburg. Within just a few years, Coke became Biedenharn's best-selling product. Consequently, he upped his contract from just 5 gallons of syrup to over 2,000 gallons annually by 1894, but there were still more sales to be had. As Biedenharn put it, "I wanted to bring Coca-Cola to the country people outside the limits of the fountain. Even in the cities the fountains were limited in number and scattered here and there. I could see that many town folks wanted Coca-Cola, but it was not easily available." So in 1894, Biedenharn began to put Coke in bottles. Uncle Joe used a rudimentary bottling system he had purchased "second-hand" from the Liquid Carbonic Company in St. Louis, Missouri, a firm that would become a major supplier of carbon dioxide to soft drink bottlers in the years ahead. The pilot project was so successful that he decided to contact Candler about a bottling franchise for Mississippi. His approach was direct— he sent Candler a case of his bottled Coke. Candler responded to Biedenharn minimally, stating that the bottled Coke was "fine" but adding nothing more. Despite this tepid response, Biedenharn continued to sell many hundreds of bottles to his customers and hand-somely increased his profits.[25]

None of this shook Candler's skepticism toward bottled Coke, but it inspired imitators. In 1899, two Chattanooga attorneys, Benjamin F. Thomas and Joseph Brown Whitehead, came to Candler with the proposition of developing a Coca-Cola bottling franchise that would reach markets well outside the South. Candler, believing the bottling enterprise to be a passing fancy, dismissively signed a fixed-price contract with Whitehead and Thomas. The contract, quite broad, gave them exclusive and perpetual rights to sell Coke in "bottles or other receptacles" anywhere in the United States except Texas, New England, and Biedenharn's Mississippi territory. Years later, the company would fight a bitter battle to gain back the rights to bottle Coca-Cola that Candler so flippantly granted the Chattanooga attorneys, but at the time, Candler did not suspect it would be of much consequence.[26]

He could not have been more wrong. With contract in hand, Whitehead and Thomas began to build a bottling empire that would spread across the country, making the Chattanooga lawyers rich. But their success was contingent upon the support of others. Neither Whitehead nor Thomas was a wealthy man capable of financing national expansion. Whitehead was the son of a Baptist minister from Oxford, Mississippi, who lived most of his childhood traveling the itinerant preacher circuit. He had scraped together enough money to attend law school at the University of Mississippi and secured a job as a Chattanooga tax attorney in 1888, beginning a twelve-year legal career that "was more rewarding in experience than financially." Benjamin Thomas enjoyed a more privileged upbringing. The son of a successful wholesale grocer in Maysville, Kentucky, he was able to go to school out of state at the University of Virginia and later completed his Juris Doctor at the Cincinnati Law School. He committed himself to a variety of business ventures, briefly working in the banking world and later forming several boutique legal firms in Chattanooga. Yet by 1899, the year he signed the Coca-Cola bottling contract, he was still struggling to strike it rich. Thomas had just enough money to open a rudimentary $5,000 Coca-Cola bottling enterprise in Chattanooga, whereas Whitehead had to request the assistance of another friend, John Thomas Lupton, to front half the cost of building his bottling plant in Atlanta. From the very beginning of the Coca-Cola bottling business, then, both Thomas and Whitehead had to rely on independent franchises to make their distribution system work, and they began, almost immediately, to license their contractual rights to bottle Coke to local bottlers across the country. In this way, Whitehead and Thomas sought to win expansive growth of the Coca-Cola bottling enterprise while effectively managing the capital risks associated with national growth.[27]

And the system worked. The Coca-Cola Company bottling network expanded from just a few bottlers in 1899 to roughly four hundred by 1910. Whitehead and Thomas became wealthy almost overnight, extracting a small fee for every gallon of syrup they shipped to a franchisee. Because they owned virtually no physical assets, simply negotiating the trade between the supplier of syrup and those that bottled and distributed it, fees quickly accumulated into tremendous profits. The parent bottlers were ultimately middlemen, not true bottlers. Thomas's and Whitehead's franchisees were expected to front the capital to build the physical bottling plants in towns across America. The majority of the risk was on the shoulders of these local investors.[28]

The Coca-Cola Company profited from this system, too. By 1914, net income topped $1 million, up from $200,000 a decade earlier, but profits did not tell the whole story. Revenues totaling more than $8 million far exceeded the property, equipment, and real estate costs of running the company's syrup plants, of which there were eight in the United States by 1923. These plants were small, as a letter from

Asa Candler to his son Howard in 1899 indicated. Hoping to open a syrup factory in Kansas City, Candler wrote: "We ought to be convenient to R. R. freight depots. Not necessary to be on high priced commercial street. We would need a good basement and one floor say 30 × 100 feet in size, where we could have water and light privileges. A suitable place we would have to take a lease on, hence ought to be able to get a low rate." Spending little capital on such small plants allowed Coke to create a huge advertising budget. In the mid-1910s, Coke spent over a million dollars a year on a flurry of advertising materials, including metal signs, serving trays, calendars, playing cards, wall paintings, and much more. According to one estimate, Coke distributed over 100 million promotional items in 1913 alone. Net income statements, in short, reflected only a fraction of the revenues the parent company was able to accumulate from syrup sales to bottling franchisees, much of which was reinvested in promotional accoutrements.[29]

The early success of Coke's bottling system inspired imitation. In New Bern, North Carolina, Caleb Bradham, an enterprising pharmacist and graduate of the University of North Carolina, partnered with local bottlers in 1905 to distribute his soft drink, Pepsi-Cola. Bradham had always been one step behind his Atlanta rival. He had introduced a beverage called Brad's Drink in 1893, which was essentially a knock-off of Pemberton's product. In 1898, he would rename the product Pepsi-Cola. True, there were differences in the formulas— Pepsi, for example, did not contain coca leaves—but for the most part, Bradham and Pemberton were trading in the same product: a caffeinated, sugar-charged, caramel-colored drink, laced with kola nut powder. Bradham, in other words, did with Coke what Pemberton had done with Vin Mariani: steal market share from a successful brand by mimicking its marketing strategy. Bradham took his cues from Atlanta, and when Coke proved bottling could make the company millions, Bradham decided to follow suit.[30]

• • •

BY 1911, CANDLER STOOD in awe of the bottling network he had reluctantly approved. "I cannot refrain from expressing my cordial appreciation for the high character of men who represent the bottling department of this corporation throughout the country," he said. "Without exception they rank with the best and most respected business men of their communities." Candler and the other executives in the Atlanta office knew that these local businessmen were pushing their product to new heights. They had supplied the cash—often generated by taking out loans—needed to build Coke's distribution plants.[31]

But franchisees offered more than just money to get Coke's bottling empire off the ground. They also provided important political and social capital that helped make Coke a "respected" brand in places far removed from the company's Atlanta headquarters. Consider the story of Georgia's third bottling franchisee, Columbus Roberts, who first began selling Coke in Columbus, Georgia, in 1901. Roberts was the son of a tenant farmer from a small town just outside Columbus, a native son of southwest Georgia attuned to the parochial peculiarities of the region. He was a man-about-town: president of the local chapter of the YMCA and the Kiwanis club, deacon at the First Baptist Church, and a member of the city water board. Every Sunday he could be found in church, and his contributions to the offering were always generous. He would spend more than $2.5 million over his lifetime supporting community causes in southwest Georgia and was even credited with saving the Baptist Mercer University from going bankrupt. Considering his place in Columbus society, when Roberts said Coca-Cola was the thing to drink, people listened. Starting with just one mule-drawn cart in 1901, he quickly convinced businesses around the city to sell bottles of Coca-Cola, bringing in enough sales in just his third year of operation to make over $17,000 in profits. For decades to come, the Roberts family remained the face of Coke in Columbus. They got rich making Coke rich.[32]

The Roberts family was not alone. There were the Sams of Athens, Georgia, the Harrisons of Greensboro, North Carolina, the Biedenharns of Mississippi, and many others, all of whom offered their family name to the Coke brand. It was their friendly smile and handshake, their local goodwill, that offered Coke its most effective advertising in towns across America. Coke became popular in part because popular people pitched the product. In the years ahead, Coke would lean on these small-town allies to fight a never-ending barrage of attacks from critics claiming that Coke was harmful to human health. It was Coke's bottlers, respected members of the local community, who would silence the critics and convince people that drinking Coca-Cola led to happiness and fun.

This was not charity work. Parent bottlers, local bottlers, and the retailers they served had a material interest in upping Coca-Cola sales because from top to bottom selling Coke generated profits. Like a toy that expands in water, Coke syrup's value ballooned at each step in the distribution network. The system worked like this. Between 1901 and 1914, Coca-Cola sold syrup to Whitehead's and Thomas's parent bottling operations for about a dollar a gallon. Considering the fact that the ingredients in a gallon of syrup cost around 60 cents, Coke made profits on these sales, but parent bottlers made money, too. This was because even though they purchased Coke syrup, they never took on the responsibility of shipping it to actual bottlers. By 1903, both Whitehead and Thomas sold their bottling plant facilities and focused on managing actual bottlers. They required their franchisees to pay a 6-cent royalty on every case they brought to market, a fee they justified for having brought the franchisee into the Coke family. This meant the parent bottlers made about 30 cents on every gallon Coca-Cola sold just because they owned the rights to the syrup under the original 1899 contract. By 1914, the parent bottlers had accumulated millions in profits. But the golden stream did not end there. Local bottlers receiving syrup at markup prices then diluted the concentrated mixture to make finished beverages in an 8-to-1 ratio, water to syrup. On average they could sell Coke to retailers for about 80 cents a case (24 bottles), which meant they were selling a gallon of syrup costing roughly $1.20 for over $4.00. Yes, these bottlers had substantial overhead costs, but with modest increases in volume sales, it was not uncommon for them to see substantial profits in a few short years. This was because retailers' demand for Coke was insatiable given the handsome returns soft drinks yielded at retail. The average grocer found that he could sell a case of Coke for about $1.20 (5 cents a bottle for 24 bottles), or a 50 percent markup from costs. This was a huge margin that brought in significant cash for small businesses.[33]

Still, even though there were profits to be made, bottlers had to take on substantial risks to get the revenue stream started. George S. Cobb, an early bottler from LaGrange, Georgia, put it well when he said, "Today so many people think that Coca-Cola was a gold mine, even to begin with, but that is far from the truth. . . . The early days were hard, very hard." J. J. Willard, a successful Coke distributor for many years, described the meager funds many bottlers had when they began their careers in the early 1900s. He noted that setting up a bottling plant required "capital of around $3,500"—approximately $80,000 in today's currency—which was often a major strain on cash-poor owners, forcing many bottlers to take out loans. There were many "plants where the owners found plenty to keep them awake at night." In Willard's account, several Coke bottling plants "ran out of working capital and ownership changed hands three and four times before becoming self-supporting." Willard told the story, for example, of one plant owner who later in life had "given away sums of six figures to hospitals, colleges and orphans' homes" but at first "frequently did not have carfare and was given credit by the street car conductors in his home town." Again, often the key to success was the connections Coke bottlers made to local credit-lending agents who could offer liquid cash to the bottling plant in critical times of need.[34]

By building plants and paying for trucks and truck drivers, bottlers allowed Coca-Cola to expand into new markets without substantially increasing the parent company's overhead costs. True, the Atlanta home office offered its bottlers a popular marketing label and substantial advertising support, but it did not offer much else in the way of pipes, power-engines, or pumps, equipment essential to turning gallons of concentrated syrup into a bottled product for consumer sale.

In fact, the main material investments that supported the growth of company bottlers flowed not from the Coca-Cola Company or from local businessmen but from city governments. The key ingredient was water: small bottlers with limited resources depended entirely on public water systems built, managed, and operated by municipalities.[35]

BY THE LATE 1880s, American businesses began to receive a huge boost from a host of new public works projects. This was the dawn of what would be called the Progressive Era, a period in which idealistic middle-class reformers began to call on state and city governments to take a more active role in ensuring the health and safety of Americans. In Coke's case, perhaps no other Progressive intervention was as important as the expansion of publicly funded, capital-intensive municipal water systems. As scientists began to uncover the mysteries of the bacteriological world during Reconstruction, municipal planners began to rethink water resource management strategies. The "sanitary idea," first made popular by English statesman Edwin Chadwick in the 1840s, had stressed that environmental pollution bred disease, and this certainty gave way to the germ theory by the

1880s, as engineers began to focus on combating the microscopic organisms that harbored fatal diseases such as typhoid, cholera, and yellow fever. By 1900, epidemiologist Theobald Smith's technique for spotting and rating coliform bacteria concentrations showed that many city residents were drinking filthy water. Bacteria levels were dangerously high, and municipalities responded by building mechanized filters, complex cast-iron pipe networks, and primitive chemical treatment systems to improve their water supplies.[36]

This marked a major expansion in the role of local government. In 1830, private companies owned 80 percent of the nation's waterworks, but by the 1880s, public agencies began to take over water system management. By 1924—a decade after the US Public Health Service implemented the first federal drinking water regulations—public utilities owned over 70 percent of the nation's municipal waterworks; by 1941, the figure stood at 80 percent.[37]

Waterworks, it turned out, required sewers to handle wastewater lest it foul what citizens drank, so governments began to replace open sewers with underground networks, curbing the dangers of overflow. They invested heavily to make sure that wastes were transported safely to locations far from the urban core. By 1920, over 80 percent of the country's urban citizens utilized public sewers, up from 50 percent fifty years earlier.[38]

Just how expensive were these water projects? They often required building reservoirs, dams, aqueducts, and new filtration systems powered by mechanical water jets to clean sand filters. For large cities the bill for constructing these systems could be enormous. For example, between 1905 and 1914 it cost New York City roughly $220 million to build two dams and an underground aqueduct system that channeled water to the city from the Catskill Watershed some hundred miles north of Manhattan, infrastructure that still serves the city today. New York also invested in improvements in what became known as the New Croton Aqueduct, which siphoned water from the Croton reservoir in Westchester County (almost forty miles outside the city). These two aqueduct systems, which were designed to serve over 6 million people, represented far and away the largest public waterworks system in the country, but other cities spent proportionally. Chicago and Philadelphia, both with populations over 2 million in 1917, managed water systems valued at over $30 million. The *Coca-Cola Bottler*, a publication of the Coca-Cola Bottlers' Association launched in 1909, praised Philadelphia's investment in a million-dollar water filtration plant, noting that before this public expenditure the city water "was often so dirty as to make one debate whether to bathe or not to bathe." In 1910, *American City* reported that the Kansas City government had issued $3,100,000 in bonds "for the purchase of waterworks, thereby exhausting the city's debt-making power for a number of years to come." In Coke's hometown, the Atlanta city government floated $950,000 in municipal water bonds to pay for the expansion of the city's water system between 1901 and 1907. In 1910, the city raised over $2 million to pay for further improvements. The Atlanta Board of Water Commissioners had an easy justification: this debt would help Coke and other city businesses, and without it "almost all our manufacturing industries, hotels, railroads and other large consumers of water would have to close down." By 1915, the total value of municipal public waterworks systems in the 204 American cities with populations over 30,000 people exceeded $1 billion.[39]

The costs to municipalities would rise over the next several decades, as cities still had to pay for labor, filtration equipment, and replacement parts to ensure steady service. After 1914, wartime demands for raw materials drove up the price for basic water system maintenance. *American City* reported in 1918 that "important waterworks construction materials, pipe, valves, hydrants, etc. have more than doubled in cost" because of the war, and labor costs, too, were on the rise. Lacking a means of generating enough revenue to cover expenses, cities perforce had to take on more debt. United States per capita municipal debt increased from around $12 in 1902 to over $60 by the end of World War I, driven in good part by water costs. Cities with high water treatment demands were the hardest hit. Knoxville, Tennessee, for example, spent roughly $100 a day, or $34,000 per year, to purify water coming from the Tennessee River, a stream that the US Surgeon General claimed in 1915 was "undoubtedly subject to pollution" and unfit for untreated consumption. Charlotte, North Carolina, which sourced its public water supply from the Catawaba River, faced similar costs.[40]

While cities paid big bucks to keep mechanical filtration machines running, Coke bottlers spent little for the large amounts of water they used. In 1921, there were over a thousand Coca-Cola bottlers operating in the United States, the vast majority using public water supplies, and they enjoyed remarkably low water rates. Milwaukee, for example, offered water to residents and businesses alike for just .005 cent per gallon. Prices would vary from city to city, sometimes dramatically, but competition among metropolitan centers kept rates down. In fact, most cities tried to entice industries by offering lower rates for higher water use. In New Orleans, where Coke was first bottled in 1902, city water sold for .01 cent per gallon for the first 100,000 gallons consumed but decreased in price to .007 cent for every additional gallon. Other cities, such as Pittsburgh, Kansas City, and Seattle, featured similar scaled pricing. At base, municipalities knew that cheap water attracted business, and they did whatever it took to remain competitive, even if this meant going into the red. The real winners were heavy industrial water users. In cities across the country, Coke bottlers often paid less than .01 cent per gallon for the public water they used.[41]

Even more than bottlers, the Coca-Cola Company accrued huge savings because of public investments in municipal water systems. Between 1891 and 1920, the company did little in the way of building infrastructure to support its growth. In the United States, Candler had approved the construction of just eight syrup-manufacturing facilities in commercial transportation hubs such as Chicago, St. Louis, Dallas, and Los Angeles. In so doing, he sought to capitalize on the expansive railroad networks that now radiated from these bustling commercial centers.[42]

Here was another instance where public infrastructure investment had paid off for Coke, and this time the federal state was doling out the cash. The West and Midwest had become checkered with railroad lines in the final decades of the nineteenth century, thanks in no small part to federal government financing. During the Civil War, Congress had approved bond issues and land grants to help pay for the construction of the nation's first transcontinental railroad, the Pacific Railroad, which was completed in 1869. Over the next two decades, similar federal aid supported the construction of the Southern Pacific Railroad and the Northern Pacific Railway. Although these lines connected cities, they also traversed thousands of miles of country where there were no people or markets for goods. Since revenues generated by these lines failed to keep up with costs of maintenance, railroad companies required continued government assistance well after rail lines were built. Without state support there would have been no transcontinentals, and without the transcontinentals there would have been no way to move goods along smaller branch lines from major commercial centers, such as Chicago, St. Louis, and Dallas, to towns in rural portions of the country.[43]

Railroads built in large part with public subsidies were the commercial veins that would feed America's heartland, and Coke flooded these channels with sugary syrup. In the years ahead, Coke increased the flow of syrup to soda fountains and the company's many bottlers, with total syrup sales reaching nearly 18 million gallons in 1923, a remarkable increase from about 881,000 gallons two decades earlier. All this syrup came from only eight United States factories—in

Atlanta, Baltimore, Chicago, Dallas, Kansas City, Los Angeles, New Orleans, and New York—and seven overseas plants in Canada, Cuba, and France (more on this international story later).[44]

IN THE 1920s, COKE'S national conquest through outsourcing would continue, but under new leadership. By 1916, Asa Candler—now in his late sixties—had tired of the endless quest for profits and began to remove himself from the day-to-day business of pushing Coke. That year, after much nudging and convincing from family and friends, Candler decided to run for mayor of Atlanta, a position he handily won. After the election, he turned over the reins of his company to his mild-tempered son Howard and dedicated himself to public service. But even from his new perch in city hall, Asa Candler continued to keep a close watch on the company, maintaining title to more than half of Coke's outstanding shares, an ownership stake he had preserved since incorporation in 1892.[45]

From the beginning of his presidency, Howard Candler showed interest in handing over the company to outside investors, and in 1917 he put before the board of directors a banking syndicate's offer to buy out the company for $25 million. This initial proposal failed, however, in large part because an angry Asa Candler reentered the picture, publicly humiliating his son by voting in person at a board meeting "against the proposition of Mr. Howard Candler." Asa might have left his post as president, but he was not going to let his hard work be passed out of family hands so easily.[46]

But soon another plan for sale emerged, this time orchestrated by company vice president Samuel Dobbs. Dobbs had been miffed that Candler had passed him over when considering Coke's next president, believing he was better qualified to assume the post than Asa's son, and in many ways, he had a right to complain. Howard was a reluctant salesman who hated haggling with retailers, a fact perhaps best captured in a letter he once wrote to his father during a sales trip to New York City. In his missive, Howard griped about having "to go in frequently and talk to a proprietor and his help of soda-men and clerks" and expressed distaste for the "sociable" aspects of the trade. "I don't like that," he whined, adding in future correspondence that he preferred to be home in Atlanta.[47]

Where Howard Candler showed shortcomings, Dobbs shined. He had risen quickly in the Coca-Cola Company, from salesman to director of advertising to vice president in just over a decade and a half, gaining kudos from higher-ups for his brilliant performance throughout. He was a natural salesman noted for his excellent public speaking ability and negotiating prowess. Thus, when Candler began to hint at retirement, Dobbs believed that he himself was the ideal candidate for company president. Naturally, Howard's appointment hit Dobbs hard. To make matters worse, when Asa Candler doled out his company stocks to family members in 1917—further distancing himself from the Coke business—Dobbs did not receive a single share. He was hurt, but instead of brooding over what he saw as an act of blatant nepotism, he did something about it. In 1919, he conspired with his friend Ernest Woodruff, one of Atlanta's most powerful banking barons, to organize a potential buyout, determined to gain back his proper standing in the company.[48]

Ernest Woodruff, then fifty-six, had gained notoriety in his long career as president of the Trust Company of Georgia. The Georgia native was a prickly man, noted for his frugality and cutthroat business strategies. Combative and unsociable at times, he was nevertheless a talented dealmaker who had helped to raise capital for some of Atlanta's most prominent businesses, including the Atlantic Ice and Coal Company, Atlantic Steel, and the Continental Gin Company. But his tactics had often proved questionable. He was accused of such scandalous actions as breaking into his competitors' law offices to peruse important business documents, an allegation that was never proved in court but nevertheless colored people's perception of him for years to come. Woodruff's win-at-all-costs reputation made him unpopular among many of Atlanta's most respected businessmen, including Asa Candler, and for this reason, Dobbs worked hard to obfuscate the Trust Company's involvement in the buyout. He pulled in representatives from Chase National Bank and the Guaranty Trust in New York to help broker the deal and kept Woodruff's name out of the paperwork during negotiations, even though Woodruff was the one who brought the banking interests together.[49]

The ploy ultimately worked. The banking syndicate created the Coca-Cola Company of Delaware, which carried out the buyout of the Atlanta business, offering the Candler family $15 million in cash and $10 million in preferred stock in the new company (Coke chose Delaware because it offered lax incorporation regulations and a favorable corporate income tax rate). The Delaware corporation planned to raise enormous amounts of capital by issuing 500,000 shares of stock to the public. Believing this would be a boon to original investors, Howard Candler and Coke's board of directors approved the deal in August of 1919.[50]

The decision to take Coke public proved profitable. In the first day of trading on August 26, the newly incorporated firm unloaded over 417,000 shares at $40 a pop. The Candlers got rich, and so did Woodruff and his cronies. As part of the deal, members of the syndicate negotiated purchase of stock at just $5 a share. Some estimates suggest that this underpriced stock yielded an immediate $2 to $5 million in profits for the insider collective.[51]

Yet not everyone was happy with the windfall, most notably Asa Candler, who saw in the Coke deal an unfortunate turn of events: his immediate family was no longer in charge of Coke. After the buyout, Sam Dobbs was appointed president of the newly incorporated company and Howard Candler was given the chairmanship, a move simultaneously designed to keep the Candlers happy while removing Howard from a key operational role. Corporate hegemony remained with Woodruff and Dobbs, who, along with Eugene Stetson, another member of the banking syndicate, held on to enough stock to form what constituted a "voting trust" on the board. They would make all the important decisions at Coke in the years immediately ahead. Asa Candler saw through the hollow gesture and expressed outrage when he learned what Woodruff had managed to do. He knew the Candlers had lost control of the company, and for the rest of his life he would lament the sale.[52]

From the very beginning of the new regime, the hard-nosed Woodruff sought to streamline Coke's business, and he targeted the bottlers, especially Thomas's and Whitehead's parent operations, as a major source of waste. He believed the company could make greater profits by cutting out the middlemen. As it was, the company was forced to offer the parent bottlers syrup at a fixed price, even if the cost of raw ingredients increased. This became a major problem after World War I when sugar prices rose precipitously. Woodruff was frustrated that these costs could not be passed on to bottlers and believed the company's franchisees were getting a free ride. As a result, in the winter of 1920, the company told the bottlers that their franchise agreements were "contracts at will," meaning that they could be revoked or rewritten by the Coca-Cola Company. In response, the parent bottlers sued in the Fulton County court in April of 1920.[53]

Veazey Rainwater and George Hunter headed the bottlers' fight in court. In 1906, Rainwater had taken over Whitehead's parent bottling operation in Atlanta, at the young age of twenty-four. Eight years later, George Hunter, Benjamin Thomas's nephew, had assumed responsibility for the Chattanooga-based parent bottler. Both young businessmen found the Atlanta corporate office's position contemptuous, a slap in the face to the many local businesses that had made

Coke a nationally recognized brand. It was the bottlers, they claimed, that had put forward the capital to make Coke's distribution system work, they who had worked day in and day out to push the product into new markets, and the cost of growth had been enormous. Collectively, Hunter and Rainwater explained, Coke bottlers had spent approximately $20 million to build bottling plants and pay for trucks and other equipment vital to the business. Some bottlers had failed, assuming risks the parent company was not willing to take. The company had no right to bully these enterprises that had sacrificed so much for the Coca-Cola brand.[54]

Rainwater's and Hunter's claims rang true for local bottlers on the ground but were less accurate when applied to their own operations. After all, the parent bottlers were much like Coke: sleek businesses that made money by outsourcing industrial operations. Like the Atlanta syrup-manufacturing business, Rainwater's and Hunter's bottling firms did very little. They made large profits by essentially passing on syrup contracts to actual bottlers. Considering the limited investments they put into the system, they were making a lot of money, and, from Coke's perspective, if anyone should be asked to contribute a little more during tough times, it was the parent bottlers who deserved to be targeted. Woodruff was determined not to give in to these profit leeches.[55]

By May of 1920, with no resolution to the conflict in sight, the parent bottlers and their franchisees decided to take their case to the federal level, refiling their complaint in a Delaware district court. Simultaneously, sugar prices skyrocketed, from 9 cents a pound to over 20 cents, and in the next several months, the Coca-Cola Company ate huge losses totaling some $7 million. The Coke system was in jeopardy, and both parties in this protracted fight realized that something had to be done. Finally, in May of 1921, as the case came before the Third Circuit Court of Appeals, compromise prevailed. In a move that bucked standard civil procedure, the presiding judge in the case brought both legal teams to the bench and urged them to get over their differences. He pointed out that both the Coca-Cola Company and the bottlers would ultimately lose out if they did not come up with some way to share the burden associated with changing commodity prices. The justice's suggestion seemed wise. After all, attorneys for both parties had watched as Coke's stock prices continued to drop as the conflict persisted. With self-preservation on everyone's mind, the parent bottlers, their franchisees, and the Coca-Cola Company agreed to amend the bottling contracts to include adjustments for fluctuations in sugar prices.[56]

The crisis had been averted, but the struggles of the past year had seriously shaken the Coca-Cola Company and suggested to many a dire need for a change in leadership. In the wake of the sugar debacle, the board had criticized both Howard Candler and Samuel Dobbs for not finding a way to avoid losses. The directors wanted a new, inspirational leader, and they found him in Ernest Woodruff's thirty-three-year-old son, Robert W. Woodruff.

LOOKING AT ROBERT WOODRUFF'S early life, few would have predicted that he would become the leader of one of the most profitable companies in the world. As a cadet at the Georgia Military Academy in College Park, Georgia—now my alma mater, Woodward Academy—he had been at best an average student despite his father's efforts to keep him focused on his studies. At Emory College in Oxford, Georgia, he did not fare much better, flunking out after just one semester. But if he wasn't very book smart, he certainly showed promise in the business world. After leaving Emory in 1909 at the age of nineteen, he soon accepted a position in the Purchasing Department of Atlantic Ice and Coal, a business his father had helped to incorporate years earlier. After just weeks on the job, he initiated a bold move to replace the company's horses and buggies with brand-new trucks from the White Motor Company of Cleveland, Ohio. Walter White, president of the Cleveland operation, had witnessed Woodruff's bargaining tactics in the deal and decided to poach the young businessman from Atlantic. At White, Woodruff quickly stood out among his peers and gained promotion after promotion. By the time Coke began looking for its new leader, he had risen to become vice president of the motor company. His salary was substantial— over $75,000 a year—so large, in fact, that when Coke offered him the presidency, which came with a salary of $36,000 a year, he was initially hesitant to accept. Stock prices were down in the wake of the sugar scare of 1920, and Robert was unsure a rebound was on the horizon. Later, he would claim that it was his 3,500 shares of Coke that changed his mind: "The only reason I took the job was to get back the money I had invested. . . . I figured that if I ever brought the price of stock back to what I had paid for it, I'd sell and get even. Then I'd go back to selling cars and trucks." But considering the fact that he purchased his stock at the insider price of $5, compared to $40 offered on the open market, making good on his investment was hardly his biggest worry.[57]

Whatever the case may be, Woodruff never returned to the White Motor Company. Over the next six decades he would help make Coca-Cola one of the most popular brands in world history.

Woodruff's strategy was by no means revolutionary. In fact, he believed the best way forward was to capitalize on Coke's unique corporate structure, one that had been in existence since Candler took over the company. Woodruff believed outsourcing, rather than growing larger through integration, would remain an effective strategy for making profits. He captured this business philosophy in his oft-used motto, "If you can get somebody to do something better than you can do it yourself, it's always a good idea."[58]

If Woodruff was willing to let go control of some things, though, he was monomaniacal about preserving the uniform taste profile of Coca-Cola, and in the early years of his presidency, he became increasingly concerned about ensuring that bottlers used water that would not affect the taste of finished products.

One major concern was chlorination, which came into commonplace use in public water supplies in the late 1920s. Commenting on the positive effects of chlorination, the *Southern Carbonator and Bottler* noted in 1922, "Bacteria are destroyed by the chlorination process now used in nearly all municipal water supplies. . . . There is little danger that it [municipal water] will be unsanitary." In the final analysis, the journal advised bottlers against using "private wells for your carbonating plant water supply, unless you are prepared to put in the wells as carefully and to watch over them as jealously, as should the people who are responsible for your public water." Reflecting on the radical advancements of the Progressive Era, Dr. William Pratt Heath, Coca-Cola's leading chemist and a company vice president, praised the nation's public water systems in 1932, exclaiming, "Any water which is pure enough from a sanitary point of view to be used by cities and communities is pure enough for the beverage industry."[59]

Despite the benefits, the new age of chemical water treatment presented real problems for Coke bottlers. While chlorine killed a host of pathogens, it also distorted the flavor of many soft drinks and in some cases even altered or bleached the color of carbonated beverages. For a company that prided itself on preserving a uniform product, this was a major problem, especially considering the broad reach the company had attained.[60]

Robert Woodruff was obsessed with ensuring that a Coke in Alabama tasted the same as it did in California. Coke, Woodruff believed, was in the business of satisfying people's taste buds, and its profitability came through its consistent delivery of a product that tasted the same no matter where it was sold. Summarizing Woodruff's mission, Coke president Paul Austin explained years later, "We sell only one thing, taste. We use water as a vehicle to carry that taste to the customer." Water with certain impurities, even if harmless to health, threatened the Coca-Cola system.[61]

In response to these growing concerns, Coke's water quality team in the 1920s began research into carbon filtration technology developed by the military during World War I for use in gas masks. Dr. Heath, one of the only Coke executives to know the company's secret formula, headed the Quality Control Division. A graduate of Georgia Tech, Heath had run the Crystal Carbonic Laboratory in Atlanta, which produced the carbonation equipment needed to produce the bubbles in Coke's finished beverages. When Coke acquired Crystal Carbonic in 1919—a rare early instance of vertical integration—Heath became a key company chemist. Heath recognized that gas mask technology had produced a workable dechlorination system, and before long he pushed Coke bottlers to start installing carbon filters at their plants. By 1939, these systems existed in twenty-five bottling plants nationwide. As it always had, Coke required bottlers to front the cost for innovation.[62]

The quest for the perfect taste, however, was not complete. Each region of America had aquifers containing "impurities" that thwarted company desires to create a uniform product. Water supplied by cities in the Midwest tasted different from municipal water in the Northeast. As the *National Carbonator and Bottler* noted in 1937, "In some few sections of the United States, the water furnished by municipalities can be used directly in the preparation of beverages without any further preparation," but in other regions of the country "the supplies are so highly mineralized that products prepared from the untreated water are of inferior quality."[63]

Woodruff knew that Coke had to become more involved in the day-to-day operations of independent bottlers if it wanted to achieve the uniformity it desired, so in July of 1941 he created traveling laboratories in the Bottlers' Service Department, a group of water quality specialists and company chemists tasked with enforcing water quality standards for company bottlers. Members of the traveling laboratories motored around the country in whitewashed trailers, advising local bottlers on how to decrease the alkalinity of their water supplies, eliminate unwanted organic materials suspended in source water, and improve the overall operation of their filtration and treatment equipment. These chemists were soft drink sommeliers, astutely sampling small vials of water from bottling plants, giving grimaces or nods of approval depending on sample quality. Ultimately, however, the parent company insisted that it would only diagnose problems, not fix them. Bottlers paid for repairs and installations that traveling laboratory chemists recommended.[64]

Fortunately, thanks to continued government investment, public water remained safe to drink in the 1940s. The Great Depression had certainly diminished cities' ability to finance capital-intensive public works projects, but in the end the federal government saved the day. Its vehicle, the Public Works Administration (PWA), created under the National Industrial Recovery Act of 1933—part of President Franklin D. Roosevelt's New Deal—began to channel money toward municipal infrastructure projects. In 1936, for instance, the PWA provided over 80 percent of the funding for municipal wastewater system improvements, offering $109 million to local governments across the country for sewer construction. By the end of the New Deal, the PWA had constructed over 2,400 water projects, at a cost of over $300 million.[65]

In light of the growth of public waterworks infrastructure and improvement of older networks, the Coca-Cola Company admitted that many of its bottling filtration and treatment systems were merely "insurance" in case of "seasonal variations or emergency conditions." Not all bottlers invested in the best equipment to purify public water supplies. In 1957, when an agent of the Food and Drug Administration (FDA) stopped by for an unannounced inspection of an Atlanta plant, C. R. Bender, a company official at the Atlanta branch, explained "that only in very rare cases was the installation of water treating equipment based on a need to bring the water up to US Public Health Service standards but rather because of some objectionable chemical quality of the water which would affect the quality of the beverage. For this reason, it was pointed out, he might not find complete water treating systems in every bottling plant he inspected."[66]

As usual, it was all about money. Coke bottlers chose to use public water because it cost them virtually nothing. Between 1900 and 1950, bottlers rarely mentioned any concerns about the price of public water. In fact, it was so cheap that the Central Coca-Cola Bottling Company of Richmond, Virginia, America's tenth-largest Coke bottler, did not even list water as a separate expense in its company ledgers. Rather, water costs were bundled into "Heat, Light, Power, and Water" charges. In 1951, all four of these items totaled an expense of just under $49,000, or less than 3 percent of the bottler's total operating expenses.[67]

The expansion of public waterworks into increasingly rural areas of America allowed entrepreneurs outside the country's major metropolises to invest in the Coke system. A businessman in a small rural town had an advantage over big-city bottlers because he could tap into public piping right in his own backyard and service consumer outlets close to his plant. City distributors would not be able to compete, because the cost of shipping bulky finished beverages out to the country would be punishingly high. As a result, the number of bottlers operating in rural areas increased dramatically. By 1950, there were roughly 1,050 Coca-Cola bottlers operating in the United States, up from just 400 in 1909. Each bottler controlled a small, circumscribed territory, virtually all happily tapping into public pipes constructed and maintained by local governments.[68]

With the help of these investments, successful Coca-Cola bottlers brought in seven-figure profits. In 1944, for example, Central Coca-Cola of Richmond posted a net income of over $1.2 million, with a profit margin of about 14 percent. To be sure, to make these profits bottlers had to invest a great deal of cash. Central, for example, reported operating expenses totaling over $4.6 million—a far cry from the first bottlers' $3,000 start-up costs—but so long as returns seemed promising, bottlers were willing to make these immense commitments. Nevertheless, the question remained, would these investments continue to yield riches in the postwar era? Looking back at over fifty years of growth, many bottlers considered the prospects for prosperity endless.[69]

BY MIDCENTURY, THE COCA-COLA Company had achieved a remarkable feat: it had completely outsourced the extraction and transportation costs of its product's largest ingredient by volume. It was literally all over the map thanks to the hard work of hundreds of independent bottlers and municipal governments that invested their own capital to build the pipes and plants needed to channel Coke's finished beverages to American consumers.

But while Coke succeeded in off-loading the cost of water extraction in the first half of the twentieth century, it still had to buy many syrup ingredients that could not be so easily sucked out of the ground—or indeed come from America at all. Most of Coke's key ingredients came from environments outside US borders. Bringing them into the country at low cost would require the help of the federal government and powerful international business partners.

2

Waste Tea Leaves

Recycling Caffeine Found in Other Industries' Trash

C affeine, a white, crystalline stimulant in its pure form, is every-
where. It is the most ubiquitous drug in the modern industrial
food system, found in a variety of natural and synthetic beverages,
from coffee and tea to sodas and energy drinks. People consume it
every day, when they get up in the morning, at lunch, and after din-
ner; many confess that they cannot function without a morning cup of
joe. Caffeine is thus an intimate part of most people's lives, something
so familiar, so commonplace that few stop to question its presence.

But do we really know caffeine? If you asked a Coke drinker, for
example, where the caffeine in her soft drink comes from, do you
think she would have an answer? Would you?

As it turns out, caffeine is more enigmatic than its mundane
place in our lives might suggest. The commercial conduits that channel this drug to consumers' bodies are complex and have remained
largely hidden over the years. Yes, most people know something of

the coffee and tea trade, but what of processed caffeine? How did companies like Coke acquire this drug in copious quantities and at low cost? To answer these questions, we have to return to the late nineteenth century, when the modern industrial apparatus for caffeine processing emerged.

AT THAT TIME, JOHN Pemberton, Coke's creator, was fixated on using caffeine extracted from the West African kola nut, the fruit of the evergreen kola tree indigenous to West Africa's tropical forests. Pemberton erroneously believed that the caffeine from the kola nut was superior to caffeine "as obtained from tea or coffee in this country." He was convinced Coca-Cola could outcompete rival beverages by using this exotic variety of caffeine, rather than commonly available stocks. But the issue with kola trees was that they were grown far away and not in great numbers; extraction costs would be high. By the late 1800s, England and Germany had invested in colonial kola nut operations in West Africa, hoping to stimulate production, and they even experimented with transplantation at New World outposts, such as Jamaica. Despite these colonial investments, production remained modest by the end of the 1800s, with total annual exports to England totaling just 18,000 pounds by 1899. Coke needed to find another—and more economical—source of caffeine.[1]

Pemberton never abandoned kola nut extract entirely, preserving a small quantity of ground-up powder in his final formula, but he nevertheless decided to pursue alternative ways of acquiring the majority of Coca-Cola's caffeine from other, low-cost sources. Fortunately, there were ample caffeine stocks available elsewhere. Tea and coffee production reached unprecedented heights by the end of the nineteenth century, as vertically integrated producers used new industrial machines to increase throughput and annual yields. In this world of abundance, Western consumers could afford to be picky and often preferred only select coffees and teas. The inevitable result was that low-grade beans and leaves—produce that failed to meet quality standards—often languished in warehouses. By the late nineteenth century, international tea exchanges in Europe had become inundated with "tea sweepings" (broken or damaged leaves), which were long prohibited by law for use in consumer products, both in the United States and England. This waste became a gold mine for Coke as major chemical processing firms transformed it into a powerful drug.

In the late 1880s, Merck of Darmstadt, Germany—one of the world's leading pharmaceutical firms—and other chemical processing companies began to buy damaged leaf fragments at international tea warehouses. Considered garbage by tea traders, this refuse could be processed with lead acetate to extract caffeine. Recycling damaged tea leaves, Merck reduced its front-end expenses and expanded caffeine sales. The German firm also produced a kola nut extract, but the majority of its caffeine came from cheap tea sweepings. The pharmacological love affair with kola nut had begun to wear off, and by the turn of the century, few scientists in the United States or overseas saw any reason to prefer caffeine derived from kola nut to that from tea or coffee. As one Ohio State University scientist explained in October 1901, extensive studies had shown that the kola nut "does not possess any marked properties" not found in other caffeine-containing materials. Nonetheless, Coke's first president, Asa Candler, remained loyal to Pemberton's kola nut extract. He kept it as a component of the trademark formula, albeit merely in trace quantities, fearful the government might attack the company for misbranding if it completely removed kola nuts from Coca-Cola.[2]

The soft drink industry did not immediately realize the full benefits of the tea-waste reclamation system because Merck had no incentive to pass on savings to Coca-Cola and other American buyers. The United States had yet to develop a chemical-processing enterprise that could compete with Germany's, and very few European suppliers serviced international markets in the 1890s. Enjoying a virtual monopoly, Merck could control caffeine prices without fear of being undersold by rival suppliers abroad.

In 1895, however, Dr. Louis Schaeffer, an immigrant chemist from Stuttgart, Germany, came to Maywood, New Jersey, to build the first caffeine extraction plant in the United States. Schaeffer, now thirty-nine and having trained at German universities and worked in the German chemical industry for over two decades, was not alone in Maywood. He would be one of several German chemists and pharmacists that would come to town in the 1890s and early 1900s, converting it from a sleepy suburb of New York City, fifteen miles distant, into an industrial center specializing in chemical manufacture. The main attraction for these entrepreneurs was a rail line running right through town that would make shipping in raw materials and delivering finished products to consumers easy. By the start of World War I, Maywood boasted no fewer than five major chemical-processing firms engaging in a variety of pharmaceutical enterprises.[3]

Building the caffeine processing plant in Maywood was costly, especially considering US trade laws that required all imported tea sweepings to be mixed with lime and a pungent flavoring extract (a provision of the 1897 Tea Importation Act designed to keep adulterated tea out of the United States). The Schaeffer Alkaloid Works complained that it had to pay higher duty and freight costs for the heavier blend. Even so, Schaeffer managed to turn a profit, and by the beginning of the twentieth century, the company had become one of Coke's chief caffeine suppliers. In 1910, the company combined with other businesses in town, becoming the Maywood Chemical Works.[4]

Other American chemical firms quickly followed Schaeffer's lead. In 1904, the Monsanto Chemical Works began commercial production of caffeine from imported tea sweepings. Monsanto was a new player in the chemical industry. In 1901, just fifteen years after Coke got its start, John F. Queeny, a native Chicagoan and thirty-year drug industry veteran, founded the Monsanto Chemical Works in St. Louis, Missouri, naming the firm in honor of his beloved wife, Olga Mendez Monsanto. The company began with one product line, saccharin, an artificial sweetener derived from coal tar that was slowly becoming popular among industrial food producers. This was a risky undertaking considering market conditions. Queeny was the only saccharin producer in the United States, and he was up against a powerful German monopoly that frequently cut prices to drive the new competitor out of the market. He also did not have a lot of money, having drained his savings to get his $5,000 operation up and running. Queeny needed a friend, and he found one in Coke. At that time, the Coca-Cola Company was looking for a cheap sweetener that it could blend with sugar to make Coke syrup. Coke wanted to reduce ingredient expenses, and this seemed like a reasonable means of doing so. In 1903 and 1905, Coke purchased Monsanto's entire saccharin supply, which provided a huge boost to the chemical company in its infancy. Today, Monsanto's website still credits Coke with helping the company "survive" in those early years. Without Coke there would be no Monsanto.[5]

When Monsanto diversified into caffeine processing in 1904, it offered Coke yet another domestic supplier. Monsanto and Schaeffer's Maywood firm grew apace throughout the decade, curbing Merck's domination in the international caffeine market. In 1908, both American companies successfully lobbied for a law allowing tea sweepings to enter the United States without being doused with lime and asafetida. The amendment made Maywood Chemical Works and Monsanto even more competitive with foreign producers; by 1914, domestic caffeine producers filled over two-thirds of America's processed caffeine needs.[6]

This tickled Asa Candler, Coca-Cola's president in the 1910s. He, like John Pemberton before him, wanted to find the cheapest supply of caffeine possible. He could now reap the benefits of a competitive market that allowed Coca-Cola to buy its chief stimulant at just $3 a pound. Considering that 6 ounces of Coca-Cola in 1914 contained around 76 milligrams of caffeine, the caffeine cost in one serving of Coke was less than .06 cent.[7]

For the time being, cost was not an issue, but what did threaten Coke's caffeine delivery system in the Progressive Era was a rising concern about the adverse health effects that accompanied caffeine consumption. Indeed, powerful cultural forces challenged the idea that the company's caffeinated beverages were safe for society. Profitable relationships with front-end suppliers were well settled; now Coke had to worry about a different segment of the commodity chain: the human body.

BY THE BEGINNING OF the twentieth century, the United States had become the earth's largest coffee importer. Americans had long preferred coffee to tea in part because tea retained lingering associations with British imperial rule. By 1910, America's per capita consumption of coffee reached a hefty 12 pounds, up from 9 pounds in the 1880s and just ⅛ of a pound in 1783. Annual tea consumption, more modest, stood at 1 pound per capita by the 1910s.[8] Coffee, in short, was the more patriotic beverage.

All that caffeine made people jittery. Caffeine's molecular structure is similar to that of adenosine, a neurological depressant—akin to alcohol or sedatives—made naturally by the body. When caffeine replaces adenosine in receptors in the brain, signals that provoke sleepiness or inhibit arousal never fire. As a result, high concentrations of caffeine in the blood can disrupt the normal functioning of neurochemical pathways, leading to a host of physical ailments including dyspepsia and nervousness. Feeling these physiological effects, heavy caffeine consumers and public health officials began to question whether this drug was in fact an innocuous stimulant appropriate for daily consumption.

Concerned about the human health costs of the nation's caffeine craze, public health reformers began an anti-caffeine movement in the early 1900s. This movement was part of a much larger pure food and drug campaign that blossomed after 1906, the year muckraking journalist Upton Sinclair published *The Jungle*, which offered a horrifying exposé of the unsanitary conditions in Chicago's meatpacking industry. Sinclair's work touched off a debate about the safety of the modern industrial food system and sparked new interest in government regulation of major food producers. Many came to believe that federal experts should play a more significant role in deciding what foods and chemicals were safe for public consumption.

The anti-caffeine crusade was in many ways fueled by opportunistic businessmen. Entrepreneurs such as C. W. Post, one of the biggest American cereal tycoons, diligently fed growing fears about caffeine in the early 1900s through advertising campaigns that pushed coffee substitutes as the healthful alternative to caffeine beverages. Post developed a famous coffee imitation in 1895, a potpourri called Postum made from various cereal grains. To sell his product, he published ads in national newspapers that featured testimonies from coffee drinkers complaining of nervous disorders allegedly connected to excessive caffeine consumption.[9]

The caffeine debate also heated up in local and state politics. Throughout the country, state legislators proposed bans on caffeinated beverages following the turn of the twentieth century. In North Carolina, a state senator submitted a bill to the 1907 general assembly that would have prohibited the sale and distribution of all caffeine drinks in the state. Despite considerable support, the bill's opponents ultimately defeated it by a narrow margin of 51 to 39. In Alabama, Texas, Louisiana, Mississippi, and Georgia, state representatives proposed similar restrictions on caffeine beverages.[10]

Local beverage bans often singled out Coca-Cola as a particularly injurious consumer product, in large part because it appeared to be a perversion of nature. Progressives highlighted the fact that caffeine was added to Coca-Cola by company chemists, suggesting that there was a conspiracy to imbue the beverage with addictive properties. Speaking in favor of a caffeine ban in 1909, a Texas representative argued before the state assembly, "The reason they put this dope in Coca Cola is to create craving and to have such an influence upon the human system as to cause a constant craving for more and thus sell the drink."[11]

Coke defended itself against such accusations by countering that its drinks contained only "pure caffeine" identical to that found naturally in coffee and tea. Asa Candler, Coke's evangelical president and a churchgoing man who was staunchly opposed to intemperate behavior, stressed this point in a letter designed to discourage support for the proposed 1907 North Carolina caffeine ban. Writing to his "friends in North Carolina," Candler reassured consumers that Coca-Cola "does not contain as much caffeine as is to be found in the average cup of good coffee or tea." There was nothing dangerous, much less sinful, about the soft drink, Candler insisted.[12]

This argument reflected Victorian assumptions about what purity meant in the context of Progressive Era debates about food and drug policy. In the late 1800s and early 1900s, the terms "pure" and "natural" became increasingly interrelated. In a world where urban citizens had begun to live far from the main centers of food production, the field and pasture became romanticized landscapes and the food-processing plant the site of adulteration. In many ways, to be pure was to be from the land, to be from "nature." In linking his products to agricultural products such as coffee and tea, Candler sought to dispel any concerns that his beverage could be harmful to human health.[13]

Food purity advocates were not convinced, especially USDA Bureau of Chemistry chief Harvey Washington Wiley. Popularly known as the "crusading chemist," Wiley was deeply concerned about rising caffeine consumption in America and vowed to do something about it. Since 1902, he had headed a division known as the "poison squad" at the Bureau of Chemistry, a group responsible for testing various preservatives and chemicals that were entering the nation's food supply. Under the Pure Food and Drug Act of 1906, Wiley's division acquired enforcement powers to seize any food or beverage product shipped across interstate lines suspected of containing an "added poisonous or other added deleterious ingredients which may render such article injurious to health." For Wiley and his team of chemists, a primary mission was to protect public health by terminating the production and distribution of misbranded consumer products.[14]

It was with this objective in mind that Wiley ordered the seizure of forty barrels and twenty kegs of Coca-Cola syrup shipped from Coke's Atlanta factory to a Chattanooga bottler in October of 1909, which was interstate cargo subject to federal regulation under the commerce clause of the Constitution. Outlining his grievances against the Coca-Cola Company, Wiley explained, "The extraction of caffein [*sic*] from any of its natural sources and the use of it in beverages which by their manner of use give no suggestion of containing this product, appear to me to be an objectionable practice, irrespective of any opinion regarding the injurious qualities of this alkaloid." In filing a lawsuit, he was determined to open consumers' "eyes to the dangers of extending use of caffeine beyond those beverages in which it naturally occurs."[15]

Wiley had long waited for this moment. His superiors in the US Department of Agriculture had denied his numerous requests to prosecute Coca-Cola for violation of the food and drug law. He had first petitioned for seizure of Coke syrup in November of 1908 but was told by George McCabe, the USDA solicitor, that there was no case to be made against Coke. In February, the response was the same. The Board of Food and Drug Inspection rebuffed another Wiley appeal, suggesting that if the department moved against Coke it would have to take on coffee and tea importers as well, an absurd proposition.[16]

But Wiley was persistent, full of confidence, and not one to take no for an answer. Here was a Harvard-educated man who would begin his autobiography with the immodest assertion that he had "studied" his "accomplishments" and "found them more interesting than my theories." Since joining the USDA in 1882, Wiley had sought a landmark case that would bring him fame and posterity. Twenty-five years later, he was still searching for his big break. Though he had helped push through the Pure Food and Drug Act and professionalized the Bureau of Chemistry, he still felt hemmed in by the higher-ups at the USDA. In his mind, this was his moment to shine, to show the world his true mettle.[17]

Wiley's case against Coke went to trial in the United States District Court for the Eastern District of Tennessee in the city of Chattanooga starting March 13, 1911, calling forth headlines all across the country—"Claims Coca-Cola Unsanitary," "The Caffeine in Eight Coca-Cola's Would Kill," "Coca-Cola on Trial." The *Charlotte Daily Observer* called the trial "one of the most important" tried in a southern federal court, while the *American Druggist and Pharmaceutical Record* labeled it "a record case in many respects." Wiley was in the spotlight. National newspaper coverage included anecdotes about his weekend excursions into the countryside with his new fiancée, Anna Kelton, a beautiful young librarian over thirty years his junior. Wiley attended extravagant dinners and gave public lectures to Chattanooga's finest aristocratic societies, reveling in his celebrity status.[18]

Supporting Wiley in his starring role was a team of famous personalities and international scientists, including Oswald Schmiedeberg of the University of Strasbourg, considered by many to be the leading pioneer in pharmacology at that time. Wiley also leaned on Reverend George R. Stuart, a well-known Southern Methodist preacher based out of Cleveland, Tennessee, who served as a government witness in the case and sermonized about the moral depravity of caffeine addicts. The state was not holding back, appealing to both science and God to make its case.[19]

The government's legal team—headed by the United States district attorney for the Eastern District of Tennessee, J. B. Cox, and his assistant W. B. Miller—focused its argument on proving two main points: that Coke contained an "added ingredient, caffeine," considered "injurious to health," and that Coke was misbranded because it no longer contained coca leaves even though its name suggested it did. In the case of caffeine, the emphasis was on the words "added ingredient." The government believed that it could easily show that the caffeine in soft drinks was not a natural component of the consumer product, but rather an adulterant added with the express intent of stimulating addiction.[20]

Miller and Cox had their work cut out for them. They faced the talented and experienced Atlanta law firm of Candler, Thomson, and Hirsch, Coca-Cola's general counsel. Name partner John Candler, Asa's younger brother, had served on the Georgia Supreme Court from 1902 to 1906, and his colleagues, Harold Hirsch and W. D. Thomson, were both graduates of the prestigious Columbia University Law School. Hirsch, who took over chief responsibility for the firm's Coke dealings in 1909 at the young age of twenty-seven, was a particularly pesky legal adversary. Born into a wealthy Jewish family from Atlanta, Hirsch had captained the University of Georgia football team in 1901 and had a reputation as a hardworking center linebacker. He brought a similar pugnaciousness to the courtroom, evidenced by dozens of trademark cases he brought against Coke imitators by 1911. Now in his early thirties and with numerous successful suits under his belt, he would lead Coke's charge against the government.[21]

Of course, it did not hurt that the fight would take place in Coke's backyard. People loved the company in Chattanooga, the birthplace of Coca-Cola bottling. This was Coke country, and it was also a southern city suspicious of federal meddling in local affairs. Miller and Cox needed to show that they understood the concerns of local people in the community, that they understood Tennessee culture and customs.

Race became the mechanism Miller and Cox used to appeal to local jurors. On the first day of the trial, they called Food and Drug Inspector J. L. Lynch, who had conducted an extensive investigation of Coca-Cola's Atlanta syrup plant in July of 1909. Lynch testified that he had witnessed the making of Coca-Cola syrup and described the room where ingredients were blended together. Lynch offered that a "negro cook" did most of the work: measuring out various ingredients from labeled containers, dispensing these ingredients into a steam-heated copper kettle, and then stirring the heated mix with a large wooden ladle. The prosecution focused on the dress and demeanor of the black cook:

MILLER: This negro cook that was on the platform and dumping ingredients into the kettle, could you state how he was dressed?

LYNCH: Well, very scantily, a dirty undershirt, his shoes were badly broken, the bare feet were sticking out through them in parts, and he had on an old, dirty pair of trousers.

MILLER: State whether or not he was perspiring?

LYNCH: Yes, freely.

MILLER: Could you state whether or not he was chewing tobacco?

LYNCH: Yes, sir.

MILLER: Did he expectorate from time to time, and if so, where.

LYNCH: Whenever he happens to want to, just wherever it fell, on the platform and on the floor.

MILLER: Was that the same platform that he was dumping these barrels from over into the kettle?

LYNCH: Yes, sir.

MILLER: Now, in dumping the barrels, or contents of the barrels, in the kettle, state whether or not a portion of the contents were left on the platform.

LYNCH: Yes, sir, a considerable amount of the sugar fell on the platform.

MILLER: And how would the cook get that sugar on the platform, the sugar that fell on the platform? How would he get it into the kettle?

LYNCH: Shove some of it with his feet and also part of it with a board.

MILLER: With his feet?

LYNCH: Yes, sir.[22]

Here was an egregious violation of Jim Crow segregation, one Miller and Cox believed would assuredly disgust the southern jurors. How could they bring themselves to drink this stuff, a beverage tainted with the spit and sweat of a racial outcast? If there ever was a drink that was contaminated, impure, surely this was it.

The horror story continued as the government called more witnesses to testify to the dangers of Coke. John Witherspoon, a physician in nearby Nashville, Tennessee, and a government witness in the case, testified that he had treated numerous patients suffering from the "Coca-Cola habit." He spoke of "young people" who consumed "eight, ten, fifteen or twenty" Cokes a day, quantities that disrupted the normal functioning of the heart. According to Witherspoon, they looked like "morphine habitués so far as their efforts to try to control" their Coke cravings. Coca-Cola, in his telling, was corrupting Tennessee's youth. Physician Louis Le Roy from Memphis, Tennessee, maintained that kids were not the only victims. He admitted that he himself had become a Coke addict, consuming "half a dozen or so bottles a day," and that only with great resolve was he able to "leave it alone."[23]

In some instances, the government contended, Coke consumption could even prove fatal. Two pharmacologists testified that rabbits and frogs given experimental doses of Coca-Cola syrup had died in their labs, but J. B. Sizer, an attorney for Coca-Cola, later proved these claims to be overblown. In one case, rabbits had been given unreasonably huge quantities of Merchandise #5, Coke's kola nut and coca extract. If a human were given a commensurate gargantuan dose, Sizer argued, no doubt there would be harmful side effects. And as for the frogs, they were fed enormous quantities of caffeine given their body weight, proportional concentrations no coffee addict could ever hope to guzzle down.[24]

In the end, none of this jousting mattered. Coke's legal team realized that they had a way out. If they could prove that Coke was not misbranded and that caffeine was not in fact an added ingredient, they could circumvent the question of whether or not caffeine was harmful to human health. Though Coke's attorneys called witnesses to counter government expert testimonies about the adverse physiological effects of excessive caffeine consumption, they decided less than twenty-three days into the trial to approach the bench and ask Judge Edward T. Sanford to dismiss the case on the grounds that the government had failed to prove Coke was misbranded, proof needed in order to bring suit against the company under the Pure Food and Drug Act. R. H. Williams, another Coke attorney, explained Coke's case to Judge Sanford: "My legal proposition is this . . . if we can show that it [Coca-Cola] is an article known and sold under its own distinctive name, and which does not contain any added poisonous or deleterious ingredient, we are excepted from the provisions of this law." Williams went on to say that Coca-Cola was a distinctive trademark whose properties were well known to the public. People knew caffeine was an ingredient in the drink. How could it be considered an adulterant?[25]

After mulling over Williams's argument for a few days, Judge Sanford instructed the jury to decide in favor of Coke, stating that the lack of evidence to support the government's contention that Coca-Cola was misbranded provided grounds for the dismissal of the case. Explaining his findings to the jury, Sanford held, "I am constrained to conclude that the use of the word 'added' as applied to poisonous and deleterious ingredients in articles of food other than confection-ery, in sections 7 and 8 of the Act, cannot be regarded as meaning-less." He offered an example: "Sausage cannot be deemed adulterated within the meaning of the Act, however deleterious to health some of its normal ingredients may be, provided that, as manufactured and sold, it does not contain any other poisonous or deleterious ingredi-ents added to its normal and customary constituents." Coke was like sausage, "a distinctive name which clearly distinguishes this particu-lar compound from any other food product." It was a beverage known to have caffeine in it. In fact, in Sanford's reasoning, "Coca-Cola without caffeine would not be 'Coca-Cola' as it is known to the public and would not produce the effect which the Coca-Cola bought by the public under that name produces." He therefore concluded "that as a matter of law the Coca-Cola in question is not to be deemed as adul-terated by the presence of caffeine as an 'added' ingredient within the true intent and meaning of the Act."[26]

Coke and its supporters popped the champagne and worked the press. Georgia's *Columbus Daily Enquirer* labeled Sanford's verdict a "sweeping" success for Coca-Cola, adding that the "decision failed to sustain the government in any of its contentions." A company advertisement run in the *Daily Oklahoman* featured Dr. Schmiede-berg's expert testimony about the healthfulness of caffeine paired with the statement that the testimony "was brought out at the trial in Chattanooga—U.S. Gov't vs. The Coca-Cola Co.—at which trial the

Government lost." In Chicago and New York, the company offered free booklets "telling of Coca-Cola vindication at Chattanooga."[27]

But the government's legal team was not done with Coke. After a five-year battle in the Court of Appeals, the government finally took the case to the Supreme Court in 1916. There, the Court reversed Judge Sanford's verdict, with Chief Justice Charles Evans Hughes stating that caffeine was indeed an added ingredient in Coca-Cola. In his opinion, Hughes cited the technicality that caffeine was mixed by hand in the "second or third melting" of the syrup to justify his classification of the ingredient as "added." Furthermore, he described Sanford's decision as "inadequate" because it "failed to take account of the design" of the Pure Food and Drug Act "to protect the public from lurking dangers caused by the introduction of harmful ingredients." If the lower court's finding was upheld, "the statute would be reduced to an absurdity. Manufacturers would be free, for example, to put arsenic or strychnine . . . into compound articles of food, provided the compound were made according to formula and sold under some fanciful name which would be distinctive." He therefore ordered that the case be retried on the issue of whether caffeine was in fact "a poisonous or deleterious ingredient," a question, he believed, "was plainly one of fact which was for the consideration of the jury." In those words lay potential disaster for Coca-Cola.[28]

THE RETRIAL WAS NOT the only major threat facing Coke in 1917. Even if the company won the suit in Sanford's court, the company's source of cheap and abundant caffeine, waste tea leaves, was under threat. As we will see in the next chapter, sugar was perhaps the biggest concern in 1917, as the company struggled to acquire enough sweetener to meet increasing market demands, but military interdictions during World War I also threatened caffeine procurement chains. Blockades cut US companies' access to waste tea leaves needed for caffeine production, and Axis-power embargoes totally halted the importation of processed caffeine from German chemical companies, which theretofore had supplied roughly 98 percent of US caffeine imports. Freight costs for transporting waste tea leaves increased dramatically from 65 cents per 100 pounds in 1914 to over $1.50 by the end of the war. Considering that chemical-processing companies needed over 45 pounds of damaged tea leaves to produce just 1 pound of caffeine, the new freight charges put punishing burdens on US producers.[29]

Caffeine prices naturally skyrocketed. Prewar, in 1912, the Monsanto Chemical Works, now one of the largest caffeine suppliers in the United States, reported international prices hovering around $3.22 per pound, but by July of 1916 prices approached $17. Coca-Cola had no choice in the short run but to dip into its inventories and wait out the wartime market. Company vice president Sam Dobbs highlighted Coke's grave situation in April of 1917, just days after the US Congress declared war on Germany: "We are finding it exceedingly difficult to secure sufficient amounts of sugar and other material to keep our plants running."[30]

Dobbs and Coke's top leadership proposed a radical solution to the company's problem: reduce Coke's caffeine content. Besides drastically lowering the company's demand for a scarce commodity, doing so would appease government attorneys waiting for retrial of the *Forty Barrels* case. On November 12, 1918, the company approved a 50 percent reduction in the caffeine content of Coke—from over 76 milligrams per serving to approximately 38 milligrams (about the same amount as can be found in a 12-ounce Coke today and about half the amount contained in a strong shot of espresso). Coke's action proved good enough for the government's legal team in Chattanooga. They never requested a decision on whether caffeine in Coke was in fact injurious to public health and returned all confiscated kegs and barrels to the company.[31]

It seemed the storm had passed, but Justice Hughes's 1916 Supreme Court decision would cause serious problems for Coke as it sought to protect itself against imitators. Just three years after the *Forty Barrels* Supreme Court case ended, Coca-Cola was embroiled in the fifth year of a trademark suit against J. C. Mayfield's Koke Company of America. Ever on the lookout for imitators, Coke attorney Harold Hirsch had initiated the case, arguing that Mayfield's signature beverages, Dope and Koke, clearly infringed on Coca-Cola's trademark. This was standard practice for Hirsch. He had joined Coke's legal team just a year before the passage of the landmark Trademark Act of 1905, which strengthened an 1881 law granting corporations legal powers to protect their brands in federal courts. He was determined to use the new law to quash Coke's imitators and helped organize the company's Investigation Department in 1915 to help carry out this objective. Hirsch's team included professional detectives from the distinguished Pinkerton National Detective Agency, an outfit renowned for hunting the great Western outlaws of the late nineteenth century—Jesse James, Butch Cassidy, and the Sundance Kid. Pinkerton's motto was "We never sleep," and that aptly described Hirsch, who filed hundreds of injunctions over the next three decades against imitators, almost a suit every week by some calculations, in order to prevent potential competitors from piggybacking on Coke's success.[32]

The Koke case proved particularly unnerving for Hirsch. Mayfield had lots of money and every intention of fighting Coke to the bitter end. This was not some backwoods businessman who could be bullied or overwhelmed by a corporate giant. Mayfield had been one of John Pemberton's business partners in Atlanta and even claimed title to the original Coke formula. He had been in the soft drink business since the 1880s and was doing quite well with Koke. Here was a worthy challenger for Hirsch, now in his second decade as Coke's head attorney.

The suit originally went to trial in an Arizona district court, the state in which Mayfield organized his company in 1911. Hirsch won this first trial handily in 1916, as District Judge William H. Sawtelle gave a resounding decision in favor of Coke. He was "convinced that when the witness Mayfield adopted the name 'Koke,' he did so with the deliberate purpose of representing his goods to be the product and manufacture of the Coca-Cola Company." The decision was in some ways surprising since Coca-Cola had not trademarked the word "Coke" at this point (that would come in 1945). Nevertheless, Coca-Cola was colloquially known as Coke by 1920, and the judge believed Mayfield was trying to capitalize on this fact. There was no doubt, Sawtelle continued, that Mayfield designed Koke "for the purpose of reaping the benefit of the advertising done by the plaintiff." He therefore issued an injunction against any further distribution of Koke or Dope.[33]

But Mayfield would not give up. He appealed to the Ninth Circuit Court of Appeals in San Francisco, where the case took a decidedly unfavorable turn for Coke. In 1919, the appeals court reversed Sawtelle's decision, arguing that Coke could not seek trademark protections because it was a misbranded product. This, the court stated, was in keeping with Justice Hughes's decision just three years earlier. Judge Erskine M. Ross explained the court's position, noting that since its founding Coke had engaged in devious marketing practices, suggesting through its advertisements that it contained coca leaves and kola nuts, when in fact "the drug cocaine was practically eliminated from the drink, and the caffeine, of which it has since been mainly composed, still comes mainly, if not entirely, from other sources than the cola nut." The court found Coke engaged in "such deceptive, false, fraudulent, and unconscionable conduct as precludes a court of equity from affording it relief."[34]

This was a serious problem. Coke stood stripped of federal trademark armor, thereby exposing it to would-be competitors once kept at bay by the threat of lawsuits. This was 1919, before Coke had become one of the world's most dominant consumer brands, and there were now a host of soft drink firms—including Chero-Cola of Columbus, Georgia (today RC Cola), North Carolina's Cheerwine founded in 1917, and Pepsi-Cola, among many others—competing against the Atlanta company. The only way to increase brand equity—the most important, if intangible, asset Coke owned, valued at approximately $20 million in 1919—was to remain distinct from other beverages. Without federal protections for its trademark, aspiring businessmen could appropriate Coke marketing material to promote their product. This was a free-market, dog-eat-dog world that scared everyone at Coke.[35]

For stockholders considering purchasing Coke shares in 1919, Judge Ross's decision was a cause for concern. Skeptical investors saw Coca-Cola for what it was, a hollow company with few physical assets. Coke's trademark value had increased markedly over the past several decades, but would brand equity continue to increase if Coke lost its trademark protections? If not, what would the company have left? The company owned just $5 million in buildings, equipment, and land in 1919. Coke was a risky investment if indeed its brand strength was in jeopardy, and share prices reflected this investor concern, plummeting to less than half of the 1918 value in the days after Ross's decision.[36]

For Ernest Woodruff, the prominent Georgia Trust banker who was organizing a banking syndicate to buy out Asa Candler in 1919, the recent court case proved particularly unnerving. Members of his arranged syndicate expressed reservations about buying Coke from Candler with the Koke case still in limbo. They wanted assurances that Hirsch would win the case on appeal and only agreed to the buyout after hearing from Hirsch and the entire Georgia Trust legal team that the situation would be resolved in the coming months.[37]

Given the huge stakes, there was a lot of pressure on Hirsch to follow through on his word and settle the Koke case once and for all when it reached the Supreme Court in the winter of 1920. Hirsch was up for the challenge, writing a masterful brief that explained why Coca-Cola could not possibly be considered a misbranded product, an issue that had been reopened under Judge Ross's Ninth Circuit decision of 1919. He went back to the founding of the company and showed how Pemberton and Robinson's alliterative name for their beverage was not designed to be "a recipe or formula reciting every-thing that entered as an element into the composition." Nor was it intended to signify the most "potent elements" in the company's bev-erage. "Coca-Cola" was merely a catchy and attractive name, one that accurately reflected the presence of coca leaves and kola nuts but by no means reflected all the ingredients that went into the product. As for whether Coke had attempted deception in adding caffeine from tea leaves rather than sourcing from kola nuts, Hirsch had an easy answer: "Caffeine is caffeine and it is nothing else. To distinguish caf-feine derived from the coffee bean from that found in the cola nut or the tea leaf, is like distinguishing *aqua pura* from *aqua pura*." What-ever its natural source, caffeine was not "deleterious to health" and could not therefore reasonably be considered an adulterant.[38]

Chief Justice Oliver Wendell Holmes agreed with Hirsch's argu-ment. In his opinion, Holmes described Coca-Cola as a "single thing coming from a single source, and well known to the community." He admitted that Coke's caffeine "comes mainly from other sources" but stated that this did not affect Coke's right to appeal for trademark protections. Coke never claimed that its caffeine came solely from kola nuts and was therefore free to source this ingredient as it chose. Holmes issued an injunction against any further distribution of Koke but allowed Mayfield to continue to sell Dope, stating that Coke had no right to restrict the use of a name that did not closely resemble its trademark.[39]

Coke was saved. Assured the backing of the state, the company mowed down competitors in court. By 1940, Coke would win over 240 trademark infringement cases, and those were just the competitors that could afford to challenge Coke in court. Many others folded before seeing a judge, no doubt intimidated by Coke's impressive record of success. To scare the competition, the company published compendiums of its trademark victories in 1923 and 1939, a record of success requiring nearly three volumes and two thousand pages. The distribution was widespread: these records can still be found at law libraries all across the country today. With each passing victory, fewer and fewer businesses entered the soft drink market, and as imitators slowly disappeared, Coke's brand equity grew larger, increasing to over $30.5 million by 1935.[40]

The trademark protection federal courts offered Coke was another instance where an enlarged federal state helped Coke become great. America's legal infrastructure had grown immense. In 1789, in the first year of the New Republic, there were just thirteen district courts in the United States, but by the 1930s, there were dozens of lower federal courts hearing thousands of civil cases a year. This judiciary expansion, which intensified in the late nineteenth century, was a response to the demands of the new American marketplace. No longer was this a world of mom-and-pop shops operating within circumscribed regional boundaries. This was a national economy dominated by powerful interstate corporations that had new rights to federal protections following a series of Supreme Court decisions that confirmed their status as legal persons under the Fourteenth Amendment. As citizens, corporations could now bring suit against any firm infringing upon their constitutional right to "life, liberty, or property." And the suits came in a flood. Between 1900 and 1930, the federal district court civil caseload more than quadrupled, and as a result, the government appointed more judges to deal with the huge trial volume. The growth of the judiciary was crucial to companies like Coke who saw in the federal courts a way to codify, once and for all, property rights to both tangible and intangible assets. And it seemed the courts were willing to consider almost any kind of property claim. As early as 1873, in the *Slaughterhouse Cases,* Supreme Court Justice Noah H. Swayne had stated, "Property is everything which has an exchangeable value," a view later supported by the majority of Progressive Era judges. Coke knew it had to take advantage of this court protection after 1919. It had to protect its trademark before competitors tarnished its image. Thankfully, it had a strong federal court system backing its crusade.[41]

By 1920, Coke could revel in the fact that it had averted a potentially devastating procurement crisis. In a series of high-profile cases, the federal courts had sanctioned the use of processed caffeine in American consumer goods, leaving Coke free to source its caffeine from whatever source it saw fit. The timing could not have been better for the soft drink company. As World War I came to an end, so too did trade embargoes that had slowed imports of caffeine. Monsanto and other chemical processors now faced renewed competition from overseas suppliers, forcing them to reduce prices to record low offerings. A new era of caffeine cornucopia had arrived, and Coke gorged on the excess.

But if Coca-Cola had circumvented one ingredient disaster in 1920, it now faced another that would shake the corporate empire to its core: the collapse of the world sugar market.

3

Sugar

Satiating Citizen Cane's Sweet Appetite

Humans love sugar (sucrose), a disaccharide consisting of one glucose molecule bound to one fructose molecule, and for good reason: it provides in dense, crystalline form the basic primers needed to produce energy in our bodies. Because sugar is such an effective source of energy, humans have evolved a neurochemical regulatory mechanism that stimulates the release of dopamine, a pleasure-inducing neurotransmitter, when sucrose is consumed. While this psychotropic system helps humans optimize caloric intake, it can also stimulate overindulgence in sugary products when sweet foodstuffs are available in abundance. Recently, scientists have even found evidence to suggest that sugar may be as addictive as cocaine.[1]

It is no small wonder, then, that Coke's first customers loved, even craved, a daily dose of Coca-Cola. After all, Pemberton's original formula called for over 5 pounds of sugar per gallon of syrup. At the turn of the twentieth century, each 6-ounce Coca-Cola serving contained more than four teaspoons of sugar, a concentration that would likely have overloaded consumers' taste buds were it not for the high concentration of acids that helped to balance Coke's flavor profile. (Today, phosphoric acid makes Coca-Cola syrup's pH so low that trucks transporting the concentrated mixture require hazardous material placards to be in compliance with federal transportation laws.) Pemberton had come up with the perfect sugar delivery system, one that made people feel good without overwhelming the tongue. As a result, by the mid-1910s, Coke was the single largest industrial consumer of sugar in the world, funneling roughly 100 million pounds annually into customers' bodies.[2]

All that sugar cost Coke money, and since its founding, the company had scoured the world, seeking out suppliers that could offer the lowest prices for its most important ingredient. Without cheap sugar, Coke had no business. The company made its millions selling an inexpensive, nonessential beverage in volume, and it could only turn a profit on bulk sales if it kept raw material costs down, especially for sugar, its most expensive ingredient by far. Customers simply were not willing to pay a premium price for soft drinks. Remarkably, from 1886 to 1950, Coca-Cola maintained a 5-cent price for its beverage. This was due in part to Coke chairman Robert Woodruff's constant vigilance. He insisted that company bottlers and soda jerks maintain this price for Coke, even when operating expenses increased, and he spent millions on advertisements featuring Coke's nickel price in an attempt to ensure local bottler and retailer compliance with his policy. In the 1930s, when Coke began a concerted campaign to sell its beverages in coin-operated vending machines that only accepted 5-cent coins, Woodruff had an added incentive to preserve the nickel policy. Technology dictated that any price increase in Coke would require a jump to 10 cents in order to meet single-coin vending machine requirements, a change, executive Ralph Hayes noted, that would have been "murderous" to the company. With no way to pass

increased commodity costs on to consumers, Coke's future solvency
was contingent upon the perpetuation of cheap sugar production.[3]

FORTUNATELY FOR COKE, THERE was lots of sugar available
for purchase when Coke was first invented, as sugarcane fields covered the tropical world, but this was truly an ecological conquest
replete with historical contingencies. While today many people think
of sugar as a ubiquitous commodity closely linked to the economies
of the Caribbean and South America, especially Cuba and Brazil,
not a single sugarcane stalk would have been found in these tropical regions before the fifteenth century. First domesticated in New
Guinea 12,000 years ago, *Saccharum officinarum* (sugarcane) was native
to Southeast Asia and first came to the West via Persian traders in
the eighth century AD. Though sugar quickly became a desired spice
and a medicinal dietary supplement for wealthy aristocrats, European sugarcane cultivation nonetheless remained modest up to the
1400s, confined to rich soils abutting the Mediterranean Sea.[4]

But sugar proved popular, and Westerners soon looked to expand
sugarcane cultivation into new regions of the world in order to satiate their cravings. As they had with black pepper, cinnamon, and
other coveted spices, Old World elites turned to state institutions to
help them acquire greater quantities of the "sweet salt" they desired,
and by the fifteenth century, aristocrats in Western Europe secured
government financing for colonial sugar cultivation projects in the
imperial periphery. For the next three centuries, European powers
cultivated sugar throughout the tropical world, relying on the labor
of enslaved men and women. As a result, the sweet foodstuff became
a cheap commodity by the end of the eighteenth century, available in
abundance for the West's working class.[5]

Sugar offered incredible caloric density, making it the ideal dietary
staple for both plantation field hands in the Caribbean colonies and

factory laborers working long hours in the burgeoning industrial centers of nineteenth-century Europe. It made factories and plantations productive because it kept laborers on their feet. Along with coal, sugar would become a critical fuel feeding capitalist expansion in the nineteenth century.[6]

The United States government recognized the value of this dense energy source in the early 1800s and offered subsidies to help develop a domestic sugar empire. Beginning in 1803, when Thomas Jefferson executed the Louisiana Purchase, Congress imposed tariffs on imported raw sugar as a means of insulating Louisiana growers from international competition. Tariff-protected Louisiana growers expanded their operations between the War of 1812 and the 1890s, producing over 17,000 tons of sugar by 1823, with total US imports topping 30,000 tons that year. By the end of the twentieth century, the government helped expand sugar cultivation to the American West and Midwest, offering subsidies and tariff protections to sugar beet growers in the temperate climates of California, Colorado, and Nebraska.[7]

American farmers were not the only ones benefiting from the federal government's sweet sugar deals; industrial refiners got a big boost as well. Refiners developed the infrastructure that turned raw sugar from sugarcane and beet farms into refined white crystals fit for the consumer market. In the early 1800s, these factories were often quite rudimentary, often using open fires to vaporize juices mashed from sugarcane, but by the end of the century, refineries featured steam-powered engines and complex centrifuges capable of distilling lily-white crystals from beets and sugarcane. Investments were substantial and included railroad construction, sugar barrel manufacturing, and processing plant operation. After the Revolutionary War, the United States was far behind its European counterparts in refining, so in the tariff of 1789, the government placed heavy duties on imported refined sugar in order to help American processors gain a foothold against foreign competitors that could otherwise outsell them by a wide margin. This was part of a larger government tariff initiative to stimulate American manufacturing across all industries.

Throughout the nineteenth century, the federal government would continue to shield domestic refiners, increasing duties on imported refined sugar to as high as 9 cents. With government protection, over fifty refineries emerged in the United States by 1870, up from just a handful seventy years earlier, but the success of many of these operations would be short-lived. Ultimately, the real beneficiaries were not small businesses but a handful of wealthy elites that gobbled up competitors to form huge monopolies.[8]

No one did this better than Henry O. Havemeyer, the co-owner, along with his brother, of Brooklyn-based sugar refinery company Havemeyer and Elder, incorporated by Henry's father in 1863. By the 1880s, Havemeyer had taken over leadership of the New York–based firm, which had become one of the biggest refinery concerns in the country. The family had amassed a fortune totaling more than $3 million by the 1880s, and Henry was determined to add to the coffers. By the time he became a partner in Havemeyer and Elder in the 1860s, he was dismayed at how competition cut into profits, and he set out to buy out struggling rival firms.[9]

Havemeyer was a cutthroat businessman with a reputation for being a brutal taskmaster. In 1893, for example, after several workers in his Brooklyn plant suffered heat exhaustion and severe burns in boiler rooms, he refused to grant a modest request for work reduction, believing the concession would reduce productivity and thereby hurt profits. Havemeyer told his workers that if they did not want to work for twelve hours a day, he would find someone else to fill their shoes. He would treat his competitors with similar ruthlessness, driving down prices in particular markets to force small refiners into bankruptcy. For those with limited savings, it was hard to survive, the margin between refined and raw sugar dwindling to less than 1 cent by the 1880s.[10]

In 1887, Havemeyer turned up the heat. He approached several of the major refineries and proposed forming a trust. The Sugar Refineries Company, as this alliance came to be known, took over ownership of roughly twenty refineries and quickly closed about half of them. Havemeyer had struck at just the right time, when businesses faced meager profit margins due to competition and were therefore willing to sell at low cost. He had paid bargain prices to become the world's biggest sugar refiner.[11]

The Sugar Trust, one of the most iconic corporate monopolies in American history, thrived in the early years of operation, Henry Havemeyer earning an estimated $2 million a year, but the monopoly's remarkable profits quickly drew criticism from Havemeyer's remaining rivals. Disgruntled competitors urged state attorneys in New York to bring suit against the Sugar Trust, charging the monopoly with unduly hindering competition in the industry. In June of 1890 the Court of Appeals of New York State ruled that the Sugar Refineries Company's buyouts "tended to the public injury" and declared the trust illegal, but Havemeyer, always persistent, found a way around the decision. He and his partners decided to take their business to New Jersey, where new incorporation laws allowed companies to buy and sell stock of businesses operating outside the state. The trust became incorporated as the American Sugar Refining Company in 1891 and quickly came to control over 90 percent of the entire sugar-refining business in the United States.[12]

Havemeyer had taken advantage of a radical change in corporate law, one that would nurture the ascendancy of other great monopolies in America. New Jersey's incorporation code, which Governor Leon Abbett and a cabal of local businessmen revised in 1888 with the specific objective of attracting corporate revenue to the state,

allowed colossal conglomerates to become legitimate businesses entitled to legal protections denied them as trusts. Whereas in the early
nineteenth century states generally granted corporate charters to
companies that could prove some public service objective, New Jersey
allowed businesses to incorporate for almost any reason, and it placed
few restrictions on where businesses spent their money or whom they
partnered with. It was a ploy to attract capital investment, and it
worked. Businesses flocked to New Jersey, but soon other states, in
an attempt to remain competitive, copied the Garden State's model.
The net result was rapid corporate consolidation, as big companies
forced potential competitors to merge with them or die. The age of
monopoly had arrived.[13]

In these high times for big business, Havemeyer made record
profits, in part because the federal government continued to offer
his refining interest special tariff protections. Trade policies that had
first been created to promote the growth of small American refining
businesses now served to increase Havemeyer's profits.[14]

Flush with cash, Havemeyer chose to increase throughput—that
is, the flow of goods through the corporate system—in order to make
money. He figured he could generate the most profit by selling more
for less. The ten operating plants owned by the Sugar Trust produced more barrels of sugar per year—roughly 34,000—than had
been produced by the entire industry prior to trust formation. As a
result, wholesale prices for refined sugar declined from 6.2 cents per
pound in 1890 to 4.1 cents per pound in 1894.[15]

THIS WAS THE WORLD Coke president Asa Candler inhabited in
the 1890s. He was living in a time of abundance, when sugar could
be had in unprecedented volume at dirt-cheap prices. Five times as
much sugar flooded US markets in the 1890s as at the time of his
birth in 1851, and all this had been made possible with the help of

state subsidies and tariffs that fueled domestic sugar cultivation and refining around the world. After all, the United States government was not the only one encouraging sugar production through its trade policies. European countries also offered tariff protections and bounties for their domestic producers. The collective result was more sugar on the world market. In the years ahead, Candler would attack the US government for artificially inflating sugar prices and petition for a return to a time when the company enjoyed "free market" offerings. But from the very beginning, Coke's access to cheap sugar was guaranteed not by market mechanisms—Adam Smith's invisible hand—but by interventions of state institutions and monopolies that structured markets to meet the needs of a new corporate oligarchy.[16]

Candler was happy to do business with the sugar giants. They offered cheap prices (around 4 cents per pound) and took on all the risk associated with transporting and refining raw materials. All Candler had to do was scavenge off the mountains of white crystals that piled up at these refineries. For the remainder of the 1890s, Candler purchased virtually all of Coke's sweetener—over 380,000 pounds in 1895 alone—from Revere Sugar Refining Company of Boston, Massachusetts, a sugar operation that technically remained separate from the Sugar Trust but was closely affiliated with Havemeyer's consolidation, owning a large amount of stock in American Sugar Refining.[17]

Relying on others to process sugar meant that Coke could stay lean. While companies like American Refining spent millions on labor and machinery, Coke kept its operating costs down. By the end of the nineteenth century, there were around twenty people working at Coca-Cola's Atlanta office, and its machinery expenses were equally modest. The production process in Atlanta's syrup factory was about as streamlined as it could get, akin to something you might find in a charity soup kitchen. It was basically a mixing operation, the majority of the work carried out by an African American worker who poured various ingredients into a huge copper kettle, stirring and heating the mixture to produce a dark brown syrup. That was it. The syrup was shipped out in barrels or jugs on rail lines or via horse and buggy to retailers, who mixed the product with water. In the grand scheme of its production flow, from the cultivation of raw ingredients like sugar to the distribution of its fizzy beverage, Coca-Cola did relatively little and could therefore efficiently turn sales into profits.[18]

While Coke stayed out of the sugar business, Havemeyer and his remaining rivals went all in, integrating further backward into management and ownership of Caribbean production facilities in the wake of the Spanish-American War in 1898. American businesses were taking advantage of the federal government's new imperial presence in the Western Hemisphere. As early as 1875, the US government had pushed for the territorial acquisition of sugar-producing polities in the tropical world, beginning with the Kingdom of Hawaii, with which it negotiated a reciprocity agreement in 1875 granting island growers duty-free status in US markets in return for an elimination of tariffs on many American imports to the island and US access to Pearl Harbor. The treaty stimulated the growth of the sugar industry in Hawaii, as island producers made profits selling their sugar at premium prices made possible by US tariff policy. In other regions of the world, especially the Caribbean, powerful US sugar refineries put pressure on the federal government to use its military might to protect American investment in tropical sugar isles. Defeating the Spanish empire in the Spanish-American War, the United States gained control over the Philippines, Puerto Rico, and Cuba in 1898, and by the end of the nineteenth century, the federal government's tariff protections for these territories stimulated a sugar production boom with growers and refiners benefiting from guaranteed US markets offering premium selling prices. Puerto Rico and the Philippines enjoyed duty-free status, while Cuba, by 1903, enjoyed a 20 percent reduction in raw sugar tariff rates. The Platt

Amendment, signed into law in 1901, further encouraged US private investments in Cuba. The amendment stipulated that the US government was authorized to use military force to protect US investments in Cuba. With state backing, American refineries poured their capital into developing Cuban sugar mills and plantations.[19]

The federal government's forays into the tropical world marked a new era in US foreign policy. Prior to this time, the United States had largely adopted a noninterventionist diplomatic agenda. Though never truly isolationist—the United States always engaged in protecting its foreign trade through negotiations and, at times, military action—for most of the nineteenth century, the federal government showed no interest in colonizing or acquiring overseas territory. After the Civil War, however, economic pressures forced the US government to alter its course. One impetus for change was the perception that America's new businesses might be hemmed in if new markets for their goods could not be found overseas. In 1893 Frederick Jackson Turner, a renowned University of Wisconsin professor, delivered his famous essay declaring America's western frontier closed for further expansion, and it seemed that the only way to grow would be to stretch beyond the country's borders. Doing so would allow American businesses not only to acquire new vital resources overseas but also to tap into new retail markets.

But those who would direct this policy change from within the government—most notably Secretary of State William S. Seward, Rear Admiral Alfred Thayer Mahan, and President William McKinley, among many others—did not want to repeat mistakes made by European nations in centuries past. They envisioned a new expansionist policy, one in which the United States would not seek traditional colonial acquisition of foreign lands. Rather, their neocolonial strategy called for the creation of American protectorates and military satellites that would help to ensure that US interests received preferential treatment overseas. As for the day-to-day responsibilities of running a nation, this should be left to host governments. This way, America did not have to pick up the tab for providing public services overseas. In many ways, then, the government was following Coke's organizational model: create low-cost satellites that can connect to established networks of trade, but stay out of the risky business of directly managing large overseas assets. Governments as well as businesses were experimenting with Coca-Cola capitalism.[20]

The government's foreign policy strategy worked amazingly well in the Caribbean. In 1903, the Cuban investment craze became frenetic when Congress approved a reciprocity agreement that allowed Cuban raw sugar to enter the United States at a duty rate 20 percent below other foreign imports. US refineries with investments in Cuban plantations were ecstatic. They could now import the raw sugar they needed below the full-duty price placed on other foreign imports. As a result, American Refining Company and other independent processing industries bought cane fields and expanded raw sugar milling operations in Cuba. Big Sugar could invest with confidence, knowing that they had the support and protection of the US military. By 1915, US refineries owned roughly 25 percent of all raw sugar mills in Cuba.[21]

With transnational integration, sugar came flooding into United States markets. American Sugar Refining Company's Cuban plants produced more than double the output of rival Cuban-owned operations in the country. Furthermore, American Sugar had developed an incredibly efficient and highly integrated transportation network for bringing refined sugar to market. In 1916, Earl Babst, the company's president, provided a portrait of this international industrial octopus. He explained that the American Sugar Refining Company had become invested in industries as diverse as barrel manufacturing, not only owning and operating the factories that produced sugar barrels but also managing "reforestation" programs to ensure adequate supplies of raw materials. According to Babst, the company planted "about one-half million of white pine and spruce trees . . . in the open Adirondacks" in order to meet demands for barrel production. The company also owned and operated over "130 miles of railroad" tracks channeling raw materials to refining plants on the East Coast. "Today," he said, "only a large corporation is able to compete successfully in the world's sugar markets. . . . Not only does it require large organization, but vast capital, resources, and plants to draw the necessary raw products from quarters of the world sufficient to make a year-round campaign." Asa Candler would have cringed at the thought of managing such expensive equipment.[22]

All these investments had been made in an attempt to root out competition. The goal was to become so massive, so powerful, that no company could possibly undersell American Sugar Refining. Here was a window of opportunity, company leaders thought, the government having cleared new fertile ground for investment in the Caribbean. Havemeyer and his successor Babst would spare no expense to quash their rivals once and for all.

But wise as these investments may have seemed at the time, considering the political context in which they occurred, they nevertheless failed to deliver the hoped-for crushing blow to the trust's rivals. Old competitors had survived, and new mass marketing companies, such as United Fruit and Hershey Chocolate Company, began to buy up large sugar plantations and refineries for the first time, believing—unlike Coke—that they could make more money by becoming their own suppliers. The costs of entry into the business were cheaper than they had been fifty years earlier, and more businesses were willing to risk capital to take advantage of the new shift in foreign policy. They believed integration assured greater profits in the future. As a consequence, by 1907, American Sugar Refining's marketshare was cut in half, and just five years later, the firm would control only 28 percent of the refined sugar market, a remarkable change in fortunes.[23]

Coke had encouraged this trend, using its purchasing power, the largest in the sugar business by 1919, to keep the trust's competitors in business. During the 1920s, with over 1,000 Coca-Cola bottlers serving the county, Coca-Cola consumed more than 100 million pounds of sugar per year, up from roughly 44,000 pounds in 1890. The company learned that it could drive down prices by simply playing suppliers off against one another and spreading out its purchases. By the 1920s, Coke bought from multiple sugar refineries, acquiring roughly half of its sugar from the American Sugar Refining Company but purchasing thousands of pounds of sugar from other businesses, such as the Texan grower and refiner Imperial Sugar, Louisiana's Godchaux Sugars Inc., and, somewhat later, Hershey.[24]

Coke's power to shape markets, however, was not absolute, and during World War I it discovered its vulnerability to the vagaries of international politics. As supply networks connecting US refineries to overseas sugar sources crumbled, Coke feared that it would be unable to acquire its most important ingredient at low cost. Not owning sources of supply, it needed help, and it looked to the government to restore order.

At first, Uncle Sam appeared more an adversary than a savior. In 1917, the US Food Administration, headed by future president Herbert Hoover, began imposing rationing restrictions on industrial sugar users in an effort to stabilize prices. Under the new FDA regulations, Coke and other confectionery companies had to cut back their sugar use to 50 percent of prewar levels. These restrictions extended into 1918, when the administration created the Sugar Equalization Board, which froze sugar prices at 9 cents per pound. Though the price ceiling was a welcomed intervention, the Coca-Cola Company had fought hard against government rationing programs and sent corporate attorney Harold Hirsch and vice president Sam Dobbs to Washington, DC, to lobby for exemptions, but ultimately the company gave in to government demands. In a magazine layout entitled "Making a Soldier of Sugar," it stated that it was a "privilege to comply with the Government's request." Throughout the war, Coke bombarded the public with similar messages of corporate sacrifice, presenting itself as an altruistic citizen willing to "enlist" its sugar for the public good.[25]

Coke's publicity campaigns paid dividends. To the American public, Coca-Cola appeared a patriotic company selflessly committing its resources to the national cause. Few Americans knew about the company's closed-door politicking and its attempts to receive special exemptions from the Sugar Equalization Board. Even fewer citizens recognized how Coke and other commercial users benefited from the government's price-stabilizing measures. No doubt the government's rationing program temporarily affected Coke's bottom line, with annual sales dropping from 12 million gallons in 1917 to 10 million gallons in 1918, but by 1919, as the government removed purchasing restrictions, Coke made record profits, in part because government price controls kept sugar costs down. The Equalization Board's market interventions insulated Coke from the chaos of the world market, stabilizing prices during a period of great uncertainty. In 1919 alone, Coke witnessed exponential growth, posting volume syrup sales of almost 19 million gallons. The indirect, yet no less tangible, benefits of federal government market management remained out of sight.[26]

But in the spring of 1920, everything changed. By March, the Sugar Equalization Board expired, and so did government price controls. As a result, sugar prices skyrocketed from roughly 7 cents per pound to over 20 cents per pound by May, causing Coke and its soft drink rivals to panic. The instability stimulated speculative buying. Coke and Pepsi frantically signed contracts for large futures from foreign suppliers, paying just over 20 cents per pound, hoping to satiate their sweet appetite before prices rose even higher. But as tropical growers rushed to plant new crops in an effort to capitalize on

high prices, a global sugar surplus piled up, dropping prices precipitously to 9 cents a pound by December and further to 3½ cents just
months later. [27]

For Pepsi, the decision to buy futures in the spring of 1920 led to
the brand's temporary demise. Caleb Bradham, Pepsi-Cola's founder
and owner, had been unable to push his product as far and wide as
Candler had Coca-Cola. By the 1920s, Pepsi's distribution was limited, having spread to just over twenty-five states. It simply did not
have the revenue stream that Coke enjoyed and was therefore more
vulnerable when the sugar crisis hit. Bradham declared bankruptcy
in 1922, unable to recover from the financial losses he incurred for
carrying overpriced sugar in a deflated market.[28]

Coke hung on, but not without suffering serious losses. Company
executive Howard Candler, who in 1920 once again became president
of Coca-Cola after a short stint as chairman, reported a year later
that the ill-advised sugar purchases cost the company an estimated
$2 million. These losses had to be eaten by the parent company,
which could not raise the price of bottlers' syrup according to its
contractual obligations. Though the company had been able to force
its bottlers to amend their contracts to allow for marginal increases
in the price of syrup during the war, the amended agreements still
did not permit Coca-Cola to pass on the increased cost of sugar to its
bottlers after the war.[29]

Coke's losses, however, were not as severe as those incurred by
other industrial sugar consumers that had become heavily invested in
Cuban sugar plantations. The lure of high prices in the early months
of 1920 had enticed many companies to sink large amounts of capital
into Cuban landholdings and milling operations. The "Dance of the
Millions," as it came to be called, had begun, with Cuba's planter
class spending freely on extravagant fiestas, casino escapades, and
other festivities. The tempo of investment increased every day as
prices continued to rise. Everyone was betting that the bubble would

not burst, and at first, it seemed the gamble was going to pay off.
High prices in the spring of 1920 brought in hefty revenues, so much
money that even tenant farmers in the field earned a little extra cash
for their backbreaking labor. But by the summer of 1920, the party
was over and the hangover began. All this investment yielded surplus, and prices plummeted. American and Cuban sugar interests
were stuck with more sugar than the international market could
absorb, and questions remained whether heavy debts and weak cash
flows would force some businesses to fold.

One of the hardest-hit enterprises was the Hershey Chocolate
Company, which had become a major player in Cuba during World
War I. Structurally, Hershey could not have been more different
than Coca-Cola in 1920, in large part owing to the peculiar corporate vision of its founder, Milton Snavely Hershey. No hard-hearted
tycoon, Milton Hershey belonged to that special breed of Progressive
Era businessman that believed corporate profits should be reinvested
in communities to promote the public weal. As he would later muse,
he "could never see what happiness a rich man gets from contemplat-
ing a life of acquisition only, with a cold and legal distribution of his
wealth after he passes away." He wanted to make a difference while
he was alive and believed strongly in corporate social welfare programs, initiatives many wealthy business barons promoted during
this period, including Henry Ford, Andrew Carnegie, and others. In
1906, when he founded the Hershey Chocolate Company in Derry
Church, Pennsylvania, he set out to do more than just sell chocolate;
he intended to create a utopian factory town.[30]

Childless and nearing fifty, Milton envisioned himself as the
paterfamilias of a new corporate community, one that would use
company earnings to enhance the public good. He renamed his host
village Hershey and over the next several years used the profits
from his business—which totaled over $6 million in 1919 alone—to
develop the town's infrastructure. The scope of his improvements

was truly remarkable. In addition to building recreational facilities that included a zoo and an amusement park, he created the Hershey Water Company, the Hershey Electric Company, and the Hershey National Bank. He also built the Hershey Industrial School, an orphanage that provided schooling for abandoned children from surrounding townships. If Coke shunned investment in large-scale development projects, Hershey welcomed it with open arms.[31]

What Milton Hershey built in Pennsylvania he would attempt to re-create in Cuba. After the death of his beloved wife, Kitty, in April of 1915, Hershey, now fifty-seven, traveled to the Caribbean isle to contemplate his ambitions for the future. Like most other people in the confectionery business, he was worried about fluctuating commodity prices during the war and believed his company might gain greater security by becoming its own supplier. Cuba seemed like the right place to invest as it was only ninety miles away from the US mainland and enjoyed preferential duty treatment under federal tariff policy. So in 1916, ready for a new adventure, Hershey bought 35,000 acres on the island's northern shore between Havana and Matanzas, prime real estate directly facing Key West. As he had in Pennsylvania, Hershey set about creating a model town in the middle of his plantations, calling it Central Hershey. In addition to building a modern processing and refining mill on the site, Hershey constructed the country's first electric railway to bring his products to port. The line extended from Mantzanas to the outskirts of Havana and totaled over 120 miles when it was completed.[32]

In Central, Hershey spared no expense. He built state-of-the-art housing for his workforce, which totaled some four thousand Cuban laborers at peak production in the 1920s. Community houses featured indoor plumbing, electricity, and beautiful gardens, all the amenities of modern life. For recreation, townspeople could partake in a soccer match on one of the many athletic fields or take a stroll down a palm-lined avenue to a verdant park. There was a school, medical center, and orphanage as well. For the Cubans that lived in Central, Hershey offered a dream world, and many were sincerely grateful.[33]

At the beginning of 1920, Hershey gave no signs that he was willing to quit his experiment. Not only had he invested nearly $25 million in Cuba, he had also laid down his own roots. Hershey loved the "Queen of the Antilles" and retreated from business in Pennsylvania whenever he could to enjoy life in his Caribbean utopia. Soon after arriving, he had bought a hundred-year-old mansion called Rosario for $6 million, and throughout his sixties, this would be his preferred residence. Descriptions of Hershey in Cuba during these years portray the aging baron as a contented Panama Jack, parading through the streets of his utopian village, chewing a sloppy cigar and often carousing with workers. On weekends he could frequently be found at one of Havana's many casinos, enjoying a round at the roulette table or a burlesque show. He was savoring the moment.[34]

But when the sugar crisis hit in 1920, Hershey's dream turned into a nightmare. Hershey was exposed in ways Coke was not with heavy assets in sugar plantations. When the bubble burst, Hershey's losses were severe. The hit reduced the chocolate company's net income to just over $362,000 by December of 1920, down from roughly $6 million the year before. In order to meet payments on outstanding debts in the coming months, the company had to find outside financial support. As a result, the National City Bank of New York, the lending institution that helped finance the construction of Hershey's Cuban factories, took over ownership of Hershey's operations and began to manage the company's property in the Caribbean. By 1922, with sugar prices stabilized, Milton Hershey was able to take back control of the company, but Hershey's profitability remained contingent upon the perpetuation of state policies that permitted cheap imports of Cuban sugar.[35]

After the panic, Milton Hershey would return to business as usual. He would not pull out of Cuba. On the contrary, he increased his landholdings and sugar operations. Over the next few years he would buy new mills, ultimately acquiring five factories, and purchase more land, increasing his holdings to over 60,000 acres by the end of 1923. Hershey was determined to make his Cuban experiment work, but in time, it would become clear the utopia would not last.[36]

While Hershey doubled down on investments in Cuba, Coke company boss Ernest Woodruff sought insulation from volatile sugar price fluctuations. In March of 1921, he had successfully amended the company's bottling contracts to include a sliding scale that would take account of sugar price increases. Under the new agreement, parent bottlers would receive syrup at a base rate of $1.17½ per gallon but would be required to pay an additional 6 cents for every 1-cent increase in sugar prices above an established market price. More importantly, the parent company in Atlanta could now pass along raw material costs to its many distributors, significantly decreasing its front-end purchasing risks.[37]

Abroad, Coca-Cola adopted an even better plan for outsourcing costs. In the early 1920s, the company's international presence remained modest. The company had first ventured beyond US borders around 1900 when it expanded sales to Canada and Cuba. Two decades later it had a handful of bottling plants in countries around the world. Yet as late as 1927 distribution was limited to eleven countries, and not until after World War II would foreign sales make up a significant chunk of revenues. Nevertheless, the company sought to streamline overseas distribution in the 1920s in an effort to squeeze as much cash out of its satellite operations as it could. To this end, company chemists developed a dehydrated, sugarless Coca-Cola concentrate for export to foreign bottlers. This concentrate allowed the company to pass off sugar purchasing responsibilities to bottlers operating in host nations. The Atlanta home office had masterminded another astonishing feat of shifting costs onto others.[38]

On its face, the new domestic bottling agreement and the company's overseas concentrate policy appeared to give the corporate office the kind of insulation it had always wanted against sugar market fluctuations. In reality, however, the parent company still had to be concerned about how sweetener costs would affect retail prices. Coke's empire depended on volume sales that in turn depended on low retail prices. If sugar costs increased precipitously, bottlers would have to raise prices in order to cover their operating expenses. Such increases would inevitably lead to decreased consumption, ultimately affecting the parent company's profitability. Thus, even after the 1921 contract amendments, the parent company still needed cheap sugar to make profits.

For companies that had limited assets tied up in the sugar production business, the best strategy for success, considering fluctuating trading policies, was to remain flexible, and this is exactly what Coca-Cola did. The company diversified its purchasing contracts in the 1920s, buying sugar from domestic suppliers as well as overseas producers. It patronized massive refineries, such as American Sugar Refining, as well as smaller enterprises, such as Savannah Sugar Refining, which had begun operations in Georgia in 1917. In this way, Coke kept its options open and limited its financial exposure to radical sugar production changes in particular host nations.[39]

With the worst of its sugar woes behind it, Coke made lots of money in the 1920s. The company's stock price soared from $40 a share in 1919 to around $200 a share by 1927, at which point the company decided to split its stock two for one. In less than a decade, Coke managed to double its net profits, from $6.2 million in 1922 to $12.8 million in 1929. People who had invested in the company in the late 1910s got rich, especially Ernest Woodruff's family and cronies who helped form Coca-Cola International in 1922, a holding company that accumulated more than half the outstanding stock in Coca-Cola (more than 250,000 shares). The decision to form the company was driven by Ernest Woodruff's concern that he was slowly losing control of Coke as New York investors began to buy up shares in the company. For Robert Woodruff, the decision to go along with his father's plan proved a wise decision. By 1927, just thirty-seven years young, he became a millionaire.[40]

A bearish sugar market was not the only good news for Coke and its investors in the 1920s. By then, the company had finally concluded its decade-long caffeine battle with the government and avoided a potentially devastating divorce with disgruntled bottlers. No longer did the company have to combat Progressive Era fears that its product was unfit for habitual consumption. It could hawk its beverage as a whimsical treat ideal for almost any occasion. Archie Lee, who ran Coke's advertising account at Atlanta's D'Arcy marketing firm in the 1920s, recognized this change and began to develop a new line of promotional material for the company designed to encourage Coke consumption throughout the day. Lee preferred pithy pitches to detailed scientific diatribes, recognizing that postwar Americans had disposable income to spend on leisurely activities. This was the Jazz Age, a frenetic time marked by the emergence of the automobile, moving pictures, and bustling dance halls. It was a time of liberation, when both working-class and middle-class Americans sought to forget about the troubles of the war by engaging in cheap amusements. In this new era of mass consumerism, Lee hoped Americans would think of Coke as "the Pause That Refreshes," a frequent indulgence at work, home, or play.[41]

Still, even if the Roaring Twenties encouraged a culture of copious consumption, expansion in the 1920s would never have been feasible for Coke without cheap sugar. Only by tapping into a host of global sugar supply channels in the postwar era could Coke capitalize on the new commercial outlets of 1920s America.

·   ·   ·

BY THE END OF the 1920s, Hershey came to see what Coke had realized all along: that there was more money to be made in buying sugar than in making it. The chocolate company recognized that it was going to have a hard time selling stock with the increasingly problematic Cuban assets on its books. So, in 1927, Milton Hershey's attorney John Snyder persuaded the chocolate baron to separate his company into three firms. The newly created Hershey Chocolate Corporation would be responsible for selling company goods to consumer outlets. It was to be the profit maker. Hershey Estates, on the other hand, would take over management and maintenance of the company's transportation networks, housing units, and recreational properties in Pennsylvania, and, likewise, the Hershey Corporation would assume responsibility for the company's Cuban plantations, rail lines, and refining operations. The accounting books for these firms remained separate.[42]

Hershey had taken the first step to become more like Coke. It began to separate the cash cow of its operations from those industries that threatened profitability, and as a result, it presented a more attractive portfolio to its investors. In the waning years of his life, Milton Hershey would remain committed to his utopian projects, but the reality was that his orphanages, railroads, and refining factories drew little stockholder interest. What investors liked was the Hershey Chocolate Corporation, a leaner business that posted hefty profits.

But neither the newly formed Hershey Chocolate Corporation nor Coca-Cola was as insulated from the vagaries of the sugar market as their pristine financial ledgers suggested to investors. Both needed cheap sugar, so both continued to fight to keep Cuban sugar prices down.

A budding partnership between the two companies had begun to form by the late 1920s. Though Coke bought from both domestic and overseas producers, it increasingly looked to the Hershey Corporation for supplies. The soft drink company purchased over 2.2 million pounds of refined sugar from Hershey in 1928. As a result, when a Republican pro-tariff Congress met to discuss raising Cuban raw and refined sugar duties in the spring of 1929, Chairman Robert Woodruff reached out to Milton Hershey and expressed his interest in establishing an advertising campaign that would "bring to the public's attention the evils of the contemplated increase in the raw sugar tariff and the proposed differential against imported refined." The key was anonymity. Woodruff suggested that appeals be made through third-party agents who would appear to represent the interests of the masses. He envisioned "cartoons and editorials" and anti-tariff articles in "sympathetic mediums" read by the average consumer. Coke and Hershey would supply the promotional directives and commissioned writers would plant the material in popular media outlets. Hershey agreed to the proposition, offering to pay up to half the cost of the campaign. By 1932, Coke and Hershey collectively spent over $50,000 on anti-tariff propaganda, working with publicity agencies to produce opinion pieces, editorials, and other publications designed to motivate consumers to push for sugar duty reductions.[43]

No one worked harder to secure cheap sugar for Coca-Cola than Ralph Hayes, the company's colorful vice president. Hayes had become Robert Woodruff's right-hand man by the mid-1930s and would oversee Coke's sugar procurements in the years ahead. He had joined the company in 1932, after successfully running the New York Community Trust, where he gained a reputation of "going out and accomplishing," as one business executive put it. He had proved himself no less competent as a government official in the 1910s, having served as an assistant to the secretary of war during World War I.[44]

Like many Coca-Cola executives who would follow him, Hayes had that perfect mix of private business acumen and public sector experience, and he would therefore prove a vital asset as Coke increased its lobbying efforts in Washington during the 1930s. A flamboyant bow-tie wearer with a flair for the dramatic, Hayes always spoke his mind to Woodruff, at times pushing the boundaries of propriety. In 1952, for example, Hayes wrote to Woodruff to complain about not being able to sleep one night after reading the story of an Indian prince who had seventy wives. He said the story led him to think of Nell, Woodruff's wife, and "what it would be like if 70 copies of Ole Mis' were simultaneously in operation." If Woodruff found Hayes's indiscretions unnerving, he never said so, writing to Hayes throughout his life as one would a beloved confidant. In the sugar matter, as in so many other critical issues the company faced, Woodruff turned to Hayes, trusting in his diplomatic abilities to make legislators see Coke's interests as their own.[45]

As the nation entered the Great Depression in the 1930s, Hayes worked hard to persuade Congress to eliminate tariffs protecting domestic growers, believing the elimination of such support would yield cheaper sugar prices. He made his case to Georgia senator Walter F. George in 1936, complaining that American consumers spent an additional $116 million to pay for sugar protections that benefited a "tiny fraction of our agricultural population." He described domestic beet and sugarcane growers as perpetual beggars, "standing at the doors of the federal treasury seeking more and greater tariffs, benefits, bounties and gratuities from the public till." He was particularly concerned about a proposed processing tax that would add to the subsidies growers were already receiving. Of course, if it passed, Coke would have to pay a hefty portion of this impost, but Hayes focused attention on America's poor, a constituency, he claimed, that would be hit hard by the new measure when food prices rose as a result of the tax. Even if import quotas had to be established, the government should not impose an additional tax that "would bear as indefensibly as this one would, on the housewife, the market-basket, and the breakfast table." George's decision on this matter,

Hayes made clear, could affect his reelection: "Every consideration of equity, and economics—and, I venture to add every proper political consideration—should militate against [the] levy." A few days later, George wrote back to Hayes to say that the processing fee had not passed in the Senate and added that he would not support any "additional bounty" in future legislation. Hayes, for the moment, was satisfied.[46]

Considering Hayes's voracious appeals for tax relief, one might think the company in the mid-1930s was barely scraping by, but this was not the case. The company stock price took a small hit on Black Tuesday in 1929, dropping by just 6 percent of its value, but by 1930, it had returned to pre-crash levels. Even the repeal of Prohibition in 1933, which many predicted would drastically reduce soft drink sales, only temporarily affected Coke's profits. In 1935, Coke split its stock four to one after it reached $200 a share. Net income, totaling just over $10 million in 1928, jumped to over $25 million a decade later.[47]

Robert Woodruff, serving his eighth year as president of the Coca-Cola Company in 1930, had charted the course for this growth. He had professionalized Coke's sales team in the 1920s, creating the Statistical Department, which conducted sophisticated surveys to determine ripe markets for Coke sales. Through this new branch of the company, Woodruff kept close watch on bottlers and retailers and worked to ensure uniform delivery of the company's product across the nation. He was most insistent that bottlers preserve Coke's 5-cent price, recognizing that even some of the poorest Americans could afford a nickel drink despite the tough economic times. He hired a host of new brilliant company managers, Ralph Hayes chief among them, who had experience working with government officials to protect Coke's procurement needs at the back end of the business, and he promoted to managerial positions veteran talent who demonstrated a knack for developing innovative sales techniques in the retail sphere. This included stalwarts like Harrison

Jones, the company's imposing, redheaded vice president of sales, who had started as a Coke attorney back in 1910 and had long displayed a single-minded obsession with making the company's signature beverage available in every corner of the country. By the 1930s, Harrison had become famous within the company for organizing impassioned speeches designed to embolden company bottlers to increase sales. He came up with one of Woodruff's beloved rallying cries, urging salesmen to make sure Coke was just "an arm's length from desire." Harrison constantly brainstormed ideas to increase Coke sales and in 1923 came up with the idea for the six-pack carton as a way to facilitate bulk consumer purchases. During the Great Depression, Harrison's six-pack, along with coin-operated vending machines, made it easier than ever for consumers to make impulse purchases, especially at one of the more than 500,000 gas stations around the country, venues Woodruff identified as prime targets for expansion. The result of these new marketing initiatives, executed by experienced middle management, was record sales as the company sold more than 56 million gallons of syrup in 1939, an increase of nearly 30 million gallons from sales a decade earlier. While millions of Americans struggled to get by in the hard years of the Depression, Coca-Cola was thriving.[48]

Troubles, however, surfaced with the onset of war. Beginning in 1939, heavy sugar users in Europe, fearing future embargoes and other trade disruptions, signed huge sugar contracts with international growers, hoping to stockpile reserve supplies. This made prices rise precipitously. As a result, the federal government, through the recently created Office of Price Administration (OPA)—an arm of the Office for Emergency Management—took aggressive steps to halt the price inflation stimulated by increased demand, capping duty-paid raw sugar prices at 3.5 cents per pound in August of 1941.[49]

Coke—whose annual sugar consumption now totaled over 200 million pounds—welcomed the OPA's August 1941 price ceiling; the company recognized that the government's intervention prevented exponential increases in sugar prices at a time when wartime demand and trade disruptions threatened runaway inflation. With the OPA putting a cap on sugar prices, it appeared that the government would help Coke avoid costly losses in the face of uncertain international market conditions.[50]

The company's praise for the government's price control interventions, however, was tempered with frustration about sugar-usage restrictions imposed by the Office of Production Management (OPM), the predecessor agency to the War Production Board (WPB). These restrictions went into effect on January 1, 1942, limiting sugar usage for Coca-Cola and other soft drink manufacturers to 70 percent of 1941 consumption. Coke executives were livid about the measure and believed that the government controls would severely impact domestic sales.[51]

Determined to get around the OPM restrictions, Benjamin Oehlert, a Coca-Cola executive and company lobbyist in DC, wrote to Robert Woodruff just weeks after the OPM restrictions went into effect suggesting the company look into "the practicability of manufacturing Coca-Cola syrup in Canada, Mexico, Hawaii, Cuba, Puerto Rico, the Virgin Islands, and any other place outside the territorial confines of the United States, for shipment to and use in the United States." Ultimately, the Atlanta office tabled the proposal, recognizing that transportation and import fees would make the plan cost-prohibitive. Oehlert, unfazed, decided to approach the OPM to see if he could secure a better sugar deal for Coke.[52]

Ben Oehlert was well suited to act as Coke's liaison to the government, having spun in the revolving door separating private and public worlds. Before joining Coke's legal team in 1938, he had served as an attorney for the Department of State since 1935. He was just the type of recruit Robert Woodruff was looking for in the 1930s, someone with the diplomatic acumen to help the company break into new markets. An Ivy League graduate, he was bright and confident, a man with a knack for brokering tough deals, a talent both businessmen and public officials recognized (including President Lyndon Baines Johnson, who in 1967 snagged Oehlert from Coke, sending him to Pakistan to serve as US ambassador). Woodruff initially brought Oehlert in to handle issues related to foreign sales but soon recognized that his talents could be better used negotiating tough deals with Washington bureaucrats. Within a few years, he became one of the company's chief government liaisons.[53]

Oehlert, drawing on his State Department experience, knew that he had to prove to the government that increasing Coke's sugar quotas was a matter of national security. He recycled World War I propaganda that positioned Coke as a dedicated public citizen committed to the war effort, a product that brought much-needed energy to a war-weary nation. Oehlert also sold thousands of pounds of Coke's inventoried sugar to the US military to improve the company's "psychological and public relations position." The ploy worked, with major newspapers, such as the *Washington Post*, praising Coke's government sales, citing the company's claim that it sold the sugar below market price. Citizen Coke was once again coming to the aid of its mother country. In the eyes of the American public, the Coca-Cola Company was sacrificing its bounty for the common good, aiding the federal government while asking nothing in return.[53]

Behind closed doors, however, Coke worked hard to capitalize on its "charitable" donations, relying heavily on its inside man, Ed Forio, a Coke executive well versed in DC lobbying tactics. Again, the boundary between Coke and government was blurred. In addition to working for Coca-Cola, Forio was also a consultant for the Beverage and Tobacco Branch of the WPB. Working from within the government, Forio sought to raise Coke's status on WPB quota charts from a luxury item associated with candies to a wartime necessity. Explaining his chief objective, Forio told the *Coca-Cola Bottler* after the war that "an untiring effort was made to point out the tremendous part that soft drinks play in the ordinary every day lives of average people to those highest in authority in government. This effort was crowned with the publication of the Civilian Requirements Bedrock Report, which stated that a minimum of 65 per cent of the products of this industry was necessary to the maintenance of civilian morale." The Bedrock Report also treated tobacco as a wartime essential, suggesting that the government take action to ensure civilian access to at least 71 percent of all tobacco products produced in 1941. Coke and cigarettes were apparently provisions essential to the good health and happiness of American citizens.[54]

In addition to its Washington lobbying efforts, Coca-Cola leaned on the talents of its advertising men to shape public policy in the company's favor. Coke's promotional team produced a series of publications in 1942, such as "Importance of the Rest-Pause in Maximum War Effort" and "Soft Drinks in War," that portrayed Coke as an essential foodstuff of the American worker. These propaganda pieces proclaimed that Coke was simply channeling energy, both chemical and psychological, to the working men and women of America. To silence those individuals who questioned the company's scientific assertions about the benefits of soft drinks, Coke brought in a team of scientists to fight for its cause. One passionate appeal came from US Surgeon General Thomas Parran, who exclaimed, "In this time of stress and strain, Americans turn to their sparkling beverage as the British of all classes turn to their cup of tea and the Brazilians to their coffee. From that moment of relaxation, they go back to their task cheered and strengthened, with no aftermath of gastric repentance. There is no undue strain upon the purse; no physiological penalty for indulgence."[55]

Ultimately, the federal government bought Coke's pitch and increased the company's sugar quota to 80 percent of 1941 consumption. The OPA transferred the company from the Beverage and Tobacco Branch to the Food Section, a division overseeing production and consumption of basic agricultural necessities.

But the government deal got even sweeter. The US Army persuaded the OPA to offer sugar credits to Coke for all company shipments to military installations both at home and abroad, including post exchange stores at domestic army bases. Under the arrangement, Coke could sell virtually unlimited supplies of syrup to US soldiers without affecting its 80 percent cap on civilian sugar sales. This request for exemption came from the top: General Dwight D. Eisenhower issued an order on January 23, 1943, for equipment, bottles, and Coke syrup adequate to supply 6 million monthly servings to the troops.[56]

Coke's military contracts allowed the company to make immense net profits, $25 million in 1944 alone, not only because it enjoyed exclusive access to army markets but also because it could purchase unlimited supplies of sugar at government-controlled prices—ceiling prices that would have been far higher in a turbulent wartime economic climate had the OPA not intervened to regulate inflation. With government controls keeping the cost of sugar down and new military contracts being signed as the war progressed, Coke expanded its operations and increased its sugar consumption throughout the war.[57]

Coke's industry rival, Pepsi-Cola, was furious. It did not receive the same military contracts as Coke, and there were those at Pepsi who feared the government's preferential partnerships might eliminate the company's recent hard-won gains. After going bankrupt in 1923, Pepsi had reemerged in the 1930s, the pet project of Charles Guth, president of Loft Inc. in New York City, a business that owned several candy stores in the Big Apple. Before taking over the Pepsi brand, Guth had sold both Coke and Pepsi at his New York stores. A hot-tempered businessman who had shot his chauffeur after a heated argument in the 1910s, Guth had it in for Coke after the company refused to offer him a discount on a bulk sale of syrup. In his typical bellicose manner, he retaliated to the perceived slight by selling Pepsi-Cola in 12-ounce containers for just a nickel, twice as much product as Coke offered for the same price. The marketing ploy worked. Guth made over $450,000 in Pepsi sales by 1934, a total representing less than 1 percent of Coke's business that year, but early success that nevertheless disturbed Woodruff and Coke's legal team. Fearful of losing market share, Coke tried to quash Pepsi before it could get any bigger.[58]

John Sibley, who took over the reins of Coca-Cola's Legal Department from Harold Hirsch in 1934, led the charge. He filed a trademark infringement suit in Canada in May of 1936, hoping to capitalize on the fact that Pepsi was a relatively new competitor to Coke in that country. Four years later, however, the Canadian Supreme Court ruled in favor of Pepsi, leaving Woodruff with no choice but to broker an uneasy truce. It seemed Pepsi was here to stay.[59]

Fortunately for Coke, by the fall of 1938, reasonable minds now occupied Loft's highest offices. Guth no longer owned Pepsi-Cola. He had resigned from Loft in 1935, hoping to take Pepsi with him, but four years later lost a decisive court case that allowed Loft to retain ownership of the soft drink company. Walter Mack, a much less acrimonious character, now headed the rival soft drink firm, and he worked quietly behind the scenes to resolve differences with Coke. By 1941, he had convinced Woodruff to drop any further lawsuits against his company and, in exchange, offered to deemphasize "cola" in all future Pepsi advertisements. With Coke off his back, Mack built on Guth's success, nearly tripling the company's profits in his first four years with the company. In 1941, the company posted net profits exceeding $9 million.[60]

Considering how hard Pepsi had scrapped and clawed just to gain a small portion of the soft drink market from Coke, Mack was appalled when the government refused to extend the same military contracts it offered Coke. He complained that the government had established a prejudicial sugar system, one that gave Coke an unfair competitive advantage. Mack wrote a scathing letter to the OPA in the fall of 1944 expressing frustration that some soft drink companies were allowed, through military rationing exemptions, to do "160%" of 1941 sales while competitors without government contracts were "held down to only 80% of 1941" production. He requested that the OPA not offer "replacement sugar" or rationing credits to preferred companies and pleaded with the OPA to abandon an inequitable sugar program that fueled the monopolistic growth of industry giants.[61]

Pepsi's pleas went unheeded, and for the remainder of the war, Coca-Cola continued to enjoy exclusive contracts with military installations across the globe. Thanks in large part to the government, Coke gained a huge lead over its chief rival, the margin between the firms' net incomes widening from $19.9 million in 1941 to $26.3 million six years later. By some estimation, Coke sold over 10 billion bottles at military bases and home post exchanges during the war, controlling 95 percent of all military soft drink sales. Due in large part to its overseas operations, between 1942 and 1944 the company increased its syrup sales from 74.4 million to 95.8 million gallons.[62]

Coke's military contracts would sow the seeds of global expansion after the war. Rudimentary bottling plants designed to serve troops in Europe (discussed in chapter 6) were reconverted for civilian markets in peacetime, and there was a ready market for these plants' finished goods. After all, Coke had become the libation of liberation. As GIs swept through devastated cities and towns in 1944 and 1945, so too did Citizen Coke. For many war-weary Europeans, the soft drink was seen as the fuel of the freedom fighters. Thus, what the government offered Coca-Cola was more than just financial support and special privileges in the sugar market; it also offered the company invaluable cultural capital in new markets. Bedecked in government-issue garb, it was easy for Citizen Coke to make promises of public betterment in foreign lands. For those who had never heard of the Coca-Cola brand, the US Army's imprimatur offered the best kind of advertising Coke did not have to buy.

BY THE END OF World War II, the Hershey Corporation decided it was time to get out of the Cuban sugar business. Milton Hershey had passed away in the fall of 1945, and Percy A. Staples, who had run Hershey's Cuban operations since 1921, had taken over leadership of the company. Staples had no lofty ambitions to change the world through corporate welfare programs. Unlike Hershey, he was an introvert, more comfortable crunching numbers late at night at his desk than socializing in Cuban casinos. The bottom line mattered to Staples, and when he surveyed Hershey's Cuban assets, he saw only risks and no benefits. The company's sugar plantations were not generating sizable profits. The real moneymaker was its retail business back in Pennsylvania. So, in 1945, Staples sold Hershey's Cuba properties, worth some $30 million, to the Cuban Atlantic Sugar Company. Hershey had moved even closer toward Coke's model of doing business.[63]

Staples's streamlining made Hershey better adapted to the globalized marketplace of the mid-twentieth century. In the postwar period, no business wanted to have heavy assets tying it down in one host nation. International politics and federal trading policies were too erratic to ensure that these place-specific investments would continually produce profits. Integration was therefore more risky than staying out of the commodity production business. Diversifying purchasing contracts among a host suppliers was a much more prudent way of reducing risk.

AS A THIRD-PARTY BUYER, Coke reaped the benefits of a stable global sugar market in the late 1940s and through the 1950s, one regulated by Uncle Sam. After the war, the federal government controlled the sugar market through import quotas by regulating how much producing countries could export to the United States each year. Preventing wild price spikes allowed Coke to make steady increases in sugar purchases without suffering major financial losses. Here at midcentury was a company that channeled over 600 million pounds of sugar into customers' bodies. With huge purchasing contracts, even the most minuscule price fluctuation could prove devastating to Coke. The company could only thrive in a predictable market environment, and this artificially stable world only existed because the federal state intervened to make an otherwise chaotic trade legible to big buyers.[64]

Going back to the late nineteenth century, Coke had been the beneficiary of tariffs protecting American refiners, state-sponsored military expeditions in the tropical world, and bounty payments to domestic growers, all of which amplified global sugar production. Quota price regulation was just the latest iteration of state aid, and it proved no less important than earlier government interventions in keeping bloated commodity supply chains from collapsing. Coke suffered major profit scares precisely when the state relinquished protective sugar controls in 1920 and again in 1974 (more on this 1970s scare in the final chapter). In these moments, a basic truth was revealed: unregulated competition produced boom-and-bust commodity price cycles that clashed with American corporations' perpetual growth models. As it turned out, the best thing for sleek Citizen Coke was big government.

4

Coca Leaf Extract

Hiding the Cocaine-Cola Connection

What's in a name? In the case of Coca-Cola, it could be argued, quite a lot. Coke's trademarks were worth over $6.7 billion in 2013. Considering this fact, it is no surprise the company has fought long and hard to secure the exclusive right to trade its flagship product under a distinctive label, relying on federal enforcement of trademark law to prevent potential rivals from stealing one of its most important assets.[1]

But the fact is, Coke never really owned the name Coca-Cola, at least not the "coca" part. After all, the first half of Coca-Cola's moniker was merely appropriated from the ancient language of the Quechua people of South America. Over five thousand years ago, these Peruvian highlanders first used the term "coca" to describe a shrub that grew along the steep, verdant slopes of the Andes. The Quechua became attached to this plant because they found that chewing its leaves kept them energized throughout the day. Coca

leaf contained small quantities of cocaine, an alkaloid later identified in the pharmacological world as a triple reuptake inhibitor,
which meant it prevented the human body from storing important
neurotransmitters that regulate blood flow and mood states. The
result was that Andeans felt more alert and invigorated over longer
periods of time while consuming coca leaves.

Thus, long before there was Coca-Cola there was coca, and for
millennia it belonged to the people of Peru. The story of how Coca-
Cola came to claim title to this Andean crop is long and winding.

FOR CENTURIES, EUROPEANS TREATED coca chewing as an
indigenous practice unfit for civilized society. Though the first
batch of coca leaves made its way back to the Old World in 1544, it
was not until the mid-nineteenth century that scientific discoveries
transformed the plant from a colonial curiosity into a conspicuous
commodity.[2]

The major breakthrough came in the late 1850s when German
and Italian scientists simultaneously isolated the coca leaf's most
potent chemical constituent: cocaine. Since 1554, Europeans had
been intrigued by people chewing coca leaves, and by the mid-1800s,
they began to try in earnest to isolate the potent substance therein.
This was part of a larger chemical quest trailblazed by European
scientists, especially from Germany, which had already led to the
discovery of morphine (derived from opium) in 1817, caffeine (1820),
and nicotine (1828), among other plant-based drugs. The honor of
discovering the coca leaf's chemical stimulant belonged to Göttingen
University doctoral student Albert Niemann and Italian physician
Paolo Mantegazza, both of whom belonged to this growing community of European biochemists interested in isolating the elemen-
tal chemicals within tropical biota. Cocaine was indeed a powerful
drug, capable, as Niemann described in his dissertation, of creating a

"peculiar numbness ... when applied to the tongue." Niemann's and Mantegazza's studies showed that there was magic in the coca leaf after all and that modern science could distill its powers for the world to enjoy.[3]

Just what cocaine would be used for in the Western world was not clear, but experimentation began almost immediately. As we saw in the first chapter, perhaps the greatest European promoter of the Peruvian drug was the Corsican Angelo Mariani, who introduced his coca-laced wine, Vin Mariani, just a few years after Niemann and Mantegazza published their findings on cocaine, but numerous other businesses, both in Europe and America, jumped into the fray, hoping to strike it rich in the coca bonanza. There seemed to be no limit to what people would try: coca cigarettes, throat lozenges, wines, and tinctures. Almost anything was fair game.[4]

While Angelo Mariani relied on the solvent properties of alcohol in his wine to extract the cocaine he needed for his beverages, other businesses sought cocaine supplies from commercial manufacturers. In 1879, Merck of Darmstadt, the German-owned chemical company that would also become one of the world's biggest caffeine producers, began the first commercial extraction of cocaine from coca leaves, and soon it enjoyed a healthy trade in wholesale distribution of purified, white cocaine crystals. Some of Merck's early clients were doctors who had found new surgical uses for cocaine. German physician Karl Koller was one such early buyer, who put cocaine to use as a numbing agent while performing eye surgery on a patient. Following Koller's discovery, interest in cocaine spread rapidly within the medical community. Citing Koller's experiment, the *American Druggist*, a popular publishing organ of the pharmaceutical industry, reported in June of 1885, "Coca leaves and Cocaine—are undoubtedly the lions of the day, no other drug having caused such a stir, professionally or commercially, for many years past."[5]

The surge in coca demand inspired new investment in supply

infrastructure. By 1887, Merck had competition from a host of new chemical companies in the United States and Europe. The entry of Parke-Davis, New York Quinine, Mallinckrodt, and other similar companies made cocaine available in larger quantities, and whole-sale prices for the narcotic dropped from over $10 a gram in 1884 to just 25 cents per gram two years later. In the United States, the federal government encouraged domestic output by placing, in 1896, high import duties on cocaine entering the United States while reducing the impost on raw coca leaves needed for domestic nar-cotic production. Shielded from international competitors, American chemical-processing companies expanded their cocaine production exponentially in the 1880s and 1890s.[6]

Andean cocaine manufacturers did well, too, encouraged by local politicians interested in modernizing South American polities. Peru-vian scientists pushed for the construction of cocaine-manufacturing infrastructure in their country during the 1880s. They helped turn coca consumption from a tabooed native custom into an instrument of modernization. These Peruvian nationalists believed that the pro-duction of crude cocaine for international pharmaceutical compa-nies could help bring cutting-edge industry into remote corners of the Andes.[7]

The coca production boom expanded in the late nineteenth cen-tury. Angelo Mariani commented on this trend in 1896: "For some time, as a result of the extended consumption of Coca and for a still stronger reason, now that the day is at hand when the consumption of Coca will assume greater proportions, numerous plantations of Coca trees have been laid out in regions where that shrub was formerly unknown." Another commentator echoed Mariani, commenting that the "shrubs are [now] found scattered along the entire eastern curve of the Andes, from the Straits of Magellan to the borders of the Caribbean Sea." One estimate had it that the global cocaine supply for licit consumption increased by over 700 percent between 1890 and 1902, with Peru leading the world in exports of both coca leaf and crude cocaine.[8]

But would the production surge continue to meet the growing demand for coca? This would become a paralyzing fear at Coca-Cola. As we have seen, John Pemberton's Coca-Cola, a kind of temperance knock-off of Vin Mariani, contained coca leaf extract, and though it is unclear exactly how much coca went into Pemberton's syrup in the 1880s, a copy of a formula acquired by the great-grandson of Pemberton's business partner, Frank Robinson, suggested that some 10 pounds of coca leaves were needed to produce 36 gallons of syrup. If this were so, Coke would have needed over 59,000 pounds of coca leaves by 1898 in order to produce the syrup it sold that year. Considering this demand, Coke had to have a steady supply of coca, and only a special type would do. For decades, Coke's leaders insisted on using only Trujillo leaves cultivated in Peru, even when new coca producers emerged in Java and Formosa, arguing that this variety offered the only flavor profile suitable for Coca-Cola flavor extract. Too many buyers chasing too little Trujillo supply could surely hurt, perhaps fatally, Coke's bottom line. Pemberton foresaw this problem in 1885, arguing, "The greatest misfortune that can ever arise, in regard to the coca question is that we may not be able to get sufficient supplies for all when once its great properties are known to the people."[9]

By 1900, Coke had no internal fix for this problem. It did not own coca plantations in Peru and therefore had no leverage over supply. The company was at the mercy of Trujillo producers because they had a monopoly on an ingredient Coke needed. This made coca different than other commodities Coke purchased. Coke acquired its caffeine and sugar from multiple producers around the globe and relied in part on interfirm competition to help keep costs down. But coca suppliers in Peru, who enjoyed exclusive control over production of the Trujillo leaf Coke wanted, were free to serve buyers at the highest bidding price, a price that was bound to rise if new buyers continued to increase demand. The Coca-Cola Company needed to eliminate competitors for precious coca resources; it needed monopoly control, but it was not willing to invest in coca production itself to achieve this goal. It needed help—and found it, perversely, in the growing anti-cocaine movement.

BY THE START OF the twentieth century, concern over the rampant use of alkaloid drugs—caffeine, morphine, cocaine, and other organic bases extracted from plants—had begun to grow. In 1901, over 1.8 million pounds of coca leaves entered the United States, much of it used to produce purified cocaine crystals. For some, this was a sign of a dangerous national addiction. Progressive reformers—many of whom also questioned the healthfulness of caffeine—believed cocaine turned otherwise law-abiding citizens into wide-eyed criminals. In the South especially, cocaine increasingly became seen as a drug contributing to black crime. Such fears also gained momentum even in the North. The *New York Times*, for example, reported in June of 1903 that "cocaine sniffing" was "increasing among negroes of the South" and argued that the drug "habit is growing with wonderful rapidity, and its evil effects are being seen in all the towns and cities of the Southern States." In 1902, playing up such racist fears, Georgia legislators outlawed the distribution of cocaine in Coke's backyard, and soon other states followed suit.[10]

In light of growing public concerns about cocaine, Coca-Cola president Asa Candler decided to remove all traces of cocaine in his formula around the time of the ban. Candler, then in his early fifties, had become sensitive to growing reports that his drink contributed to iniquitous transgressions. The brother of well-known Atlanta bishop Warren Candler of the Methodist Episcopal Church, South, Asa was a devout Christian and a Sunday school teacher, someone who shunned intemperate behavior and preached moral rectitude to his children.

He would expect the same moral purity of his company. He would not sell an ingredient many considered to be a primer for devilish vice.

Yet, even as Candler made the decision to remove cocaine from the secret formula, he insisted that the beverage contain a new decocainized coca leaf extract so as not to alter Coke's flavor profile. The new ingredient, known within the company as Merchandise #5, consisted of trace quantities of decocainized coca leaves mixed with kola nut powder. In an attempt to further distance Coke from any association with the cocaine industry, the company chose to rely on its caffeine supplier, Schaeffer Alkaloid Works of Maywood, New Jersey (later Maywood Chemical Works), to manufacture this decocainized extract.[11]

The Maywood firm was critical in securing Coke's coca supplies because, as a wholesaler servicing other pharmaceutical industries, it was largely invisible to the public. The company made profits from the sale of intermediate products to pharmaceutical distributors, not from the sale of branded products in retail outlets. Schaeffer could thus distinguish itself from increasingly discredited quack medicine makers who sold directly to consumers. In the early years of the Progressive Era, reformers insisted that medical experts become the primary dispensers of medicinal products. As a drug wholesaler rather than a brand-name retailer, Schaeffer could claim that its cocaine would only go into products prescribed by credentialed physicians, the new trusted custodians of professionalized public health.[12]

Coke used Schaeffer to shield its involvement in the increasingly controversial coca trade. The soft drink company did not build processing plants to decocainize its coca leaves and it did not conduct the day-to-day business of extracting or transporting leaves from Peru. Rather, it let Schaeffer do these things and remained a third-party buyer in the trade.

Anonymity was key, especially as anti-cocaine agitation intensified after 1902, when local bans inspired federal legislation. By

1906, the USDA Bureau of Chemistry required products containing cocaine to say so on product packaging. Strict federal restrictions on imports and use of coca, however, did not clamp down until after passage of the Harrison Narcotics Tax Act of 1914, which, among other measures, restricted the use of cocaine to prescribed medicines. For enforcement, the act created the Federal Narcotics Control Board and the Narcotics Division within the Department of Treasury. These agencies would be the cocaine gatekeepers in the United States. Finally, the Jones-Miller Narcotic Drugs Import and Export Act of 1922 further circumscribed the market for cocaine by officially closing off importation of coca leaves into the United States except for distribution to select licensed cocaine manufacturers.[13]

The coca leaf and its cocaine, once items of vibrant international trade featuring multiple commercial buyers, had thus, by the early 1920s, become restricted commercial commodities dominated by a few chemical processors—a select few. The federal government sanctioned just two companies to bring coca leaves into the United States after passage of the Jones-Miller Act in 1922; they were Merck of Rahway, New Jersey, and the newly renamed Maywood Chemical Works.[14]

This supply-channel constriction in the United States came about not because private reform interests captured federal narcotics agencies but rather because the state actively pursued construction of a monopoly to facilitate regulation. At bottom, the federal government needed to simplify oversight of coca imports. Regulating just a few coca distributors was far easier than trying to trace purchases made by a variety of small buyers at ports around the country. In short, Progressive Era counternarcotics regulation, conceived of as expanding the role of government to curb the excesses of corporation growth, often had the unexpected consequence of encouraging monopoly.[15]

During debate over the Harrison Act and later legislation, Coca-

Cola did not seek rights to become a direct importer of coca leaves. Rather, it preferred to deal with a middleman. Doing so meant that it could remain insulated from a tabooed international drug trade. But to stay at arm's length required an exemption permitting Coke to use Maywood's spent coca leaves in its production of Merchandise #5, and Coke began an extended lobbying effort to ensure it got what it wanted. Attorney Eugene Brokmeyer of the National Association of Retail Druggists, an organization that represented over 50,000 drug businesses in the country, led Coke's lobbying effort. The result was section 6 of the Harrison Act, a clause sanctioning use of "de-cocainized coca leaves or preparations made therefrom, or to any other preparations of coca leaves that do not contain cocaine." Since Coke was the only major company using this extract, some congressmen dubbed the exemption the "Coca-Cola joker." It turned up in the Jones-Miller Act of 1922 and the Porter Act of 1930, and it remains in all cocaine legislation to this day.[16]

Maywood also benefited from the "Coca-Cola joker," which kept alive a market for a waste by-product of the cocaine-manufacturing process. Maywood, of course, continued to make money from the sale of cocaine to pharmaceuticals for "medicinal or scientific purposes." But the joker legalized the sale of waste coca leaves to Coke, a trade that increasingly became an important source of company revenue. Coke had secured a virtual monopsony, single buyer access to deco-cainized Peruvian coca leaf.[17]

Only one problem remained—Maywood did not have enough coca leaves to satisfy Coke's growing demand. By 1930, Coca-Cola required roughly 200,000 pounds of coca leaves annually for its Merchandise #5, more leaves than the Maywood Chemical Works needed to supply its medicinal cocaine buyers. Maywood did not have federal permission to import the additional leaves Coke required. Coke was being squeezed, and its coca leaf extract reserves were dropping rapidly. Company syrup manufacturers predicted that they would run out of sufficient supplies of decocainized coca leaf extract by February 1, 1930. What to do?[18]

An answer perhaps lay offshore. By 1928, Coca-Cola and Maywood had invested in an experimental coca processing plant—managed by Maywood—in Callao, Peru. That year the plant produced over 4,000 pounds of coca leaf extract for Coca-Cola and 18 kilograms of cocaine as a by-product. Because it was operating outside of American narcotics oversight, the Coke official in charge, Claude Gortatowsky, figured the Peruvian plant could sell its cocaine any place in the world other than the United States, which it did for over $1,000 (roughly 41 pounds at about $28 per pound). Before long, however, the State Department muttered about the plant's potential to flood the international market with cocaine. Fearful of losing its state-sanctioned coca supply, Maywood and Coca-Cola abandoned the experimental plant by 1933 and never attempted to reopen it.[19]

With overseas production ruled out, relief would have to come from Washington. And it did, via new legislation, the Porter Act of 1930. This new counternarcotics law created the Federal Bureau of Narcotics (FBN) within the Treasury Department and permitted Maywood's coca import quota to include "special leaves" specifically reserved for production of coca leaf extract in beverages. Any cocaine generated by decocainizing the leaves had to be destroyed under supervision of FBN inspectors stationed at the New Jersey plant. For Coke, the arrangement was not ideal because it required Coca-Cola to assume costs once covered by the sale of cocaine to Maywood's clients. Coke now took on transportation and impost expenses, as well as a higher decocainizing processing fee. All told, it cost the company an estimated 35 cents more per pound of coca leaves imported for the Merchandise #5 it needed, actually a modest investment to avert supply shortages.[20]

But these technicalities aside, the state had once again sweetened Coke's supply situation. Special leaf imports from Peru, all of which went to prepare Coke's extract, exploded after the Porter Act, from 217,124 pounds in 1931 to over 639,000 in 1941, dwarfing by 200 percent medicinal imports that year. For its part, Maywood was making money at both ends.[21]

THE IMPORTATION PROBLEM SOLVED, questions remained regarding domestic competition for Maywood's finished product. Once cocaine had been drawn from coca leaves in New Jersey and shipped off to medical facilities or burned at Coke's expense, federal narcotics agencies did not regulate distribution of what was left. Since passage of the Harrison Act, no law prevented other businesses than Coke from bidding for Maywood's decocainized coca leaf extract. What if a host of new buyers drove up the price of Merchandise #5?

While simultaneously battling sugar taxes in the US Congress, Ralph Hayes, Coke's vivacious vice president and top political lobbyist, expressed his concern about the coca situation to company boss Robert Woodruff in 1936. He explained that Maywood's vice president, Marion J. Hartung, had contacted him and indicated that "the pressure on Washington was heavy to prevent applicants other than [Coke] from being shut out from a source of supply of extract." One applicant in particular, the Better Kola Company—a small Louisville, Kentucky, firm with just $900 in fixed assets—had submitted multiple petitions to the Federal Bureau of Narcotics seeking relief. Maywood appeared amenable to extending a contract to Better Kola but first wished to know whether Coke would object. Maywood proposed two solutions. To stem a flood of new coca extract buyers, Maywood could sell "a small quantity" of coca leaf extract to a wholesale intermediary, such as Schieffelin & Company. What Schieffelin did with it would be its own business. Alternatively, the company could process small quantities for Merck, which would in turn supply extract to specific soft drink companies.[22]

Neither option found favor with Coke since both, in its view, would diminish the company's brand strength. A competitor with access to extract produced from Trujillo leaves would no doubt sing loudly that their product was "made from the same source" as Coca-Cola. Whatever coca leaf extract might actually add to the taste of a competitor's beverage was clearly of secondary importance to Hayes. His company had, and meant to keep, exclusive access to an exotic ingredient because it increased the value of its trademark.[23]

The Federal Bureau of Narcotics did not push Maywood to sell to Coke's competitors. Rather it chose evasion. When beverage companies wrote to the FBN to learn more about Maywood's operations, the agency responded with stock letters to all of them, including RC Cola, Hoffman Beverage Company, Great Bear Water Company, and the National Fruit Flavor Company, declaring, "The further processing or extraction of any non-narcotic alkaloids from these decocainized leaves is not under the jurisdiction of this Bureau." If these companies wanted to learn more about procurement possibilities they should contact the two companies licensed to distribute this product, Maywood and Merck.[24]

Though the government offered de facto support for its monopsony, Coca-Cola still could not be certain Maywood would refuse future contracts from other companies, so to help Maywood make up its mind, Coke raised the stakes. In March of 1936, Hayes wrote to Hartung, explaining that Maywood's acceptance of competing contracts might force Coke to seek a new supplier. Coke "would be willing," he said, "to negotiate an extension of" its established contract with Maywood, but "if circumstances were so to change as to make us one of a number of purchasers of extract from the present source, we would have freedom of discretion to consider the utilization of an alternative source ourselves." The loss of Coca-Cola's contract, which generated hundreds of thousands of dollars in revenue for the chemical company by 1930, would have hurt Maywood's profitability. Clearly, this was a risk the New Jersey firm should not take. From that point on, Maywood evaded other companies seeking access to their coca extract.[25]

Coke was such a dominant Maywood client by the mid-1930s that Hartung approached Hayes about buying the chemical company's facilities in New Jersey. When Hayes mentioned the overture to company attorneys in March of 1936, the Legal Department wrote back sharply, "We should be more interested in seeing the plant in good hands than in owning." For fifty years Coke had dodged the risks and liabilities associated with direct production of its ingredients. Merchandise #5 would be no exception. Some twenty-five years later, Maywood would renew its merger proposal, but Coke's vice president Benjamin Oehlert once again rebuffed the invitation, arguing that ownership of coca production facilities "would violate our general policy of nonproduction of ingredients." The company's historic partnership with Maywood had been "highly satisfactory in that [Maywood had] done a most commendable job in terms of raw material acquisition, maintenance of exclusivity, maintenance of formula and process secrecy, conduct of delicate government relationships here and abroad, and mutually agreeable pricing arrangements." For Oehlert, ownership "might raise troublesome problems of public relations," and nobody wanted that. A heightened public awareness of Coke's links to the international coca trade would surely pose an existential threat.[26]

Such fears were elevated in 1937 when commissioner Harry Anslinger of the Federal Bureau of Narcotics suggested creation of a regulatory commission to oversee the export of Merchandise #5 to Coca-Cola plants outside the United States. Seven years into his commissionership with the FBN, Anslinger had befriended Coke and sought to work with it in designing new trade regulations. He saw the new commission as a way to protect Coke from pending changes in federal narcotics policy that would have banned the sale of Merchandise #5 to international distribution facilities. These proposed amendments ultimately failed, but Coke all the while balked at Anslinger's plan because it believed the Coca-Cola Company "would possibly be grouped, as beneficiaries of the amendment, with some manufacturers of" other "narcotics." Coke had worked hard to keep its name clean from association with "contraband substances," and it wanted no part of a government program that would in any way expose a link to coca traders. With the federal spotlight on international coca trafficking growing brighter, the obfuscation Maywood offered Coke was too important to give up.[27]

But exposure was not the only problem Coke had to worry about. After World War II, new developments abroad sparked concerns about supply. The newly created United Nations Commission on Narcotic Drugs showed signs of initiating stricter regulations on international cocaine traffic. In 1947, that body set up the Commission of Enquiry on the Coca Leaf to study coca export patterns and cocaine production around the world. Coke feared this would be the beginning of a new international crackdown on coca.[28]

Further, the Peruvian government was moving steadily to take over management of coca production within its borders. Beginning in the 1930s, Paz Soldán, editor of the influential South American medical reform journal *La Reforma Médica* and former subdirector of the Pan-American Sanitary Union, launched a campaign to end foreign domination of the Andean coca trade. Soldán proposed a new state-run organization in charge of buying coca from Peruvian producers and managing sales to international buyers. It was a long battle, but in 1949, Peru's government passed Decree-Law No. 11406, creating a government coca monopoly, Estanco (later the National Coca Enterprise or ENACO).[29]

Coke believed that these new state institutions and international counternarcotics agencies might have agendas that would spoil the company's favorable monopsony position. Benjamin Oehlert had expressed his alarm in a company memorandum in February of 1948, just months before the official announcement about Estanco. He disliked the renewed attention "being given by governments and by the United Nations to narcotics problems" and predicted "that it is entirely within the realm of possibility that the cultivation and harvesting of coca leaves might be banned in Peru and elsewhere in the world" in the not too distant future. "Such a development," Oehlert continued, "could have such drastic results to the Coca-Cola Company as practically to destroy it, regardless of the actual physical importance of coca extracts."[30]

Was all this fretting worth it? After all, how important was the coca leaf to Coke's taste? All evidence suggested not very. Indeed, Federal Bureau of Narcotics commissioner Harry Anslinger—an official with considerable knowledge about the process of creating decocainized coca-leaf extract for Coke—suggested that if one compared "the limited quantities of coca extract manufactured with the huge volume of finished coca cola extract sold and exported," it appeared obvious "that the contribution of the former to the ultimate flavor is insignificant and suspect that it continues to be used merely to enable the Company to retain the word 'Coca' in the name which it has spent millions to advertise."[31]

As Anslinger suggested, Coca-Cola saw magic in the coca leaf not because it added special flavors to beverages but because it was an important component of what Coke chronicler Frederick Allen termed "the cult of the formula." In 1948, Benjamin Oehlert explained the company position, saying that if Coca-Cola removed coca from its product, "it would, of course, become known that that ingredient was no longer used, and the psychological impact of that public knowledge could be disastrous."[32]

There was no abandoning coca, and in the next two decades Coke would experiment with new ways of getting its special ingredient. In 1948, Oehlert proposed a solution involving the company becoming stronger in biotechnological research and development. He recommended that "a reasonably substantial sum of money be appropriated each year, for as long as may be necessary . . . to try and develop a strain of coca plants whose leaves would have the flavor qualities we desire without any cocaine or other narcotics." For Oehlert, the venture was important enough "to completely justify substantial expenditures."[33]

This was not the first time Coke had sought alternatives to Peruvian sources of supply. In the 1910s, the company had tinkered with using leaves produced in Java but ultimately found them to have an off-taste. Then, early in 1937, Hayes wrote Woodruff touting Brazilian coca leaf as a way to ameliorate predicted shortages, saying it would be "advantageous to know whether we are limited to one satisfactory source or have a serviceable alternative." But Brazil's leaves fell short as well. Nothing, it seemed, could match Peru's Trujillo leaves.[34]

Nor could chemistry solve the problem. Initial experiments to isolate a cocaineless variety of coca in the 1950s proved fruitless. Little is known about these projects, which were conducted in complete secrecy by Maywood. In 1959, Hayes reported only that "Maywood's experimentation at our request a couple of years ago to find an alternative for the tabooed component was less than successful, both because the resultant product was sub-standard and because, even if it were not, the compositional change might have left us vulnerable to essentially the same objection that we were trying to obviate," namely that raw materials needed for Merchandise #5 production contained cocaine. Even so, undeterred, Hayes urged Coke to continue financing Maywood's operations: "My layman's notion is that if the chance of success were even half what it is, we ought to keep the scientists at work."[35]

Despite Coke's fervent quest for a cocaineless coca shrub, the company ultimately had no real trouble meeting its procurement needs via Peruvian suppliers, well into the late 1950s. The FBN continued to protect Coke's Peruvian trade, and because new buyers were prevented from entering the restricted market, prices for Coke's special ingredient remained low.

Nonetheless, Coke never gave up hope of cultivating cocaine-free coca. In the 1960s, the company began discussions with the Stepan Chemical Company—now Maywood Chemical Works's owner—to renew its search for a cocaineless coca variety in nature. Coke had begun discussions with the FBN about this prospect in the fall of 1962.

What Coke proposed was astonishing: the development of secret coca farms on United States soil. Ralph Hayes, now in his late sixties, still with the company and serving in his third decade as a Woodruff consigliere, corresponded with narcotics commissioner Henry Giordano in October 1962, suggesting that the Virgin Islands might be a suitable site for such a project. By comparing coca crops in the US Virgin Islands with crops in Peru the company might "learn something of the combination of soil, altitude, moisture, temperature, fertilizing, etc. that is conducive to the growth of leaves high in flavor elements and, hopefully, low in alkaloidal content."[36]

This overture intrigued the FBN because of its potential assistance to US counternarcotics initiatives. John Maher of the Bureau of Narcotics supported the initiative and explained that altering "the alkaloidal content of the coca plant would certainly be a noteworthy project and if successful a meritorious contribution . . . to the sciences."[37] Commissioner Giordano also came on board, and by the spring of 1963, Coca-Cola began to negotiate with the federal government to move forward with the operation. In April, Ralph Hayes contacted Giordano and explained that the Virgin Islands would not be ideal for growing coca. He argued that "the factor of altitude (or lack of it) can better be assayed" in Hawaii than in the Virgin Islands and requested that the island of Kauai serve as the base for future experiments.[38]

Once again, having no wish to manage anything regarding manufacture of its ingredients, especially not coca leaf, Coke enrolled several public and private sector partners in the Hawaiian venture, now called the "Alakea project." The research contract negotiated between the University of Hawaii, the Federal Bureau of Narcotics, Coca-Cola, and Stepan specifically stipulated that Coca-Cola not be listed as a contributor to the Kauaian initiative. William Tollenger, narcotics agent for the Honolulu Branch of the FBN, explained that the Tropical Agricultural Department of the University of Hawaii would direct the operation. Further, all funding for research would come directly from the Maywood Chemical Works Division of the Stepan Chemical Company "so that the name of the Coca-Cola Company is not generally associated with the coca leaf." The federal government had its own reasons for obfuscation. In 1963, no federal law prohibited cultivation of coca leaves on US soil, and the FBN feared the Alakea project would foster imitation. Commissioner Giordano even held that if the Hawaiian experiment succeeded, the federal government should develop a new law specifically banning coca growing in the United States, except for research purposes.[39]

In Honolulu, University of Hawaii officials did not like the nondisclosure clauses in the draft proposal. University president Thomas H. Hamilton maintained that the school simply could not honor contract provisions banning it from listing Coca-Cola's connection. Writing to Oehlert, Hamilton explained, "Dean Rosenberg has told me of your desire not to bring the name of Coca-Cola into this project. Certainly we shall not volunteer such information. On the other hand, should questions be raised I shall have to answer them. Being a public university we really can have no secrets!" Hamilton added that "grants such as this go on the agenda among others, and we do not spell out any details," suggesting only that the name of the project be changed from Alakea to the scientific name of coca in order not to "excite curiosity." Back and forth it went.[40]

The university's reluctance worried Coca-Cola executives. Vice president Benjamin Oehlert, Woodruff's trusted Washington diplomat who had fought successfully for Coke's sugar quota exemptions during World War II, wrote to Giordano in January of 1964 outlining his grievances: "We are concerned about a number of points in this proposed agreement and the covering letter, principally the University's unwillingness to agree not to publish any of the experiments or their results." He asked for Giordano's advice "as to what we might say or do to persuade the University that under the very special circumstances involved, they should be willing to undertake the research with a commitment not to publish." Giordano responded that the FBN could not support the Alakea project unless the University of Hawaii agreed to a nonpublicity clause; it was a matter, he said, of national security: "Knowledge of the existence of the research program could lead to an illicit production of the coca leaf and subsequently cocaine. Furthermore, other countries of the world with whom the United States cooperates under treaty obligations concerning the international controls on narcotic drugs could very possibly misinterpret the United States' intentions in granting approval for this proposed research program."[41]

Oehlert used these arguments—the specter of domestic cocaine production and deterioration of American diplomatic relations—to put pressure on Hamilton to keep quiet about Coca-Cola's involvement. He said that committing to nondisclosure was "in the public interest, both national and international," and flatly refused to go forward with the project unless Hamilton agreed not to mention Coke in project documents or public statements.[42]

The move proved effective. In February of 1964, Hamilton wrote to Oehlert explaining that he could "withhold any publicity on projects which are classified, and it would seem to me I could justify that action in this case because Commissioner Giordano indicates that such action is in the public interest."[43]

A jubilant Oehlert nevertheless reiterated that the Coca-Cola Company could only support the project if its involvement remained secret, adding, "We feel that if, as and when such an agreement is executed in the name of Maywood Chemical Works Division of Stepan Chemical Company, the identity of that Company is adequate to respond to any questions which need to be answered as to the sponsorship of the project. The fact that The Coca-Cola Company was involved in putting the parties to the agreement together should, we feel, be of no consequence to anyone other than the parties themselves and the Bureau of Narcotics."[44]

By May of 1964 the University of Hawaii, the Stepan Company, and Coca-Cola had crafted a nonpublicity clause satisfactory to all interested parties. The contract now stipulated that "no publication or publicity regarding the research project will be released except by the prior, mutual consent of the parties to this agreement." In the section outlining funding for the project, the Stepan Company was listed as the sole donor, offering $105,100 for the project to be distributed over the course of four years beginning in 1964. In December, FBN agent Tollenger reported that the Hawaiian coca project was under way.[45]

Under the terms of the agreement, Coca-Cola did not purchase land to grow coca in Hawaii or provide the manpower to oversee the project. This support came from the state university in Hawaii, which provided the scientists as well as the publicly owned experimentation centers for the project. Some of the Hawaii field studies took place at the University's Lyon Arboretum, an old cattle ranch restored by the Hawaiian Sugar Planters Association beginning in 1918. Other experiments occurred at the Foster Botanical Garden (owned by the City of Honolulu) as well as the university-owned experimental station located on Kauai. University officials ultimately sent coca leaves from all four sites to the Stepan Chemical Company for processing.[46]

Between April 21 and May 3, 1965, University of Hawaii agronomists reported that over 101 shrubs were "surviving" at various sites owned by the institution. Coca-Cola seemed on the verge of securing a reliable and cheap domestic supply of coca leaves, grown and distributed under the complete jurisdiction of the Federal Bureau of Narcotics, one that was not subject to the vagaries of political changes in the developing world.[47]

But nature soon interceded. Within ten years of commencing coca cultivation in Hawaii, the Coca-Cola Company learned that a mysterious fungus was killing off its entire Kauaian coca crop. The fungus, later identified as *Fusarium oxysporum* EN-4, attacked the coca shrubs by injecting toxins into their roots that essentially deteriorated plant cells, causing the crops to wilt. *Fusarium oxysporum* EN-4 was particularly devastating because it remained in the soil for years, preventing University of Hawaii agronomists from growing new crops, of any kind. Coke's secret coca farms were no more.[48]

Quietly, Coca-Cola abandoned the Hawaiian project, and capital investments made by Stepan, estimated at about $100,000, became lost research costs. Losses, however, were minimized by federal and state commitments to the project. Coke and Maywood did not have to worry about the depreciation of the public property used for their projects. Not owning the sites that now lay fallow, devastated by the fungal blight, they had no obligation to restore them. The companies simply walked away.[49]

As it turned out, the failure of the Alakea project did not affect

Coke's ability to acquire coca leaves in the years ahead, for fears of UN or ENACO interventions restricting Coke's access to Andean suppliers never materialized. ENACO ultimately respected Stepan's contracts with local purchasing agents, placing no onerous price increases on Coke's coca supplies. Likewise, the UN worked with Coke and Stepan to make sure that all counternarcotics programs simply bypassed these companies' established trade. This result, however, did not come without hard work. Both companies had sent multiple representatives to a United Nations conference organized to draw up the 1961 UN Single Convention on Narcotic Drugs, a document restricting international drug trafficking. Stepan executive Marion Hartung and Ralph Hayes were present, and both lobbied aggressively for the preservation of exemptions. In exchange for protection, Coca-Cola and Stepan cheerfully supported UN-sponsored coca eradication projects in South America that targeted illicit producers. In 1966, Stepan vice president Donald H. Francis expressed this allegiance: "Our commercial interests and the social interests of the United Nations and United States Government are peculiarly the same. We all believe in effective control of Coca and the elimination of the blight of Coca mastication and illicit Cocaine manufacture." Francis also praised ENACO, saying that though Stepan "did not welcome the intrusion of this agency in the 1950s," his company had "learned to work with it and [understood] the need of it."[50]

After the Alakea failure, Stepan continued to procure coca leaves from Peruvian suppliers for Coke under state supervision. By the 1980s, the chemical company had a lock, being the only firm licensed to process coca leaves in the United States, and all of its decocainized coca leaf extract went into Coca-Cola beverages. Naturally, competitors continued to seek access to Stepan's supplies, but to no avail. In 1964, Ralph Hayes crowed, praising Stepan for its persistent efforts to "brush off" beverage competitors seeking coca leaf extract. Without a doubt, in Hayes's view, Coke's exclusive partnership with Stepan would enable the company to "tire out an applicant hopeful of hitching on for a free ride." Its monopoly buying power seemed assured.[51]

The real losers in all this were the Peruvian coca farmers, who slipped into poverty or, in many cases, into dangerous partnerships with South American narcoterrorists. Andean cocaleros had little control over their own destiny. There simply was no legal international coca trade, and the buyers coca farmers did have wielded powerful weapons to keep prices dismally low; Coke had the Peruvian and US governments backing its contracts, while drug cartels turned to machine guns and grenades to get the coca they needed. One study revealed that less than 1 percent of all revenue generated from coca and cocaine sales between 1985 and 1988 made its way back to peasant farmers in Peru, Colombia, and Bolivia.[52]

What Peruvian farmers wanted was freedom to sell their products in an open market, and the possibilities seemed endless. There was a host of potentially marketable products, from coca teas to candies and flours, all of which could generate cash for growers. But in order for these products to make it to market, counternarcotics policy had to change.

By the 1990s, a host of activists and nonprofit organizations were beginning to rally against criminalization of the coca leaf trade. In Peru, scientists and political activists called for government-commissioned studies to reconsider restrictions on legal coca sales. In Bolivia, a cocalero trade union run by coca farmer Evo Morales began to attack state-supported coca eradication programs. All of these activists pushed for a revalorization of the sacred Andean plant, believing that decriminalization was the key to opening up new international demand. A coca renaissance, they claimed, promised tremendous financial rewards for poor farmers in the country.[53]

But as late as 2014, little had changed. The 1961 UN convention restricting coca leaf trafficking remained in place, which, though devastating to poor farmers in the Andes, was a good thing for Coke. The Atlanta company kept its monopoly on legal coca exports, and prices remained low. Coke might not have had absolute legal title to Peru's coca, but it had the next best thing: exclusive access.

IT MAY SEEM ODD that Coca-Cola continued to obsess over a tabooed agricultural product, considering its tiny contribution to the secret formula. Surely, Coke could have removed coca extract without drawing public ire. After all, barely anyone knew about the company's hidden coca connection. Some at Coke agreed. In 1985, the Coca-Cola Company launched what became known as New Coke. The new product was a desperate attempt to gain back market share that had been lost to Pepsi-Cola over the past several years. The company believed that a new, sweeter Coke might revitalize sales and help Coca-Cola edge out its chief competitor. But New Coke held out the promise of solving another problem for Coca-Cola: eliminating the company's delicate dependence on coca leaf extract. With President Ronald Reagan's War on Drugs heating up, it seemed Coke's connections to coca farmers in Peru might be jeopardized in the years to come, and if the company planned to mess with the secret formula anyway, Coke's leaders thought they might as well take out the Merchandise #5 as well.[54]

To put it bluntly, New Coke was a disaster. Despite a huge marketing rollout, Coca-Cola faced a blitz of consumer complaints. People wanted "old" Coke back. Over 40,000 Coke loyalists called the company's 800 customer line to protest the switch. "Give us the Real Thing," they ranted. "Coke was it." Ultimately, the company had no choice but to listen, swiftly returning to its coca-laced formula (now advertised as Coca-Cola Classic).[55]

If the company had considered experimenting with formula changes to Coca-Cola before the New Coke fiasco, it robustly recommitted to preserving the flavor profile of Coke Classic after 1985. It seemed changing the formula to eliminate a tabooed ingredient was not as simple as some might have thought. Coca-Cola continued to gobble up huge amounts of Peruvian coca leaves to create its secret Merchandise #5, but few people knew about the trade. This was the real secret ingredient for Coke: the company's unique and invisible partnerships that made it all work.

5

Cocoa Waste

Synthesizing Caffeine in Chemical Labs

C oke's effort to isolate a cocaineless coca shrub after World War II was not the first time the company had tried to redesign nature to meet its supply needs. As early as the 1930s, fears about pending shortages in other supply channels sparked creative discussions about lab synthesis of key ingredients, especially caffeine. Less than fifty years into its corporate existence, Coke was already looking to break free of limits imposed by the natural environment. The firm would seek salvation in the corporate laboratories of the world's chemical giants.

By the end of the 1920s, Coca-Cola was still purchasing the majority of its caffeine from Monsanto Chemical Works, but it had become clear that waste tea leaves, Monsanto's raw material for caffeine production, would not meet future demand. With its Progressive Era battles against anti-caffeine health reformers behind it, Coca-Cola's sales had exploded in the Roaring Twenties, and the company needed more of its chief narcotic. As a result, Monsanto proposed the idea of adding a new, lab-created caffeine to its supply.

Since 1907, US chemical companies had experimented with producing caffeine from theobromine, a stimulant found in cocoa beans, the fruit of the tropical cacao tree. The process involved changing the molecular structure of theobromine by adding various hydrocarbon compounds. Maywood Chemical Company had begun using theobromine for caffeine production in 1911, depending largely on Dutch and German suppliers, who had ample inventories of cocoa waste from domestic chocolate industries. Cocoa waste was essentially organic matter unwanted by chocolate companies that desired only the rich cocoa butter and solids within the bean. By the 1920s, the Monsanto Chemical Works began sourcing caffeine from cocoa waste as well. In order to do so, Monsanto had to invest in new infrastructure, which required substantial capital investments; the company spent over $200,000 in 1925 to build a theobromine extraction plant in Norfolk, Virginia. The plant was quite impressive, including massive warehouses for receiving cocoa beans, milling factories for grinding up raw materials, and a series of extraction and distillation facilities that allowed Monsanto to isolate various chemical constituents of the cocoa bean. All told the facility sprawled over twenty-two acres along the banks of the Lafayette River in Norfolk. It was an investment the company was happy to make because it believed buyer interest in its product would only grow in the years to come.[1]

As usual, Coca-Cola let others make the risky investments and weighed its options before committing to a new purchasing policy. Company president Robert Woodruff was at first hesitant to buy caffeine produced from theobromine because he believed the public would consider the ingredient unnatural and attack the company for adulterating its beverages with a synthetic chemical. As chronicled in chapter 2, the company had just waged a major battle against the

Bureau of Chemistry over the purity of its product in which its chief defense hung on a claim that caffeine was a "natural" constituent of its product. In all their briefs, Coke attorneys had said that the caffeine the company used was no different than that found in coffee or tea. Woodruff feared Coke's exposure to renewed attacks from pure food and drug zealots if it now switched to a new form of caffeine, one created in a laboratory.

Monsanto founder John F. Queeny sought to reassure Woodruff that using caffeine made from theobromine would in no way jeopardize Coke's reputation. Citing reports from a series of distinguished scientists, Queeny explained that "the complete synthesis from chemicals is what every chemist would have primarily in mind if he hears the term synthetic caffeine." He concluded that if Woodruff chose to use caffeine made from theobromine in his product, he could "properly make the positive statement that the ingredients used in Coca Cola are obtained from naturally occurring products, instead of the negative announcement that no synthetic products are used in Coca Cola." He ended the letter as a friend would.

Woodruff had good reason to trust John Queeny. After all, Coca-Cola and Monsanto had grown up together. Since 1901, Coca-Cola had been a Monsanto client, buying the St. Louis firm's entire stock of saccharin in 1903 and 1905 and keeping the firm afloat in its infancy by consistently purchasing large quantities of artificial sweeteners and caffeine. Queeny knew that Coke had made Monsanto possible, and he was not about to jeopardize a relationship that continued to bear fruit for his firm.[2]

When John Queeny gave Robert Woodruff his word that the new caffeine would not cause problems for Coke, his promise carried weight. Robert Woodruff agreed to buy the new product, and in the years ahead Coca-Cola would become one of the world's largest single buyers of caffeine processed from cocoa waste. With two natural sources of supply, broken tea leaves and cocoa waste, Coke succeeded in buying caffeine at historic low prices, which dropped from a pre–World War I price of over $3 per pound to just $1.65 by 1933. Throughout the 1930s and the first few years of the 1940s, Coca-Cola enjoyed such bearish markets, continuing to stock caffeine at prices lower than those at the turn of the century, between $1.58 and $2 per pound up through the start of World War II. Cheaper ingredients mixed into the same 5-cent product meant even greater net profits: $29 million in 1939, up from $14 million in 1934.[3]

For its loyalty, Coke received special deals from Monsanto—the kind of deals only close friends brokered. By this time, Edgar Queeny had replaced his father as head of the Monsanto Chemical Company (renamed in 1933) and forged an even tighter bond with Robert Woodruff. Edgar and Robert went on hunting and fishing trips together and frequently wrote one another to stay abreast of family affairs—"Your suggestion about a duck shoot in Arkansas in December certainly sounds good to me"; "Thanks, again, for sending us the salmon." They had a lot in common. Both came of age in the Progressive Era South. Both had taken over businesses run by their fathers. Both loved mucking around in the woods. This was a special relationship, and with it came certain business perks, namely cheap prices for caffeine. In early 1942, for example, Coke received caffeine from Monsanto for $1.61 while Pepsi received price quotes at $2.18.[4]

Special deals for Coke cost Monsanto money. The St. Louis firm had invested hundreds of thousands of dollars in its factories—a projected half a million dollars in 1935—and was feeling pressure to generate larger returns from its caffeine business. Monsanto expected Coke to help, and in the summer of 1935, Queeny wrote to Woodruff to explain that Monsanto was making a pittance on past investments: "A few scratches on your desk pad will convince you we are not getting very rich at present prices." Considering Monsanto's substantial investments in infrastructure so critical to Coke's growth, Queeny believed Woodruff would be amenable to channeling more money to his longtime business partner.[5]

But while Woodruff did indeed consider Queeny a close friend, his loyalty to Monsanto Chemical Company only extended so far. By the start of World War II, the Coca-Cola Company was the world's largest buyer of caffeine, consuming over 900,000 pounds annually, and although Monsanto was Coke's chief supplier—shipping 300,000 and 360,000 pounds to Coke in 1939 and 1940, respectively—Woodruff also relied on Monsanto's competitors to satisfy its demands. Coke bought from Maywood Chemical Company in New Jersey, as well as foreign companies, such as Orquima, based in Brazil. In the fall of 1942, Coke listed six main suppliers on its caffeine-purchasing ledgers.[6]

During World War II, Coke had no choice but to turn to Monsanto's rivals. As in World War I, its supplies were in jeopardy, and the company had to consider new ways of acquiring the chief drug for its beverages. The downside of Coke's exponential sales growth was almost no caffeine inventory before the war and therefore vulnerability to market supply shortages that inevitably developed in the years following Pearl Harbor.[7]

Restrictions on transatlantic shipping cut deeply into imports of tea leaves and cocoa waste, causing a serious crisis for Coke's chief caffeine suppliers. Monsanto sourced the majority of its cocoa waste from Dutch chocolate manufacturers in Holland, with only "small quantities" coming from Great Britain. Waste tea leaves, likewise, came mainly from European suppliers. In December of 1941, Monsanto wrote to Coke purchasing agent Horace Garner explaining that owing to the shortage of raw materials, Monsanto would only be able to meet about 50 percent of its contractual obligations. Eleven months later, the Beverage and Tobacco Branch chief for the War Production Board reported that domestic caffeine producers were "literally 'scraping the bin' as their supplies of caffeine bearing raw materials are about to reach the vanishing point."[8]

Monsanto was also facing another resource shortage: manpower. Its theobromine extraction plant in Norfolk required over 120 employees to function, and Uncle Sam was calling up veteran employees to serve overseas. Between 1941 and 1944, the company lost twenty-six men to the armed forces. As a result, Monsanto turned to "the use of minority groups" and even employed as many as thirteen women in its plant by 1944, up from just two in 1941, but even then, the company was having a hard time competing with the naval bases in the area. Coca-Cola might not have needed a large staff in order to keep its syrup factories running during the war, but Monsanto needed more men—and women—if it was going to expand caffeine production.[9]

As the supply and labor shortages worsened, caffeine prices quadrupled, but this time Coca-Cola was willing to make purchases at almost any price. In December of 1942, the company had just enough caffeine to cover twenty-six days of production. Facing complete liquidation of its caffeine supplies, Coke sought to purchase its chief stimulant at $7 a pound, over four times the price it paid in early 1942, but Monsanto and Maywood simply did not have the supplies to satisfy regular customers, with most production reserved under government contracts for use by the US military.[10]

Coke needed a radical solution, and company executive Ralph Hayes provided one: approve the use of a synthetic substitute made from compounds found in coal tar, a thick black liquid produced as a by-product of coal refining. Considering the success of theobromine conversion to caffeine, Hayes held out hope that modern chemistry could once again provide a solution to the pesky caffeine procurement problem. At the time, a host of chemical companies had begun experimenting with synthesizing caffeine from coal by-products, but no firm had yet proved that this could be done on the cheap. Hayes approached the American Cyanamid Company, DuPont, and Merck's American subsidiary in New York in the fall of 1942 to discuss the prospects of constructing a synthetic caffeine processing plant, but he was discouraged by the talks. All three companies begged off, explaining that serious capital commitments would have to be made to get such an operation up and running. Sadly, Hayes concluded that the "likelihood of such a development coming sufficiently soon and in adequate volume . . . is virtually non-existent."[11]

Only one option remained, and Woodruff took it: once again reducing the caffeine in Coca-Cola. By the end of the war, Coca-Cola contained only around 16 milligrams of caffeine per serving, an amount that was 60 percent less than prewar levels and almost half the caffeine content found in a 12-ounce Coke today. This reduction, however, only lasted until 1945, when the opening of transoceanic trade allowed Monsanto and Maywood to renew their international purchasing agreements with tea and cocoa waste suppliers abroad. Immediately, prices dropped to around $5 per pound, but went no lower largely because of increased demand for these raw materials.[12]

Market conditions had changed after the war. Chocolate and tea companies had begun to sweep up their own garbage, rather than sell it to others, realizing that they too could make profits turning waste into wealth. Kentucky-based company Duncan Hines made ready-made chocolate cake mixes, while the Swiss firm Nestlé sold hot chocolate powder, both utilizing cocoa waste residues. Tea companies also began to sell tea bags containing sweepings and damaged leaves. Smaller merchants had sold tea bags for steeping as early as 1908, but after the war, major labels entered the market. By 1952, Lipton had patented its "Flo-Thru" tea bags, and a year later, Tetley, one of the world's largest tea distributors, began selling tea bags in the United Kingdom. Waste that had once been considered cheap commodities for chemical-processing companies had become consumer items branded for commercial sale. Coke and its business partners had no control over this shift in consumer tastes, but once again the question of supply presented a serious threat to Coke's future profitability.[13]

By the end of World War II, Coke was a radically different company than the one that faced the caffeine and sugar supply shortages of the 1910s. It now had lots of capital to deal with the problems it faced: $25.1 million in net profits in 1945 alone. Theoretically, Coke could make unprecedented investments in caffeine production facilities. It could throw more money at this problem than it ever had in the past. But in its fifty-ninth year of operation, Coke also had a history, and executives at Coke began to take note of established ways of doing business that had proved fruitful for the company in its first half century of growth. In the 1910s, the company had weathered many storms, often fumbling and bumbling to find solutions, approaching problems with a can-do attitude but often with little data on which to base sound business decisions. Now, Coke could survey its past and create prudent policies based on precedent. Coke was no longer simply an unwitting beneficiary of Coca-Cola capitalism: it was consciously shaping this new strategy for business growth.[14]

In 1945, strong, veteran leadership ran the company, with Robert Woodruff still serving as the undisputed boss of the firm. Woodruff had temporarily handed over the presidency of the company in 1939 to Arthur Acklin, a former IRS man who had helped Coke reduce its tax liability in the 1930s, but never fully gave over control of the company, serving as chairman of the board throughout the war. When Acklin begged relief from his pressure-filled post after the war, Woodruff became an interim president. In 1946, Woodruff appointed new leadership at the top but retained the chairmanship. He also continued to enjoy the support of dedicated executives, such as Ralph Hayes and Benjamin Oehlert, men replete with institutional memory. Anybody who knew anything about Coke understood that Woodruff and his cronies were still in charge.[15]

What struck Woodruff and longtime company loyalists when they surveyed Coke's history was that it was better to outsource problems than fix them internally, better to let other companies experiment with untested ventures than to go it alone. In addition, they knew Coke could be persuasive in making other companies do its bidding. By the end of World War II, Coca-Cola had nurtured decades-long business partnerships with a host of suppliers, all of whom were eager to keep Coke's huge contracts. Beyond purchasing power, Woodruff was also good personal friends with many of his suppliers and knew he could call in a favor whenever he needed one. In the case of Monsanto, Woodruff had Edgar Queeny, and he would encourage Queeny to pursue investment in experimental synthetic caffeine production. Whether Coke would ultimately buy Monsanto's finished product was never put down in writing, but Queeny had to think that Woodruff would never leave him high and dry.

In 1945, Monsanto renewed its efforts to develop synthetic caffeine production facilities. The St. Louis firm hoped to create a production system that would "not be subject to the vagaries of nature, politics, or international economics," and it believed Coke would be ecstatic about such a stable supply source. The new factory would follow "nature's synthesis," according to Monsanto, drawing on "basic materials from a variety of sources," such as "charcoal or coke, air, water, salt, and lime."[16]

Thus began an expensive experiment by Monsanto. The company's $1.5 million synthetic caffeine plant in St. Louis began operation in the winter of 1948, an accomplishment the company called "another chemical victory over nature." The caffeine project was not a one-off but rather part of a larger company campaign to produce chemical products that would replace "scarce, variable, expensive natural products." As the company's international branding manager explained, Monsanto believed that "modern mass production requires that raw materials be available in dependable supply and of a high purity. If this is improving on nature, it must be done again and again as industrial needs surpass nature's unplanned production." The company went all in, becoming a pioneer in a host of new chemical manufacturing enterprises in the postwar years, producing consumer items such as "soapless soap," synthetic rubber, and inorganic herbicides. Synthetic caffeine was just one of many products designed to make the company "independent" of foreign suppliers as well as nature's contingencies.[17]

Coca-Cola, of course, agreed with Monsanto that liberation from the international tea leaf and cocoa waste trade would reduce contingencies that could threaten corporate profitability, especially in light of postwar political revolutions abroad and recent unforeseen environmental catastrophes. On the political front, Ralph Hayes wrote in January of 1948 that the partition of India and Pakistan created "chaotic social and economic conditions" in Southeast Asia that hindered the tea leaf trade. In the Ivory Coast, the main center of cocoa cultivation, a devastating tree blight known as swollen shoot disease laid waste to cocoa farms between 1936 and 1949, worsening what Hayes called a "serious, if not critical, undersupply" of caffeine. For farmers, losses were devastating. In what is now Ghana, costs for rehabilitating cocoa tree groves totaled over $2.8 million. Farms were restored only after the British parliament offered huge grants to pay for the removal of diseased trees on infected plantations. As always, those hit hardest by the natural disaster were those on the ground, who often lost everything because of the blight. Without formal commitment to or investment in these farms, Coke simply moved on to other sources of supply.[18]

Considering these realities, Monsanto's synthetic product should have appeared attractive to Coke, but Woodruff and his top advisers had reservations. In April of 1948, Hayes wrote to company chemist W. P. Heath, admitting that Coke's chief executives were "still making up [their] minds." The Publicity Department "would refrain for the present from any comment outside the company concerning our not using this material." Whether or not Coca-Cola adopted its product, Hayes did not want the chemical company to halt production. He wanted synthetic caffeine to be "acceptable to every other Monsanto customer" so that "prices of raw materials going into non-synthetic caffeine" would plummet. After all, competition among chemical companies was a good thing for Coke. If rivals thought Monsanto had a viable synthetic, they would cut prices to attract contracts. If indeed the synthetic failed, Coke would be no worse off. Monsanto, not Coke, would be left to pay the tab for the experiment.[19]

Coke's chief worry had to do with the raw materials used to make the new synthetic. Would customers accept Monsanto's caffeine, considering it was in part synthesized from coal-derived urea, a nitrogen-rich molecule commonly found in human urine? Coke thought not. Years after retiring, Monsanto research scientist William S. Knowles reported on the controversy. It "sounded too much like urine," he remarked. If word got out that Coke was using a molecule found in people's pee, Knowles explained, it "would really kill them." As a result, Monsanto established a policy prohibiting "any public announcement of the starting material or intermediates in the synthesis" of its caffeine, hoping to lure Coca-Cola to purchase its product. Labels for synthetic caffeine read "caffeine anhydrous," making no "reference to its synthetic origin."[20]

Whatever it was called, Coke executives believed customers would discover the synthetic caffeine-urea connection. In fact, the company suggested that it might be advantageous to expose the details of Monsanto's operations if indeed Coke decided to remain disconnected from the fossil-fuel-based synthetic market. That, Hayes believed, would give Coke a competitive edge against rival brands using the anhydrous coal derivative.[21]

With Coke wavering on approving new contracts, Monsanto went on the attack, setting out to prove that Coke's foreign suppliers had already surreptitiously shipped large amounts of synthetic materials made from coal by-products to Coca-Cola syrup plants beginning in the late 1940s. To prove the point, Monsanto developed a method for determining whether caffeine came from fossil fuels or natural vegetable extracts, drawing on cutting-edge carbon-dating technology. Using this new technique, Monsanto showed conclusively that some of Coke's caffeine from abroad was in fact coal-based material and not generated from tea leaves or cocoa waste.[22]

Monsanto hoped that such an exposé would force Coca-Cola to accept synthetic materials from domestic suppliers, but it in fact inspired a more rigorous crusade within the Coca-Cola Company to make sure that all future supplies of caffeine met "natural specifications." As Ralph Hayes put it, Monsanto's studies forced Coke "to greatly enlarge and supplement our Quality-Control analysis" in the 1950s "by arranging for carbon-dating facilities at three outstanding laboratories" across the country. And when the company identified caffeine samples that appeared to come from fossil fuels, it took "rigorous remedial and preventive action" against the offending supplier.[23]

In the wake of carbon-dating discoveries, Coke could no longer afford to be ambivalent about sourcing from artificial or natural sources. The company doubled down and strove for molecular purity, knowing that new sophisticated technologies could reveal truths about a microscopic world once hidden from consumers' eyes. Before Willard Libby developed carbon-dating technology in the mid-1940s, a product could be chemically constructed to look, taste, and smell like a natural foodstuff with no one the wiser. Now scientists could see things in, for instance, Coca-Cola's carbon molecules that exposed synthetic imitations of natural products. If Coke had considered using Monsanto's anhydrous caffeine before the 1950s, it now backed further away from the idea.[24]

Monsanto was the loser in the struggle. Coke's decision not to use its anhydrous materials led to serious financial losses in the late 1950s. Monsanto simply could not make a return on its investments without sales to Coca-Cola, the largest industrial consumer of caffeine in the world. Further, the halving of US tariffs on imported caffeine between 1936 and 1957 had allowed foreign suppliers to offer American buyers competitive prices that barely covered the cost of production in the United States. Signing contracts with new suppliers in Western Europe, Coke used its unmatched purchasing power to stimulate competition in a globalized economy. As a result, international prices dropped to $2.50 per pound by the end of the decade, and it appeared that new sources of supply would help push prices even lower in the 1960s. As Coke reduced its contracts with Monsanto, the chemical company was unable to cover the costs of operating its theobromine plant. Monsanto closed its Norfolk, Virginia, cocoa processing plant in 1956, and by the end of the decade, the company's caffeine sales were half of what they were in 1955.[25]

Edgar Queeny, Monsanto's chairman, was naturally stung. In 1955, he wrote to Woodruff, to say that Coke's refusal to buy larger stocks of Monsanto caffeine "disturbed me very much." Monsanto had spent almost $3 million to build its Norfolk plant, and that did not include the "power plant, roads and other ancillary facilities." All this was done with the assumption that Coke would remain a preferred client. He appealed to their long-standing relationship, saying, "I have more than a material interest in caffeine and our association with the Coca-Cola Company; I have a sentimental one. . . . I would be remiss," he added, "both in my duty to Monsanto and in my friendship, if I failed to apprise you of" Monsanto's need for Coke's contract.[26]

Woodruff pleaded ignorance. He wrote back to Queeny to say that he knew "very little about the details of the situation your letter describes." He promised to "get together with those of our people who are directly responsible for the procurement of this material and talk the situation over." In the end, however, he said he would have little pull. A new president, William E. Robinson, had just been appointed, and it would ultimately be Robinson's responsibility to make the decision about caffeine purchases. "In the meantime," Woodruff assured Queeny, "I want you to know that I deeply appreciate your personal interest."[27]

Despite his kind words, Woodruff knew more than he let on to Queeny. In May of 1954, less than a year before this exchange, Coca-Cola vice president Ralph Hayes had sent Woodruff a comprehensive letter summarizing the Coca-Cola Company's caffeine procurement practices. He explained that the company had entered "on a militant and sustained campaign to" find new sources of supply after the war, making "contracts with various new suppliers, namely foreign manufacturers in England and other parts of Western Europe." The company had been well aware of its ability to influence domestic markets by opening new contracts overseas and believed that "successive purchases were the very weapon we had to use in forcing prices to low and then to lower levels." Monsanto and other domestic manufacturers, he assured Woodruff, were "understandably" miffed by the arrangement, but prices were dropping, and this was good for Coke.[28]

In the end, Woodruff made the economical choice and approved new caffeine contracts with Monsanto's rivals. It was just business; Coke wanted the bargain deal. Between 1943 and 1954, Coke had spent $46.4 million on caffeine. It had doubled its annual consumption of the drug, consuming well over a million pounds per year by 1955. If it could get caffeine for cheap overseas, it was going to do so. There was nothing personal about the transaction. The company had made new friends overseas and left Monsanto with heavy machinery it no longer needed. Coke approached the future with confidence, believing that it had the power to control global trading systems with its purchasing power. In its hands lay the fate of hundreds of businesses around the world.[29]

Here at midcentury was a strange corporation, a leviathan whose purchasing contracts were so valuable that they influenced market prices for international commodities, but at the same time a slender operation with virtually no investment in the extractive industries, chemical-processing factories, or the vast majority of bottling businesses that supported its growth. Fewer than 1,060 employees worked at Coke's US syrup factories in 1945. In fact, at the Atlanta syrup plant, only 7 people were listed as being involved in "Production." In total, fewer than 7,000 employees across the globe received Coca-Cola Company paychecks that year. Sure, there were hundreds of independent bottlers paying salaries, but these costs never ended up on Coca-Cola's books.[30]

For such a wealthy enterprise with limited manufacturing and distribution overhead, the allure of internalizing outside operations must have been strong, but company executives would resist the temptation. They had learned an important lesson after a half century of growth: that integrating backward into ownership and management of commodity production industries was risky business full of unforeseen pitfalls that could destroy a company's profits. In the second half of the twentieth century, Coke would capitalize on its sleek organizational structure, reaching into new markets in untapped regions of the world.

But expansion through franchising and outsourcing placed heavy costs on host communities, costs that were not confined to the fiscal balance sheets of firms like Monsanto, Maywood, Hershey, or local bottlers. These were costs that were borne by the public at large, costs that became increasingly visible to Coke's customers. Coca-Cola could alienate a supplier or two, even force them to eat substantial investment losses, but it could not make money if it lost consumer support. It needed the world, but the question remained: did the world need Coke?

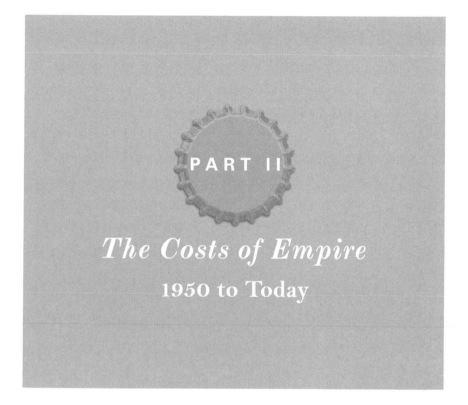

PART II

The Costs of Empire
1950 to Today

AT MIDCENTURY, COKE WAS DOING BIG business. In 1950, annual syrup sales totaled over 130 million gallons, 350 times what the company had sold fifty years earlier, and the company was a recognized symbol of refreshment in more than a hundred countries. That year, *Time* magazine's cover featured a smiling Coke sign force-feeding the world the company's soft drink from its signature hourglass bottle. The message was clear: Coke was an unrivaled global brand, dominant in all corners of the world.[1]

As a result, Coke had money, $118 million in gross profits in 1950, up from roughly $26 million twenty years earlier, and there were those at Coke who wanted to put this money to good use.[2]

New faces inhabited Coke's highest offices. Aging fast were

old-guard watchdogs that had kept the company afloat in its adolescence—men like Ralph Hayes and Robert Woodruff. To be sure, Woodruff would hold on to the company's reins for some years to come, remaining the irrefutable boss even after he officially retired in 1955, but gradually new leaders began to assert control. They came from Ivy League business schools that had been gaining prominence in the country since the 1920s. These were men imbued with contagious ambitions to conquer the world, with a belief that a well-managed company could do anything. It seemed self-evident that Coke's past success warranted experimentation in new enterprises, new product lines, and they set about making this happen.

They wanted more. They surveyed a map of the world and saw an endless frontier, millions of people in hundreds of countries that had yet to hear the good news. These people would drink Coke, if only they had access, and Coke's leaders committed themselves to a crusade to make their product, as Woodruff would put it, just "an arm's reach from desire." With the help of hundreds of franchisees, they would paint the world red and make Coke the most-recognized brand in human history.

Coca-Cola claimed that this global conquest would be good for the world. It would bring not only "refreshment to its buyers" but also "jobs and business and profits all along the line to a ramifying multitude of people." And they were in part right. Many people did make money peddling Coke; overseas retailers and bottlers, representing a third of company business in 1950, earned a collective $150 million in profits in 1950.[3]

But all this business would come at great cost. As Coke stretched its reach into distant markets, the company consumed precious natural and financial capital in host communities. Decade after decade, Coke asked for more raw materials, more land, more machinery, and more cheap labor to make its system work. What Coke had created was more than it could manage, more than its independent suppliers could support on their own. The company needed help, and it turned to the public to absorb the costs of relentless growth, but it was not at all clear whether people would accept the burden they were asked to bear.

6

Water from Abroad

Securing Access to Overseas Oases

Soaked and cold, my college roommate and I made our way down the darkened back alleys of Coimbatore, the third-largest city in the southern Indian state of Tamil Nadu. My longtime friend, whose family was from India, had signed up for the adventure, acting as my translator in the foreign country. We had just finished a harrowing trek through a dense jungle surrounding Palakkad, a small town in the adjacent state of Kerala. We had been searching for a Coca-Cola bottling plant in the secluded village of Plachimada that had been shut down six years earlier in 2004 by local authorities. Villagers alleged that the plant had sucked their wells dry and polluted their streams. We wanted to see for ourselves.

That night, having survived a rickshaw journey that included a precarious through-water crossing over a flooded dam, we reflected on the day's events. We had met with Plachimada villagers who had told us how the Coca-Cola plant had significantly depleted their local water resources and pumped untreated effluent into streams. One villager who had worked as a part-time mechanic at the bottling plant spoke of mysterious skin and stomach diseases that appeared in the community after the company came to town. By the time we made it to our hotel in Coimbatore several hours later, we had heard a lot of tales of corporate misdeeds, and there were many unanswered questions.

We walked out into the darkness, famished and parched, in search of food and water. Down a dimly lit corridor we found a restaurant that was open for late-night customers. There, glistening in the storefront, was a refrigerator containing ice-cold Coca-Cola. I wanted to resist the temptation to grab the shiny red-labeled plastic bottle. After all, I was still digesting some pretty grim allegations about Coke's unethical practices. But my fellow traveler, more familiar with water conditions in India than I, advised going with Coke. After all, I could get sick from drinking water from the tap. Strange situation. It seemed I had become trapped in the history I had come to investigate.

EXPLAINING WHY COKE WAS my only viable beverage choice that night in Tamil Nadu requires going back to the years after World War II, when Coke worked feverishly to expand its global empire. By 1950, a third of Coke's profits came from foreign sales, but just twenty years later, more than half of company net income would come from overseas markets. The company had made its first foreign shipment of syrup to Canada around the turn of the twentieth century and soon after began doing business with local distributors in Cuba, Jamaica, and Germany. In 1927, Coke sold syrup to bottlers in eleven countries, including the far-distant Philippines. A year earlier, with the prospects for overseas expansion seeming endless, the company created the Coca-Cola Foreign Department, a branch of the firm tasked with developing a comprehensive plan for international marketing. The new branch was small—just five guys in a tiny New York office on Broadway—but it had high hopes of taking Coke to distant lands.[1]

Coca-Cola's Foreign Department actively courted overseas investors and politicians. With headquarters in New York City, the American crossroads of international diplomacy, Coke's export team rubbed shoulders with foreign emissaries from across the globe. Chuck Swan, for example, one of the department's finest hawkers, frequently visited the US Customs House and Chamber of Commerce to call on international diplomats. Swan and his colleagues wined and dined these foreign dignitaries, advertising Coke as a golden stream that could generate revenue for a host of small businesses.[2]

Their argument that Coke was a primer for local economic activity abroad was not entirely unfounded. After all, Coke bottlers overseas had to purchase glass bottles, trucks, purification systems, and other equipment from local manufacturers. They even had to purchase sugar. This was because the Foreign Department had approved the use of a new dehydrated and sugarless concentrate for sales overseas in the late 1920s, meaning international bottlers, unlike their US counterparts, had to "make use of local supplies of sugar." Coke held that this arrangement would "contribute to the economic growth of the individual countries."[3]

But while Coke boasted in company literature that the sugarless concentrate policy was designed to promote local business, in reality the decision offered profound benefits to the parent company, dramatically cutting down shipping costs and relieving Atlanta from buying sweeteners, always a headache considering the wild fluctuation of sugar prices. Coke had finally found a way to outsource sugar procurement responsibilities. This was a sweet deal for the Foreign Department.

Diplomats bought into the idea that Coke was a moneymaker and sold the idea to investors back home. By 1930, the Foreign Department had negotiated sixty-four bottling contracts in twenty-eight different countries. Coca-Cola was selling concentrate thousands of miles away, in places like Burma, Colombia, and South Africa, and it soon became clear that the Foreign Department needed a larger office. So in March of 1930 Robert Woodruff reorganized the branch into a subsidiary called the Coca-Cola Export Corporation. With a bigger budget and more staff, the new company heightened the pace of Coke's foreign expansion.[4]

Coke Export's big breakthrough came when it was able to negotiate contracts with the US government to send soft drinks to the front lines during World War II. Not surprisingly, there had been a lot of work put in to secure these military purchases. As we saw in the chapter on sugar, Woodruff had mobilized a massive lobbying campaign to convince the government that Coke was a wartime necessity for civilians back home. He also argued that the soft drink was something every soldier needed in order to survive in the harsh environment of battle. His mission was simple: to see "that every man in uniform gets a bottle of Coca-Cola for five cents wherever he is and whatever it costs." In 1942, he commissioned a promotional pamphlet called "Importance of the Rest-Pause in Maximum War Effort," which emphasized the role of soft drinks in improving soldier morale. The pamphlet marshaled scientific evidence highlighting the energetic properties of Coca-Cola. With this literature in hand, Coca-Cola executives Benjamin Oehlert and Ed Forio, two of Coke's top lobbying men, went to the War Production Board to negotiate a reconsideration of Coke's rationing restrictions so that it would be treated as an essential foodstuff rather than a trivial confectionery good. In addition to the propaganda piece, the team brought with them letters and correspondence from army bases, soldiers abroad, and civilians at home all testifying to the importance of Coke in their lives. The appeal worked, and in the winter of 1942, the WPB granted the company sugar rationing exemptions for all products sold to military outposts. This freed Coca-Cola to sign massive purchasing contracts with army and navy concessions around the world. Having convinced the government that what it sold was a public necessity, Citizen Coke was going to war.[5]

One of the main reasons Coke succeeded in gaining WPB approval was because military officials wanted it so. General Dwight D. Eisenhower, for example, believed Coke kept his troops happy, and he made special arrangements with the War Department to ship "three million bottled Coca-Cola" as well as "complete equipment for bottling, washing, and capping" to the front lines in order to "meet the two hundred thousand bottle daily demand." Quartermasters at bases all around the world echoed Eisenhower's sentiments. Lieutenant Colonel John P. Neu, for example, quartermaster at a US base in Dutch Guiana, filed a "request for priority rating" to have critical Coca-Cola bottling equipment shipped to his base in January of 1942. Neu's petition was downright desperate. Coke, he wrote, was "vital to the maintenance of contentment and well being of the military personnel stationed at this far away post." He believed that alleviating the Coke crisis was important enough to "justify whatever action is necessary." He pleaded for "prompt delivery" of an $832 Chevrolet delivery truck, six beverage coolers, hundreds of Coke bottles, and a "chilling compartment." Failure to comply with his request, he concluded, would be "pernicious to the peace and good morale of Army personnel at this base." Brigadier General H. C. Ingles of the Caribbean Defense Command echoed Neu's request and added that Coke "has the additional advantage of reducing the consumption of intoxicating liquors which are plentiful of low grade, and cheap." Dozens of other letters from the frontlines made similar pleas.[6]

Ultimately, the WPB approved many of these requests, and Uncle Sam spared no expense getting Coke to the troops. The military paid for pipes, pumps, refrigerators, and trucks to spread Coca-Cola throughout North Africa and Europe. Army aircraft and ships carried syrup dispensers and Coke bottles deep into combat theaters. In addition, the military offered manpower. Despite the fact that there were some 248 Coke employees overseeing bottling operations at military exchange stores and US bases all over the world, these "technical observers" often drew on the engineering skills of army and navy personnel. By the end of the war, the United States military helped build an estimated sixty-four bottling units overseas, many staffed by GIs. This government support gave Coca-Cola a huge boost, one, it should be noted again, that Pepsi and other rival soft drinks did not receive. It would go a long way in explaining why Coca-Cola would control such a dominant market share in the years ahead.[7]

With the military paving the way, Coke's overseas sales exploded. The company sold over 10 billion bottles of its soft drink to US soldiers between 1941 and 1945. This was a new era of international conquest.[8]

Coke had more than just the US government to thank for its global success; it also benefited from wealthy foreign elites who sank capital into building bottling businesses outside military base boundaries. During the war and in the immediate years thereafter, Coca-Cola Export began an aggressive search to find international bottling partners. Heading the quest was Coca-Cola Export's bigger-than-life chairman, James Farley. An imposing, baldheaded man standing 6'2" and weighing over 200 pounds, Farley knew how to get people to do his bidding. He had a storied political career in government before coming to Coke in 1941, having served as chairman of the Democratic National Committee and also as Franklin D. Roosevelt's presidential campaign manager in 1932 and 1936. Displeased with Roosevelt's pursuit of a third term in 1940, Farley decided to take his talents to the private sector, and Coke was happy to accept the political clout he brought. Immediately, Coca-Cola shipped Farley off on a whirlwind tour where he met with diplomats and businessmen eager to hobnob with someone so well connected to political powers in Washington. Wherever Farley went knocking, people opened doors.[9]

In seeking out bottlers, Farley and Coke Export tapped trusted members of society, people who had already amassed substantial fortunes in other enterprises. They wanted the wealthy and famous to be the face of Coke in foreign markets. In a 1950 cover story, *Time* explained how the company piggybacked on the success of financial magnates, likening the international bottler application process to "a fairy-tale king choosing a proper husband for his daughter." The magazine explained that a successful applicant "had to have money to support his bride in the manner to which she was accustomed (i.e., enough capital to withstand any possible competition and to finance any possible expansion)."[10]

As *Time* aptly noted, international bottling was not a Cinderella story. No doubt selling Coke helped to create jobs, but more often than not, the people who really got rich from the soft drink business were families that were already the commercial captains of their communities. Take, for example, Paulo Pereira Ignacio, who sought franchise rights to build a Coke bottling plant in Rio Preto, Brazil, in the late 1940s. Ignacio was a millionaire who had started what became booming textile and concrete businesses with his father. A graduate of Cornell University, Ignacio was the kind of polished professional Coke wanted as the face of the company in foreign lands. So too was Maharaja Yadavindra Singh, a famous Sikh guru and international Indian diplomat who secured contracts to bottle Coke in New Delhi, Bombay, and Calcutta. As with Ignacio, Coke trusted Singh because it believed he would have both the financial capital to keep plants in operation and the social capital to entice new consumers to try company products. As an added bonus, Singh was good friends with Prime Minister Jawaharlal Nehru and heavily involved in Indian national politics. As Coke well knew, having friends in the highest levels of governments could come in handy in times of crisis.[11]

The political implications of elite partnerships abroad cannot be overemphasized. In the years ahead, Coke's wealthy international bottlers proved integral in negotiating access to foreign countries' valuable water resources. As native citizens of the countries in which they operated, men like Singh and Ignacio could navigate familiar political channels to secure host government aid to facilitate expansion. Coke bottlers often gained tax breaks on property purchases and rights to extract water from underground aquifers. The key was using the local business argument to get what they wanted. As employers of hundreds of workers and primers of regional economic activity, international bottlers claimed they were entitled to public relief. As the pitch went, Coke was more than just a nonessential foodstuff imported from a foreign land; it was a product that was *"in* the country and *of* it" that created wealth for a variety of home grown businesses.[12]

This was the message Citizen Coke brought to US foreign aid agencies in the postwar years as it sought federal dollars to finance overseas bottling operations. By the late 1940s, the United States government had launched the European Recovery Program (ERP), a foreign aid initiative designed to restore economic prosperity to a war-ravaged Europe. Colloquially known as the Marshall Plan—in honor of President Truman's secretary of state George C. Marshall— the ERP marked an unprecedented American commitment to foreign aid investment, one that dwarfed the modest $100 million congressional appropriation for European aid in the wake of World War I. In 1948, the government committed over $5 billion to European recovery projects. To administer these funds, Congress created the Economic Cooperation Administration (ECA), an independent agency led by some of America's most successful businessmen. From the beginning, this was an organization run, as one senator put it, like a "business operation." Congress specified that the head of the ECA should not be a federal government bureaucrat but someone who had experience in the private sector. They chose Paul G. Hoffman as director, the famed head of the Studebaker corporation who had brought the failing auto giant out of near bankruptcy in the 1930s and 1940s. Hoffman believed in the power of free enterprise to revitalize economies overseas and sought to forge partnerships with American corporations to begin essential reconstruction projects abroad.[13]

Naturally, Coke tried to tap into the money this business-friendly agency had to offer. Beginning in 1948, the Coca-Cola Export Corporation began to court the ECA, requesting foreign assistance money to help support international bottlers overseas. That year, Coke requested over $7 million worth of guaranties on bottling investments in Western Europe and North Africa. Once again highlighting its efforts to be a good global citizen, the company justified its requests by saying that "local, independently owned bottle operations in each country concerned would participate importantly in the project both financially and managerially," to which one loan adviser scribbled in the right-hand column of the guaranty proposal, "Good!" The company explained that Coke production "is a business which for its success, prosperity and development in international trade relies on local or international sources of supply." Surely the government would see the benefits of financing bottling projects with clear, far-reaching rewards for foreign countries?[14]

ECA's investment chiefs, however, balked at the company's requests. In their view, such aid would go to a nonessential product that would not improve recipient nations' ability to generate revenue from exports. This latter goal was at the heart of ECA's loan policy. In his denial of Coke's request, Dennis A. Fitzgerald, director of the Food and Agriculture Division of the ECA, was diplomatic but direct, saying US foreign aid "objectives can best be achieved by restricting authorized use of ECA funds to the basic needs of the country." The ECA was not buying Citizen Coke's pitch that it was in the business of public service.[15]

Coke, not surprisingly, saw no harm in making a follow-up

request, but the ECA's response was the same. One loan officer "strongly" advised "against the extension of ECA guaranties to the investments in question." He argued that "the projects of the Coca-Cola Export Corporation" would not assist aid countries in becoming "economically self-sustaining" and "in fact . . . may well accomplish the reverse." Unimpressed by Coke's claims that its bottling operations portended "stimulation of employment and the stimulation of a number of industries which cater to the domestic market," the officer chided:

> The Coca-Cola Company makes the rather disingenuous assertion that the project will not affect the foreign exchange situation of the particular countries and requests therefore that the requirement that the approval of the particular countries be obtained be waived. As a matter of fact, it may be said that the projects will in the end adversely affect the foreign exchange situation of these countries in that it will require the application of resources to the manufacture and distribution of a product which can hardly be called essential and which is not designed for sale abroad.[16]

As the ECA recognized, Coke's bottling projects drained host communities of vital resources, transforming fresh clean water into a commodity whose sale ultimately profited a parent company thousands of miles away. In short, they were hardly development projects that would improve the infrastructural integrity of provider communities. In fact, the opposite was true: the projects were dependent on local infrastructure for survival. As the company acknowledged in its ECA application, Coke Export conducted extensive surveys of potential host communities to make sure that certain vital infrastructure was available—that, in other words, "the quality of water, the availability of electric power locally, buildings, local machinery and equipment . . . [and] distribution channels" were adequate to meet the company's needs. Summarizing its position on Coca-Cola funding mechanisms, the ECA concluded that supporting the Coke project "would be an unfortunate initial request to approve under a procedure which was developed essentially to insure private investment in serious reconstruction projects, whereas the present item is of a far from essential nature—indeed may even be considered a luxury."[17]

Some in Congress challenged ECA's Coke rebuff on the grounds that other luxury foodstuffs were subsidized under the Marshall Plan, most notably tobacco. In February of 1949, just a few months after ECA rejected Coke's initial petition, Senator John Davis Lodge (R-CT), grandson of Senator Henry Cabot Lodge (R-MA), brought this issue up in a hearing concerning the extension of the European Recovery Program. He maintained that the ECA had already apportioned funds—an alleged $900 million—to send American tobacco to European countries. Why, then, should Coke be treated any differently? Richard Bissell, a professional economist and ECA assistant administrator, made an off-the-cuff reply to Lodge's query, saying, "I expect the actual and correct answer is simply that if you were to ask one of the proponents of austerity in Britain, he would say that he deeply regretted that the British people had long since formed the habit of smoking tobacco which they could not grow at home and that he would not care to encourage another such habit." Nevertheless, Bissell conceded that people could do what they wanted; if countries wanted to accept Coca-Cola and Marlboro, that was their own prerogative. He just felt that "such investments . . . should not be encouraged through a contingent liability of this Government."[18]

ECA director Paul G. Hoffman agreed with Bissell's assessment. Hoffman, a twenty-year auto-industry veteran familiar with capital-intensive industrial development, consistently maintained that America's objective in Europe should be to "help them help themselves" by offering financial assistance to businesses involved in the construction of large-scale infrastructure projects. If a business wanted ECA support, Hoffman insisted that it demonstrate clearly how it would enable countries to sustain productive industrial growth well into the future. As a result, under his watch, the ECA was parsimonious with its guaranty and loan assistance, only granting aid to firms that could turn nature's bounty into industrial products with broad utility. These included a railway company and a stone-cutting yard in Italy, a French chemical corporation that created drugs to treat tuberculosis, and an engineering firm manufacturing lamps for coal miners in Great Britain. Coke simply did not seem a viable competitor for guaranty support when placed alongside these other applicants.[19]

In refusing aid for Coca-Cola bottling plants, the ECA would establish a precedent later upheld by the International Cooperation Administration (ICA), the successor institution to the ECA formed under the Mutual Security Act of 1954. With Europe well on the way to recovery by this time, the ICA focused its foreign aid programs on Southeast Asia, a region of the world in which Communist political factions had made major gains since the end of the war. In 1949, Mao Zedong brought the Communist party to power in China, and a year later, Stalin-backed autocrat Kim Il-sung invaded South Korea, hoping to create a united People's Republic of Korea. India also became a major concern as local Communist parties won a series of elections in 1952. Many in the United States Congress believed something had to be done to stop this red tide and therefore voted to appropriate billions of dollars of aid—almost $3 billion in 1955 alone—toward foreign assistance programs. In the 1950s, Coca-Cola sought to exploit this growing anti-Communist fervor to serve its own ends and renewed its appeals for federal dollars, arguing that it could serve as a capitalist antidote to the menacing authoritarianism of the Soviet Bloc.[20]

In 1957, Coke filed an application to the ICA for guaranties that would underwrite the building of a concentrate plant as well as fifteen bottling operations in India. The Indian government was not particularly keen on these investments, especially the concentrate plant, which it saw as generating more profits for the Coca-Cola Company than for the people of India. The ICA calculated the total annual profit transfer back to Atlanta would be roughly $62,500 on a $250,000 initial investment. Coke claimed that "such earnings are justified since these result from years of research in soft drink manufacture and marketing and world-wide advertising which has to be paid for."[21]

ICA investment chief Charles Warden did not agree with Coke's calculations. In his blunt reply to Coke's request for aid, he stated that funding Coke "appears to be very bad business for the Indian Government in its present state of short exchange. I believe it should not be encouraged as a guaranty prospect either to the Coca-Cola Company or to the Indians." He went on to say, "It is going to be pretty hard to justify some of the loans that these people are going to need and if they are willing to undertake some of the less essential investments, as this certainly appears to be, I would find it most difficult to justify it as being in accords with the Mutual Security Act objectives."[22]

Thus, as late as the mid-1950s, the federal government's foreign aid agencies argued that Coca-Cola bottling projects abroad were not worthy of government-backed insurance because they did not significantly contribute to the basic needs of developing communities. Coke depended on the resources and public water infrastructure that foreign host countries could provide more than these communities needed the investments the bottling projects offered. To finance Coke's bottling enterprises, the federal government held, would give the American company an unfair advantage against foreign competitors looking to use vital resources for development purposes.

This was bad news for a company that was suffering through a series of disappointing financial quarters. By the 1950s, Woodruff was having a tough time finding someone to become Coke's president. He had installed William J. Hobbs to head the company in 1946 but soon discovered that his appointee alienated top talent. Hobbs, who joined the company's legal team in 1942 after serving as a loan officer for the Reconstruction Finance Corporation, had very little experience in the soft drink business. Before the RFC, Hobbs had been trained as an ad man for the *Washington Post.* As a result, he lacked a firm understanding of Coke's day-to-day operations, a fact that irritated longtime executives, such as Ralph Hayes and Benjamin Oehlert, both of whom opted for early retirement in 1948 (they would both return after Hobbs's tenure ended in 1952). In 1950, net earnings declined, and Coke's end-of-year profit report was $6 million short of its posting a year earlier. This was the largest profit decline the company had yet experienced. Coke was languishing under Hobbs, and many within the company felt this was because he lacked the brass to push for a much-needed brand refurbishment. Woodruff, still chairman of the company and the ultimate decider in all company matters, did little to alleviate the problem. Ever wary of messing with Coke's time-tested strategies, he ultimately promoted preservation over change.[23]

Coke's torpidity in these years allowed Pepsi to make major inroads in the soft drink market. While Coke's net income plummeted from a high of $37.8 million in 1949 to $25.9 million five years later, Pepsi's surged from $2.1 million to $6.2 million over the same period. Coke's rival was now under the leadership of Al Steele, who had left Coca-Cola during Hobbs's listless tenure. Steele was a tireless salesmen and a talented manager. He sought to overhaul Pepsi's supply-side operations and rejuvenate its marketing image. In sharp contrast to Hobbs, Steele relished remodeling his firm and took aggressive steps to gain a competitive edge against Coke. He even messed with Pepsi's formula, reducing the sugar content in an effort to pare down front-end

costs. On the advertising front, he launched an aggressive TV advertising campaign, with one commercial featuring a young and attractive James Dean in one of his first on-screen performances. Steele
also bombarded consumers over radio airwaves with catchy tunes
trumpeting Pepsi's 5-cent price for its 12-ounce beverages—"Twice
as much for a nickel too. Pepsi-Cola is the drink for you." Coke, on
the other hand, did little to boost its exposure in these media outlets.
The company seemed content not to rock the boat even though profits
stagnated. Not until 1960 did company net income surpass the high
reached in 1949.[24]

By the end of the 1950s, however, Coke finally began to pull itself
out of its financial slump, in part because of the strong leadership of
Alabama native Lee Talley, who became president of Coke in 1958.
Talley had become a Coke employee in 1923, the same year Robert Woodruff assumed the presidency of the company, making him
a thirty-five-year veteran when Woodruff tapped him for the top
post in the firm. Coke ran through his veins. At fifty-six, he had a
sound understanding of company history and was well liked by other
longtime executives. But though he respected Coke's past and understood company traditions, he was not stuck in his ways. In 1955, he
got Woodruff to approve the development of larger serving sizes for
Coke, presaging an era of supersize containers that would yield exponential profit gains later in the twentieth century. He would show
similar innovative prowess as president. Most notably, he pushed the
company into new product lines, such as coffee and fruit juice, buying
Tenco (a wholesale coffee firm) and Minute Maid in 1960. Abroad, he
oversaw the franchising of more than forty bottling plants in 1960
alone. By the time he left his office in 1962, he had augmented Coke
net profits to an impressive $46.7 million, the highest they had ever
been in company history.[25]

Some of Talley's success was not of his own doing but owed to
an emerging fast food giant: the McDonald's Corporation. Founded

in 1937 by brothers Richard and Maurice "Mac" McDonald, this California-based business became a national icon by the end of the 1950s under the visionary business leadership of Ray Kroc, who took over management of the McDonald's business after 1954. One of several fast food chains—including Taco Bell (1946), Burger King (1954), and Kentucky Fried Chicken (1952)—taking advantage of President Eisenhower's highway expansion programs in the 1950s, McDonald's quickly opened franchises all across the country, 250 by 1960 and roughly 3,000 ten years later. In many ways, McDonald's followed the Coca-Cola capitalism model, letting small investors across the country foot the bill for brand expansion. The McDonald's Corporation made most of its money by buying up land along major interstates and then leasing that land to franchisees at a markup. Local restaurant owners were ultimately responsible for fronting the costs of buildings, operations, and supplies. Offering a succinct summary of this sleek business model, one of McDonald's executives from the 1950s once quipped, "We are not basically in the food business. We are in the real estate business. The only reason we sell fifteen cent hamburgers is because they are the greatest producer of revenue from which our tenants can pay us our rent."[26]

McDonald's franchisees offered Coke new commercial arteries to exploit. Ray Kroc loved Coca-Cola, and he made the company the exclusive supplier for McDonald's soft drinks. As McDonald's grew, so too did Coke's fountain sales, and by the end of the twentieth century, McDonald's would become Coke's largest customer. All of this sales growth once again required Coke to build very little infrastructure. The Atlanta firm relied on its local bottlers to supply these restaurants with what was known as postmix syrup (as the name implied, syrup that could be mixed at the point of sale). Of course, it was the local McDonald's franchisee that had to pay for the water in the finished beverages.

Sourcing water at the fountain was not new. Coke had demanded this of its soda fountain partners throughout the twentieth century, but with drugstore fountains disappearing in the 1950s, McDonald's and other fast food restaurants became the new wells for Coke's hydrological expansion. These restaurants were oases along America's highways that would quench Coke's thirst for national conquest.

BUT IF COKE WAS happy about finding new sources of water at home by the end of the 1950s, it was eager to uncover untapped well-springs abroad. Fortunately, it seemed the US government might at long last be willing to offer Coke assistance in this international quest for blue gold.

The end of president Lee Talley's successful tenure in 1962 coincided with a radical transformation of America's foreign assistance programs. In the spring of 1961, President John F. Kennedy assembled an advisory panel made up of prominent American businessmen to discuss a "new and more effective approach to foreign assistance." Robert Woodruff was invited to weigh in on the government's future plans "in the areas of investment guaranties [and] private participation in international development, including surveys of investment opportunities." The State Department was in charge and set up a task force "to face candidly the lessons of our fifteen-year experience with foreign aid programs, and to reformulate our progress to take full advantage of that experience."[27]

Among many changes to foreign aid policy, the State Department Task Force on Foreign Economic Assistance wished to turn private industry into a more signficant partner in US overseas development projects. The task force maintained, "A large portion of the resources and skills available to us lies in the private sector. If we are to approach a truly national effort in assisting the economic and social modernization of the less developed nations, we must find and utilize more effective means of enlisting these private resources."

Because private industry offered resources unavailable to the government, foreign aid agencies would need to "provide special incentives, protection, or financial assistance which will mobilize U.S. business" toward overseas enterprises. To be sure, guaranties were not new to aid agencies, but the State Department believed they needed to be expanded and former restrictions on loan contracts removed. Woodruff's proxy on Kennedy's business panel, company attorney John Sibley, agreed with the government's position, writing to task force head Henry Labouisse after the meeting, "My conclusion is that the distribution of money and credit and the adaption of those tools to local needs, can only reach maximum effectiveness through corporate form."[28]

With Coke's support, Congress enacted into law many of the State Department's recommendations, passing the Foreign Assistance Act of 1961. The law, later strengthened by House amendments in 1963, portended a new era of government support for private industry abroad. Explaining the significance of the legislation, Clarence Miles, chairman of the Legislative Committee in the International Economic Policy Association, a DC consulting firm, wrote to Robert Woodruff, "A series of House amendments have materially changed the thrust of the aid program. If approved by the Senate the future will see less reliance on government-to-government grants. In lieu thereof, there will be both stimulation and protection of private enterprise through A.I.D."[29]

As Miles stated, under the amended Foreign Assistance Act, newly created bureaucracies, such as the United States Agency for International Development (USAID), would channel government aid away from public institutions and into the pockets of private corporations operating abroad. Commenting on the new direction of federal lending agencies in 1967, a Coke executive stated, "Massive government aid, if it is regarded as a pump-primer, is justifiable; but to make a lasting imprint, to avoid sand castles from being swept back into the sea, free enterprise is the only answer." Coca-Cola would lift the "unsophisticated almost pastoral economies" of the developing world up through its effective investments abroad. At first these programs did not have a lot of cash to fund large-scale projects overseas, but by the 1970s, Coke would tap into this new reserve of federal dollars to finance its global expansion.[30]

Times were changing at Coca-Cola in the 1960s. Under the presidential leadership of Georgia native and Harvard graduate Paul Austin, the company had begun to make a series of unprecedented investments in major businesses outside the sparkling beverage industry. Austin took over the company from Lee Talley in 1962 when the company was doing very well, with gross profits totaling over $279 million. He had served in a number of posts at Coca-Cola since 1950, including assistant to the president and head of Coca-Cola Export, and saw the company increase its cash reserves in the postwar years. In 1962, Coke was a very different company than the one Candler had managed in the 1890s. There was money lying around at company headquarters, and Austin intended to use it.[31]

Diversification was a growing fad in American business at the time. Business executives at wealthy firms thought that they could increase their profits by investing accumulated capital in innovative enterprises outside core operations. By betting on a series of enterprises, rather than consolidating capital in the development of one product line, companies believed they could minimize risk.[32]

Austin subscribed to this line of thinking and felt Coke was too slender for its own good. As a result, in 1970, Austin purchased Aqua-Chem, a company specializing in water filtration, water recycling systems, and desalination technology. He explained the merger to the press: "The Coca-Cola Company already is in the water business. Water is what carries our product and the water condition in this country is deteriorating. . . . For The Coca-Cola Company to use its resources to bolster a company that is one of the leaders in anti-pollution was a logical approach to take." In a conversation with the *Wall Street Journal*, Austin added that the company's new water projects were a response to the fact that "the world's supply of water is getting increasingly worse, not in quantity but in quality."[33]

By 1971, roughly 53 percent of Coke's profits flowed from overseas sales, and the number was rising. Coke was especially eager to tap into new markets in Southeast Asia and Africa but faced serious hurdles, as local bottling facilities in developing countries were poor and public water supplies were limited. To purify water in, say, India or Nigeria, required substantial investment. If Coke wanted to bring its beverages to these places, it was going to need the water filtration equipment its new subsidiary possessed.[34]

The purchase of Aqua-Chem was a radical departure from established company policy. Coke would now at last learn firsthand the costs associated with extracting and treating hydrological resources.

At first Aqua-Chem seemed like a smart investment. In addition to providing the company clean water in arid regions of the world, Aqua-Chem appeared a valuable asset in Coke's international campaign to cast itself as a service-oriented corporate citizen focused on solving real problems for local communities. In the Middle East, for example, Aqua-Chem became involved in a series of high-profile water projects in the late 1970s, including a $15 billion project financed by the government of Saudi Arabia to build twenty desalination plants by the 1980s. This move bid fair to improve relations with Arab nations that had boycotted the company after Coke's efforts to open a bottling plant in Israel. Citizen Coke found similar success in Chile, where it used its Aqua-Chem machinery to provide desalinated water to the city of Valparaíso after a major earthquake that destroyed the town's aqueduct system.[35]

But though Aqua-Chem proved useful in improving the company's public image overseas, it ultimately yielded weak profit margins for Coke. Aqua-Chem was a company with huge overhead costs.

It owned multimillion-dollar desalination plants in port cities all around the world, including Ilo, Peru; Tijuana, Mexico; Taranto, Italy; and Jeddah, Saudi Arabia. With operating expenses at these facilities eating into revenues, Coke simply could not create the kind of margins with Aqua-Chem that it enjoyed in its syrup business. Thus, in 1981, roughly ten years after acquiring the company, incoming Coke chairman Roberto Goizueta sold Aqua-Chem to Suez Lyonnaise des Eaux, giving as an explanation that "the worst waste of time for a company is to try to do well something which we had no business doing." In an interview with the *Wall Street Journal*, he remarked that the sale "reflected Coke's recently established strategy of concentrating on consumer products rather than industrial markets." Analysts were not convinced, highlighting Aqua-Chem's slim profits—roughly 7 to 8 percent annually, "a far cry," the *Wall Street Journal* noted, "from the corporate Coke average of more than 20%."[36]

Thus, Goizueta should have learned an important lesson from the Aqua-Chem experience: that engaging in large-scale hydrological infrastructure projects was a costly affair, one filled with capital risks that threatened the profitability of the Coca-Cola enterprise. The best thing for Coke's bottom line was not to buy heavy machinery.

Flush with cash, however, Goizueta could not resist the temptation to internalize outsourced operations, believing the company could become more profitable by doing more. Like Austin, he had worked his way up through the company at a time when Coke's profits were growing exponentially year after year. He started as a chemical engineer at a Coke bottling plant in his home country of Cuba in 1954. In 1962, he joined the Atlanta office as vice president of technical research and development and quickly became a rising star among executives. By the time he became chairman of the company in 1981, he had seen gross profits rise from roughly $137 million in 1954 to $2.58 billion.[37]

Goizueta was an engineer by trade who found himself at the

helm of one of the richest corporations in the world. He had hands-
on experience with company machines, both in bottling plants and
in corporate labs—experience, no doubt, that gave him confidence
when managing technical operations at Coke. Yes, he had seen the
failure of Aqua-Chem, but this did not mean he rejected the idea of
building better production and bottling networks. Here was a man
who loved solving engineering problems, a man who believed systems could always be improved.

So, in 1986, Goizueta approved the creation of Coca-Cola Enterprises (CCE), a megabottler managed by the Coca-Cola Company. In
so doing, he initiated a major break with the company's time-honored
ways of doing things. For almost a century, Coca-Cola capitalism
had been built on a decentralized bottling franchise system. There
was no way of knowing whether this new distribution arrangement
could sustain Coke's growth in the years ahead. But Goizueta was
confident, believing CCE would allow the company to create a much
more streamlined, elegant bottling network that could be managed
by the Atlanta office.

The financial architect of CCE was Goizueta's right-hand man,
Coke's savvy CFO, Douglas Ivester. A good ol' boy from the University of Georgia, Ivester was an accountant by trade, having worked
for the global accounting firm Ernst and Ernst before joining Coke
in 1979. He was one of many financial whizzes brought into the company at this time by Goizueta, who believed strongly that trained
financial managers were the key to Coke's future success. Ivester was
a number cruncher with a keen eye for identifying fat in company
operating expenses. Nothing gave him more satisfaction than figur-
ing out how to create greater profits for the company.[38]

Ivester's plan for capitalizing CCE was brilliant and helped generate risk insulation for the parent company. Technically, Coke owned
just 49 percent of the bottler, the other 51 percent controlled by private investors. Although a minority shareholder, Coke controlled the

board of directors and could dictate how much syrup CCE would buy each year, even if such purchases did not reflect consumer demand for products. In this way, Coke could artificially boost sales in order to make its portfolio look stronger. The trick was that the company's 49 percent stake meant that it did not have to list any CCE losses on its books. It was a clever system that allowed Coke to have greater control over its bottling system while simultaneously limiting the company's financial risks. In the years ahead, CCE would buy out hundreds of independent bottlers and quickly became the single largest distributor of Coke in the world.[39]

Having entered the bottling business in a major way in the 1980s, Coke now had an even greater, more urgent, reason to lower bottling costs.

The timing was fortuitous. Nascent foreign aid programs with limited funding in the 1960s now, twenty years later, had big budgets to help big business. By the late 1970s, USAID and the Overseas Private Investment Corporation (OPIC)—a newly formed federal aid agency that began operation in 1971—were funding multimillion-dollar projects for multinational corporations. Coke represented one of their key business partners. In 1978 and 1979, OPIC approved Coca-Cola Export's insurance request for a $1.7 million agricultural expansion initiative designed to increase sugar production in Swaziland as well as a guaranty on a $4.5 million arid-land reclamation project that would help Coca-Cola Export acquire citrus fruit in Egypt for its Minute Maid juices (more on Minute Maid in the following chapter). Coca-Cola also received over $1 million of insurance to build a concentrate plant in Korea in 1979. By the 1980s, bottling plants were added to the list. The Coca-Cola Bottling Company of Jamestown in Haiti received OPIC aid in 1982, and six years later, the Coca-Cola Company held over $19 million in OPIC insurance coverage for a "bottling and marketing facility" in Swaziland.[40]

In the years ahead, Coke defended the government aid it received by claiming the company offered more than just jobs and economic prosperity. In communitites lacking advanced water infrastructure, Coke explained, it also offered hydration, and not just from soft drinks but also via a new corporate product: bottled water.

THE IDEA THAT BOTTLED water could be a suitable replacement for inadequate public water systems was something that began to take root in the United States in the mid-1980s. Municipal water supplies were crumbling back home, as city governments struggled to come up with the financial resources to pay for public works repairs. By 1986, municipal debt across the country totaled over $164 billion. There simply was not enough money to pay for much-needed water infrastructure improvements.[41]

The federal government provided little assistance. Washington had changed. In office was a Reagan administration dedicated to eliminating government regulations on American business. It offered meager funding to municipal public works programs, allowing them to languish.

Coke praised the supposedly pro-business climate. President and chief operating officer Donald Keough credited Reagan with unleashing "the force of free enterprise system in this country" by cutting corporate taxes and supporting private industry. Echoing Keough, Roberto Goizueta dubbed the 1980s the "era of deregulation," predicting a "general movement away from big government, and recognition of the stifling effects of over-regulation."[42]

With government stepping out, Coke believed it had an opportunity to "assume new responsibilities." The company initiated relief projects trumpeting the superiority of company bottlers' filtration systems. Private industry, not government, the message went, was best equipped to serve the public's water needs. In 1983, for example, a coliform bacteria outbreak in Grand Rapids, Michigan, had thousands of citizens flocking to the Coca-Cola Bottling Company of Michigan for water. According to the *Coca-Cola Bottler*, the plant informed reporters that "the company's three-part water treatment system . . . surpasses any municipal purification network." The journal noted that the bottler's relief program spurred "record demand" for Coke products as "media coverage of water donations influenced the public's buying not only by promoting goodwill, but reinforcing confidence in the bottler's products."[43]

This was not the first time Coke had tried this marketing technique. In 1960, for example, when an oil refinery leaked contaminants into New Orleans city water, the local Coke bottler took a fleet of tankers to a spring sixty miles away and drew some 4,000 gallons of water an hour, which it shipped back to the city. The bottler bombarded radio stations and print media with notices proclaiming Coke's value as a replacement for city water. One ad exclaimed: "New Orleans water tastes funny right now? Then drink Coca-Cola. No funny taste there from water because Coca-Cola . . . is using only water brought in by tank trucks from deep spring wells and the water supplies of nearby Coca-Cola bottling plants."[44]

In the 1980s, Coke would use similar relief projects to promote its brand. Coke positioned itself as more than just a soft drink company; it was an essential contributor to community development, providing not simply an enhancement of public services but a replacement of government goods altogether. To fix growing infrastructural problems, Coke contended, Americans should put their faith in private industry, in companies like Coca-Cola, whose staggering net profits, $422 million in 1980, were a testament to its masterful ability to transform natural resources into valuable goods.[45]

As the American public lost faith in city managers, they drank more Coke. Between 1965 and 1982, average per capita tap water consumption in the United States declined from 269 liters to 178 liters, and as the 1980s progressed, more and more consumers turned to soft drink companies for hydration. By 1986, Coke could rejoice that "right now, in the United States, people consume more soft drinks than any other liquid—including tap water." Roger Enrico, then president and CEO of Pepsi-Cola Worldwide Beverages, praised the industry hallmark, exclaiming that same year, "You choose soft drinks—more often, these days, than you pour yourselves a glass of water or any other beverage—because soft drinks have become a part of American life."[46]

What Coke came to realize was that the public would indeed consume repackaged public tap water distributed by a trusted brand, something the company did not think was possible back in the 1970s. Executive C. A. Shillinglaw had proposed the idea of going into the bottled tap water business in 1971, arguing that "the future quality of the public water supplies in the U.S. will continue to deteriorate, thereby generating for bottled water an increasing physical quality advantage." The key, according to Schillinglaw, was to develop a "national trademark for drinking water" that "need not necessarily be tied to water from a single source." He suggested the use of "factory purified water."[47]

But critics within the company had doubts this would fly. After all, why would people pay for a product that they could easily get out of their tap at virtually no cost?

By the end of the 1980s, this idea seemed less absurd in light of experience. Coke bottlers in towns like Perdido, Alabama, Springfield, Missouri, and Paterson, New Jersey, had organized wildly popular bottled water relief programs during times of city supply crisis. Bottled water was becoming less of a novelty and something consumers had come to expect in times of need.[48]

Still, Coke was cautious in investing capital in a new enterprise. In fact, Pepsi, not Coke, initiated the first major foray into the bottled tap water business, introducing its label Aquafina in 1994. Unlike other popular water companies of the time, such as Poland Spring or Perrier, who sourced their products at special springs, Pepsi decided to use purified local tap water for Aquafina, exploiting its widespread bottling network and its low-cost civic supplies.[49]

As it always had, Coke waited and watched, letting another company take substantial risks. To do what Pepsi had done, in Coke's view, might undermine the company's unique partnership with its bottling affiliates. Coke made its money selling syrup to its bottling partners, and though Coke had kickstarted CCE, there were still a lot of independent bottlers in the Coke system in 1994. If the company began selling bottled water, surmised Doug Ivester, who was now company president, bottlers would have no reason to send profits back to the parent company because these local distributors had perfect access to local water supplies. What would prevent them from running a bottled water enterprise on their own?

To solve this problem, the crafty and calculating Ivester came up with a brilliant solution. As Constance Hays explained, "Ivester decided that a dose of mineral salts, including potassium chloride, had to be added to the water. The minerals amounted to a concentrate that the bottlers would have to buy from Coke." Under this business model, Coca-Cola could preserve its franchise system, and local bottlers countrywide would remain dependent upon the parent company. By the spring of 1999, Coke was selling its own purified water label, Dasani.[50]

Right away, the numbers were thrilling. In his work on bottled water, Tony Clarke, director of the Polaris Institute, a citizen's advocacy group based in Ottawa, Canada, revealed the disparity between what Coke paid per liter for municipal water supplies in the late 2000s and what it charged consumers per liter for Dasani. According to Clarke, Coke paid roughly .002 cent for a gallon of water from the Marietta, Georgia, municipal water supply in 2007 yet sold a gallon of its Dasani product for $4.35. In other words, in that particular municipality, a gallon of Dasani water cost over 200,000 times more than a gallon of municipal water supplied through the tap.[51]

There was in that equation a lot of money for promotional campaigns designed to decrease consumer use of tap water. In 1998, for example, Coke began an aggressive promotional effort to reduce "tap water incidence" at Olive Garden franchises. The campaign, named "Just Say No to H_2O," taught Olive Garden's servers selling techniques to steer customers away from tap water to "a profitable beverage." PepsiCo also disparaged public water supplies. In 2000, Pepsi vice chairman Robert Morrison labeled tap water the "biggest enemy" of the soft drink industry, claiming that water from public sources was only good for "irrigation and cooking."[52]

COKE TOOK THE SAME argument it used on Olive Garden to the federal government as it sought federal assistance for bottling plants abroad at the end of the twentieth century. Governments were failing their people overseas, Coke argued. They simply could not build safe and clean water systems. What soft drink companies were doing at home, they could do abroad. Coke could bring fresh, clean bottled water to millions of dehydrated people worldwide.

The government bought Coca-Cola's pitch, and in the 1990s, government-Coke federal aid partnerships grew. By 1992, OPIC received the backing of the pro-business Clinton administration, which was eager to make the agency a tool for American companies in emerging markets. Six years later, the OPIC budget had grown from $100 million to $4 billion.[53]

This was a growing federal treasure chest that Coke executives were eager to exploit, and they acted fast to become a preferred beneficiary of the federal largess. In 1990, Coke secured OPIC guaranties for bottling plants in Swaziland, Russia, Turkey, Barbados, Jamaica,

Egypt, Ghana, and Nigeria. These were large contracts. OPIC, for example, agreed to provide up to $233 million of insurance for Coke's Russia projects and $48.6 million for those in Nigeria. These guaranties came with very few strings attached. In fact, the aid agency allowed Coca-Cola to "self-monitor" its compliance with federal development policies regarding foreign projects' "effects on the U.S. economy, on development in the host country, and on the environment." OPIC felt certain that by financing Coke's bottling enterprises in developing nations, such as Nigeria, it "contributed strongly to U.S. and host country job creation," promoting "the dissemination of strong technology and knowledge transfer impacts to one of the world's poorest countries."[54]

Neville Isdell, Coke's executive overseeing all company operations in Eastern and Northern Europe, the Soviet Union, Africa, and the Middle East in the 1990s, could not have been happier with the OPIC arrangement. For years, Isdell had felt Coke was not doing enough to boost its presence in the developing world, especially in Africa, a continent he knew well, having grown up as a Northern Irish expat in Northern Rhodesia and served in various Coke bottling operations in Zambia and South Africa. Now, Isdell envisioned the company forming unique public-private partnerships that would bring Coke to more people in Africa, something he saw as good for both Coke and local economies.[55]

Isdell earnestly believed in Coca-Cola's public service mission. As a young student at Cape Town University, he had originally set his sights on becoming a social worker and showed a deep sensitivity for the racial inequality he saw in South Africa. He participated in local rallies to oppose apartheid at his university and conducted research on child abuse in impoverished black townships on Cape Town's outskirts. When he decided to become a Coke man, he did not abandon this service-minded mentality. He was a "firm believer that capitalism is the most potent form of foreign assistance" and that government could do the most good by offering "tax credits to encourage companies to invest in poor countries." OPIC represented the Isdell ideal, a public-private partnership that would not only increase corporate profits but also bring happiness to millions of people.[56]

All seemed quite rosy, and it was, for Coke. But a close look at OPIC contracts hinted at the hollowness of development promises. For example, buried in OPIC's Nigerian bottling contract was a note stating that the "original clearance" for the project "did not provide information on developmental infrastructure improvements." Rather, OPIC noted, Coke's major "infrastructural" contribution was supplying "bottled drinkable water in the host country." OPIC's $48 million would do a lot for Coke's sales but very little to improve the quality of Nigeria's meager public water infrastructure. The gap between public funding and demand for improvements was staggering. The same year Coke received its OPIC funding, only 58 percent of the Nigerian population had access to an improved water source, defined by the World Health Organization as a source that is protected from contamination from human waste and other toxic pollutants. The country, in other words, needed more than just a bottling plant. It needed massive investment in large-scale public waterworks infrastructure.[57]

To be fair, not all of Coke's projects were solely self-serving. In November of 2005, for example, Coca-Cola and USAID launched the Water and Development Alliance (WADA), an initiative meant to bring better water to impoverished communities across the globe. According to USAID, WADA "showcases the potential of the U.S. Government to partner with the private sector to make a long-term impact on pressing global challenges. By matching USAID's development expertise with the resources, capacities, and commitment of The Coca-Cola Company, we are making a positive impact on community water issues throughout the developing world." By 2012, the partnership was building water projects in twenty-three countries.[58]

USAID and its other government partners put up 50 percent of the money for WADA water projects, with the Coca-Cola Foundation and the Coca-Cola Africa Foundation, charitable arms of the parent company, providing most of the private sector support. Here are some of their accomplishments:

- In Mozambique, extended municipal water systems to semi-urban neighborhoods.
- In Ghana, constructed "decentralized water treatment centers" in the capital city of Accra.
- In South Africa, improved and repaired broken water mains in towns and cities.
- In Nigeria, supplied point-of-use water treatment products for poor communities.
- In the Philippines, offered technical service to city water managers.
- In Honduras, financed green technology investments and environmental training at a Coca-Cola bottling plant.

In all, the company boasted in 2012 that WADA had helped in bringing "clean drinking water to over 500,000 people, ensuring access to basic sanitation to over 55,000 people, and protecting more than 400,000 hectares of critical watersheds."[59]

At the same time WADA was taking off, Coke launched a host of other water projects with the help of international agencies and NGOs. In 2008, for example, the company began a partnership with the Nature Conservancy to carry out a diverse array of development initiatives in impoverished communities around the world. Four years later, the two organizations could boast over 250 water programs around the world. Likewise, a new alliance with the World Wildlife Fund bore fruit, most notably in Asia, where the partners helped to restore wetlands in the Yangtze and Mekong river basins. Africa became a prime focus of Coke's charitable work as well. Its Replenish

Africa Initiative (RAIN), a six-year, $30 million program launched in 2011, enlisted the help of the World Health Organization and a host of nonprofits to begin development of large-scale public drinking water infrastructure on the continent.[60]

In 2013, Coke piloted a bold initiative to install modular units called EKOCENTERs equipped with state-of-the-art Slingshot water treatment technology in impoverished regions of Africa. (Slingshot is so named because it suggests the small technology's capability to defeat a giant problem, à la David and Goliath.) The inventor of the Segway, Dean Kamen, introduced the Slingshot back in 2004 but needed a way to get his product to poor communities around the world. Considering its global reach, Coca-Cola seemed like an ideal corporate distributor for this small water treatment system, which is not much bigger than a hotel minifridge. The first EKOCENTER, essentially a 20-foot-wide solar-powered shipping container, opened in August of 2013 in Heidelberg, South Africa. The company planned to launch over 1,500 similar units by 2015, partnering with female entreprenuers in Africa, Asia, and other parts of the world who would receive microloans to run the centers. Again, Coke argued, it was in the business of empowering local people and creating new jobs. Of course, in addition to offering clean water and vaccines, these units also peddled ice-cold Coca-Cola.[61]

Coke has been widely praised for these water projects, and deservedly so, as they have improved water supplies and forced many other companies to begin thinking about corporate water stewardship initiatives. But the truth is, Coke's programs have not cost the company much. As of 2010, Coca-Cola's total contribution to WADA over five years stood at roughly $15 million, a drop in the bucket for a company that made over $11.8 *billion* in net profits that year alone. Considering what many host communities have offered Coke—access to their precious water resources—such donations might more aptly be treated as partial payments for services rendered rather than altruistic do-good handouts.[62]

Coke could claim that its OPIC- and USAID-backed investments in company bottling projects abroad, though modest, have generated significant tax returns for foreign governments, but Coke has received a number of tax breaks from foreign political leaders, money that could have been devoted to the common good. One example: in addition to OPIC's $45.6 million liability coverage granted to Coca-Cola Nigeria Limited in 1990, Coke also enjoyed a "five year tax holiday" from the Nigerian government.[63]

Along these lines, the Mexican case proves instructive. In the 2000s, the Mexican government cheerfully granted Coke attractive tax breaks as it looked to expand into the country's interior. In the town of Chamula, near San Cristóbal de Las Casas, Coke came under attack in the early 2000s from local activists who claimed that the company was depleting local water resources without paying for what they took. According to townspeople, Mexican president Vicente Fox—a former chief executive at Coca-Cola's Mexican office—had overseen the issuance of the federal permit that allowed a Coca-Cola bottler in central Mexico to extract thousands of gallons of water from the Huitepec Aquifer. That water was "not metered, and the municipality [of Chamula] does not receive reimbursement."[64]

Much the same happened in Australia, where Coke paid next to nothing for its water supplies in the early 2000s after the national government overruled a municipal government's decision not to allow Coke to extract water from a local aquifer. The Australian Land and Environment Court gave Coca-Cola Amatil, Coke's fifth-largest bottler and a distributor to Asia, permission to pump millions of liters of water from underground reservoirs. This was much to the chagrin of the Gosford City Council, which rejected Coke's plan for increased water extraction during one of the worst droughts the region had faced in a hundred years. The court set the extraction fee at a token $200.[65]

In these battles, and there were many around the world, Coke won more than it lost against local governing bodies. But in Plachimada, the small Indian village located in the southern state of Kerala I visited in November of 2010, Coke was less successful. There, local activists organized in 2002 as the Coca-Cola Virudha Samara Samithi (Anti-Coca-Cola Committee), urging the village governing body to close down a Hindustan Coca-Cola Beverages Pvt. Ltd. (HCBPL) bottling plant. HCBPL's production facilities were allegedly stressing underground aquifers and dumping pollution into local streams and fields. By April of 2003, the local governing body revoked HCBPL's license, forcing Coke to file an objection petition with the Kerala High Court. In February of 2004, in the wake of scientific studies that revealed evidence of point-source pollution, the state government of Kerala issued a restraining order on HCBPL, barring plant operations until mid-June of that year. In April 2005, however, the High Court of Kerala reversed that order, freeing HCBPL to resume bottling in Plachimada.

Even so, the anti-Coke forces continued to protest, and a year later, the state government of Kerala stepped in once again. Focusing on new reports detailing high concentrations of pesticides in Coke and Pepsi products, the court banned the sale of Coke and Pepsi in the state of Kerala on August 9, 2006. However, Coca-Cola renewed the challenge, suggesting that the state government had no jurisdiction. Back and forth the legal battles went, but as of 2014 the Plachimada plant remained closed. Coke still denies that its bottling partner contributed to the depletion of water resources in the region.[66]

Very few communities have been as successful at blocking Coke's entrance as Plachimada. In Rajasthan, for example, a desert state in northern India I traveled to in 2010, Coke's bottling operations have worsened water scarcity in the region. Unlike Plachimada, which is in the middle of a jungle, much of Rajasthan receives less than 23 inches of rain annually. Yet HCBPL approved the siting of a plant in Kaladera, an agricultural village a few miles away from the heavily populated city of Jaipur. The local government welcomed the investment and offered real estate in an industrial park, believing the plant would bring much-needed jobs. By 2004, the plant had placed heavy demands on the overtaxed aquifer, and farmers in the surrounding area noticed well water levels dropping as a result. Protests erupted, making headline news around the world. Facing pressure from the University of Michigan student body, which threatened to ban Coke on their campus if the company did not look into these issues, Coca-Cola ultimately approved a third-party study of the plant in 2006. Two years later, Coke's approved environmental investigator, the New Delhi–based Energy and Resources Institute (TERI), produced a report stating clearly "that the plant's operations in this area would continue to be one of the contributors to a worsening water situation and a source of stress to the communities around." Villagers and activists continued to protest after the issuance of the report, but HCBPL refused to shut down this plant. When I went to visit the bottling facility in the fall of 2010, it was still in operation.[67]

This was the brilliance of the Coca-Cola capitalism. By not owning its many distributors and by relying on native intermediaries in foreign nations, Coke could claim that it was a critical component of the local economy, a company that encouraged a variety of regional purchasing transactions, and therefore a worthy beneficiary of local public resources and natural capital. Once embedded in host communities, Coca-Cola became very difficult to dislodge, even in places where it caused serious environmental problems, because killing Coke meant killing jobs. In impoverished communities, few politicians were willing to risk their careers to protect natural capital from overexploitation. The argument of dollars and cents won the day.

But whether in Africa, Australia, India, or Mexico, Coke's expansion in the early 2000s revealed a sad truth: Coke was extracting water from communities that were the least able to sacrifice precious water resources. And Coke gave no sign of halting its relentless growth. In its 2012 Sustainability Report, the company made clear that it had every intention of using more water in the long run, not less. The company would grow, it proclaimed. In a clear gesture to shareholders fearing the potentially unprofitable repercussions of Coke's greening efforts, the company's Sustainability Report declared: "Greater efficiency in our water use does not mean making less product. To the contrary, we intend to reduce our water use ratio—the amount of water we use per liter of product produced—while growing our business." We will be "responsible water stewards," another company publication proclaimed, "even as we increase our production volume."[68]

If the company was going to sell more Coke, it was going to need more water, so it set out to discover where the world's remaining blue gold could be found. In 2004, the company invested over $1.5 million to create a digital atlas indicating water stress levels around the world. The goal was to create a kind of color-coded treasure map that would help Coke visualize water-rich and water-scarce regions of the globe. When Coke's team of researchers finally produced images from their data, the portrait was disturbing. Much of North Africa, Australia, and the Middle East was covered in red, indicating "extremely high" water stress. The map also showed similar dire conditions in large portions of China, India, Mexico, and the American Southwest. In short, Coke's database revealed a world in crisis with many populated communities facing unprecedented hydrological shortages.[69]

Despite what its researchers saw, Coke kept its bottling operations in arid regions of the world running. We know this because we now have the map that Coke created in 2004. Coke donated its atlas and the supporting database to the World Resource Institute's Aqueduct project in 2011. Anyone can now peruse the geographic information system (GIS) data online here: aqueduct.wri.org.

Below is a table featuring just a few of Coke's bottling operations that remained in operation as of 2012 in areas marked on the map as being at high or extremely high risk for serious water shortages. Some of these plants were capable of extracting over 300 million liters of water annually from the ground.[70]

LOCATION	STRESS LEVELS
Riyadh, Saudi Arabia	Extremely High
Kaladera, Rajasthan, India	High
Dire Dawa, Ethiopia	Extremely High
Al Ain, United Arab Emirates	Extremely High
Baku, Azerbaijan	Extremely High
Mashhad, Iran	Extremely High
Manama, Bahrain	Extremely High
Amman, Jordan	Extremely High

Figure 1: Select Coca-Cola Bottling Plants in 2012 and Water Stress Levels
Source: Water risk assessments came from the Aqueduct Water Risk Atlas, World Resource Institute, aqueduct.wri.org; data generated by the Coca-Cola Company.

If Coke had created its 2004 map to assess whether it should close down operations in particularly water-scarce regions of the world, it did not act on the information it had on hand. Business continued, despite all indications that expanding extractive practices in certain regions of the world would worsen serious water shortages. The company claimed that it could become more efficient, and that by reducing its water use ratio it could become a good water steward. It also argued that it could help "replenish" water resources via reforestation programs, watershed management, and the construction and distribution of barrels designed to capture rainwater (a practice called "rain harvesting"). For places lacking adequate precipitation, in other words, Coke promised to be a rainmaker.[71]

But despite its promises to give back, Coke always preached a message of expansion. In the long run, Coke would need more water, not less.

Not surprisingly, governments have urged Coke on, believing growth good for their communities. They have given tax breaks, access to land, and special subsidies to encourage the growth of Coca-Cola, even though the company places heavy demands on precious ecological resources. Coke has committed to expanding sales in the driest portions of our planet in the years ahead, all in pursuit of greater profits. Some believe this means more jobs and economic prosperity. Still, the question remains: are communities giving more than they get? Coke's million-dollar investments in public water projects can only put a dent in the billion-dollar infrastructure problems many nations face. In the United States alone, the Environmental Protection Agency has projected a $500 billion gap between allocated funds for public water system improvement and anticipated development and maintenance costs by 2020. For developing countries overseas, the price tag is much higher. Considering these steep demands, it seems citizens in water-stressed regions of the world would be better served spending their public resources to fix public pipes rather than to buy bottled water. If not, Coke may be the only thing citizens in these countries will have to quench their thirst. In some places, as I found out, this is already a reality.[72]

7

Coffee Beans

Capitalizing on the Decaf Boom

For Coke, selling caffeine was always a negotiation. To keep its commercial veins flooded with this all-impotant drug, the company needed commitments from both consumers and suppliers. What Coke asked of its patrons was no small solicitation: the use of their bodies as repositories for large quantities of caffeine. Americans were downing unprecedented doses of the drug in the second half of the twentieth century, and questions emerged: might this binge have harmful physiological consequences? If Coke was going to increase sales, it had to convince the public that science was on its side, that there was no penance to be paid for gorging on supersized soda.

Working with suppliers was no less a balancing act for Coke. The company had to assure its business partners that there was money to be made in expanding their caffeine production further and further, despite the fact that such growth often made little economic sense for producers. Coke encouraged longtime suppliers to invest in expensive expansions of fields and factories, even as it sought new sources of supply. The trick was getting as many players into the game as possible without antagonizing loyal business partners whose margins were inevitably squeezed by increased market competition.

In the latter half of the twentieth century, Coke's negotiating skills would be put to the test as the hidden ecological, economic, and biological costs of both caffeine production and consumption threatened to cause ruptures in the company's commodity chains. Important questions faced the corporation. Would Monsanto and other caffeine suppliers continue to satisfy Coke's demands for more caffeine considering dwindling profit margins for production? Would tropical farms continue to yield the raw materials needed to produce Coke's potent drug? Most importantly, would consumers agree to ingest more and more caffeine into their bodies? If Coke was going to succeed, it was going to have to convince consumers and business partners alike that more caffeine was good for their physical and corporate bodies.

BY THE 1950s, AN anti-caffeine movement, which Coca-Cola had worked hard to suppress since the early battles with government chemist Harvey Wiley in the 1910s, had gained momentum. In the 1930s and 1940s, the FDA received a mountain of letters from health-conscious Americans expressing concern about the correlation between caffeine consumption and nervous jitters or insomnia. Many said they were done with the drug once and for all, while others called for government action. Coke, a caffeine culprit, was again in the crosshairs of consumer critics.

But what at first seemed like a disturbing trend for Coke soon turned out to be a boon for the soft drink giant. Growing fears about caffeine created a niche market for stimulant-free beverages of all kinds, with businesses heavily advertising new caffeine-free drinks as healthy substitutes to regular coffee brands. As the decaffeinated market expanded in the 1950s, large amounts of caffeine became available as waste at coffee processing plants around the world. Coke had a new and bountiful source of caffeine because a consumer culture driven by a desire to limit stimulant availability ironically generated an unprecedented production of the same drug.

Decaf coffee had been around for a while. In 1906 a German businessman named Ludwig Roselius had patented a method for treating green coffee beans with steam in a way that permitted caffeine extraction. Using this decaffeination technique, Roselius began production of a concoction he called Kaffee HAG, the first decaffeinated coffee blend branded for commercial sale. Over the next ten years, Roselius distributed Kaffee HAG in France under the label Sanka (a creative coupling of the French words meaning "without caffeine") and in the United States as Dekafa—though the name for the American brand would be changed to Sanka later.[1]

In the 1910s and 1920s, consumer demand for decaffeinated products was limited, in part because caffeine-free beverages were expensive. Large capital outlays were required to process beans into decaffeinated coffee between 1900 and 1920, which forced distributors to price their product at over a dollar a pound, more than four times the cost offered by retailers for regular coffee. Even given decaf's appeal, few consumers were willing to pay high prices for a product stripped of its key ingredient; it did not help that most of the caffeineless beverages did not taste very good.[2]

But eventually prices for decaffeinated coffee declined as big corporations made major investments in coffee-processing plants. In the 1930s, food giants, such as the Kellogg Company and General Foods, bought out foreign decaffeinated producers, spending heavily to improve and streamline decaffeination systems. General Foods, the major distributor of Maxwell House Coffee, developed a decaffeination plant in Hoboken, New Jersey, and bought out Roselius's Sanka decaffeinated brand in 1932. In 1937, General Foods purchased Kaffee HAG from Kellogg, becoming the sole producer of decaffeinated coffee in the United States.[3]

Having achieved economies of scale, General Foods dropped the price of its decaffeinated brands by almost 70 percent in 1939. In an interview with the *New York Times*, the company's merchandising manager reported, "Sanka Coffee, which ten years or so ago retailed at a dollar is now priced to sell at a little more than a third of that amount." By the end of the Great Depression, consumers could buy a pound of decaf coffee for just a few cents higher than regular coffee, which averaged 22 cents per pound in 1939.[4]

As General Foods expanded its decaffeinated coffee operations, it produced as a by-product a lot of caffeine. In 1944, the company supplied over 300,000 pounds of caffeine to commercial buyers, almost 20 percent of total domestic production and just 50,000 pounds less than Maywood Chemical Works. Coke, however, was not one of General Foods' original customers. For years, Coca-Cola contended that the caffeine produced at the Hoboken coffee plant was inferior to that from other sources. The problem was that General Foods was unable to eliminate coffee by-products and solvents used to extract caffeine from green coffee beans. "Impurities sometimes found in the finished material" made General Foods caffeine unsuitable for use in Coke products.[5]

But in the final years of the 1950s, General Foods would work hard to meet Coke's purity standard. These were boom times at General Foods, and the company was willing to risk capital to make more money. Here was a corporation that ranked thirty-first on the Fortune 500 list of the largest businesses in 1955, with revenues exceeding $780 million. Coffee was the biggest division of the company that year, but General Foods also experienced strong sales in its other packaged food lines, which included brands such as Jell-O, Swans Down Instant Cake Mixes, Minute Rice, and Post Toasties cereal.

With cash to spend, company president Charles G. Mortimer reinvested revenues and took out loans in order to build state-of-the-art factories and facilities, increasing its long-term debt to $44 million in 1959. Coffee was a major focus of investment precisely because this division generated so much revenue for the company. Between 1955 and 1965, General Foods expanded the Hoboken plant's capacity and built decaffeination facilities in Jacksonville, Florida; Houston, Texas; LaSalle, Quebec; and Itami City, Japan.[6]

These investments paid off. By 1959, General Foods had perfected its decaffeination system to the satisfaction of Coke chemists and was producing caffeine for $2.10 a pound, the best price Coca-Cola had seen since 1942. Coke vice president Ralph Hayes was ecstatic: "This price is, of course, our lowest and will be serviceable in dealings with other sources." As a result, General Foods became Coke's dominant caffeine supplier, provisioning Coke with 350,000 pounds of caffeine annually, roughly 49 percent of the company's total annual demand.[7]

Monsanto, Coke's main caffeine provider before the decaf coffee boom, was the loser in all this. The St. Louis chemical company had sunk lots of money into developing synthetic caffeine-processing plants, believing Coke would renew its contracts, but this never happened. Monsanto simply could not match General Foods' prices or those of foreign competitors that now, due to collapsing tariff barriers in the postwar period, could offer cheap caffeine to Coke. Monsanto ultimately cut bait and got out of the caffeine business, eating the cost of manufacturing investments.[8]

Coke, on the other hand, was thriving. On the caffeine front, it happily reported in 1962 that one of the company's "minor current embarrassments is to prevent our inventory from becoming unmanageably large." Hayes even wrote to Ira Vandewater, General Foods sales agent, to explain that contract prices were "too low," adding, "The frankness of our relationship has been such that, when I thought prices were high in 1954, I did not hesitate to tell you so. Now the pendulum has, I believe, swung too far in the opposite direction."[9]

But General Foods was not overly concerned about returns on caffeine sales. It could afford to offer low prices because it was enjoying record profits from its coffee division, both from its regular coffee labels—Instant Maxwell House, Maxwell House, and Yuban—as well as from its decaffeinated brand, Sanka. This was partly due to the fact that raw material costs were down, the result of bumper crop yields in South America. In a familiar agricultural story, Brazilian growers had dramatically expanded coffee cultivation in the wake of a devastating frost in 1953. Commodity prices were high then, but when the trees matured four years later, a huge glut resulted—more coffee than buyers needed. This was the problem with investment in a perennial crop. Unlike sugarcane fields that had to be stripped and replanted each year, coffee trees were expected to produce beans for up to twenty years. As a result, speculative planting one year led to wild overproduction down the road. By 1957, new crops began to fruit and a flood of coffee beans rolled onto the international market, dropping prices steeply. Growers in coffee-producing countries received a pittance for their labor, even as American companies made money on the markup of cheaper raw materials.[10]

By this time, per capita coffee consumption in the United States was over three cups a day, just below an all-time high achieved in 1946. In the fast-paced automobile age, Americans were hooked on cheap instant brands. These were solubles, as they were then called, packaged ground coffee beans that simply needed to be mixed with hot water. The US military had first perfected freeze-drying technology for instants to supply caffeine to war-weary troops on the front lines during World War II, but after the war, companies like General Foods began to market solubles to frenetic consumers on the move who wanted the convenience of a cup of coffee without the hassles associated with brewing beans. Instants became Americans' preferred way of getting a coffee fix, and quite a fix it was. By 1960, America consumed more than double the amount of coffee imported by any other country, roughly 40 percent of all coffee produced in the world, and most of it was processed and distributed by General Foods. Decaffeinated coffee represented a significant share of this growing market. Sanka, the country's leading decaf brand, ranked fourth among all instant coffees sold in the United States in 1957. Caffeine sales were merely a bonus by-product of General Foods' booming decaffeinated business.[11]

IN THESE FLUSH TIMES for American coffee roasters, Coke began to consider a foray into the industry. There seemed to be huge profits to be had, and Coke believed it possessed the marketing power and capital resources to become a major player in the coffee business.

This was a radical change in company strategy, one directed by company president Lee Talley, who took over leadership of the company in 1958. Though stumpy in stature and noted for his disarming Alabama accent, Talley was an aggressive businessman with big dreams for Coke's future. He had joined the company in 1923 and served as a top executive at Coke Export from 1943 to 1958 at a time when Coke was slowly losing market share to its pesky rival Pepsi-Cola. As discussed in the previous chapter, Talley believed that Pepsi's postwar success came from its willingness to adapt to changing market conditions. He felt Coke, by contrast, had become complacent, stuck in its ways, unwilling to risk profits by diversifying into new industries. For seventy-five years, the Coca-Cola Company had sold one product; Talley wanted the company to do more.[12]

In 1960, Coke's new president acted upon his ambitions, spending $72.5 million to acquire the Minute Maid Corporation, the world's largest producer of frozen orange juice concentrates and the second-biggest processor of instant coffee. This was a huge merger that required Coke to take on assets it had never managed before. Not only did Minute Maid own or lease over 20,000 acres of citrus groves in Florida—making it the world's largest citrus grower and processor—it also had substantial investments in coffee processing plants through its subsidiary Tenco. In 1952, ten regional coffee producers servicing markets in New England, the Mid-Atlantic, the Southeast, and on the West Coast had formed Tenco in order to finance the construction of an instant coffee processing plant and decaffeination facility in Linden, New Jersey. One of Tenco's founding members, Albert Ehlers of Albert Ehlers Inc., explained the economics: "No one of us could afford to gamble a million on such a plant. Nobody ever knows when a new process might make this new field obsolete. But by uniting, each of us taking a tenth of the stock of the new corporation, we believe we have developed a fine quality process and we have acquired a fine, adaptable plant." In the years ahead, Tenco would manage packaging and processing facilities in San Francisco, California; Ajax, Canada; and Hamburg, Germany. It would remain a wholesaler, processing and packaging coffee for private labels marketed by the ten company members of the conglomerate—which included brands like Fleetwood in Nashville, Tennessee, and Old Mansion in Richmond, Virginia. By 1961, Tenco had grown to become the third-largest coffee wholesaler in the world.[13]

Of course, one of the more attractive features of the Tenco/Minute Maid acquisition was that Coke now had its own in-house caffeine supply. By 1960, the caffeine that Tenco extracted from its coffee to make its decaf brands went directly into Coca-Cola's soft drinks. Coke had done something it had always avoided: it had become its own ingredient supplier.[14]

Recognizing this as a departure from standard practice, some top executives at Coke questioned whether the Minute Maid merger and Tenco acquisition were prudent. After all, as analysts pointed out,

Minute Maid carried heavy debts compared to Coke, and there were early signs that revenues from sales would be modest. In July of 1961, Benjamin Oehlert, now head of the company's Minute Maid Division, announced that Tenco's earnings report had "been very disappointing." He explained that the "only reason we bought [Tenco] . . . was our conviction that we could improve the stability, value and earning power" of the company. Coke was not interested in keeping Tenco as its in-house caffeine supplier if the subsidiary continued to post sluggish sales.[15]

But Talley's successor, Paul Austin, who became president of the company in 1962, would not heed the warning signs, seeing great promise in Coke's further expansion into the coffee industry. He too believed in diversification as a means of stimulating new growth at Coke and was a strong-willed leader who was willing to take risks. In 1964, he continued Talley's legacy of expansion and oversaw the acquisition of Duncan Foods, a company based in Houston, Texas, that processed and distributed several popular coffee brands, including Maryland Club, Admiration, and Bright and Early. Duncan and Minute Maid were now part of a new Foods Division run by Charles Duncan, the former owner of Duncan Foods Company.[16]

Throughout the 1960s, Coke had trouble making profits on the coffee it sold. Members of the Tenco conglomerate, companies whose names few consumers would recognize today—Cain's Coffee Company, William S. Scull, John H. Wilkins Company—did not have the marketing capital or brand strength to compete with major labels, such as Maxwell House and Taster's Choice, produced by General Foods and Nestlé, the industry leaders. Coke had no direct role in marketing roasted beans from its coffee plants, acting merely as a wholesaler to its small, regional coffee partners. As Tenco head Ed Aborn put it, the company was "strictly a supplier of private brands" and therefore "helpless to defend itself against aggressive promotional activities of the national brands." Coke's greatest strength lay in exploiting the gap between commodity prices and the branded products it sold to consumers. With Tenco, it had no such power. Buyers were not willing to pay a premium price for Coke's coffee.[17]

Coke's Duncan brands did not do much better. They were only popular in circumscribed, regional markets—no match for Maxwell House favorites. Coke now knew what it felt like to be the little guy taking on a huge national behemoth. Being the first company to establish a nationally recognized brand meant everything in this business. As a coffee producer, Coke was playing catch-up from the very beginning, and it was having a tough time competing.

To make matters worse, by the 1970s, erratic fluctuations in world coffee prices caused headaches for executives in Coke's Foods Division. Beginning in 1962, the major coffee producing and consuming nations had come together to create the International Coffee Organization (ICO), a trade body tasked with establishing yearly import and export quotas. Through the early 1970s, the organization used quotas to reduce volatility in the market, but in 1975 another unexpected frost in Brazil forced the ICO to suspend quota restrictions until 1978. In the meantime, shortages caused prices for imported coffee beans to spiral upward, severely diminishing the margin between wholesale prices and commodity costs and effectively eliminating Tenco's earnings. With little hope of making substantial profits in the coffee business, Coke sold Tenco in 1981. After nearly two decades of market experiments, company chief financial officer Sam Ayoub explained, "We don't really care much to manufacture coffee we can't market." Within seven years, the company also unloaded its Duncan coffee brands.[18]

Even the key ingredient that had partially coaxed Coca-Cola into the coffee business in the first place—caffeine—was not enough to keep it in the decaffeination business. In fact, despite supply shortages in the 1970s caused by Brazilian frosts, by the 1980s, there was actu-

ally an oversupply of Coke's chief stimulant because of the booming
decaffeinated coffee market. Sanka had made significant gains in the
1960s, spurring General Foods to release three new decaf brands by
1985: Brim Decaffeinated, Maxwell House Decaffeinated, and Yuban
Decaffeinated. Nestlé also offered a host of new brands, including
Taster's Choice Decaffeinated and Nescafé Decaffeinated. Annual per
capita decaffeinated consumption quadrupled between 1962 and 1984.
Over the same period, regular coffee consumption fell by more than
40 percent, from more than three cups a day to less than two cups.
According to an industry spokesman, decaf was the fastest-growing
segment of the coffee industry in 1984. The result was more caffeine
available for soft drink companies.[19]

And there were also new caffeine producers, outside the coffee
industry, helping to drive prices down. By the mid-1960s, Pfizer Inc.,
one of the world's largest pharmaceutical concerns, known mainly
for manufacturing popular prescription medicines and antibiotics,
had succeeded where Monsanto had failed, developing a marketable
synthetic caffeine produced from materials other than tea leaves, coffee beans, or other plant sources (exactly what the chemical inputs
were is unclear, but urea derived from fossil fuels was probably the
base compound). The drug company had first invested in caffeine production facilities in 1947, buying out one of Coke's marginal caffeine
suppliers, Citro Chemical, and for the next two years Pfizer manufactured caffeine from natural materials, such as waste tea leaves.
In 1949, the company expanded its operations to include a synthetic
processing plant in Groton, Connecticut. Like Monsanto, Pfizer faced
pressure from General Foods and foreign competitors in the 1950s,
but it nonetheless remained committed to improving its synthetic
process, and by 1965, the company could happily report to its shareholders that it had succeeded in marketing its synthetic to soft drink
companies as well as to cold and headache medicine producers.[20]

Whether Coca-Cola signed a purchasing contract with Pfizer in the 1960s remains uncertain. To this day, caffeine production is a highly obfuscated industry. But while records available to the public do not indicate exactly when Coke approved the use of synthetic caffeine, ultimately the company made the switch. Today, the company admits that it sources its caffeine from "coffee beans, tea leaves, or synthesis from appropriate sources." However, Coke is still clearly sensitive to past concerns about natural sourcing, voluntarily offering in its public statements that caffeine is a "naturally occurring substance" found in over "sixty types of plants."[21]

Whether Coke made the switch to synthetic in the 1970s or later, the effect of Pfizer's entry into the caffeine market certainly benefited Coke. By 1970, Pfizer could offer caffeine for just $2.14 a pound, roughly 25 percent less expensive than General Foods' offer some twelve years earlier (adjusted for inflation). Pfizer had become a major caffeine supplier, the sole synthetic producer in the country, generating over 1.6 million pounds of synthetic each year by the end of the decade, and soon there were new synthetic producers that became major players in the US market. By the 1990s, American companies had begun purchasing large quantities of synthetic caffeine from China, and as a result, prices continued to remain low.[22]

This was a buyer's market in the 1980s, one Coke would exploit in the coming decades to increase profits. It had no reason to internalize caffeine production operations. Caffeine was cheap. The smart thing from Coke's perspective was to return to being a third-party buyer and let global suppliers, whether they be coffee processors in the United States or synthetic chemical manufacturers in China, compete with each other.

Coke regretted the failure of its foray into the coffee business, but things could have been worse. The company owned just a few coffee-packaging and -processing plants and easily found willing buyers to purchase these assets. Fortunately, Coke's integration only extended so far. The company did not own coffee farms in Brazil nor heavy agricultural equipment.

Coke had resisted integration into agricultural operations overseas, even though there were those at Coke who wished the company had done otherwise, especially Paul Austin. In 1973, Austin, now company chairman, had approached Woodruff about buying sugarcane fields, citrus groves, and other farm properties in Brazil, purchases he thought would help the company reduce raw material costs in the future. Austin described Brazil as a kind of ecological horn of plenty that could feed American businesses that had laid waste to the natural bounty of their native country. "At a time when the U.S. has all but depleted its natural resources," he wrote, "Brazil is opening up." It is the "treasure house of the entire world," he told Woodruff, who was ultimately unmoved by Austin's appeals. The aging boss, now eighty-three, flatly rebuffed Austin's proposals to invest in Brazil.[23]

Woodruff simply did not see things the same way Coke's new scion did. He knew how quickly market conditions could change, how seemingly smart investments one year could nearly bankrupt a company the next. Woodruff had taken over the company at a time when company profits were just a fraction of what they were when Austin became president. He was more cautious, committed to doing things the way they had always been done, and he counseled the much younger Austin, fifty-eight in 1973, against making purchases that would create liabilities for the company. In the end Woodruff prevailed, and Coke stayed out of the farming business in Brazil, but Austin remained unconvinced that this was good for Coke.

AUSTIN SHOULD HAVE KNOWN better. Back in 1970, Coke's Minute Maid farming operations put the company's brand in serious jeopardy as activists exposed the horrible working conditions on company-owned orange groves. In order to make a profit, Coke paid field hands next to nothing, some less than $1,500 a year with no benefits, and did little to develop suitable housing projects for its employees. In 1960, CBS had exposed these labor practices, airing a documentary called *Harvest of Shame* that showed African American field laborers working long hours without proper food or water in Coke's groves. A decade later, conditions had not improved, spurring NBC to produce another documentary, *Migrant*, that took American viewers into the homes of Coke's farm laborers. What they saw was shocking: run-down shacks lacking toilets and other basic amenities. The press was appalled, and so was Senator Walter F. Mondale (D-MN), a future US presidential candidate, who called a special congressional hearing in July of 1970 to discuss ways to make companies improve migrant working conditions across the country.[24]

A farmworkers rights movement had been building in America during the 1960s. This was the era of countercultural revolution, when young, college-educated idealists partnered with labor activists to expose corporate injustices inflicted on destitute agricultural workers. The face of this new movement was César Chávez, a Mexican American agricultural laborer from California who helped to form the National Farm Workers Association (NFWA) union in 1962, which became the United Farm Workers (UFW) four years later. Throughout the 1960s, Chávez and the UFW led a series of successful boycotts against commercial grape and fruit agribusinesses in the American West and brought the California vintner industry to the negotiating table to broker contracts with organized labor groups. By 1972, the UFW boasted roughly 70,000 "dues-paying members" and had plans to expand across the country.[25]

Coke president Paul Austin was scared of Chávez and the UFW. In a private letter to Woodruff in 1969, Austin foresaw dark times ahead if UFW turned its attention to Coke: "Antiestablishmentarianism is a very real force in American life today. If Chavez could polarize it against us by using the migratory worker technique which he has perfected in California, we could be engulfed." After all, Austin candidly admitted, Coke's "situation in the [Minute Maid] groves [was] vulnerable." As he explained, the company had "as many as 6,000 itinerant workers" recruited "from pockets of poverty throughout the South," all of whom lacked access to "indoor sanitary accommodations," many "housed in barrack-like structures." The company even put to "work some of the children." And the situation in Florida was only part of the problem. Austin believed that if Chávez "were to widen the attack to include Coca-Cola and not just Minute Maid products, we could be in an extremely serious situation."[26]

Austin had to get to work to save Citizen Coke's public image. He attended the July 1970 migrant worker hearing called by Senator Mondale and expressed Coke's willingness to right wrongs. Striking a humble tone, he said that Coke executives "did not pretend to have all the answers to this complex question" but that the company was "determined to do something about it." Austin proposed radical changes, including raising Minute Maid workers' salaries to levels "on parity with all other company employees." He also proposed offering health care and retirement benefits, paid leave for up to four weeks, and life insurance to all field workers. To improve living conditions, the company promised to invest in "modern sanitary housing and dormitories" and pay for the "maintenance services necessary to keep that housing clean, decent, and livable."[27]

Austin delivered on his promises, and the press responded with praise. Newspapers published stories about Coke farmers like Willy Reynolds, who with better pay and job security under Austin's new contracts was able to purchase his first home. It seemed Coke was finally taking responsibility for the workers who produced its agricultural raw materials and making a real difference in the lives of America's poor. Major publications gave Coke kudos and offered vignettes about workers whose lives had been changed by Coke's new policies. In 1970, *Business Week* honored Coca-Cola for its initiatives with the Award for Business Citizenship.[28]

But while Austin's move temporarily quieted the storm, operating costs rose, something company executives always loathed. Paying workers higher wages cut into profits and hurt the company's bottom line. Minute Maid's earnings were sluggish, and ultimately the company decided it wanted out of the growing business. In 1993, the company would sell its groves in Florida, saying it would "focus on citrus-juice processing and marketing" in the future. By that time, the company had begun contracting out growing responsibilities to companies in Latin America, thereby erasing large amounts of heavy assets on its books.[29]

This strategy of outsourcing had served Coke well in the coffee business. While the debate raged about the problems in Minute Maid's Florida groves, no network cameras ever ventured to southern Brazil or Central America to see what effect Coke's Foods Division was having on peasant coffee farmers there. No doubt this was due in large part to the distance between Coke's suppliers and American consumers. After all, what made the Minute Maid story so shocking, and therefore appealing to the press, was that it was happening in Americans' backyard, and there was a clear villain, Coke, which had direct links to the injustices taking place on United States soil. In the case of coffee, the story did not line up so nicely. Coke bought from multiple, independent coffee producers from all over the world. There was no clear footprint, no way of tying Coke directly to agricultural problems in the coffee business.

Though Coke never owned coffee plantations, it nonetheless fueled the growth of agriculture systems in the tropical world that were rife with social inequity and environmental problems. By the 1970s, Coca-Cola was the third-largest instant coffee producer in the United States and the world's largest industrial buyer of processed caffeine made from coffee. The company depended on steady supplies of cheap coffee beans from the tropical world. To satiate Coke's demand for caffeine, growers in Latin America converted some of the world's finest and most diverse ecological landscapes into monocrop coffee plantations.

LONG BEFORE COCA-COLA TOOK over Tenco in the 1960s, trouble had been brewing in the coffee-producing regions of South America. In Brazil, which was by a wide margin the chief coffee exporter to the United States by the mid-twentieth century and one of the main sources of supply for instant coffee makers, such as Tenco and General Foods, problems were particularly pernicious. There, much of the Atlantic Forest in the southern region of the country had been slashed and burned to make way for massive coffee farms. The roots of this ecological transformation extended back to the mid-nineteenth century. At that time, wealthy growers in Brazil expanded cultivation to feed the increasing coffee demand in the United States, which totaled 750 million pounds a year by 1900. Railroads reduced transportation costs from inland regions, and planters abandoned farms around Rio de Janeiro and cleared new land in the Brazilian Atlantic Forest for *fazendas*, or plantations. The expansion was relentless as growers devoured primal tropical forest in the states of Paraná and São Paulo. It was a vicious cycle, growers clearing land, producing coffee for twenty years or so, and then moving on to new fertile ground. Land was cheap, and so was labor, as slaves did most of the work of felling trees, tilling land, and planting groves. The ability to force unpaid laborers to work grueling hours allowed growers to expand their plantations at a reckless pace. By the time Brazil abolished slavery in 1888, over 2,700 square miles of dense tropical forest had been converted to coffee fields.[30]

Coffee's spread in southern Brazil continued in the first half of the twentieth century, this time with the help of poor immigrant laborers from Italy, Spain, and Portugal, whose passage across the Atlantic had been subsidized by the Brazilian government. Coffee was Brazil's most valuable export, responsible for generating large tax revenues and therefore a commodity whose production state officials encouraged. The government happily helped new workers come to Brazil, so long as they signed contracts that committed them to years of work in coffee fields. Over a million European laborers accepted subsidies between 1888 and 1914, with big dreams of creating a new life in a new world. Most, however, would fail to break free of the peonage they had signed themselves into. Wealthy barons hoarded profits or reinvested them in railroad companies that built thousands of miles of rail lines (over 7,400 miles by 1950) stretching farther and farther into Brazil's hinterland. Little money trickled down to the field hands on the ground. At midcentury, coffee pickers could expect little more than a dollar a day for their work and were given few benefits by their employers. Most had to build their own homes on the margins of the coffee fields, further exacerbating the destruction of the Atlantic Forest.[31]

The ecological costs of this coffee conquest were incalculable. By 1910, over half of the Atlantic Forest had been cleared, and by the end of the century, only 10 percent remained unspoiled. Coffee was by no means the only cause of deforestation, but it was certainly a prime contributor, remaining the top export for Brazil well into the second half of the twentieth century. One of the reasons why coffee was so destructive was that the majority of Brazilian farmers preferred full-sun rather than shade-grown coffee, which meant that they rarely, if ever, embedded their properties in existing forest. They used slash-and-burn tactics, cutting down millions of ancient trees that stood in their path. Over eight hundred different species of trees were cleared, but this was just part of the tragedy. Estimates suggest that the forest canopy and floor were once home to over a thousand species of insects and dozens of different kinds of birds, reptiles, and mammals, many of which were endemic to the region. Though no one knows how many species went extinct, coffee's expansion endangered many living communities.[32]

Soil fertility was also irreversibly damaged. It had taken centuries for the Atlantic Forest floor to accumulate the rich soil that coffee growers found so attractive for cultivating their crops, but it only took a few years of intensive farming to deplete the land of its nutrients. By some calculations, after just twenty years of growing coffee, farmers could expect to lose up to 75 percent of the original soil content in their fields. The prospect of restoring the Atlantic Forest was thus bleak. Coffee growers had disrupted a fragile ecological system that recycled its own refuse. Once the forests were laid waste, there was no way to regenerate the nutritive soil that made this former world of abundance possible.[33]

Elsewhere in Latin America, similar patterns of ecological transformation and social stratification attended expansion of coffee cultivation. In El Salvador, wealthy elites converted over 300,000 acres of land—roughly a quarter of the country—into coffee plantations by midcentury. As in Brazil, the burden of performing the necessary fieldwork to sustain these farms fell on the poor. The economic disparity between the rich and the poor was striking, with the wealthiest 1 percent of the country controlling 70 percent of all arable land. In Colombia, conditions were analogous. Peasant farmers had helped clear forest land in order to create sprawling coffee plantations but ultimately remained impoverished. Tensions between poor coffee-growing *colonos* and wealthy landowners boiled over into civil war in 1948, as poor Colombians fought for greater control over land and profits, but elites ultimately consolidated power and intensified agricultural production in the 1950s, using new machines, chemical fertilizers, and pesticides to increase yields. In Guatemala, Mexico, and Venezuela similar patterns of development played out. By 1960,

there were over 18 million acres devoted to coffee cultivation in Latin
America.[34]

Initially in Central America, many growers preferred shade-
grown coffee cultivation, meaning they integrated their farms into
native forest cover, but by the end of the 1960s, many plantations
adopted monocrop practices touted by American agricultural scientists of the Green Revolution. Launched by the Rockefeller Foundation in the early 1950s, the Green Revolution initially focused
on increasing wheat, corn, and rice yields in the developing world
through modern industrial farming practices. In Latin America and
Southeast Asia, the apostles of the Green Revolution preached the
need for mechanization, heavy agrochemical use, and selective breed-
ing techniques in order to increase the world's food supply. This system of intensification spread to nonessential cash crops as well. Many
coffee farmers caught the "technification" bug, abandoning shading
practices for large-scale, full-sun farms. The result was native habi-
tat deforestation and toxic pollution of local land and waterways. By
the end of the twentieth century, over 68 percent of coffee farms in
Colombia had adopted monocrop coffee cultivation, consuming over
880 million pounds of chemical fertilizers annually. These fertilizers
often ended up in streams along with pesticides, such as endosulfan,
a highly toxic chemical known to cause serious developmental and
reproductive problems in humans (the UN initiated a global ban on
endosulfan manufacture in 2011). In short, the shift toward technified
coffee production resulted in the introduction of new toxins into tropical habitats that threatened the viability of native flora and fauna.[35]

Thus, by the 1960s, when Coke became the third-largest distributor of wholesale coffee in the world and a major consumer of
caffeine generated by America's coffee processors, it was feeding capital into a system that placed huge demands on the social and environmental resources of tropical provider nations. With its ingredient
purchases, it supported a system that was already in crisis, one that

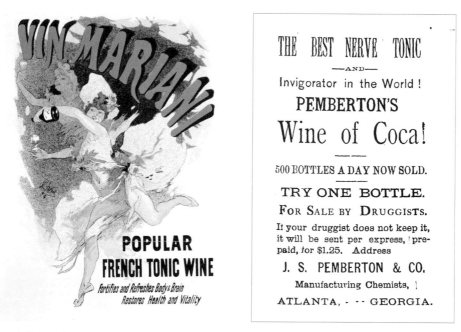

Atlanta pharmacist and Coca-Cola creator John Pemberton originally tried to knock off this French wine product, Vin Mariani (left). Popular among luminaries of the late nineteenth century, including Pope Leo XIII, Queen Victoria, and President Ulysses S. Grant, it was essentially cocaine-laced wine. Considering the buzz it created (both in the press and in consumers' bodies), it's no small wonder Pemberton piloted an imitation (right). But with the threat of temperance laws looming in Atlanta by the mid-1880s, Pemberton ultimately abandoned wine as a base, putting his hopes in carbonated water as an alternative. His new product, Coca-Cola, was alcohol-free but did contain trace amounts of cocaine until around 1903.

This 1899 photo of the paid staff at the Coca-Cola Company testifies to the sleekness of the Coke enterprise. Remarkably, a company that reportedly sold its products "in every state of the Union" by 1895 could fit virtually all of its employees on the front doorstep of the company's home office at 179 Edgewood Avenue in Atlanta. Key figures include Asa Candler (first row, second from left) and his business partner Frank Robinson (first row, first on the left). Also included is Howard Candler, Asa's son, who stands next to a woman resting her arm on the front entrance pillar (right). The African American man on the far right is Will Cartright, a wagon driver for the company.

Coca-Cola syrup trucks, such as this one in 1911, puttered around Atlanta carrying barrels of syrup to soda fountains. Syrup barrels were also shipped out of town on rail lines to distant markets. Selling concentrated syrup rather than finished beverages, which were mostly water and thus higher in volume, meant the company saved on transportation costs.

A Coca-Cola bottling operation in North Carolina, date unknown. Coca-Cola began franchising to bottlers in 1899. By 1920, there were over a thousand bottlers operating in the United States, all using returnable glass bottles.

Coca-Cola and its bottlers benefited from massive municipal investments in public waterworks during the Progressive Era in the early 1900s. Coke bottlers in Los Angeles, for example, took advantage of the Jawbone Siphon that brought water from the Owens Valley through the Mojave Desert to the City of Angels. Started in 1908 and completed in 1913, the Owens Valley aqueduct stretched over 200 miles from the coast to the Sierra Nevada Mountains. It cost the city more than $23 million to build.

Robert Woodruff (right), president of the Coca-Cola Company, with Milton Hershey (left), founder of the Hershey Chocolate Company, in 1924. They are in Havana, Cuba, where Hershey had built a massive sugar empire. Coke became a big purchaser of Hershey sugar in the 1920s.

Ox carts unloading Hershey's sugarcane harvest onto railroad cars in Cuba, ca. 1924–1945. Unlike Coca-Cola, Hershey had made expensive investments in Cuban sugar plantations and mills, and even helped to build a series of rail lines to get harvests to market. Coca-Cola still uses sugar to sweeten its beverages overseas but made the switch to high-fructose corn syrup in US markets during the mid-1980s.

Beginning in the mid-1920s, Monsanto Chemical Company, Coke's chief caffeine supplier for the first half of the twentieth century, processed cocoa beans into chocolate and theobromine at this Norfolk, Virginia, plant. Monsanto synthesized caffeine from theobromine, a chemical found in the cocoa waste that was a by-product of chocolate production. In the 1950s, when decaf coffee producers began to generate new supplies of caffeine, Coke terminated its Monsanto caffeine contract, forcing the chemical company to shut down this plant in 1957.

In 2004, citizens in Plachimada, a small village in the Indian state of Kerala, rose up against the Coca-Cola Company, alleging that a bottling plant in their town was depleting precious water supplies. Outside groups joined in the fight, as in this 2006 protest organized by the All India Bank Employees Association (above). Because of the protests of 2004 the Coca-Cola bottling plant in Kerala was shut down, and remained so when I visited six years later (left). I went on a harrowing trip through dense jungle and flooded rivers to find this factory, a journey that drove home just how far-reaching Coke's commercial arteries can be.

Peruvian cocaleros (coca farmers) picking coca leaves in Quillabamba, Peru. Today, Coke—through its buyer Stepan Chemical Company—sources its coca from Peru. Though the company removed cocaine from its formula around 1903, Coca-Cola remains the single largest licit importer of coca leaves in the United States. The company commissions the Stepan Chemical Company to remove the cocaine from the leaf. Stepan then sells the narcotic to pharmaceutical firms for medical use, and what is left over after the decocainizing process is sold to Coca-Cola as a flavoring extract.

In the early 2000s, new companies, such as Israel-based SodaStream, began marketing reusable and returnable beverage systems rather than disposable soft drink containers. This biker, a participant in the 2012 SodaStream Unbottle the World Day, bikes through New York City's Columbus Circle hauling as many bottles and cans as one person throws away in two years. Coca-Cola has sent cease-and-desist letters to SodaStream demanding that it discontinue these caged-trash advertisements that expose the hidden costs of Coke's nonreturnable distribution system.

Like packaging waste, obesity became a liability for Coke in the twenty-first century. New Yorkers for Beverage Choices is an astroturf (artificial grassroots) organization funded by the American Beverage Association, the chief lobbying group for the carbonated beverage industry. In 2012, the organization printed shirts and rallied citizens to protest Mayor Bloomberg's proposed ban on soft drink servings larger than 16 ounces.

continued to drive poor people further and further into poverty, and one that stripped producer countries of their most valuable natural resources. Without American buyers like Coke, coffee plantations in tropical South America would not have expanded or increased yields. In 1961, American companies purchased roughly 85 percent of its coffee from Latin America, over 3 billion pounds, and instant companies like Tenco represented an increasingly large portion of that buyer's market. Between 1965 and 1989, stimulated by demand, Brazil increased coffee bean exports by roughly a billion pounds, and other countries followed suit in the 1990s, especially in Africa and Southeast Asia. Coffee production became particularly important in India and Vietnam, where labor costs were cheap and soils were well suited for Robusta coffee, the variant desired by American instant coffee makers. Here, large plantations consumed forestland, repeating tragedies already played out in South America. In 1994 alone, Vietnamese coffee growers cleared over 300,000 acres of native forests to create new groves. The result was a massive global glut that sent green coffee bean prices spiraling downward. The Coffee Crisis, as it came to be known, exacerbated poverty in coffee producing regions around the world, yet the push for more and more production persisted. For dirt-cheap wages, poor laborers continued to fell trees to supply America's caffeine fix.[36]

THESE ECOLOGICAL AND SOCIAL costs were hidden from Americans' eyes, but as companies like Coke and General Foods channeled more and more caffeine from new suppliers into consumers' bodies, abundance sparked new concerns at the end of the commodity chain. Beginning around 1960 and continuing into the 1970s, new scientific evidence suggested links between heavy caffeine consumption and rising birth defects; reports also suggested that caffeine consumption was linked to bladder and pancreatic cancer. Such health complications were far more troubling than the "jitteriness" that spurred the decaf boom of the 1950s. While these oncological studies were not conclusive, they did not need to be to make a dent in commerce.[37]

Here was an issue that directly affected American consumers' bodies, an issue that hit closer to home than workers' rights or ecological degradation in third world countries. However caffeine made it into the country, the question became: was caffeine safe to consume in such large quantities? Some began to think not.

In this edgy climate, Coke did what it could to mask the caffeine content of its drinks, chiefly by appealing for special exemptions from the Food and Drug Administration. Before the 1960s, cola beverages did not have to list their caffeine content because the stimulant was considered an essential ingredient known by the public to be a constituent of all cola beverages. In fact, federal law prohibited the use of the word "cola" to describe a beverage that did not contain caffeine.

But, over time, the labeling exemptions heightened rather than abated consumers' fears. Many asked what Coke was hiding. Why were they afraid to list ingredients if there was nothing harmful in their product? Since the 1930s, the FDA had been receiving a flood of letters from Boy Scout troop leaders, physicians, and parents wanting to know whether there was something hidden in Coke. Some inquiries bordered on the ridiculous—"I have been told it contains enough poison to kill a heurose [*sic*]"—while others expressed understandable concern—"Will you kindly advise me as to whether or not Coca-Cola is harmful to a 3 year old child." By the early 1960s, in part due to these persistent inquiries, the FDA felt it could no longer support the soft drink labeling exemptions. In 1961, FDA commissioner George Larrick proposed an amendment to the Food, Drug, and Cosmetic Act of 1938 that would have required all soft drink companies to list caffeine as an ingredient on their packaging.[38]

Coca-Cola executives quickly met with Commissioner Larrick to lodge objections to the proposed labeling requirements. Senior vice presidents Edgar J. Forio and Benjamin Oehlert made a familiar argument: that caffeine was an "essential ingredient" in cola beverages, and without it no soft drink could properly be called a cola. Further, the company's caffeine was a "standard" foodstuff, well known to the public. If the FDA forced Coca-Cola to list its ingredients, the argument went, it would also have to do so for other natural caffeine-containing products, such as tea and coffee.[39]

Forio and Oehlert were quite hopeful that they would be successful in Washington, but Larrick pushed back against their pitch, vowing, at a private meeting with them, to continue his labeling crusade. If the company wanted to challenge the FDA's move, Larrick suggested, it should organize a public hearing where consumers could weigh in on the decision. Oehlert and Forio naturally opposed this option; surely a hearing would give health critics a highly visible platform from which to attack Coca-Cola.[40]

Fortunately for Coke, the company never had to face a public hearing. In the fall of 1965, Larrick retired from the FDA. In his place President Lyndon Johnson appointed Centers for Disease Control (CDC) director James Goddard to take over the agency. The decision came as no surprise to Coca-Cola. Company executives had met with Johnson in 1965 to push for Goddard's appointment, believing he would be a useful ally. A resident of Atlanta, Goddard was on "friendly terms with several company officials," according to journalist Frederick Allen; he was someone Coke could trust.[41]

Goddard abandoned Larrick's proposals for new labeling requirements and approved, in 1966, an FDA order that exempted soft drinks made from "kola nut extract and/or other natural caffeine-containing extracts." While cola beverages and "pepper" soft drinks could continue their established labeling practices, all other beverages with added caffeine, whether from natural or synthetic sources, had to say so on product labels.[42]

The Coke–US government connection, always strong, could not

in itself make the caffeine issue go away, especially in the face of growing consumer agitation. A new era in consumer advocacy had blossomed by this time. Beginning in the early 1960s, fiery political activist Ralph Nader had helped launch numerous nongovernmental organizations to increase awareness about corporate corruption in America. Nader's Raiders, as his followers came to be known, became particularly concerned about food safety issues, publishing a book called *The Chemical Feast* in 1970. The work amplified arguments made earlier by Rachel Carson in *Silent Spring* (1962), a treatise on the carcinogenic consequences of heavy pesticide use in America. Carson's work galvanized the nation to combat corporate pollution and helped spark a crusade against the toxification of the American landscape. *The Chemical Feast* was part of that movement. It attacked big business for inundating American bodies with toxic chemicals. Jim Turner, the main author of the book, lambasted the Food and Drug Administration for not doing more to regulate the introduction of potentially harmful chemicals into the nation's food supply and called for new investigations into commonplace additives in the American food supply.[43]

With the voices of dissent growing louder, Coke finally had to recognize a lost cause. In 1971 it decided to voluntarily list caffeine as an ingredient on Coke packaging. No doubt the move was tactical, taken to forestall more aggressive federal regulations that had long seemed a rising probability. As early as 1948, Benjamin Oehlert had warned that "ingredient labeling is an issue which must face us inevitably sooner or later" and noted that the company could either "continue to sit and wait for the explosion or we can do something about it now that will prevent the explosion from ever occurring."[44]

There might have been another reason for the sudden change in policy. Again, it is unclear when Coke approved the use of synthetic caffeine in its products, but if it did so by 1971, it would have had to change its labels. After all, in order to warrant exemption under FDA regulations, soft drinks had to use "natural caffeine-containing extracts." Synthetics derived from urea would not have met this standard.

WHATEVER THE CASE MAY be, caffeine was on Coke labels after 1971. Coke was now exposed and therefore deeply interested in shaping discourse within the medical community about the pros and cons of caffeine consumption. It needed to move science to its side and drown out critics attacking caffeine. To that end, Coca-Cola partnered with General Foods, Kraft, Heinz, and other major industrial food giants to create the International Life Sciences Institute (ILSI), a nonprofit organization headquartered in Washington, DC, tasked with conducting scientific research on public health issues affecting the food and beverage industry. One of ILSI's primary goals at the time of its founding was to offer a counterweight to research questioning the healthfulness of caffeine. According to caffeine scholars Bennett Alan Weinberg and Bonnie K. Bealer, ILSI's Caffeine Department was "careful to search out and support those researchers who [treated] caffeine as a relatively harmless compound" and avoided "supporting those who would like to see it removed from the market."[45]

ILSI broadcast its message far and wide. By 1980, it had begun to host a series of high-profile international conferences on caffeine consumption and human health. At these conferences, top scholars from all over the world were invited to hear the results of industry-supported research; many returned to their home institutions convinced that caffeine did not present a health threat to American consumers. In an article entitled "Good News for Caffeine Consumers?" the popular journal *Science News* reported how three leading scholars—Harvard Medical Center scientist P. B. Dews, renowned Boston pediatrician Alan Leviton, and Cincinnati Children's Hospital Research Foundation head James G. Wilson—had attended a 1982 ILSI-sponsored conference in Greece where they heard over-whelming evidence on behalf of caffeine's safety. Speaking to the press, these scientists "said they were passing on the essence of recent medical literature and scientific results reported at the workshop." The results of the conference appeared to offer "almost too-good-to-be-true news," according to the journal: caffeine was not linked to pancreatic cancer, heart attacks, birth defects, or hyperactivity in children. When asked whether any conference studies showed caf-feine to be harmful, Dr. Dews responded, "Nothing raised a serious question. We cannot manufacture bad news."[46]

ILSI did another smart thing: it funded National Institute of Mental Health research in 1982, seeking to erase the linkage between caffeine consumption and hyperactivity in adolescent males. Dr. Robert Elkins, a leading scientist in the National Institute of Men-tal Health project, admitted that he felt pressure to produce a result favorable to ILSI's view. He explained, "It was clear that proprietary concerns had something to do with whether the research continued," adding, "One needs to be freer than that." With conflicting evidence before them, Elkins's team concluded that children should determine for themselves whether caffeine should invade their diet. Elkins's co-researcher Dr. Judith Rapoport claimed, "It looks as if even children self-select diets that are right for their own nervous system," a con-clusion hotly contested by other leading scientists, who pointed out that children rarely have enough product information to make wise choices.[47]

In 1985, ILSI's ability to shape federal food and drug regulatory policy increased dramatically when ILSI trustee and executive com-mittee member Dr. Artemis Simopoulos became chairwoman of an important nutrition committee at the National Institutes of Health (NIH). Heading the Nutrition Coordinating Committee, Simopoulos oversaw and directed food and beverage research. The importance of

Simopoulos's position and her links to ILSI raised questions as to the prudence of her appointment. Peter Greenwald, a senior researcher at the National Heart, Lung, and Blood Institute, wrote to Simopoulos, voicing his reservations about her impartiality, saying, "I continue to be concerned that you personally have strong opinions about diet and cancer and are very selective about what gets presented to the NIH leadership and others." Others expressed concerns, including National Cancer Institute director Dr. Claude Lenfant, who claimed that the Nutrition Coordinating Committee under Simopoulos "operates as if it were independent and not part of NIH." These cavils ultimately led NIH director James B. Wyngaarden to reassign Simopoulos to another branch of the NIH less than a year later.[48]

Considering the muddy waters of caffeine research, the FDA could not make caffeine regulatory initiatives stick. The *New York Times* summarized the FDA's stance on caffeine in 1980, reporting, "Top F.D.A. officials tend to agree that the hazard is real. But for many reasons they are hesitant to act rapidly. Uppermost in their thinking is public reaction." This was a common regulatory problem that had dogged the agency for many years: the fear that a failed food crusade would ruin its reputation. In 1977, the FDA had lost public confidence after its efforts to ban the artificial sweetener saccharin, and the agency did not want that to happen again. Commenting on the FDA's reluctance to issue warnings about caffeine in the early 1980s, FDA general counsel Richard Cooper admitted, "Every time we face a problem like this you think about your long-term credibility." The chief worry, Cooper added, was "whether the scientific case will satisfy the public and press. You can win in the scientific forum and lose in the political forum."[49]

Uncertainty had paralyzed the FDA, allowing caffeine to remain a Generally Recognized As Safe (GRAS) ingredient available in historically high quantities for intake by consumers of all ages. With the government on the sidelines, the soft drink industry had a clear field. In 1986, Coke and its beverage partners bought over 2 million pounds of processed caffeine. That year, Americans drank more soft drinks than any other caffeinated beverage.[50]

Perversely, as had happened in the 1950s, the caffeine debate of the 1980s and the fear it inspired in consumers helped Coke reduce its caffeine procurement expenses by spurring a boom in the decaf coffee industry. By the middle of the 1980s, decaffeinated brands commanded over two-fifths of the US coffee market. As a result, caffeine continued to pile up at decaffeination plants around the country, ensuring that Coke would have ample supply of its chief stimulant at low prices for years to come.[51]

Decaf coffee brands did so well in the 1980s that Coke considered launching a new product line, Caffeine-Free Coca-Cola, hoping to cash in on the growing fad. As always, Coke had been cautious. Pepsi, Seven-Up, and others were the real trailblazers, introducing caffeine-less drinks in the late 1970s, hoping to gain an edge on the industry leader by being first in the niche market, and indeed, the decision seemed to be wise. Early financial reports suggested that there was significant room for growth. By the start of the 1980s, Coke naturally felt compelled to compete, but the company was torn. It did not want to miss out on a new beverage line that could make it money; on the other hand, it feared that by marketing a caffeine-free beverage it might awaken anxieties about the side effects of excessive stimulant consumption. Would landing a portion of the caffeine-free market jeopardize its biggest profit makers, caffeinated soft drinks? In 1983, Coke decided potential profits were worth the risk and launched Caffeine-Free Coke.[52]

But Coke without caffeine simply did not generate the kind of consumer demand that had made the Coca-Cola Company one of the world's most profitable corporations. In 2008, sales of Caffeine-Free Coca-Cola Classic represented less than 0.5 percent of Coke's total earnings. This was a trend Progressive Era USDA food chemist

Harvey Wiley presciently predicted. In 1907, he envisaged that even "skillful advertising would not be able to maintain the popularity of a beverage which did not have something more than an advertisement in its appeal to human patronage." For Wiley, caffeine stimulated psychoactive reinforcement mechanisms that encouraged repeated consumption of Coke's products. It was the drug, in other words, that made Coke sell.[53]

COKE LEARNED ITS LESSON. Success seemed inseparably linked to caffeine, and in the waning years of the twentieth century, the company decided to let go of its fears, introducing new beverages that had more, not less, caffeine. The success of Red Bull, first introduced in Austria in 1987, presaged a new era of hypercaffeinated "energy drinks," and Coke wanted part of the action. It introduced a host of new brands, all with names designed to appeal to a younger generation on the move—Full Throttle, Burn, Gladiator, Relentless. Brand advertisements promised consumers an unmatched buzz, a fix that would keep them up late at night if they were working on exams or finishing up a company report at the office. The great irony of Coke's new profit stream was that it was supplied by cheap caffeine generated, in part, by consumer demand in the caffeine-free coffee market.

For those who preferred coffee, Coke expanded their options. In the mid-1990s, the company reentered the coffee market in earnest, this time forming joint ventures with companies like Nestlé and Caribou that limited its capital risk. The company was particularly interested in canned, ready-made coffee, a product line that had produced strong earnings for Coke in regional markets overseas, especially in Japan, where the company's canned coffee, Georgia, had become a billion-dollar brand. In the United States, however, initial experiments failed, most notably in the case of Coca-Cola Blak, an iced coffee/soda mix, which was discontinued just a year after introduction. Nevertheless, as of 2012, Coke CEO Muhtar Kent remained optimistic about Coke's future coffee ventures and continued to invest in new brands.[54]

As Coke reentered the coffee market and upped its caffeine purchases, the company continued to rely on outsourcing to make profits, but it promised to be a better corporate citizen this time around. Coke admitted that the company did "not own any farms and therefore [had] less direct control over the agricultural supply chain," but it assured that it would do everything in its power to enact more equitable labor and environmental practices throughout its production system. The company told consumers it would pay a just price for the coffee it used and that its new brands would come from sustainable sources. At the 2012 Rio+20 conference, a global environmental forum held in Rio de Janeiro, Brazil, and organized by the United Nations, Muhtar Kent pledged to eliminate deforestation entirely from company supply chains by 2020. This was going to be a new era of sustainable agricultural development.[55]

YET DESPITE COKE'S PROMISES, consumers had no way of knowing whether the company could stay true to its word. After all, its supply chain remained obfuscated. In 2012, I asked Coca-Cola for information about coffee sourcing, but I was told such information was proprietary and would not be released to the public. For a company that professed a belief in "the importance and power of 'informed choice,'" this lack of transparency was striking, but nonetheless in keeping with established industry practices. Coke pushed a contradiction, preaching a message of consumer empowerment, even as it prevented customers from gaining access to the information that would help them make sound judgments about company practices.[56]

But for those seeking clarity, history offered insights. For decades, Coke made money by exploiting surplus in the coffee and tea industries. Sustainable agriculture was anathema to Coca-Cola capitalism because it did not yield the excess that made Coke profitable. The company always needed more raw materials on the front end to push more sales on the backend. To eliminate this pattern of growth would be to undermine the very economics of Coke's mass-marketing empire. The company was in the business of selling cheap commodities at a markup, and commodities like coffee were only cheap because production continued to boom throughout the twentieth century. Whether Coke could survive a world without glut had yet to be seen. Past experience suggested it would pose a serious impediment to continued success.

8

Glass, Aluminum, Plastic

Selling Curbside Recycling to America

By midcentury, Coca-Cola had become one of the most conspicuous corporations in the world. The company had placed vending machines in every corner of the globe, and bright red Coca-Cola signs dotted rural roads from Alabama to Zimbabwe.[1]

Coke's exposure, however, was not always its greatest strength. In the 1960s, Coca-Cola and its soft drink rivals began to produce prodigious amounts of packaging waste, switching from returnable bottles to throwaway containers in an attempt to secure greater profits by consolidating their domestic bottling networks. Nonreturnable cans and bottles produced unsightly waste that stirred consumer backlash against corporate profligacy. The beverage industry's most precious commodity—its image of innocent fun—was at stake, and Coca-Cola, PepsiCo, and other beverage companies had to take steps in order to control the debate about producer responsibility.[2]

Coke had not always produced so much litter. In fact, in the early years of growth, the company and its bottlers had been pioneers of a rudimentary packaging recycling system: returnable bottles. Between 1899 and 1915, most distributors—small business owners with limited capital resources—used clear, green, and brown straight-sided glass bottles to sell their products (Coke's signature "hobbleskirt" design did not emerge until 1916). Bottlers expected consumers to return these containers once they were done with them. The system made economic sense; it was a way to save on front-end costs. Though remarkably durable, glass bottles were expensive to purchase in bulk. Bottlers simply could not afford to have their valuable investments thrown in the trash.

Getting consumers to participate in this system was another matter. To prevent careless customers from trashing their packaging, bottlers placed a 1- to 2-cent deposit on their bottles, which consumers could redeem upon return of the empty containers. To receive their deposit back, customers had to bring their used bottles to a retail outlet that sold the particular beverage they purchased (not necessarily the same venue where the customer originally bought the beverage). Coca-Cola bottlers knew that money talked. Of some three hundred Coke bottlers surveyed by the company in 1929, roughly 80 percent used a deposit system, many charging around 2 cents a bottle (40 percent of the cost of the soft drink).[3]

It turned out putting a price on trash made people waste less. Though many bottles were broken or discarded by consumers, most containers made their way back to bottlers for redistribution, some making forty to fifty return trips to bottling plants. According to a study conducted by the United States Resource Conservation Committee, soft drink bottles posted a return rate of about 96 percent as late as 1948, just seven short years before the Coca-Cola Company began experimenting with one-way containers. On average, then, Coke bottles made roughly twenty-two trips from bottler to consumer back to bottler for redistribution in the 1940s. Beer bottles showed similar results, as average return rates approached thirty-two trips in 1948.[4]

Both the soft drink companies and local bottlers profited from the returnable distribution system. Local soft drink bottlers—of which there were over four thousand industry-wide by 1950—spent less money purchasing containers from glass manufacturers, such as Owens-Illinois, and were thus able to use cash on other production expenses. Parent companies, such as Coca-Cola and Pepsi, benefited because the decentralized system allowed them to service remote outlets in rural America, extending their national reach. The packaging reuse system seemed to be good business for all.[5]

The shift to throwaway containers had begun in the brewing business, not the soft drink industry, in large part because the major brewing giants desired a cost-efficient way to break into new markets opened up during Prohibition. Passage of the Eighteenth Amendment and the Volstead Act in 1919 forced thousands of saloons and public watering holes across the country to close up shop, and the number of breweries operating in the United States declined dramatically from approximately 1,500 in 1919 to 331 by the time of repeal in 1933. The four major national conglomerates, however, Anheuser-Busch, Miller Brewing Company, Pabst, and Schlitz, had hung on in these tough times of teetotaling. August Busch Sr., for example, sold baking yeast, root beer, and other nonalcoholic "near beers" to stay afloat, while Gustav Pabst tried his luck at malt syrup and soft drinks. After Prohibition, battered and bruised, these brewing giants surveyed the American market and saw the promise of a profit bonanza. Hundreds of competitors had been laid waste by the Volstead Act, and hungry corporate survivors knew old territories once controlled by local breweries were ripe for invasion. Naturally, not all ground was uncontested. In Pottsville, Pennsylvania, for example, the Yuengling family survived the dark days of Prohibition and lived on to fight against Big Beer, relying on their relative isolation from major thoroughfares to keep out conglomerate competition. But other communities around the country, penetrated by new roadways paved by the Works Progress Administration during the New Deal, lay vulnerable to large national breweries that pummeled these markets with the industry's new silver bullets: cheap and lightweight beer cans.[6]

Canned beer allowed centralized brewing operations to reach consumer outlets far removed from distribution centers at low cost. As the American Can Company would write years later, "It was the nationally-minded brewers of that time [the 1930s] who foresaw how a one-trip package could provide a profitable way of quickly renewing franchises over a broad geographical range." To be certain, the trend toward at-home consumption of beer influenced brewers' interest in new lightweight, durable packaging, but, as American Can noted, "consumers were largely satisfied with returnable bottles" in 1935 and did not call on the brewing industry to change their distribution practices; rather, the prime industry problem was to develop a new way to ship large amounts of beer across expanding national markets.[7]

The tinplated steel can offered an attractive solution to industry. The original steel cans first introduced in 1935 were a far cry from the pull-tab aluminum containers of today. To open them, consumers used a "church key" to puncture the flat top of the container. It was not the most elegant beer delivery system, but brewing companies soon found that they saved on transportation costs since they did not have to transport the empties back to bottling plants, which were now further removed from consumer outlets because of industry consolidation. In little over a decade, 31 percent of the brewing industry used steel cans to sell their beverages.[8]

While the brewing industry forged headlong into canning, the soft drink industry lagged behind, largely because of some nasty chemical complications. In 1936, the Clicquot Club Company, a popular ginger ale maker based in Massachusetts, tried to become the first soft drink company to offer its products in one-way metal containers, packaging 100,000 cases of its popular ginger ale in steel cans. However, the test distribution failed when the company discovered that the high acidity of its beverage compromised the integrity of the metal cans in just two weeks. Ten years later, Pepsi-Cola tried to can its beverages but ran into another design problem when many of the cans exploded, unable to contain the pressurized gas in soft drinks (which was some two to three times the pressure in beer cans).[9]

Despite these setbacks, Walter Mack, the savvy soft drink executive responsible for bringing the Pepsi-Cola Company back from near extinction in the 1940s, was not willing to give up, and in 1953 he became the first entrepreneur to successfully introduce one-way steel containers to the soft drink industry. Mack had broken away from the Pepsi-Cola Company in 1951 and taken over the presidency of the Cantrell & Cochrane Corporation (C&C), a firm founded in Ireland that mainly sold cider but was looking to diversify into soft drink sales in the United States. Working behind the C&C label, Mack was interested in developing a line of "Super" soft drinks that would only be available in cans. Teaming up with one of the nation's largest metal can manufacturers, Continental Can, Mack began distributing his beverage in redesigned steel containers beginning in 1953. These new cans had been manufactured to handle high-pressure soft drinks and featured a fortified lining to prevent corrosion of the tinplated steel (today soft drink cans are lined with a polymer coating). Within weeks, news of Mack's enterprise made headlines, not only in the United States but also abroad. In Britain, the popular *Daily Mirror* tabloid reported that Mack's new Super colas introduced "a wholly new way of drinking that makes old-style bottled beverages as obsolete as yesterday's horsecars."[10]

Mack prophesied that one-way containers would allow C&C to outcompete Coca-Cola and other industry rivals. In the early years,

Mack contended, the soft drink industry "was designed on the little ice box, the horse-drawn cart and a grocery store that carried about four hundred items. The horse could make a hundred and fifty stops a day, to deliver and pick up the empties. Try that at today's truckers' wages!" Rejecting the returnable distribution system of the soft drink giants, a system that would require the company to make expensive capital outlays to finance transportation costs, Mack bragged that C&C would "have no distributors. We'll be our own."[11]

Coca-Cola watched warily to see how the canning trend would develop, reluctant to force its bottlers to invest in expensive canning equipment. As Coke president H. B. Nicholson explained, Coca-Cola, like the other soft drink giants, was committed to "a healthy decentralization," whereby separate ownership oversaw bottling and syrup operations. The company claimed that a switch to canning soda pop would not be beneficial for its enterprise, considering that such a transition would require thousands of independent bottlers—roughly 1,400 for Coke (around 6,000 bottlers industry-wide in 1953)—to replace expensive bottling and washing equipment with modern canning machinery.[12]

But despite such public praise for the decentralized bottling network, corporate executives at Coca-Cola headquarters relished the thought of developing a new distribution system that would diminish the power of the local bottler and allow Coke to accrue profits siphoned off by distributors. Many at Coca-Cola, including Robert Woodruff, believed that Candler's decision to outsource bottling had cut the firm out of a lot of money. Now a multimillion-dollar corporation, the company was starting to think it could go it alone, cut out the middlemen, and channel cash earned through distribution directly to corporate coffers.[13]

With this new objective in mind, the lesson of Walter Mack's success could not have been lost on Coca-Cola executives, who realized that lightweight packaging offered the corporate office a powerful weapon in its intracompany war with local bottlers. The can would allow Coke to consolidate its bottling network and thereby eliminate hundreds of distributors. Profits that once had gone into the pockets of these local bottlers could now be channeled to company headquarters in Atlanta.

The Coca-Cola Company began to experiment with steel containers in 1955, teaming up with the American Can Company, a rival of Continental Can, to produce 12-ounce "MiraCans" for export to post exchange stores at military bases abroad. By the mid-1960s, Coke was selling thousands of cases of canned Coke to domestic markets, many in aluminum containers after 1967.[14]

Large Coca-Cola distributors enjoyed huge savings from the one-way container system. The Pacific Coca-Cola Bottling Company (one of the largest Coca-Cola distributors in the country) conducted an internal study in 1978 that revealed the bottler used just 42 gallons of gasoline per thousand cases to distribute one-way containers, compared to 94 gallons per thousand cases to distribute and reclaim returnables. The company also reported savings in labor costs with the elimination of certain collection and cleaning services needed for returnables. Other megabottlers commented on the reductions in warehouse and machinery costs associated with the shift to one-way containers, savings that totaled some $4 million, according to one Coke distributor.[15]

Smaller bottlers who depended on a returnable system to turn a profit lambasted the government for allowing soft drink giants to pass the costs of container collection and disposal on to the government. Independent distributors servicing small markets, like Peter T. Chokola, president of the family-owned Chokola Beverage Company in Wilkes-Barre, Pennsylvania, lobbied Congress to ban nonreturnable containers in the early 1970s, convinced that the containers gave soft drink giants a competitive advantage. According to Chokola, the one-way distribution system adopted by corporate titans like

Coca-Cola and Pepsi forced city governments to pay for the "recovery burden of 65,000 truckloads" of bottles and cans each day. "Centralization and intent to monopolize," Chokola contended, were "the underlying reasons behind rapid conversion of soft drink industry to throwaways."[16]

Small bottlers like Chokola had strong evidence to support their claims that one-way containers were helping large bottlers monopolize markets. The number of Coca-Cola bottlers operating in the United States had dropped dramatically from roughly 1,200 in 1929 to an estimated 500 in 1979, and the total number of bottlers in the soft drink industry declined from over 4,000 in 1960 to under 3,000 by 1972. The pace of consolidation increased after the creation in 1986 of the company-owned megabottler Coca-Cola Enterprises, which gobbled up even more local bottlers in the 1980s and 1990s. By 1997 there were approximately one hundred Coke bottlers servicing domestic markets. This was an unprecedented experiment in vertical integration for Coke. Only time would tell whether the gamble would pay off.[17]

AS CHOKOLA AND OTHER small bottlers had anticipated, the one-way container allowed beverage giants like Coke to achieve record profits by shifting key costs of distribution onto municipalities. Coke's success assured the consolidation of the soft drink industry, as corporate rivals followed the number-one brand's lead. The era of one-way metal soft drink containers had arrived by the mid-1960s, and though the beverage companies would look to develop new packaging designs in the years ahead—Coke making a major shift toward plastics in 1978—the most dramatic conversion had already taken place by 1960. The beverage industry was primed for a new era of growth in the age of convenience packaging. The only question was: would the consumer remain committed to this new distribution system?[18]

• • •

RESISTANCE TO THE NEW packaging systems developed by Coke, Pepsi, and the major beer brands began to build in the 1950s. Thousands of throwaway cans and bottles lay strewn across the American landscape, along roadsides, in national parks, and along streambeds. The costs of unregulated corporate expansion had become visible in a way that it never had before, and many Americans began to call on the brewing, soft drink, and packaging industries to clean up the mess.

This was the dawn of a new environmental movement, one that would stand in stark contrast to the conservationist efforts of the Progressive Era just a few decades earlier. At the turn of the century, to be an environmentalist was to be a utilitarian, to believe that man had a duty to employ scientific knowledge in the careful maintenance of the nation's natural resources. Men like President Theodore Roosevelt and US Forest Service head Gifford Pinchot were conservationists. They saw themselves as having the awesome obligation of conserving the nation's natural resources so that the nation's captains of industry never suffered from want. Theirs was an economic policy as much as it was an environmental policy, driven more by a desire to see the country's industrial capacity expand than by a desire simply to preserve the natural wonders of America.

Yet there were contemporaries of Roosevelt and Pinchot who had a different vision for the country, men like John Muir, founder of the Sierra Club, and Aldo Leopold, author of *A Sand County Almanac* (1949), who called for the preservation of nature regardless of what purpose it might serve for American business. By the 1950s, this strain of the early environmental movement had gained new converts among a burgeoning middle class that now had both the means and the time to enjoy America's wildlands. Gone were the days of the Great Depression when people scraped and borrowed just to get by. After World War II, middle-class Americans were immersed in a booming consumer culture, and they now had more income and more leisure time than their forefathers could have imagined. Increasingly, the intangible assets nature offered—serenity, clean air, and aesthetic beauty—became valued commodities to which middle-class Americans felt themselves entitled. They resented the corporate misuse of nature, believing it infringed on their rights as consumers to enjoy America's many environmental amenities, and they were willing to fight to preserve those rights.[19]

By 1953, the battle between this new, mobilized middle class and the beverage industry was beginning to play out in the arena of state politics. That year, in Maryland, state legislators proposed a mandatory deposit bill that would have required all one-way beer containers to carry a 3-cent deposit. In a sense, Maryland was simply copying an old incentive program promoted by soft drink and beer bottlers at the turn of the twentieth century. In the 1920s, bottlers had crowed loudly about the value of deposits in disciplining consumers not to throw away their empties. Now, with waste piling up, states turned to the same logic.[20]

Some governments went even further than Maryland in attacking the problem. The Vermont General Assembly, for example, passed a law that prohibited the use of nonreturnable glass beer bottles within its state borders (a restriction that lasted up to 1957, when "beer industry pressure" led to its expiration). Faced with the success of the Vermont campaign, one-way container producers and their beverage-industry clients knew they needed to take more direct action in combating mandatory deposit legislation and packaging bans. They needed to add a corporate voice to the new environmental movement.[21]

In 1953, American canning, packaging, and beverage companies responded to consumer concern about one-way container waste by creating the first national anti-litter organization, Keep America

Beautiful (KAB). Though relative latecomers to the one-way container system (compared to the nation's brewing giants), Coca-Cola and its soft drink industry rivals were committed KAB associates, channeling considerable capital resources toward KAB's publicity campaigns.[22]

KAB was an early pioneer in what would become known as astroturfing, a term coined by US Senator Lloyd Bentsen from Texas in the 1980s to describe corporate-financed political action campaigns made to look like grassroots initiatives. KAB's greatest strength was its ability to appear as if it were merely a third-party organization interested in public service, rather than a corporate lobbying agency with a specific agenda to protect big business. By the 1980s, thousands of corporate-run organizations would employ its tactics, but in the late 1950s, KAB was in many ways a trailblazer for this new form of corporate political activism.[23]

KAB's central objective was to deflect accusations that corporations were to blame for the country's growing litter problem. Describing the impetus for the new organization in 1954, the *New York Times* reported that "intelligent self-interest" was a prime motivating factor. Through targeted education programs, national publicity campaigns, and local clean-up drives, KAB worked to persuade consumers that private citizens, not corporate citizens, should be responsible for waste disposal.[24]

KAB produced hundreds of print and television advertisements disciplining consumers to do their part to clean up the environment. One representative TV ad from the 1960s featured staged scenes at picnic areas, beach resorts, and campsites littered with trash. The organization was direct in its message to consumers, explaining, "One thing's sure, America's litter problem is in your hands," adding, "Keeping America clean and beautiful is your job." Central to KAB's campaign was the idea of the "litterbug," a term first coined in the late 1940s. The organization worked to popularize this derisive label, which it believed properly placed blame for the nation's waste woes on careless consumers rather than corporations. Litterbugs, as KAB's promotional pitch went, were in many ways subhuman, akin to disease-ridden insects that were the target of pesticide campaigns in postwar America. They had to be eradicated.[25]

KAB's promotional material appealed to an American public firmly rooted in a classical liberal tradition that stressed rational consumers' power to solve market problems. As environmental writer Ginger Strand pointed out, KAB denied that structural changes to industrial technologies would solve the nation's litter crisis. Rather, the organization sought to preclude "any debate over the wisdom of creating disposables in the first place," in this way focusing public attention "on the symptoms rather than the system."[26]

As prime contributors to the growing litter problem, soft drink companies became increasingly concerned about anti-litter backlash in the 1960s. With nonreturnable cans representing almost 11 percent of all packaged soft drink sales in 1963 (over 65 million cases that year), soft drink giants knew that their companies were exposed targets for anti-litter agitators in favor of industry-specific pollution taxes. Coca-Cola president Paul Austin admitted this fact in 1968. "We participate in the [creation of] litter to a significant degree," he conceded, adding that the company had "earned various criticisms for littering the landscape." Austin lamented the fact that "the packaging for our products is highly visible"; he was frustrated that Coke's "colored decoration on a can or the unique shape of our bottle doesn't deteriorate as readily as paper containers." The solution to this problem of exposure, as Austin saw it, was to encourage "individuals" to "*actively* get involved in the massive job" of cleaning up the unsightly by-products of Coke's commercial growth.[27]

Austin was sympathetic to the growing environmentalist movement sweeping the nation. He too believed the country faced serious ecological problems that needed fixing, but he believed businessmen like himself could be part of the solution rather than the problem. In public speeches, he played the part of a corporate eco-warrior working from within big business to make a difference. And he did not mince words. In 1970, he gave a speech to the Georgia Bankers Association, urging those in attendance to sign on to the environmental crusade. "Unless *all* of us begin *immediately* to reverse the processes of impending self-destruction, which *we* have set in motion," he warned the bankers, "this green land of ours will become a *graveyard!*" He spoke of an impending apocalypse, a "cold and utterly dead" world overrun by the "vast hordes of humanity." "I'm concerned," he lectured, "because you and I are *killing* each other and I'm *deadly* serious when I say that." Change had to come. "We must begin now. We must begin together. There is no place to hide."[28]

But as sincere as Austin's pitch was, there were real environmental problems with the Coke system that did not have an easy fix. In the case of packaging, one-way containers were simply too profitable to give up. Austin admitted as much, noting that there were not "any serious prospects for truly degradable soft drink containers. Not now, any way." Coke needed the nonreturnable container to reach certain markets, and it knew it had to convince public citizens that they needed it, too.[29]

No expense could be spared in the battle for hearts and minds, and in the late 1960s, Coca-Cola partnered with its industry competitors to generate capital to quash the opposition. In addition to KAB, Coke leaned on the Washington, DC–based lobbying arm of the soft drink industry, the National Soft Drink Association (NSDA), to rally support for the cause. In 1966, NSDA had become the new name for the American Bottlers of Carbonated Beverages (ABCB), an organization founded in 1919 by the major soft drink companies, which acted as a kind of government liaison for beverage firms, lobbying out of a K Street office in favor of legislation favorable to the beverage industry. Consumers often think of rival soft drink brands, such as

Pepsi and Coca-Cola, as archenemies, but through the NSDA, these competitors worked closely and harmoniously to solve industry-wide problems. In the case of litter, the NSDA sought to crush state and federal government plans to impose mandatory deposits on nonreturnable containers. The stakes could not have been higher. In 1967, twenty-one states proposed bans on throwaway containers. This was no time to break ranks. The soft drink giants showed a united front against those who sought to undermine the one-way container system.[30]

The NSDA's message was clear: "people, not containers, are responsible" for the growing litter problem facing the nation. The NSDA distributed thousands of posters, bumper stickers, and billboards (an impressive amount of litter by any standard), featuring "Handy," a lone hand with a string attached to the index finger, to remind consumers that "hands alone cause litter." Targeting America's youth, the NSDA also circulated booklets entitled "A Handy Guide to Lessen Litter" in schools throughout the country. The guides not only featured lessons on how not to litter but also included a great deal of soft drink advertising that spotlighted "the history, growth and outlook for carbonated beverages."[31]

While NSDA worked the classroom, Keep America Beautiful flooded the airwaves. In 1971, the organization ran its most famous TV anti-litter promotional campaign, popularly referred to as the "Crying Indian" commercial. The ad featured Iron Eyes Cody, an Italian American actor who played the role of a Native American paddling a war canoe through a metropolitan landscape littered with garbage. The advertisement wholly embraced the myth of the ecological Indian, suggesting that Cody's Native American heritage somehow made him more in touch with the natural world. Of course, the great irony was that Cody was not in fact Native American. At the end of the advertisement, Cody stands atop a hill surveying a congested highway and is struck by a bag of fast food thrown from a passing car (interestingly, the trash featured paper packaging, not beverage containers). In this moment, the camera zooms in for an extreme close-up of a weeping Cody, and an omniscient narrator declares, "People start pollution, people can stop it." Millions of Americans watched this commercial, many noting its striking imagery. *Ad Age*, a leading advertising magazine, named the "Crying Indian" commercial one of the Top 100 ads of the twentieth century.[32]

Despite these industry efforts at persuasion, environmentalist protestors continued their clarion call against corporate polluters, some taking their fight to the front doorstep of Coca-Cola—literally. On April 26, 1970, the final day of the nation's first Earth Week, young Atlantans organized a campaign to dump hundreds of bottles and cans at the entrance of Coke's North Avenue headquarters in the heart of the city. The *Speckled Bird*, a weekly publication of Atlanta's hippiedom in the 1970s, explained that it was time to "bring the trash home to the people who make it," urging the city's residents to take part in the action. Self-described "ecology freaks" writing for the *Speckled Bird* promised to hire a pickup truck, "driven by a genuine garbage striker," that would transport some of the trash from Piedmont Park to North Avenue. Some 1,500 protestors showed up for the demonstration, making the three-mile trek from the park to Coke's headquarters, many with bags of trash in hand. There they laid down their waste, an act symbolizing their refusal to carry the burden the corporation had asked them to bear.[33]

Paul Austin, Coke's environmentally conscious president, knew his company had to do more if it was going to quell this backlash. Commenting on the political and cultural climate in the final months of 1969, Austin wrote to former company chairman Robert Woodruff, "I was getting concerned about the exposure of the Coca-Cola Company to attacks because it is an outstanding member of the Establishment." He admitted that the "Coca-Cola Company is a serious offender in a certain part of the pollution problem" and stated his belief that the initiation of a corporate greening campaign "would reap immeasurable good will from government sources, the conservationists of the country, and the public at large."[34]

With Austin at the helm, the Coca-Cola Company launched a national "Bend a Little" campaign in 1970, placing ads throughout the country featuring an attractive woman bending over to pick up empty containers. The company also distributed "Bend a Little" litter bags to its customers. The message was obvious. As Coca-Cola archivist Phil Mooney explained, "The goal of the 'Bend a Little' campaign was to remind people that cleaning up America called for a little extra effort from all of us."[35]

Coca-Cola plastered its anti-litter messages all over the country, and in many ways its environmental advertising became an aesthetic pollution in its own right. One billboard campaign featured bottles and cans of Coke anthropomorphically pleading to consumers, "If you love me, don't leave me." The advertisement also ran in print media across the country with a caption explaining that though the returnable Coke bottle was "ecologically sound," consumers demanded "a choice of containers in many products, including soft drinks. And competition gives it to them. So we have to go along." The main problem with nonreturnables, the company argued, was not that they were environmentally unsound but that they presented a "real litter problem if the consumer doesn't care what he does with the empties." The company added, "We feel if we ask you to care about keeping our countryside at its best that many of you will try."[36]

Like the NSDA, Coca-Cola produced special eco-advertising tailored for the youth market. In the 1970s, for example, it distributed to schools across the country a board game called Man in His Environment in which students were asked to make eco-conscious decisions for a fictitious riverside community. Designed for elementary school children, the game stressed the importance of consumer participation in environmental cost-benefit analysis. As archivist Mooney explained, students were "not told the answers, rather they had to become involved in the decisions and discover answers for themselves." The game taught that private citizens controlled the fate of society, directing corporate citizens toward eco-friendly development solutions. Citizen Coke was training a new generation what conservation meant in a throwaway culture.[37]

Coke, NSDA, and KAB public ad campaigns in the 1960s and 1970s certainly helped draw the public's attention away from the fact that American companies were producing prodigious amounts of packaging waste, but corporate polluters knew that litter bags would not, in the long run, solve their problem of exposure. In the Pacific Northwest and New England in particular, legislators were frustrated that little was being done to combat the nation's growing litter problem, and they had pushed for mandatory deposit legislation in the late 1960s. The beverage industry had to respond with a more aggressive campaign directed to American lawmakers if it hoped to avoid costly pollution taxes.

On October 1, 1972, Oregon implemented a law mandating a minimum 5-cent deposit for all throwaway bottles and cans. The law also banned detachable pull-tabs for beverage containers sold in the state. The measure had initially failed to receive enough votes when first proposed in 1968, but the timely support of Governor Tom McCall got the legislation passed three years later.[38]

By this time, aluminum cans with removable openers were fast replacing clunky steel containers. Coke had first made the switch to all-aluminum packaging in 1967, partnering with the Reynolds Metal Company, in large part because aluminum cans were lighter, thereby further reducing transport costs for bottlers. But throwaway tabs proved yet another pesky pollutant that aggravated environmentalists. Like cigarette butts, these one-and-done openers were carelessly strewn across the landscape. True, aluminum cans were lighter, but their ecological footprint, as far as environmentalists were concerned, was no less heavy than other nonreturnable alternatives. As a result, other states were moved to act in the 1970s to abate the growing litter problem. Vermont followed Oregon's lead in 1972, passing a mandatory deposit bill for all one-way containers sold in the state.[39]

The enactment of these statewide mandatory deposit bills occurred at the same time that the US Congress began to consider a national ban on nonreturnable containers. By the mid-1960s, President Lyndon Johnson had begun to push for federal funding for municipal solid-waste programs, in part because of pressure coming from his wife, Lady Bird Johnson, who was a strong proponent of environmental conservation initiatives. By the 1960s she was helping to lobby for a series of environmental programs, including the Highway Beautification Act of 1965, which was primarily concerned with implementing federal regulation of billboard construction along major highways. Spurred on by Lady Bird, Lyndon Johnson signed into law the Solid Waste Disposal Act of 1965 and later lobbied for a national survey of solid-waste programs in 1968. The federal government was finally becoming actively involved in addressing the nation's growing garbage problem, a concern traditionally considered the responsibility of state and municipal governments.[40]

In 1970, continuing a new tradition of federal involvement in solid-waste management issues, the House of Representatives considered an amendment to the Solid Waste Disposal Act that would have prohibited the distribution of nonreturnable beverage containers within the United States. Testifying before Congress, the mayor of Bowie, Maryland, explained that his city council had passed such a ban because "rising cost to the taxpayer in gathering and disposing of these containers was becoming unconscionable." The twenty-two House legislators who sponsored the federal ban were equally concerned about escalating waste disposal costs, arguing that corporate polluters should be expected to pay the expenses associated with nonreusable cans and bottles.[41]

Representatives from the beverage container industry attacked the proposed federal ban, arguing that the measure would hurt sales and "create severe economic dislocations in industries employing hundreds of thousands of people." Richard L. Cheney, president of the Glass Container Manufacturers Institute, explained in his testimony against the proposed legislation that "thousands of glass container plant employees would be put out of work" if the industry were limited to returnable bottle production. In 1972, when a national nonreturnable container ban once again came up for consideration in the Senate, Norman L. Dobyns of the Carbonated Beverage Container Manufacturers Association explained that doing away with one-way containers would completely eliminate the soft drink canning industry: "We won't be there any more. That is a very large, very important, very consequential industry, that is gone by that one legislative stroke." Listening to these industry appeals, Congress ultimately rejected the ban.[42]

Industry lobbyists were victorious at the national level in 1970 and 1972, and continued to be throughout the 1970s, in large part because they convinced federal legislators that a prohibition on one-way containers would eliminate numerous jobs within the soft drink and packaging industries. In 1976, when another proposed ban failed to make it off the Senate floor, Senator Adlai E. Stevenson III of Illinois said emphatically that the jobs issue struck the decisive blow.[43]

Using the specter of job losses proved effective at the local level as well. In Yonkers, New York, for example, representatives from the NSDA, Coca-Cola, Pepsi-Cola, and the United States Brewers Association testified before the city council in 1971 in order to promote a recycling program over a proposed ban on nonreturnables.

According to the *New York Times*, the ban had originally received bipartisan support and "appeared to have at least a reasonable chance of passing" when it first came up for consideration in committee. Following the testimony of ten "industry spokesmen," including the head of the NSDA, however, several councilmen removed their support for the bill. As they had done at the national level, corporate lobbyists in Yonkers used the threat of catastrophic job losses to scare lawmakers into opposing top-down regulation. Explaining the effect of the industry testimony, councilman Peter Mancusi confessed, "The streets are dirty, and everyone agrees. But talk about 500 families out of a job and the Councilmen sit up and listen." Aloysius Moczydlowski, another councilman who was admittedly swayed by industry testimony, explained his rationale for opposing the ban: "I learned that the companies are understanding and facing the waste problem themselves. No voters have spoken to me, only companies. And who can solve problems better than private industry?"[44]

The soft drink, packaging, and brewing industries held out recycling as the panacea that would solve the nation's litter problems. Companies in these industries knew that they had to take preemptive steps to combat growing consumer concerns, and they believed recycling could be touted as an effective industry alternative to mandatory deposit schemes, one that would allow them to off-load costs onto consumer and municipal governments.[45]

To be sure, brewing, soft drinks, and canning giants were not the only businesses lobbying for recycling programs in the 1970s. Early supporters of recycling included scrap metal companies, which hoped to exploit new sources of revenue for their industry. But despite their enthusiasm, many scrap companies never received lucrative recycling contracts from municipalities; most went to burgeoning garbage conglomerates like Waste Management Inc. and Browning-Ferris Industries. Supermarket owners and local grocery store proprietors also welcomed recycling programs as alternatives to deposit programs that would force them to take on the messy work of receiving and processing used beverage containers. Similar support for recycling came from paper-manufacturing companies, as well as representatives from the plastics industry, all believing this new reclamation system would generate valuable materials for their industries.[46]

Nonprofit organizations lobbied for recycling as well. Environmental groups believed that municipal reclamation schemes would help alleviate the nation's growing garbage problem. The Sierra Club, the National Wildlife Federation, and other major environmental organizations attended hearings on beverage-container-recycling programs and fought in support of funding programs that would channel federal revenue toward recycling grants. Notably, though, these groups treated recycling as just one component of their conservation agenda. As journalist Heather Rogers pointed out, organizations like Environmental Action "viewed the 'three Rs' in a hierarchical fashion: first, reduce consumption, then reuse goods in their already manufactured form as long as possible, and then, only as a last resort, recycle."[47]

Still, companies like Coca-Cola and Pepsi remained leading proponents of recycling initiatives, precisely because of consumer awareness of the beverage industry's contributions to the solid-waste problem. In 1970, the president of the National Soft Drink Association explained how company advertising on one-way packaging created this industry-specific dilemma:

> It is your and my container that may lay along the side of the road inviting public wrath, not the glass or the can companies. . . . It is our trademark on it and it carries our product. . . . They are going to be concerned with the final social consequence of your and my enterprise, and they are going to expect us to account for that consequence.[48]

Recognizing their unique exposure to environmentalists' attacks, the beverage industry bombarded the public with advertisements highlighting their efforts to recycle in the early 1970s. These ads suggested that American business was using its innovative strengths to solve the nation's litter problems. In New York City, for example, Reynolds Metals Company worked with Coca-Cola, Pepsi-Cola, and Mobil Oil on a city-wide ad campaign to highlight industry efforts to reclaim container waste. The ads, which included broadside bus posters and Sunday comics, featured descriptions of twenty-nine recycling collection centers throughout the metropolitan area run by various corporate partners. Coke claimed in its advertisements that "our city government has enough to do without setting up reclamation centers," suggesting that the company, in partnership with its consumers, had both the will and the resources to solve one "of the most important ecological problems of our day." Other businessmen echoed these claims. The American Can Company, which produced the first aluminum-can-recycling program in 1967, also spoke of corporate self-reliance: "We can solve the problem in industry and we are already working on it. . . . Industry is doing such a good job in the area of coming up with systems."[49]

Despite big-business praise for privately run resource-reclamation programs, support for these clean-up drives quickly began to wane. In February 1972, less than twelve months after Coca-Cola, Mobil Oil, and Reynolds began their recycling program in New York, the press reported that "enthusiasm for the recycling of waste on Long Island seems to be faltering." Mobil gas stations had already closed their reclamation centers by the winter of 1972, and several of the centers run by the Coca-Cola Bottling Company of New York dramatically reduced their hours of operation.[50]

The press reported similar problems with private recycling programs throughout the country. In California many reclamation programs were shut down in 1972, largely because they could not cover operation costs. The San Diego Ecology Center, a major recycling plant in Southern California, barely broke even in 1972, relying on subsidies from outside sources to cover its operating expenses. The *New York Times* reported in May of 1972, "Recycling so far is not paying its own way. And there is a growing belief that it will be years— if ever, before it makes any major dent in the nation's mounting piles of solid wastes." According to the *Washington Post*, by 1978 virtually all the "3,000 drop-off recycling centers that sprang up in the United States from 1970 to 1973" had "disappeared," unable to recoup capital expenses associated with collection and facilities maintenance.[51]

In addition to being unprofitable, recycling programs in the 1970s simply were unsuccessful at reclaiming the vast majority of refuse produced by the beverage industry. Of the 36 billion containers produced by the glass industry in 1972, only 912 million (less than 3 percent) actually made it to recycling centers. Aluminum reclamation showed similar results, as only close to 4 percent of all aluminum material made it back to producers through recycling programs. These results should not have been surprising considering the small fiscal enticements that private collectors tendered to consumers. Coke's collection centers in New York, for example, offered recyclers just one-half cent for every returned can. Small bottlers who were being pushed out of the soft drink market because of the switch to one-way containers highlighted the inconsistencies in soft drink giants' conservation rhetoric. As independent Dr Pepper bottler Eugene Norton explained in 1972, "The public is . . . being told that people will not return returnable bottles for a deposit, yet on the other hand, these same pundits say the public will deliver throwaways to a recycling center for as little as a penny apiece providing they can find a recycling center."[52]

Making recycling work was going to require more than just the Sunday sweat of Boy Scout troops and altruistic citizens; it was going to require lots of money, more money than cities facing mounting inflation and a stagnating 1970s economy could invest. So Big Soda turned to the federal government, testifying before Congress to promote the adoption of legislation that would channel federal funds toward municipal recycling programs.

Reynolds, American Can, Coca-Cola, and Anheuser-Busch supported the Resource and Recovery Act (RRA) of 1970, which called for the federal government to provide assistance to municipalities struggling to deal with the nation's growing solid-waste problem. City governments interested in constructing resource-reclamation plants could expect the federal government to provide grants for the associated development and construction costs.[53]

Many local bottlers, who valued the old returnable system, were unhappy with the federal government's new interventions under the RRA. Small, independent bottlers like Peter T. Chokola believed that federally supported recycling programs shifted "the burden of recovery of containers from the private sector onto Government." They fought against programs that did not require companies using one-way containers to pay for the waste they helped create. One small bottler opposed federal grants for recycling research, arguing that "this is added consumer and taxpayer costs, millions, perhaps billions of dollars and it isn't going to solve the problem any better than the returnable system which is already here."[54]

Despite resistance from small bottlers, Congress continued to generate legislation that would encourage government investment in municipal recycling programs. In 1976, Congress passed the Resource Conservation and Recovery Act (RCRA), which increased federal support for local resource-reclamation initiatives. The major soft drink companies supported this measure, hoping to direct general tax funds toward clean-up projects that would help them keep their waste out of sight. The former president of the NSDA, Sidney P. Mudd of the Seven-Up company, praised the RCRA for setting a "clear national objective and a suitable funding mechanism to stimulate similar planning and action for appropriate solid waste management throughout the 50 States."[55]

Finally, after decades of desperately dodging environmentalist attacks, the beverage industry found deliverance through a federal bailout. The RCRA made clear that dealing with packaging waste was going to be primarily a public problem, not a corporate concern. At last, big business could stop sinking funds in unprofitable private recycling systems. They were off the hook. Municipalities would now have to come up with a solution, whether their taxpaying citizens liked it or not.

THE TIMING WAS FORTUITOUS, as Coke by the mid-1970s had just committed to a new throwaway container made of a material that promised to change the industry forever: plastic.

Coke's foray into plastics had begun in the late 1960s. At that time, young company executives in a variety of industries were enamored with this lightweight material produced from organic compounds in oil. In many ways, the experience of a young Dustin Hoffman in the 1967 film *The Graduate* captured the spirit of the times. "There's a great future in plastics," whispered a mentoring middle-aged neighbor to the aimless Hoffman. "Think about it."

Coke's green-minded president Paul Austin had indeed thought about it in 1969 and was anxious to begin experimenting with a prototype plastic package for soft drinks. First, however, he had to know whether he could sell the switch to an increasingly environmentally conscious consumer base. Might the lightweight packaging in fact reduce the amount of fuel needed to transport finished beverages? Were there energy savings to be made elsewhere in the production chain? If so, this data could be used to keep eco-warriors at bay.

So Austin commissioned a study in 1969 to better understand the footprint of various containers used by industry. It would be an undertaking that would have far-reaching implications for corporate greening strategies far beyond the soft drink industry. Essentially, this was the first Life Cycle Analysis (LCA) study ever conducted, and it would quickly become the gold standard for environmental assessment in the United States. Today, Coke's LCA method, though adapted and amended to fit new scientific and technological discoveries, is used by businesses in almost every industry imaginable.[56]

Piloting the project was Harry Teasley Jr., an executive in the Packaging Department of the company, who partnered with the Kansas City, Missouri, environmental research firm Midwest Research Institute (MRI). Under the direction of program manager Bill Franklin, MRI produced what was then called a Resource and Environmental Profile Analysis (REPA), or LCA study, for Coke packaging containers, which essentially cataloged the various environmental consequences of packaging production and distribution. In the years after 1969, Bill Franklin, working closely with MRI physicist Robert Hunt, launched several additional LCA studies for Coca-Cola and many other major corporations.[57]

Coca-Cola never released the 1969 study to the public. In fact, most LCA experiments that Coca-Cola and other corporations conducted in the early seventies were not released to consumers. To this day, Coke has remained reticent about giving out information related to the 1969 study. In the fall of 2009, I contacted MRI to see if I could obtain a copy of the Coca-Cola report and was told that while MRI was happy to provide me with the material, I would need to seek approval from Coca-Cola USA before the institute would release the study. After contacting Coca-Cola's customer hotline, I was directed to Industry and Consumer Affairs representative Elizabeth Grimaldo, who thanked me for my "loyalty and interest" in Coca-Cola but explained, "It has become necessary for us to limit the number of requests granted by our Company. We regret to inform you that your request does not fit into our current plans for the use of our trademark. Please know that this decision is not a reflection on you or your company, but rather a matter of policy."[58]

While Coke's 1969 study remains confidential, in 1974, the EPA commissioned Hunt and Franklin to produce a similar analysis of nine beverage containers for the federal government. The study focused on beer containers but also included comparative data on soft drink packaging. According to the 1974 report, a 10-trip returnable bottle—one making 10 trips from bottler to consumer back to bottler—had a lower impact on the environment than all other containers examined in the study, which included aluminum, bimetal, and steel cans as well as plastic containers and throwaway glass bottles. Considering that in 1970 the average return rate for a returnable soft drink bottle was about twelve trips, the study suggested that throwaways were not an environmentally desirable choice. Franklin and Hunt did not hedge in their conclusion, stating that no throwaway "container will be improved to match or surpass that of [the 10-trip returnable bottle] in the near future."[59]

Despite Hunt and Franklin's 1974 finding, Coke decided that plastics would be the best packaging for its products in the future. Why? In the final calculus, it was all about energy costs. In the wake of the 1973 OPEC oil embargo and the consequent increases in petroleum prices in the United States, Coke had feared that switching to a packaging material derived from oil would be risky business. But the LCA study showed that plastic packaging would use less petroleum than originally predicted. As LCA researchers Mark Duda and Jane S. Shaw explained, "Since plastics are actually made from hydrocarbons, this result was surprising and it gave the company confidence to proceed with the development of today's widely-used plastic bottle."[60]

Like Duda and Shaw, Hunt believed that energy savings really excited Coca-Cola. Nonetheless, Hunt claimed that MRI's research on plastics at that point was limited at best. He ultimately felt that

MRI's "plastics analysis wasn't very good for Coke, because they never gave us any indication that that is what they were interested in." Whatever Coke saw in the 1969 study, Hunt explained, the 1974 study showed "that refillable bottles are far and away the best" environmental choice at high trip rates.[61]

AUSTIN, HOWEVER, LIKE DUSTIN Hoffman's neighbor in *The Graduate*, decided Coke's future lay in plastics. Partnering with the Monsanto Company, one of Coke's former caffeine suppliers, Coca-Cola experimented with Lopac bottles made of acrylonitrile-based plastic in the late 1960s, first test-distributing 3 million containers to consumers in Providence, Rhode Island, and Boston and New Bedford, Massachusetts, in 1970.[62]

While Coke test marketed its Lopac bottles in New England, Pepsi-Cola began experimenting with a polyethlyene-based polymer bottle. By 1975, the plastics battle was on, with both Pepsi and Coke hoping to convince the public that their container would become the industry standard.

Coca-Cola publicly reported select evidence from its internal LCA study to sell its new packaging to the public. Donald Keough, head of Coca-Cola USA, reported to the *New York Times* in 1975 that the company's plastic bottles, nicknamed "Easy-Goers," were superior to other containers because they were lightweight, durable, and "highly resistant to biodegradation and exposure to water and sunlight which makes the package more valuable in protecting the product it contains and permits recycling." Keough's claim that plastics were recyclable conflicted with FDA research from a year later, which revealed that "substantial recycling of plastics is unlikely in the near future, either for plastic or for energy, primarily for technical reasons and lack of market for nonvirgin plastics." Also left unsaid in Keough's promotional campaigns was the fact that University of

Michigan researchers had recently produced studies showing that the acrylonitrile-based plastic in Lopac bottles leached into water chemicals that caused cancer in laboratory rats.[63]

By 1976, growing concerns about the environmental and health risks associated with Coca-Cola's acrylonitrile containers pushed legislators to propose bills banning the distribution of Coke's plastic bottles. County officials in Suffolk, New York, for example, argued that while Coke's Lopac bottles "may look rather innocent, they constitute the latest example of major corporate irresponsibility," citing evidence that plastic bottle manufacturing required large quantities of petroleum fuel and that the new containers were known to produce dangerous toxins when incinerated. John Spencer, the director of Coke's Plastic Packaging Department in New York, responded to these allegations, contending, "We would not come out with a package for Coca-Cola that was environmentally unsound because of our wide exposure in the consumer market." According to Spencer's rhetoric, the enlightened consumer would not let the company make unwise marketing decisions based on the "emotional" passions of health and environmental fanatics. Appealing to a free market ideology that placed the rational consumer in control of market trends, Spencer concluded, "When the facts are rationally brought out, I think many will change their attitude" about Coke's plastic bottle.[64]

Consumers never got the chance to weigh in. While Coke continued to promote its plastic container, the FDA issued a ban on Coke's Lopac bottle in March 1977, citing strong evidence that the containers were carcinogenic. Meanwhile, Pepsi-Cola's polyethylene terephthalate (PET) bottle, produced by the Amoco Chemicals Corporation, gained approval by the FDA, and Coke, anxious not to lose out to its archrival, thus decided to shift to the PET bottles in 1977. Later that year, Coke began distributing caseloads of 2-liter PET bottles from its Spartanburg, South Carolina, bottling plant, and by 1978, Coke was selling plastic bottles to over a fourth of its US market.[65]

With Big Soda making the switch to PET, plastic came flooding into America's landfills. The FDA was right: there simply was not a market for recycled PET, and very little of it was reclaimed initially. In part, this was because various types of plastics in the waste stream, when mixed in the recycling process, produced blends unfit for resale. As a result, plastic bottles only worsened an already severe garbage crisis.

PLASTICS, HOWEVER, WERE HARDLY the only problem thwarting recycling system success in 1970s America. Despite passage of the RCRA in 1976, which promised a federal commitment to finance curbside recycling systems in the United States, the truth was that municipal reclamation programs were costly and labor-intensive. It would take years for cities to accumulate the funds and infrastructure to make recycling a reality.

In the meantime, anti-litter agitation would grow. By the end of the 1970s and into the 1980s, with curbside recycling in most cities still years from development, waste piles reached historic heights. In the Meadowlands of New Jersey, for example, some landfills stretched for over 200 acres—more than 150 football fields—and topped 80 feet in height. With no room to expand, city commissioners moved to shut many of them down in 1978. That year, the *New York Times* foresaw dire straits: "Garbage Crisis: After Landfills, What?" Almost a decade later, it seemed the Big Apple still had no answer, as a barge called the *Mobro 4000*—colloquially known as the Gar-barge—puttered up and down the Atlantic coast for months looking for a place to dump the city's trash. Conditions were much the same in other areas of the country, especially in suburbs where residents faced new landfill construction, often extension sites for larger metropolitan neighbors. For example, the quaint town of Geneva, Illinois, just forty miles west of Chicago, raised a fuss in 1979 when a waste management firm purchased 220 acres of land along the Fox River to create a landfill for Chicago garbage. The site was expected to serve the Windy City for decades, but just seven years after it opened, managers sadly predicted that the space would reach capacity in half the time originally predicted, a product of the ballooning waste stream coming from the Great Lake metropolis. In the American South, suburban and small-town residents endured similar experiences. There, a new environmental justice movement emerged in the 1980s, as citizens of color became increasingly aware of the connections between low-income residential neighborhoods and municipal dump sites. Thus, all across the country, the litter problem grew worse and worse, and legislators now had empirical evidence from Oregon's and Vermont's mandatory deposit programs that placing a price on bottles and cans might indeed be an effective tool for fighting waste.[66]

Concerned about the perceived litter crisis and following the lead of Oregon and Vermont, several states renewed campaigns to push through restrictive legislation designed to reduce one-way container waste in the late 1970s and early 1980s. Maine (1976), Michigan (1976), Connecticut (1978), Iowa (1978), New York (1982), Delaware (1982), Massachusetts (1983), and California (1986) all passed mandatory deposit laws that required nonreturnable cans and bottles to carry 5- to 10-cent deposits. Collection systems varied from state to state and would change over time; today, for example, California requires bottlers to pay deposits directly to the state upon sale of beverages to retailers. The government keeps all deposits that are not redeemed by consumers and uses that money to pay for recycling infrastructure. Other states, such as Oregon, Iowa, and Vermont, allow bottlers to keep unclaimed deposits paid to them by retailers (who in turn include deposit costs in prices to consumers). Despite variations in redemption systems, all deposit states make private corporations price their product to partially reflect the environmental costs of cleaning up packaging waste. Soft drink companies hate these programs, because even though they can pass on deposit costs to consumers, increased prices portend reduced sales.

State legislation may have frightened soft drink firms in the 1980s, but a far greater threat loomed in the US Congress: a national deposit bill. Just a year after Iowa became the fifth state to pass a mandatory deposit law in 1978, the US House of Representatives considered adopting a national bottle bill that would require all one-way containers in the United States to carry a cash deposit. The measure was ultimately defeated, in part due to the concentrated lobbying efforts of soft drink representatives like Edward Glaston, vice president and division manager of Pacific Coca-Cola Bottling Company (one of the largest Coke bottlers in the country), who testified before Congress that mandatory deposit legislation in Oregon had dramatically increased his company's operating costs and hurt business. Glaston noted that his fuel costs "more than doubled" because of deposit legislation that required the company to pick up its containers. Left unsaid was the fact that municipal agencies had been paying the fuel costs of picking up the company's waste. Ultimately, Glaston contended, consumers were hurt most, as they were forced to pay higher prices to pay for the new deposits.[67]

Major beverage companies did little to develop infrastructure that would make deposit systems work in bottle-bill states. Historian Finn Arne Jørgensen found that big bottlers "did their best to sabotage" New York's Returnable Container Law in 1982 requiring reverse-vending machine (RVM) producers to develop complicated container-scanning systems that ultimately made them too expensive for retail grocers. Jørgensen showed how Tomra, a Norwegian engineering firm, had tried to bring laser-scanning RVMs to New

York in the 1980s but was ultimately stymied by companies like Coca-Cola, which claimed that the machines would not be able to distinguish between containers of different brands, and would therefore make it impossible for Pepsi and Coke to decide the total amount each company owed in refunds. Ultimately, RVM machines never enjoyed the popularity they gained in other parts of the world, especially Scandinavia, where Tomra's systems became commonplace by the end of the 1980s. Absent the backing of the major beverage giants, high-tech, private sector reclamation vending systems lagged in New York and the rest of the country.[68]

PUBLICLY FUNDED CURBSIDE RECYCLING programs—or rather the promise of such programs—became the US industry's primary mechanism for combating legislation that would demand extended producer responsibility for packaging waste in the 1980s. Curbside reclamation programs became the alternative to mandatory deposits and returnable bans, a system pitched as a fix-all rather than as a complement to additional waste reduction initiatives. What might have made these programs so attractive to legislators was that their costs would not be visible to the voting public. Recycling programs would be paid for with general tax funds received at the state, local, and federal levels and with small user fees. As soft drink, brewing, and packaging lobbyists explained to lawmakers, recycling, unlike mandatory deposits, would not take jobs away from their district or increase taxes in ways that would draw the ire of the American consumer.[69]

The beverage industry positioned itself as the keystone of the recycling system. Through the end of the 1980s, soft drink, brewing, and beverage-packaging companies sought to convince citizens and lawmakers alike that container waste was the essential fuel driving nascent recycling programs. Industry spokesmen argued that because aluminum cans and glass containers "can represent an excess of 70 percent of the scrap value in the curbside bin," cutting out this source of revenue would destroy resource-reclamation programs across the country. In 1987, when a mandatory deposit initiative came up for city-wide vote in Washington, DC, Coca-Cola, PepsiCo, Anheuser-Busch, and Miller Brewing Company, among others, committed more than $1 million to an ad campaign promoting the idea that beverage cans were essential to recycling programs. The *Washington Post* reported the corporations' claim "that if consumers take their bottles and cans back to grocery stores to collect their deposits, those items will not go to independent recycling centers that need revenue from glass and aluminum to survive." NSDA vice president Gifford Stack summarized the industry's position on mandatory deposit legislation and the importance of keeping one-way containers in the municipal waste stream in 1989 by arguing, "If these packages were not included in curbside recycling programs the operational cost to the municipalities would, indeed, skyrocket." In a bizarre twist to the ever-evolving Citizen Coke mythology, Coca-Cola now claimed to be the thing that made the whole system work, rather than a beneficiary of public programs it in fact did little to finance.[70]

The soft drink industry had a particularly strong case to make when it came to its aluminum cans. In the 1980s, scrap aluminum was significantly more valuable than recycled glass or plastic. Beverage companies could reduce energy requirements by up to 95 percent using recycled aluminum rather than virgin materials from bauxite ore. Energy saving for glass were considerably more modest, approximately 25 percent, and the dismal recovery rate for plastics made recycling that synthetic material economically unattractive. Major corporations were eager to buy up stocks of recycled aluminum to reduce front-end costs, making that metal the clear cash cow of the recycling system. Coke and its industry allies preached that the diversion of aluminum cans from reclamation programs would spell doom for nascent recycling systems.[71]

The soft drink industry's appeal proved effective. Under the thumb of Big Soda, states shied away from deposit programs and committed themselves to the recycling revolution. After 1986, only one other state (Hawaii) passed a mandatory deposit law. Most municipalities committed substantial resources and political support to the development of what the industry called "comprehensive" recycling programs. In 1986, only Rhode Island had a mandatory statewide recycling law on the books, but just three years later, twenty-six states had passed laws requiring recycling as a component of solid-waste reduction, and seven states mandated the creation of statewide curbside programs. The number of curbside programs in the United States increased from just six hundred in 1989 to roughly four thousand in 1992. With the rise of curbside recycling, industries abandoned many of their own buy-back programs and began to rely largely on municipal services that required them to pay no extra fees.[72]

By the end of the 1990s, citizens accepted publicly funded recycling programs as the method for cleaning up industry container waste. Touted by industry as self-sustaining systems, however, curbside programs depended for years on subsidies. According to a study conducted in 1999, revenue generated from the sale of recyclable materials covered less than 35 percent of municipal expenses for recycling programs in the United States. The *New York Times* reported in 1993, "Five years after recycling took hold in this country, it has become clear that the market value of the materials left at the curbside is not likely to cover the collection and processing costs for a long time."[73]

No one really knows how much curbside recycling costs the public by 2014. The total bill was divided among millions of private citizens, most households paying small taxes or fees for service.

American citizens traditionally averse to corporate welfare were essentially bailing out industries that remained largely exempt from disposal fees, but they continued to do so in part because the decentralized funding structure for recycling kept the collective costs of the system hidden. Few stopped to question alternative financing mechanisms for the future. By the end of the 2010s, it had become clear that government-mandated source-reduction and corporate polluter-pays programs had been discredited as viable methods for reducing the nation's pollution problem.[74]

CURBSIDE RECYCLING HAS NOT been the panacea the beverage industry has claimed. In 2001, the recycling rate for aluminum cans was about 49 percent. That year, waste disposal agencies trucked 700,000 tons of aluminum cans to landfills all across the country. Conditions have not improved much over the last decade. The national recycling rate for aluminum cans hovered around 55 percent by the early 2010s, with consumers recycling only about 29 percent of PET plastic bottles. Over a hundred billion beverage containers never made it to recycling centers in 2012.[75]

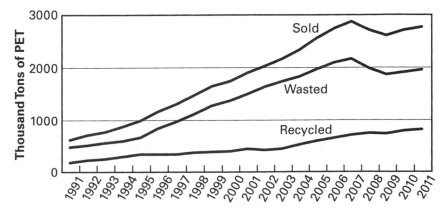

Figure 2: PET Bottle Sales and Recovery in the United States, 1991–2011
Source: Container Recycling Institute (CRI).

In short, the waste continued to pile up, and even though statistics revealed the shortcomings of waste-management practices, beverage giants continued to receive praise for their recycling efforts. Coca-Cola garnered special commendations for its commitment to packaging-reclamation programs. In 2009, the press lauded Coca-Cola for helping to finance the construction of the largest plastic-to-plastic recycling plant in the world in Spartanburg, South Carolina, despite the fact that the plant shut down just two years later because it could not generate enough revenue to cover costs. Others applauded Coke's 2007 partnership with Recyclebank, a national recycling program that offered consumers coupons in exchange for recyclable containers. In recent years, the company has distributed thousands of recycling bins featuring Coca-Cola's trademark throughout the country and has continued to produce promotional material about its "green" packaging. To the public, Coke has appeared to be the champion of sustainable business development.[76]

But despite the fanfare about corporate greening campaigns, today's curbside reclamation programs would not have been possible without public funding. Corporate recycling programs have been built on infrastructure that it took municipalities decades to construct. For years, recycling programs proved unprofitable, and private institutions failed time and time again to create comprehensive programs that would dramatically reduce litter. Expensive recycling programs survived as the preferred and exclusive solution for solid-waste disposal in this country only because private corporations used their lobbying might to shift responsibility for the collection and recycling of corporate waste onto the public sector. In the end, consumers did most of the work, subsidizing (both through their labor and through taxes) the beverage industry's packaging-reclamation system, allowing companies to expand their operations without incurring increased costs.

Coke's recycling bins scattered across the landscape may be

evidence of a new era of corporate interest in contributing to greening strategies, but past experience suggests that the company's commitments will remain a small component of a much larger effort financed by the public. Much more will need to be done. Subsidizing profligacy through public policies has not been the prescription for the country's trash problem. In the three decades since municipal recycling took hold, American companies have generated enormous quantities of packaging waste, over 150 billion pounds in 2012 alone, and they have been free to do so at virtually no cost. How long will the country continue its experiment before it asks big businesses to pay for the waste they generate?[77]

9

High-Fructose Corn Syrup

Storing Sweeteners in Stomach Silos

C oke's growth in the final decades of the twentieth century was literally littered with waste, yet much of this pollution, especially the aluminum and plastic, remained out of sight, tucked away in land-fills many citizens never saw. Packaging, however, was just one of the obfuscated problems of perpetual growth. Many other unpleasant by-products of Coca-Cola's conquest were hidden from view by 2000. Coke's bottlers, for example, relied on petroleum-guzzling trucks that emitted large quantities of greenhouse gases into the atmosphere. By 2006, over 200,000 Coke trucks puttered around the world, burning millions of gallons of fossil fuels to bring Coke to market. Likewise, for many years Coke's countless coolers and refrigerators pumped chlorofluorocarbons (CFCs) into the air, contributing to the depletion of the earth's ozone. All this was done to push a luxury item.[1]

But if many of Coke's pollutants remained out of sight, one unwanted by-product of growth became conspicuously abundant after 1985: human fat deposits. As Coke's consumers indulged in supersized soda binges, downing more and more sugary beverages each year, their bodies began to reflect the costs of excess. In response, a growing group of consumer health advocates began to attack Coke and other soft drink firms for making people fat. Their claim could not have been more damning. Coke itself was garbage, they complained, a "junk" food that was contributing to a growing obesity epidemic. Coke at one time might have been a simple treat, a "pause that refreshes," but by the 1990s it had become a staple of the average American's diet, consumed throughout the day, channeling more calories into people's bodies than they needed.

The statistics seemingly said it all. Annual per capita consumption of caloric soft drinks in the United States had more than tripled since 1955. A country that had once consumed 11 gallons per person annually in the 1950s now downed over 36 gallons fifty years later. That meant the average American in 2000 packed away over 35 pounds of sweetener a year, just from soft drinks. This was a problem.[2]

What had happened? How did this dramatic increase in soft drink consumption come about? How did Coke and other soft drinks become such significant contributors to citizens' corpulence?

THE STORY OF THE binge begins in the mid-1970s when sugar prices were once again fluctuating wildly. In December of 1974, Congress allowed the Sugar Act to expire, ending the almost three-decade-old quota system designed to protect US sugar growers and keep consumer prices steady by controlling how much sugar came into the United States each year. The Sugar Users Group, a new lobbying agency consisting of confectioners and other major sugar buyers including Coke, had campaigned for the quota collapse, mistakenly believing that the removal of federal protections would give Coke and other soft drink firms access to cheaper sugar. For years,

Coke had been prohibited from purchasing sugar from overseas at "dump" prices that were lower than the price of duty-paid sugar. Now Coke believed it was "in the driver's seat for the time-being" and looked forward to capitalizing on a deregulated market.[3]

The buyer's bonanza, however, fizzled. As protective barriers came down, prices skyrocketed, approaching 60 cents a pound by the end of 1974. With the growth of consumer markets in Asia and other parts of the developing world, sugar was in high demand, and producers all across the globe, flush with new buyers, continued to raise their prices. Overproduction, however, caused a dramatic drop in prices in 1975, threatening to bankrupt US growers, who claimed they could not sell at prices below the duty-free market price. In an attempt to provide protection to American sugar producers, the government moved to reinstate a quota system in 1976, causing industrial sugar users to protest. They wanted to return to a stable sugar market, but they did not want to pay higher prices to make such stabilization possible.[4]

Coke and its industry partners were tired of this roller coaster ride. They felt captive to the ebb and flow of global sugar market trends, and they had little faith that the volatility would ever subside. They wanted out. If there were any alternative to sugar that would free Coke from its dependence on this unpredictable trade market in the United States, the company was willing to try it.

Fortunately for Coke, there was a new sweetener on the horizon: high-fructose corn syrup. Since the 1920s, corn-refining industries in the American Midwest had experimented with processing cornstarch to produce a thick golden syrup with a molecular composition similar to sucrose, or table sugar. However, up through the mid-1960s, commercial users had largely been dissatisfied with the off-taste of these corn-based sweeteners. The sugar price scares of the 1970s, however, sparked new interest in investment, and refineries got to work to improve their processing systems. Leading the charge was the Clinton Corn Processing Company of Clinton, Iowa, which identified an artificial sweetener in 1967 that was as sweet as, if not more sweet than, sucrose and featured no unpleasant aftertaste. Clinton made the new syrup using a patented bacterial enzyme called an isomerase (first isolated in Japan) capable of transforming glucose molecules (extracted from cornstarch) into sweeter fructose molecules. The Clinton sweetener proved far superior to its predecessors in terms of taste, and in the 1970s, the company invested heavily to produce its corn syrup in mass.[5]

The name for the new syrup was a bit of an exaggeration. After all, high-fructose corn syrup 55, the main varietal of corn sweetener used in soft drinks, contained 55 percent fructose compared to about 45 percent glucose. Table sugar, on the other hand, is just a glucose molecule bound to a fructose molecule—50/50. The "high" label for high-fructose corn syrup, in other words, connoted a difference of only five percentage points between the new syrup and table sugar. In the case of high-fructose corn syrup 42, a sweetener used in some canned fruit products and ice creams, the labeling was even more misleading. This sweetener actually contained less fructose than regular sugar (roughly 42 percent).

Clinton's success was contingent upon federal aid. High-fructose corn syrup could only undersell sugar because corn was cheap, and corn was cheap because the government had made it so. During the Great Depression, the USDA began to enforce acreage-reduction loan programs for corn production through the Agricultural Adjustment Act, hoping to keep the excesses of American agribusiness locked up in silos and out of retail outlets. In short, the government was ostensibly paying farmers to produce less. The goal was to support commodity prices by limiting supply at a time when farmers were struggling to make enough money to feed their families. The American taxpayer financed the subsidy system, but not through visible sales tax. Rather, the USDA's Commodity Credit Corporation allocated tax revenue held by the US Treasury to pay for loans to farmers producing surplus corn during bumper crop years. The collateral corn was held in federal repositories, collectively referred to as the "ever-normal granary," until prices rose sufficiently so farmers could get a good market value and turn a profit.[6]

The USDA's intervention made sense during the hard times of the 1930s, but due to pressures from a consolidating agriculture sector that had grown accustomed to this cushion, the programs were extended after World War II. As with the protective policies that allowed domestic sugar growers to expand in the twentieth century, the corn support programs from the 1930s to the 1970s allowed large-scale American agribusinesses to increase their productive capacity without suffering serious financial losses. Big farmers sank government loan payments into new machines, hydrological systems, and nitrogen fertilizers that helped them intensify their land use. They benefited from technical training offered by the USDA's cooperative extension service, which taught farmers how to use high-yielding hybrid corn in the 1940s. These new varietals, created through crossbreeding techniques developed by government researchers in the early twentieth century, proved incredibly prolific in the crowded monocrop cultures of the American Midwest. As a result, between 1945 and 1971 corn production increased by 166 percent. The government's goal of actually curbing production through USDA programs had failed.[7]

This was more corn than Americans could possibly consume. Each year the government's stockpile of agricultural surplus grew, not just of corn but also of other commodities supported by similar New Deal loan programs. By 1952, the federal government held roughly $1.3 billion worth of agricultural surplus stocks in storage facilities across the country.[8]

In 1972, this excess would flood the US market. That year, the federal government dismantled its New Deal programs, recognizing that they were no longer fulfilling their original intentions. The nation was entering an energy crisis, and inflation coupled with a stagnant economy was driving the price of consumer goods ever higher. President Richard M. Nixon's agriculture secretary Earl Butz believed that the USDA was actually hurting the country through its outdated agricultural policies. The government was paying people not to produce at a time when food prices were skyrocketing. This seemed absurd. Butz thus proposed a comprehensive overhaul of agriculture policy, hoping to utilize the country's agricultural bounty to curb inflationary trends.

Urging American farmers to "get bigger or get out," Butz abandoned New Deal policies that coupled price support mechanisms with acreage reduction programs, implementing a new system under the Agriculture and Consumer Protection Act of 1973—thereafter called the Farm Bill—that favored production-stimulating bounty payments over loan programs designed to prevent farm product surpluses from flooding consumer markets. Now farmers received government payments with no strings attached. They could collect subsidies and push as much of their produce on the open market as they wanted.[9]

The consequences of Butz's policy were predictable. Because the new bounty program dismantled the ever-normal granary, the glut of agribusiness—a superfluity that for so many years had piled high within federally financed silos hidden in America's heartland—now came pouring into consumer markets all across the country, and prices correspondingly dropped, from over $3 a bushel at the end of 1974 to less than $2 a bushel just three years later. There would be price fluctuations in the coming years, but by the end of 1986, buyers could purchase a bushel of corn for about $1.50.[10]

All this cheap corn meant big business for America's corn refineries. Clinton Corn Processing Company, A. E. Staley, and Archer Daniels Midland, the three major corn refiners in the Midwest, were beside themselves with joy. Here was a golden opportunity to make lots of money; sugar prices were rising, and raw inputs for the corn refining business were in free fall. By 1978, they could offer high-fructose corn syrup at a price 10 to 15 percent lower than sugar produced from cane or beets. All they needed were buyers.[11]

AT FIRST, IT WAS not clear whether the big sugar users were going to commit to the revolution. As it did with every decision, Coke approached the prospect of switching suppliers with caution. This was a radically new product, a brown syrupy gel produced in a laboratory rather than a field. Would consumers buy this stuff? Coke was not sure, so in the summer of 1974, the company decided to try an experiment. That year, the company changed the formula for its noncola beverages (Sprite, Mr. Pibb, and Fanta) to include 25 percent high-fructose corn syrup. The plan was to test out the cheaper sweetener in its less-popular beverages before tampering with its flagship brand. Hearing no backlash from consumers, Coke gradually made the switch to 100 percent corn syrup in all of its noncola beverages in the late 1970s. This decision excited high-fructose corn syrup producers, such as Archer Daniels Midland and Clinton, who believed soft drink giants would soon commit to huge corn syrup contracts. A year later, Coke approved 50 percent corn syrup for its number-one-selling product, Coca-Cola, and by 1985, Coke made the switch to 100 percent corn syrup in all of its cola and noncola beverages sold within the United States.[12]

Coke's adaptability had once again produced dividends for the company. When high-fructose corn syrup came online, Coca-Cola did not have to sell sugar-processing plants because it did not own any. It simply switched to new suppliers. The federal government had changed the rules of the game in the sweetener production business, and Coke was ready to follow the winning team.

Coca-Cola's sweetener swap ensured the success of high-fructose corn syrup. Coke was by far the largest consumer of caloric sweeteners in the country, and, as such, its imprimatur mattered. Soon other confectionery businesses of all kinds followed Coke's lead, changing to 100 percent corn syrup by the mid-1980s. A new era of sweet excess had begun.

High-fructose corn syrup helped Coke exponentially increase its syrup sales. Rather than decrease prices for their product to reflect multimillion-dollar savings in production costs (said to be some $20 million for every cent decrease in the cost of sweeteners in 1978), Coke looked to sell greater quantities of its beverages to their consumers at marginally higher prices. In *The Omnivore's Dilemma*, journalist Michael Pollan explained Coke's mindset in the 1980s: "Since a soft drink's main raw material—corn sweetener—was now so cheap, why not get people to pay just a few pennies more for a substantially bigger bottle? Drop the price per ounce, but sell a lot more ounces. So began the transformation of the svelte eight-ounce Coke bottle into the chubby twenty-ouncer."[13]

McDonald's, Coke's largest customer in the 1990s with over 14,000 restaurants worldwide in 1993 (3,654 overseas), was the real mastermind of this supersized sales strategy. In 1993, a McDonald's retail strategist named David Wallerstein first introduced the concept of supersizing. The system was exploitative, but few consumers understood the math. Coke found that people would pay a few dimes more for a supersized product, even if that larger serving contained just 2 or 3 cents' worth of additional sweetener. Because high-fructose corn syrup was so cheap, it paid to go big. As a result, soft drink companies and retail distributors created new beverage packaging, first shooting for 20-ounce containers and later encouraging consumer purchases of 64-ounce soda buckets by the mid-1990s. The result was a dramatic increase in per capita caloric soft drink consumption, which rose from 28.7 gallons in 1985 to 36.8 gallons in 1998.[14]

The problem with the high-fructose sugar gorge was that Amer-

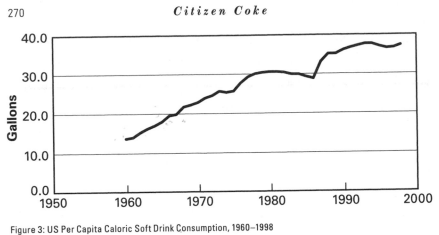

Figure 3: US Per Capita Caloric Soft Drink Consumption, 1960–1998
*Source: USDA Economic Research Service, Carbonated Beverages
Per Capita Availability Spreadsheet (2003).*

icans were not suffering from caloric deficits. They were consuming large amounts of calories their bodies did not need. In 1950, per capita consumption of caloric sweeteners had topped out at over 100 pounds per person (almost twice the per capita sugar intake of 49.2 pounds in 1885), but by the end of the 1980s, annual per capita consumption had risen to over 125 pounds. The upward trend continued into the 1990s, and by 2000, average annual per capita consumption of caloric sweeteners in the United States reached 152.4 pounds. Thus, citizens who had once thrived on less than 50 pounds of caloric sweeteners annually were by the twenty-first century consuming over three times that much each year. The country's subsidized superfarms were not recharging citizens' underfilled caloric reservoirs; they were fueling an unhealthy trend toward overconsumption of carbohydrate-rich sweeteners.[15]

Society had changed. No longer were Americans working long hours in the field as they had in the nineteenth century. By the 1990s, the country was more urbanized than it had ever been before. When Pemberton first created Coke in 1886, less than 30 percent of the population lived in cities, but that figure had risen to 54.1 percent by 1920 and 75.2 percent by 1990. In part, this was the result of government agricultural policies that benefited large agribusinesses over small farms. No piece of legislation was more instrumental in bringing about this change than the Agricultural Adjustment Act (AAA), passed in 1933, which channeled capital to rich farmers owning large plantations in the rural South and Midwest. Tenants leasing lands from these owners never saw AAA money. Elite planters were able to hoard government funds, thereby accumulating substantial federal dollars that enabled them to mechanize their operations, reducing their demand for agricultural labor. Thus, policies designed to help farmers perversely depopulated rural America and ushered in a new era of big agribusiness growth. A nation of farmers had become a nation of city workers.[16]

In the city, Americans found new opportunities for employment in the late twentieth century. By the 1990s, the typical nonfarm laborer in America worked in an office, not a factory. In 1994, 80 percent of all city workers in America were employed in a service sector industry. These jobs were typically less labor-intensive than factory jobs, meaning laborers expended fewer calories in the average workday. And Americans were not burning these extra calories outside the workplace. Only a minority of the population walked to work, many making long commutes from suburban homes to inner-city offices. Between 1960 and 2000, the number of people traveling by personal auto to work nearly tripled (from 40 million to roughly 110 million), with the average round-trip travel time approaching fifty minutes by the twenty-first century. After a long afternoon on the road, few Americans engaged in extracurricular activity once they were off the clock. A study conducted by the CDC in 1991 showed that roughly 60 percent of Americans said they engaged in virtually no physical leisure activity after work. Less than 20 percent of the population reported that they exercised on a daily basis in 2003. Life in the United States had become sedentary.[17]

At the same time as Americans' caloric demands declined, their access to cheap calories increased. Commodity support programs kept food prices down precisely at the same time that Americans' incomes were on the rise. The result was that consumers could spend a smaller portion of their salaries to buy the basic food staples they needed. In the 1930s, the average American spent almost 25 percent of disposable income on food purchases, but by 2000, this figure dropped to roughly 10 percent. Americans were not suffering from want. They had all the food they could possibly desire. In this world of abundance, Coke was a particularly potent source of excess calories few Americans needed.[18]

Despite meeting and then exceeding the country's food needs, the profligate agricultural machine grew larger and larger. What made this gluttonous growth acceptable to consumers initially was the fact that its material costs were kept out of sight. Describing the continued political success of Butz's agricultural support program in the 1990s, food journalist Betty Fussell contended that "Americans don't believe in what they can't see, and the superstructure of American agribusiness that controls the production of corn is as invisible and pervasive as the industrial products of corn." The government payments that stimulated corn overproduction, totaling billions of dollars by the late 1980s ($5.7 billion in 1983 alone), came from general tax funds, not itemized sales tax, thus limiting consumers' exposure to the cost of agricultural subsidies.[19]

Over time, however, consumers' waistlines exposed the expensive storage costs that allowed the oversupplied corn market to function. Far from receiving nutritional benefits from the supersize revolution, consumers functioned as the new repositories of agricultural surplus. Consumers' bodies became jam-packed silos, replacements for the federal repositories that had once helped stimulate scarcity by keeping excess corn off retail shelves. Consuming ever-greater quantities of calories each year, Americans became bigger and bigger. According to National Health and Nutrition Examination surveys

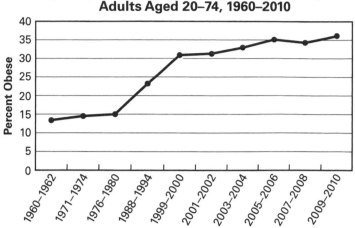

Figure 4: Age-Adjusted Prevalence of Obesity Among US Adults Aged 20–74, 1960–2010
Sources: Centers for Disease Control's National Health Examination Survey and National Health and Nutrition Examination Survey.

conducted by the CDC, only 14.1 percent of Americans were considered obese (defined as a body mass index [BMI] equal to or greater than 25.0) between 1971 and 1974 compared to 22.4 percent by the early 1990s. In 2008, over 34 percent of the US population had a BMI over 25. Consumers were taking in more carbohydrates than their bodies needed, and as a result, most Americans were turning excess sugars into fat.[20]

Americans did not bear the burden of obesity equally. Minority communities, for example, consistently reported higher incidence of obesity. In 2010, the CDC found that roughly half (49.5 percent) of all adult non-Hispanic African Americans were obese, compared to 34.3 percent of non-Hispanic whites. The obesity rate for Mexican Americans was also high, rising above 40 percent that year. While researchers continue to debate the reasons for such stark disparities, the link between race and poverty appears to be at the heart of the divide. Scientists showed that many low-income minority groups lived in "obesogenic environments," where fresh, local food was hard to find. Furthermore, many people in these communities did not earn a living wage, so that even if they did have a farmers' market in their community, they simply could not afford to sacrifice the money and time to purchase produce priced well above cheap and ready-made fast food options. In short, for impoverished minorities craving cheap calories, a McDonald's hamburger washed down with a Coke seemed like a low-cost way to satiate a hungry stomach.[21]

The only problem was that such satiation was illusory. Heavy sugar consumption resulted in a short-term buzz, as glucose and fructose molecules in the bloodstream caused the brain to release the pleasure-inducing chemical dopamine. But the chemical surge soon wore off, leaving the consumer with a strong urge to down more sugar. It was a vicious cycle, a tragic addiction. The result was bigger, not satiated, stomachs.

The consequence of sweetener binging was more than cosmetic. Distended stomachs were symptomatic of other health problems associated with excessive caloric intake. Diabetes was perhaps the most serious side effect of excessive sweetener consumption. Between 1980 and 2000, the prevalence of diabetes for citizens aged 0 to 44 doubled, rising from .6 percent of the population to 1.2 percent (over 2 million people). Again, low-income, minority communities were disproportionately affected by the disease. The CDC also registered increases in diagnoses for citizens aged 65 to 74, reporting a rise in rates from 9.1 percent to 15.4 percent over the same period. By 1996, adult-onset diabetes, a condition believed by most physicians to be linked to overconsumption of sugar and caloric sweeteners, had been renamed type 2 diabetes because so many children were exhibiting symptoms of the disease. In the early years of the twenty-first century, then, it appeared diabetes, a condition once affecting a small fraction of the population, was quickly becoming an American epidemic.[22]

America's fat problem had financial repercussions. By 2005, estimated medical costs of treating ailments associated with obesity had risen dramatically from an estimated $78.5 billion in 1998 to over $147 billion in 2008. Obesity presented consumers with immediate fiscal (in the form of medical payments) and physical (in the form of health problems) costs that forced them to scrutinize an agro-industrial complex that for decades had enriched Coke and other big food and beverage firms.[23]

COKE COULD HARDLY CLAIM it was an insignificant contributor to the crisis. Gallon sales of soft drinks had exploded during the 1980s and 1990s, and longtime Coke customers were consuming greater quantities of carbonated beverages than they ever had in history. The USDA reported that the quantity of caloric soft drinks consumed by the average adult between 1972 and 1998 increased by 53 percent. This rise in per capita consumption helped to make soft drinks containing caloric sweeteners the "largest single food source of calories in the US diet" in 2004, according to the *Journal of the American Medical Association*. Coke was a major source of the country's obesity problem.[24]

The company knew it was a prime target for food health advocates even before it switched to high-fructose corn syrup. As early as 1962, a company-commissioned study had revealed that over 28 percent of US consumers worried about how food and beverage intake affected their weight. With these results in hand, Coke decided to market new noncaloric beverages that would leave no trace on the human body once consumed. It introduced its first diet beverage, Tab, in 1963, which contained a mixture of saccharin, a coal-tar derivative discovered in 1877, and cyclamate, a synthetic compound supposedly discovered by accident in 1937 by a scientist researching anti-inflammatory medication. Within months, Tab sales produced profits for the company, and in 1966 hoping to make further inroads into the diet cola market, Coke introduced its second low-calorie beverage, Fresca. By this point, Pepsi and RC Cola had successfully launched their own noncaloric competitors, Patio and Diet Rite, respectively.[25]

Despite early success, soft drink industry giants became concerned about the future of calorie-free beverage sales when the Food and Drug Administration exposed the hidden carcinogenic risks associated with large-scale cyclamate consumption in the late 1960s. Enforcing the Delaney Clause of the Food, Drug, and Cosmetic Act, an amendment to the 1938 legislation passed in 1958 that prevented the introduction of known carcinogens into the food supply, the FDA in 1969 banned cyclamate use within the United States. The agency cited scientific studies that linked heavy consumption of cyclamate-rich solution to increased incidence of bladder cancer in laboratory rats. Almost overnight, Coke, Pepsi, and RC Cola's diet drinks came off retail shelves.[26]

In the wake of the 1969 cyclamate ban, the Coca-Cola Company asked the federal government to reverse its decision, citing the lack of sufficient evidence to prove that cyclamates caused cancer. The same year studies revealed that rats developed bladder tumors after consuming large amounts of cyclamates, company president Paul Austin claimed that the government's findings were inconclusive, saying, "We are aware, of course, of the current attention being directed to cyclamates, but to date we have seen no confirmed evidence that the substance is unsafe, particularly at present levels."[27]

Coke took its case to the public, and its argument was direct: the government should not be in the business of deciding what consumers should and should not consume. To amplify its message, in 1966, the company partnered with other artificial sweetener businesses to create the euphemistically named Calorie Control Council (CCC), another astroturf organization. Its goal was to inspire people to fight government bans on artificial sweeteners on the grounds that such interventions violated their rights as citizens. The CCC told the public that what was at stake was more than just the health of the nation.

By opposing the ban, citizens were protecting liberty itself, the freedom for consumers to choose in a free and unrestricted market.[28]

This was a familiar storyline. Coke, through Keep America Beautiful, had used the same rhetoric in its anti-litter campaigns of the early 1960s. The lesson learned in the early environmental campaigns was that consumers responded to perceived threats to their constitutional rights. This was the height of the Cold War, and the belief that a powerful, controlling state might seek to take over America was real. Tapping into this fear was the key to gaining public support for corporate causes.

But appealing as this rhetoric might have been, in 1977, the CCC had its work cut out for it. That winter, the FDA had initiated a new directive to prohibit the use of saccharin in carbonated beverages, citing recent studies that raised concerns about the potentially carcinogenic effects of the product. To counteract the FDA's efforts, the Calorie Control Council channeled $500,000 to the Coca-Cola Company's ad agency, McCann-Erickson, for the purposes of creating and distributing pro-saccharin ads in over thirty newspapers countrywide. Explaining the objective of the ad campaign, one CCC member told the press that blocking an FDA ban was "just a matter of getting consumers—diabetics and diet-conscious—to complain to Washington." CCC newspaper pieces encouraged consumers to write their congressmen expressing support for a "postponement of a ban so an independent and thorough scientific review can be made to evaluate the total evidence on saccharin." In addition to these print ads, CCC also ran a series of radio commercials that stressed how the ban would limit the common citizen's freedoms.[29]

The CCC's lobbying efforts paid off, and thousands of consumers wrote to their congressmen (often forwarding copied CCC ads) to express their disapproval for the FDA restrictions on saccharin use. Congress responded to the public uprising and granted a moratorium on the proposed saccharin ban, which allowed soft drink manufacturers to continue use of saccharin until May of 1979. Ultimately the moratorium was renewed, and by the late 1980s, saccharin had become an FDA-approved artificial sweetener.[30]

At that point, however, saccharin had begun to lose market share to a new artificial sweetener produced by the Searle Company called aspartame. Searle's synthetic additive, discovered in 1965, offered many benefits. It was some two hundred times sweeter than sugar and produced no bitter aftertaste (a problem saccharin producers never fully resolved with their product). More importantly, the FDA found no evidence that aspartame was carcinogenic. With FDA approval in 1983, the Coca-Cola Company began using the new product, adding aspartame to Diet Coke, its newest noncaloric beverage brand. But because saccharin was still significantly cheaper than Searle's new product, Coke continued to use saccharin in combination with aspartame in its diet drinks to keep production costs down. Thus, a food supplement that some scientists claimed might contribute to significant health problems remained in millions of beverages sold throughout the country. By the early 2000s, saccharin was removed from bottled and canned Diet Coke but could still be found in postmix syrup offered at retail fountains (in part, this was because saccharin helped preserve postmix syrup over longer periods of time).[31]

Consumers supporting the CCC were convinced that noncaloric sweeteners helped them lose weight, but by the 1990s, statistical evidence revealed that the promised benefits associated with diet drink consumption were less than weight-conscious consumers had hoped. Even as per capita consumption of noncaloric sweeteners rose 150 percent between 1975 and 1984, per capita consumption of sugar increased from 118.1 pounds to 126.8 pounds over the same period. After the introduction of aspartame, the trend continued, and per capita consumption of all caloric sweeteners increased by over 20 percent between the end of the 1980s and 2000. As artificial sweetener historian Carolyn de la Peña explained, the historical record makes clear that diet drinks and reduced-calorie foods have been used to "sell products[,] not create thin people." Consumers continued to gulp down larger and larger quantities of high-fructose corn syrup and sugar. Noncaloric sweeteners did not fix the country's obesity problem; they merely helped to temporarily assuage overweight consumers' guilt.[32]

Scientific research from 2008 and 2009 suggested a possible explanation for why diet drinks failed to help people slim down. One study conducted at Purdue University revealed that rats fed noncaloric sweeteners showed increased appetite and on average consumed more food than control subjects. Researchers concluded that artificial sweetener consumption "may lead to increased body weight and obesity by interfering with fundamental homeostatic, physiological processes." Perhaps the most surprising finding was that rats fed artificial sweeteners gained more weight than rats in the control group even when the test subjects consumed fewer calories than the control subjects. Physician Mark Hyman explained the potential implications of this finding: "[An artificial sweetener] tricks your metabolism into thinking sugar is on its way. This causes your body to pump out insulin, the fat storage hormone, which lays down more belly fat. It also confuses and slows your metabolism down, so you burn fewer calories every day."[33]

Whatever the case may be, one thing was clear: Diet Coke did not reduce demand for caloric soft drinks. Coca-Cola Classic remained Coke's number-one-selling product even in the era of diet drinks. Per capita consumption continued to climb in the 1980s and 1990s, and as it did, the obesity epidemic in the country worsened.[34]

WITH PRIVATE SECTOR SOLUTIONS failing to solve the country's weight problem, local governments decided it was time to deploy a new weapon: obesity taxes. In the late 1980s, Dr. Kelly Brownell, the director of the Yale Center for Eating and Weight Disorders, started promoting the idea of placing surcharges on junk food in the United States as a way to curb obesity. In many ways, this attack plan was not new. Vice taxes on other products, such as alcohol and tobacco, had become popular by the 1980s. But what made soft drinks different from, say, tobacco, a product the US surgeon general had declared a known carcinogen in 1964, was the fact that most Americans still did not think of Coke as a vice. After all, it was something parents fed to their children in copious quantities, still something many people associated with happiness and Santa Claus. How could something found in a kid's McDonald's Happy Meal be all that bad?

So one of the key tasks before health advocates in the 1990s was to change this image of soft drinks. Scientists engaged in a very public debate, showing how new science linked soft drink consumption with malady. Brownell, for example, publicly championed research that showed many people were genetically predisposed to overindulge on sugar-rich foodstuffs if given the opportunity. He published his findings in articles in the *New York Times*, emphasizing that many consumers, especially children, were not really "free" to make wise dietary choices. He called for additional federal regulation limiting junk food advertisements that targeted schoolchildren and urged the government to require the removal of snack food and soft drink vending machines from public school cafeterias and concessions.[35]

City and state officials listened to Brownell's appeal—in part because they were broke. Local governments faced mounting budget deficits in the late 1980s and early 1990s as the economy slipped into recession, making an excise tax on nonessential foodstuffs seem like a two-birds-with-one-stone proposition. Besides generating immediate revenue, fat taxes had the potential to help people slim down, which meant huge savings to public health programs tasked with treating the slew of maladies attendant to obesity. As a result, Arkansas

(1992), California (1991), Maine (1991), Maryland (1992), New York (1990), Ohio (1993), and Washington (1989) all passed some form of statewide tax hikes targeting sodas and sugary foods. Cities including Baltimore City, Maryland (1989), Chicago (1993), and Washington, DC (1993), also joined the fight. What Brownell later dubbed the "battle of the bulge" was under way.[36]

The biochemical had become political. Transformations in the molecular world of the human body inspired a health food movement that challenged a federal-corporate system costing millions of Americans billions of dollars. For years, Americans had ignored the front-end costs associated with generating a glut of corn—and thereby of sweetener. Now, they were spurred to action by the waste generated at the end of the agricultural commodity chain—excess in their bodies.

Naturally, the corporate backlash was swift and fierce. In Arkansas, Coca-Cola threatened to pull out on a bottling plant investment if the government did not repeal that state's 1992 tax. The National Soft Drink Association funded advertising campaigns in Ohio, billing the new tax hikes as symptomatic of "the ever-encroaching greed of the states." In Chicago, the soft drink industry threatened not to hold its annual InterBev conference in the city if soda imposts remained; soda spokesmen projected this would deal a $35 million blow to the municipality. Pepsi tried similar tactics in Maryland, saying it would not expand its distribution and manufacturing facilities in the state unless repeal took place. Of course, the soft drink industry did not win every battle—Arkansas and Chicago, for example, kept their soda taxes—but money talked in many places around the country. California (1992), Maine (2000), Maryland (1997), New York (1998), Ohio (1994), and Washington (1994) all repealed their taxes just a few short years after enactment.[37]

Despite such reversals, the clamor for new obesity taxes continued to mount as the 1990s came to a close. Consumer advocate Michael F. Jacobson, for example, published a report at the Center for

Science in the Public Interest entitled *Liquid Candy: How Soft Drinks Are Harming Americans' Health* (1998), promoting the imposition of federal vice taxes on carbonated beverages. The pamphlet made national news, drawing the attention of the NSDA, which challenged Jacobson's claims and argued that soft drink taxes were discriminatory because they targeted one industry rather than dealing with the full range of factors contributing to obesity in America. But even as the NSDA worked to build momentum for an anti-tax movement, new medical studies continued to erode the lobbying group's propaganda platform. These scientific reports showed that soft drinks were in fact a major contributor to America's obesity epidemic, especially among children. Dr. David Ludwig of the Boston Children's Hospital, for example, produced a report in 2001 revealing that schoolchildren who drank at least one soft drink per day increased their risk of becoming obese by 60 percent just by adding one more serving to their daily diet. Other reports provided evidence that the human body only partially registered calories consumed in liquid form, a phenomenon, some researchers postulated, that explained why heavy soft drink consumers overindulged on calorie-dense foods.[38]

The idea that soft drinks might be poisoning America's youth struck a particularly strong chord with parents across the nation, and momentum began to build for legislation that would ban the sale of soft drinks on school campuses. Armed with disturbing new evidence from the CDC that more than 15 percent of America's youth were overweight, in 2002, the Los Angeles City Council banned soft drink sales in school cafeterias and on-campus vending machines. Simultaneously, a movement emerged in Northern California, where State Senator Deborah Ortiz proposed the first statewide ban on all soft drink sales in schools, and by the end of the year over fourteen states had proposed similar bans. Ortiz's bill, though severely amended and only applying to grades K–8, passed in 2003. Talk had turned into action.[39]

THESE ATTACKS CAME AT a particularly hard time for Coke. In 1998, just months after the death of Coca-Cola chairman and CEO Roberto Goizueta, the company began to experience serious financial hardships. Douglas Ivester, Goizueta's successor, watched as sales growth halted, driving down the company's share price dramatically. The problem, according to Coke's CFO, was that the company was "bloated with overhead." Unlike the sleek Coke of years before, the company now had money invested in bottling operations, which required Coke to take on substantial debts. This hurt the company's bottom line.[40]

Coca-Cola Enterprises, the company's partially owned megabottler that had begun buying up small bottling franchises twelve years earlier, was one of the company's biggest headaches. The chief problem was that CCE was unable to sell all of the syrup that the parent company distributed to it. As *New York Times* reporter Constance Hays pointed out, the Coca-Cola Company often bailed out its megabottler, offering it just enough "marketing" support at the end of the fiscal year to cover losses associated with the expensive business of distribution. "The whole system," Hays explained, "leaned heavily on the Coca-Cola Company," and CCE remained forever dependent on end-of-year payments from the parent company to keep from going into the red. CCE shareholders remained committed to the enterprise because they were unaware of the losses. Parent company expenditures designed to prop up CCE were "buried" in the end-of-year reports. But the truth was, bigger was not better for Coke. It had violated one of its most time-honored business practices of outsourcing productive operations, and now it had to pay the price.[41]

To right the ship in 1998, chairman Ivester had tried to trim the fat, starting with the parent company's payroll, but after laying off over 5,000 employees, things only got worse. "We lost morale," Coke's CFO explained. "That is where we really started losing our way." Many of the employees Ivester fired were executives that "had special skills and deep business knowledge." Coke was crumbling from within. "These were dark days at Coca-Cola," recalled former executive Neville Isdell in his memoir. No one's job was secure, even Ivester's. In 1999, directors Warren Buffett and Herbert Allen forced Ivester to resign, replacing him with the senior vice president for operations in Asia, Douglas Daft. Everyone was shocked, including Daft, who seemed, according to journalist Constance Hays, "thunderstruck, awed, discombobulated by his fate." After all, he had been passed over for the chairmanship by Goizueta and had essentially resigned himself to being a vice president. In the years ahead, he would have few answers to the problems the company faced, further shaking people's confidence in the Coke system. In this unsettled climate, obesity weighed heavily on Coke.[42]

The most pressing concern was school bans. In the 1990s, the company and other major soft drink firms had begun to sign contracts with school districts in which they offered education grants in exchange for exclusive access to vending outlets on campus. This strategy for growth was new and had opened up a huge market that had once been closed to soft drink firms. Before 1983, the USDA had restricted the sale of soft drinks and junk foods in schools on the grounds that these products were contributing to health problems in young children, but that year, a federal court declared the USDA's meddling in school district affairs unconstitutional. Coke and other major soft drink companies entered the breach, and schools welcomed them with open arms because they needed the money. In the 1990s, many schools faced tough financial times, especially in the inner city where tax bases had been eroded in the wake of white flight to the suburbs. Coke contracts offered principals in underfunded districts a way to cover costs and even develop new programs. As a result, by 2002, over 240 school districts had signed contracts with major soft drink companies.[43]

Coke made millions on school sales, and it was not going to give up its newfound markets without a fight. In the early 2000s, soft drink and fast food businesses came together and launched a series of healthy-living campaigns targeting America's youth. Through programs such as "Step To It!" and "Balance First," the food and beverage industry offered after-school exercise and dieting courses designed to encourage young people to develop healthy living habits. Program leaders preached a message of empowerment, one that resonated with a country that believed strongly in the principles of individual freedom and personal responsibility. Students did not need the government to tell them how to lose weight. They could do it themselves, through sweat and hard work.[44]

This message of self-reliance was one Citizen Coke preached to adults as well as children as it sought to fend off a new slew of obesity tax proposals sweeping the nation at the beginning of the new millennium. In 2003, New York state legislator Felix Ortiz proposed a tax on all junk foods sold in the state, a measure that he believed would raise $50 million annually to help combat obesity. That same year, the World Health Organization endorsed obesity imposts as a viable strategy for curbing obesity around the globe.[45]

To combat these claims, Coke developed an anti-tax lobbying campaign with the help of a DC-based astroturf organization, the Center for Consumer Freedom. In this partnership, Coke had made a nasty bedfellow. The tobacco industry had launched Consumer Freedom in 1996 hoping to undermine bans on smoking in public places despite strong scientific evidence that exposure to secondhand smoke increased cancer risks. Though Consumer Freedom had lost the battle, it remained a powerful force for free-market proselytizing in the 2000s. Now under the direction of Rich Berman, an accomplished lawyer and political insider, the organization reinvented itself as a champion of "food liberty." As the CCC had done in its battle against the saccharin ban, Consumer Freedom pitched itself through national ads as a defender of America's first principles. Berman urged consumers to fight the government's "food police," to stand up for their right to choose the types of foods and beverages they would consume. Government should not have the power to decide what people should eat or drink.[46]

There were those who sought to expose the historical inaccuracy of Consumer Freedom's free-market fairy tale. Chief among these crusaders were best-selling journalists Eric Schlosser and Michael Pollan, who published widely popular books—*Fast Food Nation* (2001) and *The Omnivore's Dilemma* (2006), respectively—challenging the notion that our modern industrial food system was the product of free choice. They showed that government had always played a role in shaping the food options that were available to Americans, namely through subsidies that encouraged surplus production of high-fructose corn syrup. Since government had helped build this profligate system, they argued, it seemed reasonable to suggest that government should be called upon to right the wrongs it had helped to create.[47]

But despite Pollan's appeal to focus on what he called the "cause behind the causes," that is, the subsidies that made junk foods cheap, few people launched an assault on the corn bounty programs that created all the excess calories in the first place. The perennial Farm Bill passed in 2002 and again in 2008 with little resistance from legislators. Many people, as Michael Pollan put it, assumed that "true to its name, the farm bill is about farming, an increasingly quaint activity that involves no one we know and in which few of us think we have a stake." Fighting the Farm Bill simply was not a sexy battle.[48]

Fighting soda in schools, however, was a popular crusade, one Coke could not shake, and in 2006, the company decided to silence its critics once and for all. Neville Isdell, the social worker turned corporate executive, was now chairman of the company, having replaced Douglas Daft in 2004 after four failed years of stagnant sales, and Isdell set about making major changes at Coke. He initiated a comprehensive corporate responsibility program at Coke, dubbed the Manifesto of Growth, in an attempt to reinvigorate company morale.

A central tenet of Isdell's plan was to redefine "the company as something much more than an emotionless, profit-producing machine," to transform it into a "responsible citizen that makes a difference by helping build and support sustainable communities." When it came to curbing obesity, Isdell explained, Coke could be a part of the solution. Partnering with the William J. Clinton Foundation, the American Heart Association, Pepsi, and Cadbury Schweppes, Coke created the Alliance for a Healthier Generation and pledged to eliminate "full-calorie beverages in U.S. public schools." It seemed Coke was finally owning up to the fact that it played a major role in making kids fat.[49]

Coke's critics, however, were not satisfied. The same year soft drink companies initiated self-imposed school bans, legislators in six different states drafted obesity tax legislation that targeted soft drinks. Five years later, over fourteen states considered similar measures. Coke's highly visible public campaign to eliminate soft drinks from schools had not stemmed the health food revolt.[50]

Perhaps no one was a more committed advocate of using government regulatory powers to curb soda consumption than Mayor Michael Bloomberg of New York City, who approved a 2012 mandate to prohibit the sale of soft drinks in containers larger than 16 ounces. Bloomberg believed that the ban would force consumers to be more contemplative about their dietary choices. "We're not taking away anybody's right to do things," Bloomberg explained in an MSNBC interview. "We're simply forcing you to understand that you have to make the conscious decision to go from one cup to another."[51]

Bloomberg's ban met a predictable fate in the arena of public opinion. Few people liked such a heavy-handed use of government power, even those on the political left who were otherwise adamant public health advocates. Popular liberal media icon and comedian Jon Stewart, for example, lambasted the New York beverage container ban on Comedy Central's *The Daily Show* the day after it was passed, saying sarcastically, "I love this idea. . . . It combines the draconian government overreach people love with the probable lack of results they expect." The public agreed. Only 36 percent of New Yorkers polled supported Bloomberg's decision, and those opposed had more than a mouthful for the mayor. Jeering protesters swarmed city hall in July, lofting signs scribbled with pithy jabs, such as "Nanny Bloomberg—Stay out of <u>our</u> kitchens" and "Hands off my bladder."[52]

Industry fed the fire. New Yorkers for Beverage Choices, yet another astroturf organization sponsored by the soft drink industry, handed out T-shirts to city residents proclaiming "I picked out my beverages all by myself." Consumer Freedom ran full-page ads in city papers with provocative headlines like "New Yorkers need a Mayor, not a Nanny" and "You only thought you lived in the land of the free." They refocused the debate toward issues of individual liberty rather than important questions about how to solve the nation's obesity problems.[53]

In October 2012, the beverage companies took their fight from the streets to the courts, filing a petition to enjoin the city from imposing the beverage ban, and they brought with them a secret weapon: the support of the city's labor and minority coalitions. Named alongside the American Beverage Association in the October petition were a host of unlikely allies, including the New York Statewide Coalition of Hispanic Chambers of Commerce, the New York Korean-American Grocers Association, and the Soft Drink and Brewery Workers Union, Local 812, International Brotherhood of Teamsters, all of which opposed Bloomberg's ban on grounds that decreased soft drink sales would adversely affect low-income grocers and laborers in the soft drink industry. The state chapter of the National Association for the Advancement of Colored People (NAACP) and the Hispanic Federation concurred with the petitioners, filing an amicus curie brief supporting removal of Bloomberg's ban.[54]

It may seem odd that the NAACP and labor groups supported

the soda ban removal. After all, these organizations represented communities that bore the greatest financial and physical burdens for the nation's growing obesity epidemic. Why would these advocacy coalitions fight something designed to improve the health of their constituencies?

Some suspected that the answer had to do with the way these organizations were funded. The NAACP, for example, received thousands of dollars from Coca-Cola to launch its Healthy Eating, Lifestyles, and Physical Activity (HELP) program. Other minority organizations enjoyed similar partnerships with Coke. Thus, supporting the beverage ban could easily be construed as payback for services rendered.[55]

But even if there was some backscratching going on, there was a more fundamental and sinister economic reality at play: a soda ban was indeed bad for small business. Low-income grocers made substantial revenue from sugar-rich foods precisely because when consumed, these cheap products stimulated psychological reinforcement mechanisms that encouraged habitual consumption. Put simply, Coke fanatics—known as "heavy users" in the industry—were cash cows for small vendors. New York City movie theaters made more than two-fifths of their profits from soft drink sales in 2012, and other small businesses showed similarly impressive returns. 7-Eleven chains, for example, generated an estimated 10 percent of net income from soda sales. Ironically, Bloomberg's ban exempted these national chains from regulation because they fell under state, not municipal, jurisdiction as supermarkets. In the end, those most affected by the ban were small bodegas and restaurants, not large grocery stores—people whose success or failure hung on the thinnest of margins.[56]

Here was the sad truth. Poor communities had developed a double addiction. One was economic, the other biological. To eliminate supersized sodas from local outlets would be to deal a serious financial blow to those least able to afford it. Yes, this message came right from Coke's propaganda machines, but it was, at base, true. Hundreds of small entreprenuers had a stake in seeing Coke's empire expand. They depended on profits from selling Coke to remain afloat. The flow of dollars, not just dopamine, stimulated cravings for Coke.

THIS WAS THE GENIUS of Coca-Cola capitalism. It created local stakeholders in towns across America that could be called upon to use their political and social capital to fight government regulations that would curb soda sales. Coke had become a fixture of local economies, a product that had shaken its nonessential food status and become a vital component of small retailers' revenue streams. Applying lessons learned from the battle against anti-litter environmentalists in the 1970s, Coke knew that success lay in putting a local face on its corporate cause by mobilizing small businesses in its diffuse political action network.

And the strategy proved effective. In March 2013, the peculiar alliance of labor and industry got what it wanted. New York State Supreme Court Justice Milton Tingling held that Bloomberg had overstepped his authority in bypassing the city council to impose the soft drink ban. To allow the restriction on soda containers to stand, Tingling wrote, "would not only violate the separation of powers, it would eviscerate it. Such an evisceration," he concluded, "has the potential to be more troubling than sugar sweetened beverages." For the time being, the ban was no more, but Bloomberg would not give up, ultimately taking his case to the New York Court of Appeals—the state's highest court—in the fall of 2013, where it remained as of the writing of this book.[57]

As the battle over Bloomberg's measure played out in New York, similar events unfolded on the West Coast. In Richmond, California, the soft drink industry spent over $2.5 million to fight a proposed 1-cent obesity tax on soft drinks. Ultimately, the soft drink giants defeated the referendum, thanks in no small part to the NAACP and Black America's Political Action Committee, which threw their weight behind the corporate campaign. Again, the argument was economic. Studies showed that a modest 6.8 percent increase in the price of a soda resulted in a 7.8 percent reduction in sales. Converted to dollars and cents, this was a significant sum for retailers that depended on soda sales to turn a profit. This was the message Coke and its allies would drive home to defeat the tax.[58]

The soft drink industry's success in New York and Richmond was predictable. Poll after poll had shown that Americans across class boundaries did not like vice taxes because they saw such imposts as an unwarranted extension of state power. A 2010 CBS poll, for example, showed that 60 percent of Americans opposed fat taxes on high-calorie sweets, with over 72 percent of those polled arguing that taxation would not help in reducing America's obesity rate. Americans believed that government had no business meddling in their dietary choices.[59]

But history showed that consumers had never really enjoyed free choice. For years, major food companies had lobbied quietly for agricultural subsidies that kept the costs of raw materials for junk foods, especially high-fructose corn syrup, down. It was here, at the front end of the food system, that government had played a powerful, if invisible, role in deciding what Americans would and would not eat, and it was here that change would have to start.[60]

What the country needed was an overhaul of an industrial food system that focused on scaling up production at all cost. Ostensibly designed during the Great Depression to help America's farmers and improve the health of a down-and-out nation, the country's agricultural subsidy programs had ultimately done neither. Because of commodity support initiatives, many small farmers had been pushed off their land or been forced to sell their property to large agribusinesses, unable to compete in a market that rewarded quantity, not quality.

Those that remained were not really farming; they were overseeing the operation of huge machines designed to maximize profit. And all this was done to increase the production of a commodity glut that was making people fat.[61]

In 2013 and 2014, facing resistance from food activists spurred on by Michael Pollan and other critics of the Farm Bill, the federal government seemed on the verge of slimming down its profligate subsidy program. President Barack Obama's budget for fiscal year 2013 called for a reduction in direct payment to farmers that would total over $20 billion in savings by 2017. Describing the cuts, Obama's administration explained, "Economists have shown that direct payments have priced Americans out of renting or owning the land needed to enter into farming. In a period of severe fiscal restraint, these payments are no longer defensible." In 2014, cuts did come when Congress passed a Farm Bill that ended $5 billion in direct payments made annually to farmers. However, the roughly $1 trillion bill enlarged government-financed crop insurance programs. CNN reporter Lisa Desjardins succinctly captured the effects of the measure, saying that it would transfer risk "to the federal government, which could be even more on tap if crop prices plummet or if a disaster hits." In short, the government was once again picking up the tab for agribusiness growth.[62]

The environmental costs of this expansion were alarming. The fragile ecologies of the Great Plains states were now turned into miles and miles of monocrop cornfields—92.9 million acres in 2007—that required copious quantities of pesticides, fertilizers, and water in order to be productive. Unrelenting expansion put tremendous stress on already overburdened soils as well as waterways, which absorbed the chemical runoffs of these megafarms. Scientists have shown that fertilizers from corn country washed down the Mississippi River have contributed to recurrent algal blooms in the Gulf of Mexico, creating an ecological "dead zone" of almost 2,000 square miles. In addition, corn growers' irrigation systems have placed heavy strains on precious water sources, especially the shallow Ogallala Aquifer, which sits below the Great Plains. The water level in the Ogallala dropped year after year for over three decades, even as farms continued to expand their irrigation systems. Nature was issuing clear warning signs that the country's agricultural policies, and the foodways they supported, could not be sustained. It was time to recognize that increasing production was not the solution to our problems; it was the problem.[63]

Environmental costs associated with sweetener production were not confined to one country and its corn. Overseas, Coke's international bottlers, most still using sugar rather than high-fructose corn syrup to sweeten their beverages, continued to place heavy demands on tropical ecologies. By 2013 allegations emerged that Coke and its bottling affiliates were contributing to land grabs in the tropical world engineered by large sugar-producing firms that were turning once-diverse forests into monocrop sugarcane fields. In Mato Grosso do Sul, Brazil, which witnessed a threefold increase in sugar production between 2007 and 2012, one of Coke's sugar suppliers, Bunge, had expanded large-scale sugarcane cultivation onto lands claimed by the indigenous Guarani-Kaiowá, who reported pesticide contamination of their waterways caused by these farms and air pollution problems associated with the burning of sugarcane stalks. In Cambodia, one of Coke's sugar suppliers was accused of doing business with a local firm that dispossessed over five hundred families in order to clear approximately 69 square miles for sugarcane cultivation. Citing these and other problems with the international sugar trade, Oxfam International came out with an October 2013 report entitled "Sugar Rush," indicting Coca-Cola for failing to condemn its suppliers for these human rights and environmental violations. Ever careful to protect its brand, Coca-Cola responded to these allegations almost immediately, declaring a "zero tolerance for land grabbing" a month later.[64]

Coca-Cola was well aware that it was facing serious ecological problems in its sugar supply chain. In 2014, Coke's vice president for environment and water resources, Jeffrey Seabright, candidly admitted to the *New York Times* that sugar prices were on the rise due to global climate change and water shortages around the world. "We see those events as threats," Seabright explained, speaking of "increased droughts, more unpredictable variability, [and] 100-year floods every two years" caused by climate change. Nevertheless, Seabright assured the press that Coke was developing strategies to meet these new environmental demands.[65]

Despite its promises to halt the relentless growth of sugar cultivation overseas, addressing issues of oversupply and overconsumption was clearly secondary in its global prescriptive messages regarding obesity. In fact, Coke argued that solving obesity was not about scaling down; it was merely a matter of producing—and consuming—a greater variety of products. In a May 2012 keynote speech at the annual GBCHealth Conference, Coke CEO Muhtar Kent, Isdell's successor, laid out a dozen strategies to combat obesity, focusing mainly on new product lines. Kent championed the potential for a reformulated Coke that would contain new natural, noncaloric sweeteners, such as stevia, as well as a host of other healthy fruit juices and diet beverages offered by the company, which represented 25 percent of Coke's beverage sales in 2012. "Choice," Kent concluded, is one "way we're helping consumers avoid over-nutrition." The key was to "help consumers make informed" decisions by providing "transparency in communicating calories," something Kent explained the company was trying to do through its new nutrition labels. He also noted that the company had recently introduced smaller mini-cans that offered "delicious refreshment along with portion control."[66]

But even if Coke planned to sell smaller containers, it always intended to grow bigger. Year after year, Coca-Cola continued to feed company shareholders a healthy diet of "volume growth" statistics in year-end fiscal reports. In its 2013 end-of-year filing with the Securities and Exchange Commission, Coke noted that the company's plan for increasing value had not changed: "Unit case volume growth is a key metric used by management to evaluate the Company's performance because it measures demand for our products at the consumer level." A unit case, the company explained, was "equal to 192 U.S. fluid ounces of finished beverage." Thus, Coke made clear that future success depended on selling more stuff, not less. The company's supreme mission was to "expand marketing presence and increase our unit case volume in developed, developing, and emerging markets."[67]

The idea that Coke could somehow abandon its caloric soft drinks under this model of growth was absurd. True, since 2004, Coke's caloric carbonated beverage sales had declined, but they still represented a massive portion of the company's revenue stream. Coca-Cola with high-fructose corn syrup was still the number-one-selling carbonated beverage brand in the United States in 2012. It was biologically enticing, a product designed to stimulate repeated consumption. If Coke wanted to make money, it simply could not afford to see a significant loss in volume sales of this product.[68]

This is why in the early 2000s Coke doubled down on marketing caloric soft drinks overseas. Like the major tobacco companies that took their businesses abroad when fears about the carcinogenic effects of smoking reached their peak in the United States during the 1980s and 1990s, Coke responded to the obesity crisis of the 2000s by marketing its calorie-dense goods abroad. In 2012, for example, at the height of Coke's anti-obesity campaigns at home, the company's annual financial report heralded double-digit growth of caloric carbonated beverage sales in developing countries, such as India, and the prospects for expansion were enticing. Per capita consumption of

Coca-Cola in many countries overseas was less than half what it was in the United States in the early 2000s. The company knew that if it could get its sugary soft drinks into the hands of young consumers abroad, it stood to make huge profits.[69]

Less was not more in the fiscal rubric that made Coke profits, no matter what it preached about "portion control" in its promotional campaigns at home. The company always needed volume growth, and it could accomplish this only if it had abundant natural resources feeding its empire. Coke's solutions, therefore, always involved scaling up, not down, on both the supply and demand sides of the business. The concept of limits was something the company never considered.

In light of Coke's historic inability to regulate its own consumption of cheap sugar and high-fructose corn syrup, the country would do well to question the wisdom of nominating these corporate custodians to be our personal trainers in the years ahead. In fact, it seems more logical that private citizens should be asking corporate citizens to slim down, not the other way around. Unfortunately, many Americans do not have the economic freedom to take on this task. Coke has embedded itself in local economies in ways that make it hard to eradicate. It generates revenue for some of the most cash-strapped people in our communities, so taxing it out of existence without offering alternative revenue flows for low-income retailers is a dead-end policy. In short, solving our obesity epidemic will involve more than just taxing bad products; it will involve righting the deep-rooted inequities that make the poorest among us dependent on Coca-Cola capitalism for survival. Breaking this culture of dependency is a prerequisite for creating a healthy economy in the truest sense of the term, one that sustains a healthy citizenry, both economically and biologically, in the twenty-first century.

Sustaining Coke's Future?

Coke and Apple have suprising commonalities. Yes, one company sells soft drinks and the other computers, but in recent years both have followed similar business strategies to huge profits. Since the early 2000s, Apple, long considered a paragon of vertical integration, has chosen to outsource material production operations, siphoning off revenue as a third-party seller of materials extracted, processed, and assembled by other business intermediaries. The result has been big bucks. The company as of 2013 was the second-most-profitable corporation in the world, making most of its money off iPhones produced with cheap labor and resources in China. A year later, it replaced Coke as the most valuable global brand.[1]

Other companies at the top tell a similar story. Microsoft, the fourth-most-profitable company on *Fortune*'s 2012 chart, generates the majority of its revenue selling software—a kind of information concentrate—while letting other companies invest in expensive hard-

ware manufacturing equipment. Notably, Microsoft's recent foray
into Microsoft Surface development—the company's answer to the
iPad—and its 2013 purchase of Nokia represent untested experimental breaks with this tradition of eschewing vertical integration. Still,
for most of Miscrosoft's history, software has been its cash cow. Google (eighteenth), another giant of the digital age, has also made most
of its profits by being a pusher rather than a producer of wares. The
company confesses that it is in the business of "delivering relevant,
cost-effective online advertising," siphoning off fees from companies
using Google software to post their branded products online.[2]

In the fast food industry, McDonald's (thirtieth) has figured out
a way to make money without producing hamburgers. As we saw in
the chapter on water abroad, the company makes big revenues by
leasing property to franchisees that front most of the capital needed
to build and maintain restaurants. Other food franchise firms at the
top do much the same.

Banking and investment firms are the apotheosis of Coca-Cola
capitalism, with virtually no investment in property, plants, or equipment, making huge profits off virtual trading of commodities and
other goods produced by others. They too rank among the top money-
makers in the world. These are the companies our current brand of
capitalism rewards.

Many of the doers, that is, the companies that have built the
machines and infrastructure that fueled the twentieth-century
economy, have not fared so well. Vertically integrated companies,
such as U.S. Steel and General Motors, the titans of the first half
of the twentieth century, were sucking wind by the 2000s. General
Motors only survived thanks to a government bailout engineered
by President Barack Obama in 2008. Steel has become one of the
top money losers in the US market. Of the many problems these
companies faced, and there were many, one of the more serious
issues was revenue-draining investment in large-scale production

infrastructure. They lacked the kind of supply-side flexibility that would allow them to abandon unprofitable investments. Integration had not insulated them from the vagaries of the market; it had in fact tethered them to the ground, thereby limiting their ability to adapt to shifting cultural, political, and environmental conditions in particular production locales in a globalized twentieth-century economy.[3]

Some big companies bucked the trend. Exxon (ranking first) and Chevron (second), for example, with heavy fixed assets in extractive industries, were the two most profitable companies in the United States in 2012, but this was largely because they enjoyed oligopolistic control over some of the world's most precious natural resources. Only time will tell, however, whether Big Oil, with its large infrastructural investments, will be flexible enough to transition to a new energy regime if and when the world moves off fossil fuels. Flexibility is not the industry's greatest strength, and gambling on oil might prove costly in the long run.

Coke, of course, has not always stuck to the business strategy I have called Coca-Cola capitalism. As we have seen, the company's forays into ownership and operation of coffee firms, water purification technologies, bottling, and private recycling centers often proved a drain on company resources. For Coke, these industries often did not produce enough profits to warrant continued investment in their operation.

Take Coca-Cola Enterprises. This company-controlled mega-bottler created in 1986 has consistently posted poor earnings, piling up debt year after year. In 2006, *Fortune* listed CCE among its Top 10 money losers on the Global 500 list, with over $1.1 billion in losses. In part because of concerns about the weak earnings at CCE, Coke began in 2013 to refranchise its bottlers to independent companies. It seemed Coke was once again learning the lesson that leaving the hard work of production to others was good business for Coca-Cola.[4]

Despite forays into bottling and other industries, for the majority of its history, the company's success hinged on its ability to find partners, whether public or private, which would cover the majority of the costs of supporting these technological systems that produced the cheap commodities vital to trade in low-value consumer goods. Coke was at its best when it did less.

This is why the cult of the secret formula was so important to Coke. As a company that did not own its own systems of production, it had to convince business partners that it had something valuable to offer. The secret formula, then, was not simply a clever marketing gimmick designed to lure customers: it was a bargaining chip Coke used to keep its producers and distributors working on its behalf. Coca-Cola had to make its business partners believe that they needed the Real Thing in order to survive. This was just as important as convincing the public that Coke was the key to happiness. Naturally, the central fear at Coke has always been that, as in the climactic scene of *The Wizard of Oz*, the curtain will be peeled back, and Coke will be revealed for what it is: a business that does not have the means to produce the products—or happiness—it hawks.

Today, Coke continues to work hard to promote itself as a global citizen capable of building infrastructure that benefits the public at large. But to claim it prudent to nominate our most profitable corporations to be providers of public services in the years ahead would be to ignore history. Proponents of limited government consistently maintain that private industry should take over certain tasks, such as municipal waterworks, that are now being provided by the state. They contend that businesses could run these systems more efficiently and reduce costs to the public. But the chronicle of Citizen Coke's ascendancy offered in this book shows that some of the most profitable businesses of our time have been successful precisely because they have not invested in expensive infrastructural projects. Coke and other profitable low-value consumer goods companies were not the engineers of their destinies but rather businesses dependent upon scaffolding provided by others, and they were far more often the beneficiaries of state support programs than the material developers of technological systems that benefited the public at large. In short, Coke always needed more than it could provide. It was a consumer more than a producer, a company adept at repackaging public resources into private products for profit.

Some would say Coke should be entitled to public investments, considering the distributed financial rewards of Coke's commercial empire. After all, Coke claimed that it spent an estimated $11 billion buying ingredients from some 84,000 independent suppliers worldwide in 2006 alone. In addition, Coca-Cola reported that over 700,000 "associates" made money by selling Coke around the world in 2013 (though only a fraction of these associates—perhaps less than 15 percent—were officially on the Coca-Cola Company payroll). All this business generated over $2.8 billion in corporate income taxes.[5]

But public policies that encourage the expansion of Coke's empire on the grounds that the company stimulates economic activity fail to include in the calculus the ecological and human health costs that such growth would entail, nor do they capture the public investments that have made these profits possible. Coke is a major contributor to a growing obesity epidemic in the United States, a crisis costing Americans an estimated $147 billion a year in medical expenses, yet the company has avoided taxes that would force it to internalize a portion of these expenses. Likewise, the company depends on a host of municipal recycling and garbage programs to keep its packaging waste out of sight, avoiding pollution penalties in most communities where it operates around the world. With global costs for solid-waste management approaching $205 billion in 2012, these hidden municipal subsidies have offered Coke huge savings. No doubt, if just a fraction of these costs showed up in the price of the company's finished beverage, a Coke would no longer appear such a bargain.[6]

In sum, communities would do well to consider the ecological sustainability of Coca-Cola capitalism before channeling some of their most vital natural and fiscal capital to expand businesses that deploy this system for making money. Coca-Cola's squeaky-clean financial ledgers may make it seem that sustainability is just within reach for the company, that a little tinkering here and a patch there can turn the business into a truly green and socially just enterprise in the years ahead. But the history offered here suggests that there is a fundamental problem with the Coke system: it is a product of profligacy. For over a hundred years, the company maintained the semblance of sustainability, in both the economic and environmental senses, because the unsustainable supply chains of abundance that fueled its growth never ended up on its books. Whatever Coke's sleek financial statements might have suggested, at base the company was a product of excess. From the very beginning, Coke scavenged on surplus commodities generated by overstocked suppliers to create its cheap consumer goods in volume. It thrived when its suppliers engaged in runaway production, because it was during these times that it could get ingredients for the lowest possible prices and thereby increase its volume sales at low cost. Sustainability, in the truest sense of the word, was anathema to Coke because its business was fundamentally about gaining access to more, whether larger commodity stockpiles or bigger consumer markets.

A lot has changed at Coke over its 128-year history, even the supposedly timeless and sacrosanct secret formula, but despite new packaging and new sweeteners, the company's system for making money remained the same. This was the truly immutable aspect of the Coca-Cola enterprise, not its sugary recipe but the financial formula that earned the company profits. Coke executives never questioned the commitment to perpetual expansion first touted by the firm's nineteenth-century founders, even though the biophysical environment that spawned Coke in the Gilded Age was vastly different than the one in which company leaders found themselves a hundred years later. By the end of the twentieth century, there were clear signs that the world did not need more Coke. Bodies had become bloated with sweeteners, landfills were overflowing with company containers, and bottling plants were extracting more water than some communities could afford. Yet the mantra of more and more continued, with suggestions for reform focusing on treating the symptoms rather than the causes of unsustainable business growth. Corporate social responsibility initiatives held out the promise of efficient waste capture and reclamation as the solution to big-business problems without acknowledging the fundamental long-term dependence on using excess to create excess that made America's modern mass-marketing firms possible in the first place.

This is why history matters when it comes to designing a sustainable economy for the twenty-first century. Turning to the past requires us to grapple with the time-specific conditions that bred the modern mass-marketing firm in the late nineteenth century and to question whether these first principles of corporate governance actually apply to the environmental, political, and economic conditions of today. Why should a citizenry invest in companies that abide by a nineteenth-century commitment to perpetual growth in a twenty-first-century world facing both biological and environmental limits to relentless volume sales expansion?

Coca-Cola and its corporate partners will have a very hard time helping to engineer a sustainable economy for the twenty-first century. After all, Citizen Coke, despite its public boasting, has never been that good at engineering. The Coca-Cola Company has depended upon recycling systems, public pipes, and subsidized farms paid for and built by taxpayers the world over. Yet Coke's message to the world today is that it is a company that generates public goods rather than consumes them. In the age of corporate social responsibility, Citizen Coke asks us to give over our precious public resources for safe handling, claiming that the company's superior technology and business acumen will enable it to provide what the world needs. Give me your water, the company proclaims, and I will give you jobs, prosperity, and happiness. But must we make this bargain? The history offered here suggests not. We, the customers of corporations, have both the resources and the ingenuity to build a brighter future, but doing so will require us to keep more careful watch over our most valuable natural capital. We should be the ones setting the price for public resource use rather than the ones accepting the bill for corporate waste. Reclaiming *that* history of citizenship, one that rightfully challenges a culture of corporate dependency and restores faith in the power of private citizens to develop public systems to deal with collective problems, is the first step toward sustainability—as we must come to know it.

Acknowledgments

Many people played a critical role in helping me produce this book. I am deeply indebted to my graduate committee at the University of Virginia, who not only provided sound advice and chapter edits throughout the research and writing process but also offered encouragement when this global history became a bit much to bear. Ed Ayers was instrumental in my graduate career, taking a chance on me back in the fall of 2006 when I enrolled at the University of Virginia. Ed led by example and showed me what it meant to be a public scholar. He taught how the historian's craft could be used to better the world in which we live. I am eternally grateful to him for sticking with me and seeing me through this project. Grace Hale signed on to work with me in my second year of graduate school, at a time when her office was flooded with graduate students. She found time for me and dedicated hours to line-by-line editing of chapters. My study was immeasurably enhanced due to her persistent demands that I refine and clarify arguments in every section of the book. In the same vein, Ed Russell was a dedicated mentor throughout the process and provided day-to-day advice on how to handle the challenges of graduate school. He introduced me to the subfield of environmental history that has become my professional passion ever since. Ed is truly a selfless mentor who dedicated countless hours to teaching all his students lessons on professional development often absent in standard graduate school curriculum. Finally, I must thank Brian Balogh, who agreed to work with me on this project later in its development, but who nonetheless provided much-needed advice on how this book engaged with the American political development literature. Brian became not only a fantastic mentor but also a great friend, if at times a pesky and nearly unbeatable opponent on the tennis courts.

Several institutions at the University of Virginia and beyond helped provide critical funding without which I would have been unable to complete this project. From 2010 to 2012, I had the pleasure of serving as the Sara Shallenberger Brown Fellow in Environmental Writing at the University of Virginia's Brown Residential College, a fellowship that offers advanced graduate students funding to complete their dissertations while teaching courses on topics related to environmental history and literature. I am grateful to the Brown family for making this fellowship available and for giving me the opportunity to engage with such an amazing community of undergraduates at Brown College. I also received generous funding for this project from the Bankard Fund for Political Economy established through gifts made by Merrill H. Bankard and his wife, Georgia S. Bankard. The American Society for Environmental History (ASEH) contributed to this project in 2011 through the Hal Rothman Research Fellowship, as did the Virginia Historical Society, which granted me the Betty Sams Christian Fellowship in Business History that same year. I am also indebted to the University of California, Berkeley's College of Natural Resources, which awarded me the Ciriacy-Wantrup Postdoctoral Fellowship in Natural Resource

Economics and Political Economy for the 2012–2013 academic year, allowing me ample time to revise my manuscript.

A special thanks goes to journalists Mark Pendergrast and Frederick Allen, who wrote excellent histories of the Coca-Cola Company that proved invaluable as sources for this work. Coca-Cola had given both authors access to the corporate archives back in the 1990s, which allowed them to uncover some fascinating material not available elsewhere. I would not have been able to see broad patterns in Coke's corporate history without these texts. They are required reading for anyone interested in the history of the Coke brand. I would also like to thank Paul Gootenberg, whose work on Andean cocaine was instrumental in shaping the coca chapter in this book. He deserves the credit for discovering the declassified Federal Bureau of Narcotics documents at the National Archives in College Park, Maryland, that detail the complicated relationship between federal drug authorities and the Coca-Cola Company. Gootenberg was kind enough to read early drafts of the coca chapter and provided sound insights for ways to improve the text.

Several faculty members and students in the Corcoran Department of History were instrumental in shaping my graduate career and deserve special recognition. Though they never served in an official capacity as dissertation advisers, I nonetheless am grateful for the training and support I received from Gary Gallagher, Peter Onuf, Christian McMillen, Mel Leffler, Claudrena Harold, Chuck McCurdy, Joe Kett, and Bernie Carlson. The Russell Environmental Lab Group reviewed numerous drafts of the dissertation as well as conference talks based on the project. I would especially like to thank Jaime Allison, Adam Dean, Tom Finger, Philip Herrington, Laura Kolar, Stephen Macekura, Andrew McGee, and Katie Shively Meyer for all their assistance. I would also like to thank Raffi Andonian, Brent Cebul, David Hill, Elizabeth Ladner, Kevin Lake, Tim Lovelace, Peter Luebke, and Loren Moulds for their scholarly support and comradeship.

At Berkeley, I worked in both David Winickoff's and Nancy Peluso's lab groups. Participants in these labs read early drafts of book chapters and provided sound insights. Special thanks go to Robert Chester, Zubin Desai, and Chris Jones, who helped me work out particularly troubling sections of text. Haas Business School professor Chris Rosen also read later drafts of *Citizen Coke* and offered edits.

Environmental historian Richard White at Stanford University and business historian Bethany Moreton of the University of Georgia were incredibly gracious with their time and agreed to read sections of this work and provide comments. Bethany trudged through a near-final version of the manuscript and offered particularly illuminating reflections. It was truly an honor to have senior scholars I admire work with me on this project.

Without the tireless efforts of the talented team of editors at Norton, this book would have been a dull slog for most readers. Many thanks to Ed Barber, Steve Forman, Justin Cahill, and India Cooper for their incredibly detailed line edits and thoughtful suggestions for improvements. It was a dream working with an editorial team willing to put so many hours into the project.

Much of the primary source material in this book comes from the Manuscript, Archives, and Rare Book Library at Emory University. The hardworking archivists there, especially Randy Gue and Kathleen Shoemaker, were an absolute delight to work with. They set the standard for how a library should be run.

To Joya McMurray and her family and my friends in Charlottesville and elsewhere, I owe more than I can ever repay. To complete a project of this length, I am convinced, you have to find time to laugh, scream, and cry with those you love. I will never forget my years in Charlottesville. They have been some of the best in my life. Thank you to the Charlottesville faithful, especially Alexa and Paul Belonick, Katie Barletta, Ryan Bryant, Jerome Buescher, Ben Converse, Jon Foote, Emily Graham Teeter, Sanjay Kriplani, Rhianna Laker, Andrew and Ashley Lockhart, Zach Lucy, Theresa Macfarlan, Micah McAllister, Bret Meyer, Tim Nowaczyk, Jon and Katie Overdevest, Jesse and Kristen Pappas, Brian Renne, Joel Slezak and Erica Hellen, Nick Snavely, Justin Storbeck, Jon Zadra, and the Zocalo team. And to my friends who have known me longer than they might want to admit, thank you for sticking with me through these years. Thank you Erin Cochran, Kyle Hatridge, Hemant Joshi, Kim Krajovic, Kristian Lau, Daniel Michalow, Kip Praissman, Matt Rahn, Brad Robinson, and Joe Thistle for being my friends for so long.

I reserve my greatest thanks for my parents, Jerome and Susan Elmore, and for Collins, Scott, and Lisa. Thank you for believing in me, for loving me, and for giving me a chance to do this. This book is dedicated to you.

Notes

PROLOGUE: A CREATION MYTH OF CITIZEN COKE

1 "Mayor Makes a Bubbly Pitch for Coca-Cola Party Monday," *Atlanta Journal* and *Atlanta Constitution*, May 2, 1986, D/1 (the two papers officially merged under the name *Atlanta Journal-Constitution* in 2001).

2 Display Ad, *Atlanta Constitution*, June 20, 1886, 14. In *Rebirth of a Nation: The Making of Modern America, 1877–1920* (New York: HarperCollins, 2009), cultural historian Jackson Lears aptly described the late nineteenth century as a period of soul-searching in America. Patent medicines, he explained, served as "the focus for fantasies of regeneration through purchase," a way for consumers to experience a "magical self-transformation" not often found in the increasingly systematized capitalist markets of the period (7).

3 "Mr. Asa G. Candler, Sr.," *Coca-Cola Bottler*, April 1929, 15–21; Mark Pendergrast, *For God, Country & Coca-Cola* (New York: Scribner, 1993), 91; Frederick Allen, *Secret Formula: How Brilliant Marketing and Relentless Salesmanship Made Coca-Cola the Best-Known Product in the World* (New York: HarperBusiness, 1994), 82.

4 Michelle Ye Hee Lee, "The 30-Year Gift That Keeps on Giving," *Emory Wheel*, September 24, 2009, http://www.emorywheel.com/archive/detail.php?n=27370.

5 Speech by Ralph Hayes, 50th Anniversary Celebration of the Coca-Cola Bottling Company (Thomas), October 3, 1949, box 137, folder 7, Robert W. Woodruff Papers (hereinafter RWW Papers), Manuscript, Archives, Rare Book Library, Emory University (hereinafter MARBL); "What Coke Has Wrought," *Coke's*

First Hundred Years (Shepherdsville, KY: Keller, 1986), 86; "The Sun Never Sets on Coca-Cola," *Time*, May 15, 1950.

6 "The Sun Never Sets on Coca-Cola," *Time*, May 15, 1950.

INTRODUCTION

1 "Coca-Cola Company Announces 50th Consecutive Dividend," Coca-Cola Press Release, February 16, 2012; "Coca-Cola Retains Title as World's Most Valuable Brand," *Bloomberg.com*, October 2, 2012, http://www.bloomberg.com/news/2012 -10-03/coca-cola-retains-title-as-world-s-most-valuable-brand-table-.html; Interbrand Press Release, "Interbrand Releases 13th Annual Best Global Brands Report," October 2, 2012; Coca-Cola Company 2012 10-K Securities and Exchange Commission (SEC) Report, 1, 79.

2 Alfred W. Crosby's *Ecological Imperialism: The Biological Expansion of Europe, 900–1900* (Cambridge: Cambridge University Press, 2004) inspired what might be called the meta-strategy of this work. Crosby urged scholars to look at broad patterns in global history. As he put it, "Ask simple questions because the answers to complicated questions probably will be too complicated to test and, even worse, too fascinating to give up" (6).

3 The term "want maker" comes from journalist Eric Clark's *The Want Makers: The World of Advertising—How They Make You Buy* (New York: Viking, 1989); Mark Pendergrast, *For God, Country & Coca-Cola: The Unauthorized History of the Great American Soft Drink and the Company That Makes It* (New York: Maxwell Macmillan, 1993; New York: Collier Books, 1994; New York: Basic Books, 2000, 2013), 2. Citations in this book are to the 2000 Basic Books edition unless otherwise indicated. For other histories of the Coca-Cola Company produced by journalists unaffiliated with the company, see Frederick Allen, *Secret Formula: How Brilliant Marketing and Relentless Salesmanship Made Coca-Cola the Best-Known Product in the World* (New York: HarperBusiness, 1994); Thomas Oliver, *The Real Coke, the Real Story* (New York: Random House, 1986); Constance L. Hays, *The Real Thing: Truth and Power at the Coca-Cola Company* (New York: Random House, 2004); Michael Blanding, *The Coke Machine: The Dirty Truth Behind the World's Favorite Soft Drink* (New York: Avery, 2010); Mark Thomas, *Belching Out the Devil: Global Adventures with Coca-Cola* (New York: Nation Books, 2008). For histories written by authors connected in some form or fashion with the Coca-Cola enterprise, see Pat Watters, *Coca-Cola: An Illustrated History* (New York: Doubleday, 1978); E. J. Kahn Jr., *The Big Drink: The Story of Coca-Cola* (New York: Random House, 1960); Neville Isdell with David Beasley, *Inside Coca-Cola: A CEO's Life Story of Building the World's Most Popular Brand* (New York: St. Martin's Press, 2011). To date, no academic historian has attempted a comprehensive history of the company.

4 Frederick Allen, *Secret Formula*, 104; "Investor's Guide," *Chicago Daily Tribune*, February 3, 1940, 23; Letter from Ralph Hayes to Robert Woodruff, May 5, 1954, box 138, folder 3, RWW Papers, MARBL Coca-Cola Company 2007/2008 Sustainability Review, 34.

5 For economic theories on the boundaries of the firm and why corporations choose

to buy or make various products, see Oliver E. Williamson, "Transaction-Cost Economics: The Governance of Contractual Relations," *Journal of Law and Economics* 22, no. 2 (October 1979): 233–261, and Ronald Coase, "The Nature of the Firm," *Economica* 4, no. 16 (November 1937): 386–405. See also Ronald E. Coase, "Accounting and the Theory of the Firm," *Journal of Accounting and Economics* 12 (1990): 3–13; Oliver E. Williamson, "Strategizing, Economizing, and Economic Organization," *Strategic Management Journal* 12 (Winter Special Issue, 1991): 75–94. For recent critiques and revisions to Coase, Williamson, and early transaction cost theorists, see Anoop Madhok, "Reassessing the Fundamentals and Beyond: Ronald Coase, The Transaction Cost and Resource-Based Theories of the Firm and the Institutional Structure of Production," *Strategic Management Journal* 23, no. 6 (June 2002): 535–550. Economist Richard N. Langlois has written extensively about the 'de-verticalization' of the corporate economy in the 1970s, perhaps most notably in "The Vanishing Hand: The Changing Dynamics of Industrial Capitalism," *Industrial and Corporate Change* 12, no. 2 (2003): 351–385.

6 Scholars such as Brian Balogh, Gabriel Kolko, Thomas McCraw, Martin J. Sklar, and James Weinstein have all produced excellent works that chronicle the rise of what Louis Galambos and Joseph Pratt have called the "corporate commonwealth" in the twentieth century. These works show how corporations used the federal courts and "captured" government regulatory bodies, such as the Federal Trade Commission (FTC), the Interstate Commerce Commission (ICC), and even the Food and Drug Administration (FDA), to help legitimate monopolistic growth and create national markets suitable for the expansion of big business. Likewise, Richard White has examined the substantial public sector investments in railroad infrastructure that fueled commercial growth in the twentieth century. My work adds to this literature and highlights the critical role the state played in creating and sustaining the global extractive industries and international commodity networks so essential to the growth of low-value consumer goods enterprises. Brian Balogh, *A Government out of Sight: The Mystery of National Authority in Nineteenth Century America* (Cambridge: Cambridge University Press, 2009); Gabriel Kolko, *The Triumph of Conservatism: A Reinterpretation of American History, 1900–1916* (New York: Free Press of Glencoe, 1963); Thomas K. McCraw, *Prophets of Regulation: Charles Francis Adams, Louis D. Brandeis, James M. Landis, Alfred E. Kahn* (Cambridge: Belknap Press of Harvard University Press, 1984); Martin J. Sklar, *The Corporate Reconstruction of American Capitalism, 1890–1916* (Cambridge: Cambridge University Press, 1988); James Weinstein, *The Corporate Ideal in the Liberal State, 1900–1918* (Boston: Beacon Press, 1968); Louis Galambos and Joseph Pratt, *The Rise of the Corporate Commonwealth: U.S. Business and Public Policy in the Twentieth Century* (New York: Basic Books, 1988); Richard White, *Railroaded: The Transcontinentals and the Making of Modern America* (New York: Norton, 2011). Historians of the New Deal, the 1940s, and the Cold War have also contributed new works that help to debunk the "myth of the weak American state," showing the centrality of government in facilitating the birth of new industries in the mid-twentieth century and beyond. Bruce Schulman, Pete Daniel, and Jack Temple Kirby, for example, have illustrated how the Agricultural Adjustment Act (AAA) and other Depression-era farm aid programs helped channel federal revenue to large landowners in the South who used the new influx of capital

to create mechanized agribusinesses that pushed small farmers off their land in the rural South. Michael Hogan's and James Sparrow's works on World War II and the Cold War, among others, have highlighted the expansion of the military-industrial complex in the 1940s and 1950s and shown how federal defense funds supported the growth of new high-tech industries. Christopher Howard and others have likewise illustrated that even in the 1980s, the so-called era of deregulation, the Reagan administration helped to expand a "hidden welfare state" and developed neoliberal policies that channeled tax expenditures toward specific industries. See William J. Novak, "The Myth of the 'Weak' American State," *American Historical Review* 113, no. 3 (June 2008): 752–772; Jason Scott Smith, *Building New Deal Liberalism: The Political Economy of Public Works, 1933–1956* (Cambridge: Cambridge University Press, 2009); Bruce J. Schulman, *From Cotton Belt to Sunbelt: Federal Policy, Economic Development, and the Transformation of the South, 1938–1980* (New York: Oxford University Press, 1991); Pete Daniel, *Breaking the Land: The Transformation of Cotton, Tobacco, and Rice Cultures Since 1880* (Urbana: University of Illinois Press, 1985); Jack Temple Kirby, *Rural Worlds Lost: The American South, 1920–1960* (Baton Rouge: Louisiana State University, 1987); Michael Hogan, *A Cross of Iron: Harry S. Truman and the Origins of the National Security State, 1945–1954* (Cambridge: Cambridge University Press, 1998); James T. Sparrow, *Warfare State: World War II Americans and the Age of Big Government* (Oxford: Oxford University Press, 2011); Christopher Howard, *The Hidden Welfare State: Tax Expenditures and Social Policy in the United States* (Princeton: Princeton University Press, 1997). For a thoughtful survey of the history and historiography of regulatory capture, see Daniel Carpenter and David A. Moss, eds., *Preventing Regulatory Capture: Special Interest Influence and How to Limit It* (Cambridge: Cambridge University Press, 2014).

7 Scholars interested in the history of capitalism have recently written excellent works about the rise of financial capitalism in the 1970s. These studies see the last half century as an economic era in which corporate conglomerates divested from competitive commodity production markets and realigned themselves toward generating profit windfalls through strategic trading of financial instruments on the stock market. Summarizing the new corporate governance ideal, historian Louis Hyman wrote, "New lean corporations could spread quickly through the American and global economy, pushing operations outside of themselves and relying on the market for managerial talent, financial capital, and anything else that they could not monopolize in the value chain." This book adds to Hyman's work and others, returning to the late nineteenth century, long before American financial markets became what they were in the 1970s, to explain the origins of the lean big business. It is here in the Gilded Age that the extractive infrastructure on which financialization depended was first laid, and here that we see the progenitors of global outsourcing. For histories of corporate development in the age of financialization, see Louis Hyman, "Rethinking the Postwar Corporation: Management, Monopolies, and Markets," in *What's Good for Business: Business and American Politics Since World War II*, ed. Kim Phillips-Fein and Julian Zelizer (Oxford: Oxford University Press, 2012), 208; Louis Hyman, *Debtor Nation: The History of America in Red Ink* (Princeton: Princeton University Press, 2011); Greta R. Krippner, *Capitalizing on Crisis: The Political Origins of the Rise of Finance* (Cambridge: Harvard University

Press, 2011). Richard N. Langlois, "The Vanishing Hand"; William Lazonick, "The Financialization of the U.S. Corporation: What Has Been Lost, and How It Can Be Regained," *Seattle University Law Review* 36 (2013): 857–909; Dirk Zorn, Frank Dobbin, Julian Dierkes, and Man-Shan Kwok, "Managing Investors: How Finance Markets Reshaped the American Firm," in *The Sociology of Financial Markets*, ed. Karen Knorr-Letina and Alex Preda (New York: Oxford University Press, 2009). On the early twentieth century origins of mass investment in the securities market, see Julia Ott, *When Wall Street Met Main Street: The Quest for an Investors' Democracy* (Cambridge: Harvard University Press, 2011).

8 Alfred Chandler, one of the most influential and important business historians of our time, wrote throughout his career that vertical integration represented the hallmark of modern corporate development. He believed companies improved their profitability and reduced risks by combining "processes of mass production with those of mass distribution within a single business firm." He acknowledged that many consumer goods companies never completed the process of backward integration, but he saw these firms as sidenotes to the main attractions of the US Sugar Trust, General Motors, and U.S. Steel. This book offers a new take on the rise of big business in America, showing how Coke's nonintegrated structure enabled it to accelerate the flow of commodities through its corporate system. Following one firm from its birth and maturation in the Gilded Age through the end of the twentieth century, I argue that externalizing technological systems closely associated with natural resource extraction and processing proved an essential business strategy for many profitable, low-value consumer goods enterprises. In other words, *Citizen Coke* illustrates how big firms that eschewed vertical integration were not just exceptions to the rule of twentieth-century corporate development, but rather essential commodity conduits linking vertically integrated empires to local markets. Alfred Chandler, *The Visible Hand: The Managerial Revolution in American Business* (Cambridge: Belknap Press of Harvard University Press, 1977), 11, 285; On the resilience of Chandler's theories, see Louis Galambos, "Global Perspectives on Modern Business," *Business History Review* 71, no. 2 (Summer 1997): 287; William J. Hausman, "U.S. Business History at the End of the Twentieth Century," in *Business History Around the World*, ed. Franco Amatori and Geoffrey Jones (Cambridge: Cambridge University Press, 2003), 96–97. Interestingly, Chandler treated Coke as a vertically integrated firm. For specific references to Coke as an "integrated enterprise" in *The Visible Hand*, see 313, 390. See also Chandler's other major works that stress the importance of vertical integration, including: "The Beginnings of 'Big Business' in American Industry," *Business History Review* 33, no. 1 (Spring 1959): 1–31; "Development, Diversification, and Decentralization," in *Postwar Economic Trends in the United States*, ed. Ralph E. Freedman (New York: Harper and Brothers, 1960); *Strategy and Structure: Chapters in the History of the Industrial Enterprise* (Cambridge: MIT Press, 1962); and *Scale and Scope: The Dynamics of Industrial Capitalism* (Cambridge: Belknap Press of Harvard University Press, 1990). For an excellent survey of Chandler's work see Thomas McCraw, ed. *The Essential Alfred Chandler: Essays Toward a Historical Theory of Big Business* (Boston: Harvard Business School Press, 1988). Philip Scranton provided perhaps the most direct revision to Chandler's vertical-integration model in *Endless Novelty: Specialty Production and American Industrialization, 1865–1925* (Princeton: Princeton University Press, 1997). In this work,

Scranton exposed the economic vitality of specialty and artisanal producers in the late 1800s and early twentieth century.

9   Several excellent material-flow studies produced by environmental historians inspired my interest in this topic, namely Richard Tucker's *Insatiable Appetite: The United States and the Ecological Degradation of the Tropical World* (Berkeley: University of California Press, 2000), John Soluri's *Banana Cultures: Agriculture, Consumption, and Environmental Change in Honduras and the United States* (Austin: University of Texas Press, 2005), and William Cronon's *Nature's Metropolis: Chicago and the Great West* (New York: Norton, 1991). My work builds on Cronon's organizational methodology in *Nature's Metropolis*, a study that explored the connections between Chicago and the countryside suppliers that fueled urban growth. Replacing the corporation for the city and the globe for the Midwest, my work offers a model for a new interpretation of the rise of the modern corporation that focuses on the environmental demands that structured big business development in the twentieth century. Steve Ettinger's *Twinkie, Deconstructed: My Journey to Discover How the Ingredients in Processed Foods Are Grown, Mined (Yes, Mined), and Manipulated into What America Eats* (New York: Hudson Street Press, 2007) inspired the ingredient-based structure for this book. There are several "natural flavors" in Coca-Cola, but I chose to deal with just one, coca leaves, considering its importance to the trademark brand.

10   I am referring here to the excellent works of journalists Mark Pendergrast and Frederick Allen. Both authors explored Coke's procurement of various ingredients but largely focused on times when Coke had trouble getting what it needed.

PART I: CITIZEN COKE COMES OF AGE, 1886 TO 1950

1   Speech by Ralph Hayes to the 50th Anniversary Convention, Coca-Cola Bottling Co. (Thomas), Inc., at Waldorf-Astoria Ballroom, New York City, October 2, 1949, box 137, folder 7, RWW Papers, MARBL. For an excellent history of the economic conditions in the New South, see Ed Ayers, *The Promise of the New South: Life After Reconstruction* (New York: Oxford University Press, 1992).

1. TAP WATER: PACKAGING PUBLIC WATER FOR PRIVATE PROFIT

1   National water footprint calculations and basic cooking, cleaning, and drinking statistics were based on the following sources: United Nations Water Assessment Programme, http://www.unwater.org/statistics/statistics-detail/en/c/211765 (the UN maintains that people need on average 20–50 liters per day "to ensure their basic needs for drinking, cooking and cleaning"; M. M. Mekonnen and A. Y. Hoekstra, *National Water Footprint Accounts: The Green, Blue and Grey Water Footprint of Production and Consumption*, Value of Water Research Report no. 50, UNESCO Institute for Water Health, May 2011, 30–31. Statistics regarding Coca-Cola's water footprint came from the following sources: "Water Stewardship," Coca-Cola Company 2010/2011 Sustainability Report, 20; Coca-Cola Company and Nature Conservancy, "Product Water Footprint Assessments: Practical Application in

Corporate Water Stewardship," September 2010, 8–15; Coca-Cola Enterprises 2009 Corporate Responsibility and Sustainability Report, 24–31; Coca-Cola Company 2010 Replenish Report, 4; Coca-Cola Company 2012 Global Response Initiative Report, 69; Paul Brown, Water Technologies Director, Coca-Cola, "Our Commitment to the Environment," Presentation given to Coca-Cola employees in San Jose, Costa Rica, September 24, 2009, 19 (in Dr. Brown's presentation, he specifically noted that the 300-billion-liter water footprint often quoted by Coca-Cola did not include embedded water used to make Coke ingredients or packaging); Coca-Cola Hellenic (bottler) 2011 Corporate Social Responsibility Report, 21–24; Coca-Cola Company Water Footprint Sustainability Assessment (Europe), August 2011, 1; Coca-Cola Company 2012/2013 Global Reporting Initiative.

2 James Harvey Young, "Three Atlanta Pharmacists," *Pharmacy in History* 31, no. 1 (1989), 16; Wilbur G. Kurtz Jr., "Dr. John Pemberton—Originator of the Formula for Coca-Cola: A Short Biographical Sketch," no date, p. 1, box 14, folder 1, Mark Pendergrast Research Files, MARBL; Frederick Allen, *Secret Formula*, 18–22; Mark Pendergrast, *For God, Country, and Coca-Cola*, 19–20.

3 "The Patent Medicine Problem," *Atlanta Constitution*, September 5, 1884, 4; Classified Ad, *Atlanta Constitution*, May 10, 1888, 2; Display Ad, *Atlanta Constitution*, May 7, 1884, 3; Display Ad, *Atlanta Constitution*, April 1, 1885, 8; Classified Ad, *Atlanta Constitution*, February 20, 1887, 14.

4 Frederick Allen, *Secret Formula*, 18–22; Mark Pendergrast, *For God, Country & Coca-Cola*, 19–20.

5 "Who is Mariani? How He Came from Corsica and Grew to Be One of the Great Men of Paris," *New York Times*, May 31, 1898, 7; Frederick Allen, *Secret Formula*, 23; Mark Pendergrast, *For God, Country & Coca-Cola*, 22–23.

6 Ed Ayers, *The Promise of the New South*, 102; Mark Pendergrast, *For God, Country & Coca-Cola*, 19–20, 25; Frederick Allen, *Secret Formula*, 34.

7 Mark Pendergrast, *For God, Country & Coca-Cola*, 24, 26–27; Frederick Allen, *Secret Formula*, 24; Monroe Martin King, "Dr. John S. Pemberton: Originator of Coca-Cola," *Pharmacy in History* 29, no. 2 (1987): 86–87.

8 Of course, Pemberton's original formula is a closely guarded secret at Coca-Cola. I have not been given special access to the recipe, but in the 1990s, journalist Mark Pendergrast discovered a document in the Coca-Cola archive that closely resembled what must have been Pemberton's formula. Pendergrast detailed the fascinating account of his finding in the appendix of his book *For God, Country & Coca-Cola*, 456–460. I have chosen to list ingredients here that, based on other evidence, were almost certainly in Pemberton's syrup; phosphoric acid apparently became the chief acidifying agent in Coca-Cola later; Mark Pendergrast, *For God, Country & Coca-Cola*, 30.

9 Frederick Allen, *Secret Formula*, 26.

10 Mark Pendergrast, *For God, Country & Coca-Cola*, 28; Frederick Allen, *Secret Formula*, 24.

11 Frederick Allen, *Secret Formula*, 28–29; James Harvey Young, "Three Atlanta Pharmacists," 17.

12 Company publications state that Coke's first year of sales totaled just 25 gallons. This figure comes from a statement given by early Coke executive Frank Robinson

during a trademark suit in 1920. Mark Pendergrast, however, discovered evidence in the *Atlanta Constitution* from May of 1887 that shows much larger sales of Coca-Cola. The article stated, "The sales within the last few weeks for the coca-cola syrup amounted to six hundred gallons." *Atlanta Constitution*, May 1, 1887, 12, quoted in Mark Pendergrast, *For God, Country & Coca-Cola*, 32; Frederick Allen, *Secret Formula*, 29. The price for Pemberton's French Wine Coca at Joe Jacob's pharmacy can be found in a classified ad published by the *Atlanta Constitution*, August 5, 1888, 1.

13 Mark Pendergrast, *For God, Country & Coca-Cola*, 43–46, 53–58.

14 Ibid. For documents detailing this title battle, see numerous court records and documents in box 14, folder 1, Mark Pendergrast Research Files, MARBL.

15 Letter from Asa Candler to Dr. A. W. Griggs, September 11, 1872, box 1, folder 1, Asa Griggs Candler Papers, MARBL; Stephens's statement is quoted in Mark Pendergrast, *For God, Country & Coca-Cola*, 44–45, 49–50. A detailed history of Asa Candler's early life can be found in a biography penned by Charles Howard Candler, his son. See Charles Howard Candler, *Asa Griggs Candler* (Atlanta: Emory University, 1950), 38–94.

16 Quoted in Charles Howard Candler, *Asa Griggs Candler*, 45–46; Mark Pendergrast, *For God, Country & Coca-Cola*, 47; Frederick Allen, *Secret Formula*, 32.

17 Franklin M. Garrett, "Coca-Cola in Bottles," *Coca-Cola Bottler*, April 1959, 79; Mark Pendergrast, *For God, Country & Coca-Cola*, 47–53, 61, 65; Frederick Allen, *Secret Formula*, 37.

18 "Death of Asa G. Candler, Sr.," *Coca-Cola Bottler*, April 1929, 14; Charles Howard Candler, *Asa Griggs Candler*, 186.

19 The Coca-Cola Company was incorporated on January 29, 1892. Mark Pendergrast, *For God, Country & Coca-Cola*, 52, 57–58; Frederick Allen, *Secret Formula*, 39.

20 The formula for Coca-Cola called for "not less than one ounce of syrup to eight ounces of water." Bottling Contract between Coca-Cola Bottling Company and Alexandria Coca-Cola Bottling Company, January 21, 1910, quoted in *Coca-Cola Bottling Co. of Elizabethtown, Inc. v. Coca-Cola Co.*, 654 F. Supp. 1388, 1392 (D. Del. 1986); Mark Pendergrast, *For God, Country & Coca-Cola*, 62.

21 Display Ad, *Atlanta Constitution*, May 20, 1890, 2; Display Ad, *Atlanta Constitution*, November 29, 1896, C20.

22 Display Ad, *Atlanta Constitution*, March 26, 1886, 7; Mark Pendergrast, *For God, Country & Coca-Cola*, 14. The history of how Dr Pepper got its name is still up for debate. Tristan Donovan, *Fizz: How Soda Shook Up the World* (Chicago: Chicago Review Press, 2014), 69.

23 Deposition of Veazey Rainwater, June 3, 1920, *Coca-Cola Bottling Co. v. Coca-Cola Co.*, Fulton County Superior Court, 1920, quoted in Frederick Allen, *Secret Formula*, 68. Also quoted in Mark Pendergrast, *For God, Country & Coca-Cola*, 70.

24 "Joseph A. Biedenharn," *Coca-Cola Bottler*, April 1959, 95–97.

25 Biedenharn quoted in ibid., 95; Charles Elliott, *A Biography of the "Boss": Robert Winship Woodruff* (Robert W. Woodruff Estate, 1979), 111. In 1894, the Coca-Cola Company also began operating the first syrup-manufacturing plant outside of Atlanta in Dallas, Texas. Coca-Cola Company Public Relations Department, *Chronological History of the Coca-Cola Company* (Atlanta: Coca-Cola Company,

1971); "Early History of Coca-Cola Bottling," *Coca-Cola Bottler*, August 1944, 25; Franklin M. Garrett, "Coca-Cola in Bottles," *Coca-Cola Bottler*, April 1959, 79.

26 For an account of this early history of Coke bottling, see transcripts from *Coca-Cola Bottling Co. v. Coca-Cola Co.*, 269 F. 796, 800 (D. Del.1920); "Early History of Coca-Cola Bottling," *Coca-Cola Bottler*, August 1944, 25.

27 "Benjamin Franklin Thomas," *Coca-Cola Bottler*, April 1959, 85–86; "Joseph Brown Whitehead," *Coca-Cola Bottler*, April 1959, 87–88; Mark Pendergrast, *For God, Country & Coca-Cola*, 74–75; Frederick Allen, *Secret Formula*, 106. Again, transcripts from *Coca-Cola Bottling Co. v. Coca-Cola Co.*, 269 F. 796 (D. Del.1920) provide details about Whitehead's and Thomas's operations.

28 J. F. Curtis, "The Overseas Story," *Coca-Cola Overseas*, June 1948, 5; Frederick Allen, *Secret Formula*, 108.

29 Letter from Asa Candler to Charles Howard Candler, June 3, 1899, box 1, folder, 3, Asa Griggs Candler Papers, MARBL; Mark Pendergrast, *For God, Country & Coca-Cola*, 62, 89, 94; Frederick Allen, *Secret Formula*, 64.

30 Mark Pendergrast, *For God, Country & Coca-Cola*, 188.

31 Quoted in Charles Howard Candler, "Coca-Cola Company Bottling Company 50th Anniversary Address," November 21, 1950, box 15, folder 4, Charles Howard Candler Papers, MARBL; Charles Howard Candler, *Asa Griggs Candler*, 143; Mark Pendergrast, *For God, Country & Coca-Cola*, 80.

32 For the story of Roberts and other early Georgia bottlers, see Mike Cheatham,*"Your Friendly Neighbor": The Story of Georgia's Coca-Cola Bottling Families* (Macon, GA: Mercer University Press, 1999), 61, 65, 67, 71.

33 Mark Cheatham, *"Your Friendly Neighbor,"* 94; "Comparative Statement of Sales, Net Profits, and Net Profits per Case, for the Years Ending December 31, 1942, and December 31, 1941," box 1, folder 13, Central Coca-Cola Bottling Company (Richmond, Virginia) Manuscript Collection, Virginia Historical Society, Richmond. In 1928, bottled Coke sales topped fountain sales for the first time. Mark Pendergrast, *For God, Country & Coca-Cola*, 61–62, 79, 138, 501. For soft drink bottlers' average profit margins in 1921, see House Committee on Ways and Means, *Internal-Revenue Revision*, 67th Cong., 1st Sess., July 26–29, 1921, 220–221; Frederick Allen, *Secret Formula*, 109.

34 Mike Cheatham, *"Your Friendly Neighbor,"* 103–104; J. J. Willard, "Some Early History of Coca-Cola Bottling," *Coca-Cola Bottler*, August 1944, 27.

35 Revisionist historians interested in challenging the myth of corporate autogenesis have largely overlooked municipal public waterworks expansion in the Progressive Era as a critical state intervention that reduced supply-side costs for mass-marketing firms. Scholars that have examined government-funded hydrological projects in the Progressive Era have focused mainly on the federal projects run by the Bureau of Reclamation in the American West that contributed to the expansion of large-scale agribusiness in the region. Though perhaps not as visible as the federally supported large-scale damming projects and irrigation projects of the West, smaller, municipally financed water systems nonetheless proved critical for water-intensive industries that distributed inexpensive consumer goods all across the country in the early decades of the twentieth century. For examples of scholarship on federal water projects in the West and their influence on the growth of

American agribusiness, see Donald Worster, *Rivers of Empire: Water, Aridity, and the Growth of the American West* (1985; Oxford: Oxford University Press, 1992); Marc Reisner, *Cadillac Desert: The American West and Its Disappearing Water* (New York: Viking, 1986). For excellent revisionist work deconstructing the "myth of the weak American state" in the Progressive Era, see William J. Novak, "The Myth of the 'Weak' American State," 752–772; Martin J. Sklar, *The Corporate Reconstruction of American Capitalism, 1890–1916*; Gabriel Kolko, *The Triumph of Conservatism: A Reinterpretation of American History, 1900–1916*; James Weinstein, *The Corporate Ideal in the Liberal State, 1900–1918* (Boston: Beacon Press, 1968).

36 Joel A. Tarr and Patrick Gurian, "The First Federal Drinking Water Quality Standards and Their Evolution: A History from 1914 to 1974," in *Improving Regulation: Cases in Environment, Health, and Safety*, ed. Paul S. Fischbeck and R. Scott Farrow (Washington, DC: Resources for the Future, 2001), 46. For a discussion of municipal water supplies before the Gilded Age, see Maureen Ogle, "Water Supply, Waste Disposal, and the Culture of Privatism in the Mid-Nineteenth-Century American City," *Journal of Urban History* 25 (1999): 321–347; Michael Rawson, "The Nature of Water: Reform and the Antebellum Crusade for Municipal Water in Boston," *Environmental History* 9, no. 3 (July 2004): 411–445; Robin L. Einhorn, *Property Rules: Political Economy in Chicago, 1833–1872* (Chicago: University of Chicago Press, 1991); Ted Steinberg, *Nature Incorporated: Industrialization and the Waters of New England* (Cambridge: Cambridge University Press, 1991); Nelson Manfred Blake, *Water for the Cities: A History of the Urban Water Supply Problem in the United States* (Syracuse, NY: Syracuse University Press, 1956).

37 Martin Melosi, *The Sanitary City: Urban Infrastructure in America from Colonial Times to the Present* (Baltimore: Johns Hopkins University Press, 2000), 123, 120; Elizabeth Royte, *Bottlemania: How Water Went on Sale and Why We Bought It* (New York: Bloomsbury, 2008), 72.

38 Martin Melosi, *Sanitary City*, 153, 213; Tarr, "First Drinking Water," 52.

39 United States Department of Commerce, Bureau of the Census, *General Statistics of Cities: 1915: Including Statistics of Governmental Organizations, Police Departments, Liquor Traffic, and Municipally Owned Water Supply Systems, in Cities Having a Population of Over 30,000* (Washington, DC: USGPO, 1916), 41; Martin Melosi, *Sanitary City*, 140, 127; "Philadelphia Water," *Coca-Cola Bottler*, July 1909, 14; Ray F. Weirick, "The Park and Boulevard System of Kansas City, Mo.," *American City* 3 (November 1910): 212; John Ellis and Stuart Galishoff, "Atlanta's Water Supply, 1865–1918," *Maryland Historian* 8 (Spring 1977): 11–17; Atlanta Board of Water Commissioners, Annual Report of 1914, 18, quoted in John Ellis and Stuart Galishoff, "Atlanta's Water Supply," 5.

40 Martin Melosi, *Sanitary City*, 244, 460; "War Burdens of Water-Works in the United States," *American City* 19 (September 1918): 193; Joel Tarr, "The Evolution of Urban Infrastructure in the Nineteenth and Twentieth Centuries," in *Perspectives on the Urban Infrastructure*, ed. Royce Hanson (Washington, DC: National Academy Press, 1984), 8, 18. The trade coverage of municipal water supplies was not always glowing. The *National Bottlers' Gazette*, for example, exclaimed in 1922, "Bottlers in cities or towns—who use the general water supply—should be insistent and persistent with the authorities in control of the public water works system

to have reliable chemical analyses made at least once a month for the better protection of all." W. W. Skinner, "Beverage and Beverage Flavor: Their Federal and
State Control," *National Bottlers' Gazette*, July 15, 1922, 88; United States Department of Commerce, Bureau of the Census, *General Statistics of Cities: 1915*, 44, 148,
154; Annual Report of the Surgeon General of the Public Health Service of the
United States (Washington, DC: USGPO, 1915), 108.

41 Constance Hays, *The Real Thing*, 11; "Meters Called Best Route to Filtered Water,"
Chicago Daily Tribune, February 12, 1925, 6; "Planning New Mains," *Washington
Post*, October 6, 1911, 14; Niva Kramek and Lydia Loh, *The History of Philadelphia's
Water Supply and Sanitation System: Lessons in Sustainability for Developing Urban
Water Systems* (Philadelphia: Philadelphia Global Water Initiative, June 2007), 28;
"Industry Esteem Reflected in City Rates for Water," *Los Angeles Times*, August
30, 1973, SE1. The .01 figure is a conservative estimate and reflects a thorough
survey of metered rates for cities over 30,000 people in 1915. Data sourced from
United States Department of Commerce, Bureau of the Census, *General Statistics of
Cities: 1915*, 158–164. In 1917, John Candler reported that the average bottler spent
half a cent per case on "water, power," and other miscellaneous utility expenses.
The fact that these costs were bundled shows how inconsequential Coca-Cola considered water costs. This estimate, however, was given in testimony to the US
Senate with the intent of dissuading congressmen from supporting a soda tax, so
the figure is almost assuredly high. United States Senate Committee on Finance,
Revenue to Defray War Expenses, 65th Cong., 1st Sess., May 11, 1917, 131.

42 Coca-Cola Company 1923 Annual Report, 15.

43 On state financing of national railroad networks in the Progressive Era, see Richard White, *Railroaded: The Transcontinentals and the Making of Modern America*.
Coke paid for freight associated with shipping syrup, although an amended contract signed in 1921 would require bottlers to pay shipping costs for advertising
purchased from the Coca-Cola Company. Freight rates varied across the country,
but in 1917, John Candler, Asa Candler's brother and attorney for the Coca-Cola
Company, reported to the Senate Committee on Finance that the company spent
on average 7 cents per gallon shipping syrup. This statistic may be inflated, as
John Candler was trying to show that costs were spiraling out of control and that
a new proposed tax would be devastating to the industry. United States Senate
Committee on Finance, *Revenue to Defray War Expenses*, 65th Cong., 1st Sess., May
11, 1917, 128; Coca-Cola Company Annual Reports, 1920–1923.

44 Chart of Coca-Cola's Gallon Sales, Grand Consolidated (The Coca-Cola Co. and
Its Subsidiaries), undated, box 22, folder 14, Mark Pendergrast Research Files,
MARBL; Coca-Cola Company 1920 Annual Report, 14–18; Coca-Cola Company
1923 Annual Report, 15, 18–19.

45 Candler had planned to turn over the company to Howard for several years. In
1908, he wrote to Howard, "As soon as I can lay this Coca-Cola business on your
shoulders I intend to do it. I want you therefore to learn it thoroughly." Letter
from Asa Candler to Charles Howard Candler, July 27, 1908, box 1, folder 7. In a
letter to his brother Warren, Asa Candler announced his intentions for retirement,
ending his letter saying, "Money is not meant to be hoarded." Letter from Asa
Candler to Warren Candler, January 13, 1913, box 1, folder 8, Asa Griggs Candler

Papers, MARBL; Memorandum from Asa G. Candler Announcing Retirement, February 1, 1916, box 3, folder 1, Charles Howard Candler Papers, MARBL; Mark Pendergrast, *For God, Country & Coca-Cola*, 126.

46 Quoted in Mark Pendergrast, *For God, Country & Coca-Cola*, 127.

47 Letter from Charles Howard Candler to Asa Candler, March 12, 1903, box 1, folder 6, Asa Griggs Candler Papers, MARBL; Frederick Allen, *Secret Formula*, 54.

48 Letter re: Memorial to Mr. S. C. Dobbs, from Hughes Spalding to Robert W. Woodruff, with attachment, November 7, 1950, box 73, folder 3, RWW Papers, MARBL; Frederick Allen, *Secret Formula*, 79–83, 91; Mark Pendergrast, *For God, Country & Coca-Cola*, 52.

49 Frederick Allen, *Secret Formula*, 92–93.

50 Mark Pendergrast, *For God, Country & Coca-Cola*, 130–131.

51 Ibid.; "KO Stock Year-End Market Value Since 1919," box 43, folder 1, Joseph W. Jones Papers, MARBL.

52 Letter from Asa Candler to Charles Howard Candler, September 11, 1919, box 3, folder 1, Charles Howard Candler Papers, MARBL; Frederick Allen, *Secret Formula*, 100; Mark Pendergrast, *For God, Country & Coca-Cola*, 131–134.

53 Mark Pendergrast, *For God, Country & Coca-Cola*, 135–136; Frederick Allen, *Secret Formula*, 108–110.

54 Mark Pendergrast, *For God, Country & Coca-Cola*, 138.

55 Frederick Allen, *Secret Formula*, 108–110.

56 Ibid., 118–119, 127; "KO Stock Year-End Market Value Since 1919," box 43, folder 1, Joseph W. Jones Papers, MARBL; Mark Pendergrast, *For God, Country & Coca-Cola*, 139–142.

57 For a biography of Robert W. Woodruff written by his good friend Charles Elliott, see *A Biography of the "Boss"*; Employee History for Robert W. Woodruff, Coca-Cola Company and Domestic Subsidiary Companies, March 17, 1960, box 358, folder 6; Letter from William R. Brewster Jr., President of Georgia Military Academy, to Mrs. Lucille Huffman, Secretary to Mr. Robert W. Woodruff, September 7, 1962, box 358, folder 6; Letter from J. William Pruett to J. W. Jones, Subject: R. W. Woodruff—Biography, with attached biographical sketch, box 358, folder 6; RWW Papers, MARBL; "KO Stock Year-End Market Value Since 1919," box 43, folder 1, Joseph W. Jones Papers, MARBL; Robert Woodruff quoted in Mark Pendergrast, *For God, Country & Coca-Cola*, 153–154.

58 Quoted in Mark Pendergrast, *For God, Country & Coca-Cola*, 152.

59 *National Carbonator and Bottler*, June 15, 1932, 19; *Southern Carbonator and Bottler*, May 1922, 54; *Southern Carbonator and Bottler*, August 1926, 65; Martin Melosi, *Sanitary City*, 144. Even as chlorine became popular in many municipalities, only one-third of waterworks in the United States used the chemical in treatment processes as late as 1939. Melosi, *Sanitary City*, 223.

60 *National Carbonator and Bottler*, February 15, 1937, 32.

61 Letter from Paul Austin to Robert W. Woodruff, November 28, 1969, box 16, folder 1, RWW Papers, MARBL.

62 "The Quest for Quality Never Ends," *Coca-Cola Bottler*, April 1959, 165–166; Charles Elliott, *A Biography of the "Boss,"* 130; Martin Melosi, *Sanitary City*, 224.

63 *National Carbonator and Bottler*, November 15, 1937, 71.

64 Bert Wells, Chemist, Chemical Control Department, Coca-Cola Company, "Traveling Laboratory Control of Bottlers' Operation," *Journal of the American Waterworks Association* 34, no. 7 (July 1942): 1035–1041; "Mobile Labs Guard Product Quality," *Refresher*, June 1954, 19–21; Charles Elliott, *A Biography of the "Boss,"* 131.

65 Martin Melosi, *Sanitary City*, 240, 218, 213, 137.

66 "The Quest for Quality Never Ends," *Coca-Cola Bottler*, April 1959, 167; Memorandum from C. R. Bender dated July 22, 1957, box 123, folder 4, RWW Papers, MARBL. In 1950, the *Coca-Cola Bottler* commented on the soft drink industry's dependence on municipal water supplies, explaining that the industry used "about six and a quarter billion gallons of water" from municipalities each year with approximately twelve bottling plants within the country using "as much as 50,000,000 gallons of water a year" or "about as much as used by a town of 2500 inhabitants." "Processing Water for the Carbonated Beverage Industry," *Coca-Cola Bottler*, January 1950, 42.

67 "Statement of Income, Profit, and Loss for All Plants: January 1, 1951 to December 31, 1951," box 1, folder 22, Central Coca-Cola Bottling Company (Richmond, Virginia) Manuscript Collection, Virginia Historical Society, Richmond.

68 "Processing Water for the Carbonated Beverage Industry," *Coca-Cola Bottler*, January 1950, 42; "The Overseas Story," *Coca-Cola Overseas*, June 1948, 5; Frederick Allen, *Secret Formula*, 108.

69 "Statement of Income, Profit, and Loss for All Plants: January 1, 1944 to December 30, 1944," and "Comparative Statement of Sales, Net Profits, and Net Profits Per Case, For the Years Ending December 30, 1944, and December 31, 1943," box 1, folder 15, Central Coca-Cola Bottling Company (Richmond, Virginia) Manuscript Collection, Virginia Historical Society, Richmond.

2. WASTE TEA LEAVES: RECYCLING CAFFEINE FOUND IN OTHER INDUSTRIES' TRASH

1 Paper presented by Dr. John S. Pemberton, "Essay on Guarana, Caffeine, and Coca," Proceedings of the Twelfth Annual Meeting of the Georgia Pharmaceutical Association, April 1887, box 14, folder 1, Mark Pendergrast Research Files, MARBL; Mark Pendergrast, *For God, Country & Coca-Cola*, 29. The *New York Times* claimed that kola nut extract was "superseding all stimulants in medical practice" in November of 1895. "That Nut from Africa," *New York Times*, November 3, 1895, 11; Edmund Abaka, *"Kola Is God's Gift": Agricultural Production, Export Initiatives, and the Kola Industry of Asante and the Gold Coast c. 1820–1950* (Athens: Ohio University Press, 2005), 85. Seventy years after Pemberton created the secret formula, Coca-Cola executives Benjamin Oehlert and Ed Forio explained to the FDA why Coke chose to use other sources of caffeine for its product, claiming "caffeine from sources other than cola nut, such as chocolate and coffee, is readily available on an economical basis, whereas the derivation of all of the caffeine from cola nuts, which are in relatively short supply, would be an expensive process and would cause substantial economic waste." Letter from Ed Forio and Benjamin Oehlert to George Larrick, July 21, 1965, box 243, folder 2, RWW Papers, MARBL.

2 George B. Kauffman, Professor of Pharmacology, Ohio State University, "Phar-

macology of Caffeine," *Merck's Archives of Materia Medica and Drug Therapy* 3, no. 10 (October 1901): 394. Other industries at the time recognized the value of recycling other types of wastes, not just broken tea leaves, to produce new products. See George Powell Perry, *Wealth from Waste; or, Gathering Up the Fragments* (New York: F. H. Revell, 1908) and Henry J. Spooner, *Wealth from Waste: Elimination of Waste a World Problem* (London: G. Routledge and Sons, 1918).

3 "Dr. Louis Schaeffer," *American Perfumer and Essential Oil Review* 7, no. 10 (December 1912): 246; Edward S. Kaminski, *Maywood: The Borough, the Railroad, and the Station* (Charleston, SC: Arcadia Publishing, 2010), 8.

4 House Committee on Ways and Means, *Tariff Hearings, 1896–97, Vol. 1*, 54th Cong., 2nd Sess., December 28, 30, 31, 1896, and January 4, 5, 8, 9, 11, 1897, 133–134; Patricia J. B. DeWitt, "A Brief History of Tea: The Rise and Fall of the Tea Importation Act" (Third Year Writing Requirement, Harvard Law School, 2000), 32.

5 For a history of the Monsanto Company written by a former public relations executive at the corporation, see Dan J. Forrestal, *Faith, Hope and $5,000: The Story of Monsanto* (New York: Simon and Schuster, 1977). For Monsanto's acknowledgment of Coke's early help, see http://www.monsanto.com/whoweare/Pages/monsanto -history.aspx; "P.S. Just Got Our Special on Monday," undated document, series 3, box 1, Caffeine (General), Monsanto Company Records, 1901–2008, University Archives, Department of Special Collections, Washington University Libraries, St. Louis, MO (hereinafter Monsanto Company Records).

6 "Early Days," undated document; "Caffeine," undated document, series 3, box 1, Caffeine (General), Monsanto Company Records.

7 Senate Committee on Finance, *Schedule A: Duties on Chemicals, Oils, and Paints*, 62nd Cong., 2nd Sess., March 14, 15, 19,–22, 1912, 36; "Caffeine," undated document, series 3, box 1, Caffeine (General), Monsanto Company Records; Frederick Allen, *Secret Formula*, 90.

8 Mark Pendergrast, *Uncommon Grounds: The History of Coffee and How It Transformed Our World* (New York: Basic Books, 1999), 107; Richard Tucker, *Insatiable Appetite*, 181. Steven Topik, "Historicizing Commodity Chains: Five Hundred Years of the Global Coffee Commodity Chain," in *Frontiers of Commodity Chain Research*, ed. Jennifer Blair (Stanford: Stanford University Press, 2009), 50; United States Government Printing Office, *Summary of Tariff Information*, prepared for the Use of the Committee on Ways and Means, United States House of Representatives (Washington, DC: USGPO, 1920), 798. Journalist Murray Carpenter aptly notes that coffee was also more popular than tea in the United States because it was easier to attain from nearby producers. See Murray Carpenter, *Caffeinated: How Our Daily Habit Helps, Hurts, and Hooks Us* (New York: Hudson Street Press, 2014), 34. Carpenter's book was published as *Citizen Coke* was going to print in 2014.

9 "Like Opium Eaters, Coffee Drinkers Become Slaves," *Washington Post*, October 27, 1900, 10; "Postum," *New York Times*, October 4, 1904, 5.

10 "'Dope' Bill Defeated," *Washington Post*, January 26, 1907, 13; "Bills Favorably Reported," *Washington Post*, January 15, 1907, 13; "Bills Prohibits [*sic*] Sale of Coca-Cola," *Atlanta Constitution*, August 16, 1909, 4; "Texas House Proceedings," *Dallas Morning News*, February 27, 1909; "Many New Bills in House," *Charlotte Observer*, January 26, 1909; "The Week's News," *Cincinnati Lancet-Clinic*, July 9,

1910, 30; "Judge Stark's Bill Would Include Soft Drinks in Anti-Shipping Bill," *Macon Telegraph* (Macon, GA), November 16, 1915; "Fight on Sale of Coca-Cola in Georgia Is on in Assembly," *Macon Telegraph*, July 15, 1919; "Possible Coca-Cola May Be Barred," *Daily Herald* (Biloxi, MS), February 24, 1911.

11 "Texas House Proceedings," *Dallas Morning News*, February 27, 1909.

12 Letter from Asa Candler, January 18, 1907, box 4, folder F, James L. Fleming Papers, Collection No. 437, East Carolina Manuscript Collection, J. Y. Joyner Library, East Carolina University, Greenville, NC.

13 This analysis builds on historian Benjamin Cohen's work on food adulteration in the late nineteenth century. Cohen contended that "the environmental challenge of distance between producers and consumers was a cultural challenge of knowledge, character and ideas about authenticity from nature." Separated from the sites of food production, consumers increasingly saw chemists and nutritional scientists as the ultimate arbiters of food purity. Benjamin R. Cohen, "Analysis as a Border Patrol: Chemists Along the Boundary Between Pure Food and Real Adulteration," *Endeavor* 35 (2011), 3. See also James Harvey Young, *Pure Food: Securing the Federal Food and Drugs Act of 1906* (Princeton: Princeton University Press, 1989), 66.

14 Pure Food and Drug Act of 1906, sec. 7. Wiley did suggest that not all food products found in nature should be considered beneficial to human health. In a letter to Coke president Asa Candler in February of 1907, for example, Wiley criticized Candler for suggesting that caffeine was harmless simply because it existed in tea and coffee, arguing, "You might as well say that hydrocyanic acid is harmless because it occurs in peaches and almonds." Quoted in Mark Pendergrast, *For God, Country & Coca-Cola*, 111.

15 "Is The Drinking of Tea or Coffee Harmful to Health?," *New York Times*, September 15, 1912, SM11.

16 Mark Pendergrast, *For God, Country & Coca-Cola*, 115.

17 Harvey Wiley, *Harvey W. Wiley: An Autobiography* (Indianapolis, IN: Bobbs-Merrill, 1930), 2.

18 "Claims Coca-Cola Unsanitary," *Montgomery Advertiser*, March 14, 1911, 12; "The Caffeine in Eight Coca-Colas Would Kill If Concentrated in One Dose, Says an Expert on the Witness Stand," *Columbus Daily Enquirer* (Columbus, GA), March 19, 1911, 1; "Coca-Cola on Trial," *Times-Picayune* (New Orleans, LA), March 14, 1911, 9; "Coca-Cola Wins Fight," *Charlotte Daily Observer*, April 7, 1911; "Coca-Cola Wins in Government Suit," *American Druggist and Pharmaceutical Record*, April 24, 1911, 45.

19 Mark Pendergrast, *For God, Country & Coca-Cola*, 118.

20 Transcript of Testimony at 25, *United States v. Forty Barrels and Twenty Kegs of Coca-Cola*, 191 F. 431 (E.D. Tenn. 1911).

21 Mark Pendergrast, *For God, Country & Coca-Cola*, 102–104; Frederick Allen, *Secret Formula*, 78.

22 Transcript of Testimony at 48–57, *United States v. Forty Barrels and Twenty Kegs of Coca-Cola*, 191 F. 431 (E.D. Tenn. 1911).

23 Ibid., 499, 562.

24 Ibid., 541; Frederick Allen, *Secret Formula*, 60.

25 Transcript of Testimony at 3037, *United States v. Forty Barrels and Twenty Kegs of Coca-Cola*, 191 F. 431 (E.D. Tenn. 1911).

26 Ibid., 3179, 3184–3185.

27 "Coca-Cola's Victory Was Very Sweeping," *Columbus Daily Enquirer*, April 9, 1911; *Daily Oklahoman*, February 18, 1913; Display Ad, *Chicago Daily Tribune*, May 12, 1912, D4; Display Ad, *New York Times*, May 16, 1912, 8.

28 *United States v. Forty Barrels and Twenty Kegs of Coca-Cola*, 241 U.S. 265, 284–285, 276 (1916); Frederick Allen, *Secret Formula*, 84.

29 United States Government Printing Office, *Summary of Tariff Information*, 30; Senate Committee on Finance, *Tariff Act of 1921, Vol. 2: Schedule 1: Chemicals, Oils, and Paints; Schedule 2: Earths, Earthenware, and Glassware*, 67th Cong., 2nd Sess., 1921, 886, 898.

30 Senate Committee on Finance, *Schedule A: Duties on Chemicals, Oils, and Paints*, 62nd Cong., 2nd Sess., March 14, 15, 19,–22, 1912, 36; "Caffeine," undated and untitled Monsanto Company document, series 3, box 1, Caffeine (General), Monsanto Company Records; Dobbs quoted in Frederick Allen, *Secret Formula*, 88.

31 Frederick Allen, *Secret Formula*, 90; Murray Carpenter, *Caffeinated*, 5.

32 Mark Pendergrast, *For God, Country & Coca-Cola*, 102; Letter from Samuel C. Dobbs to Robert W. Woodruff regarding Hirsch's courtroom tenacity, May 4, 1937, box 73, folder 3, RWW Papers, MARBL.

33 *Coca-Cola Co. v. Koke Co. of Am.*, 235 F. 408, 414 (D. Ariz. 1916); *Coca-Cola Co. v. Koke Co. of Am.*, 254 U.S. 143, 145 (1920).

34 *Koke Co. of Am. v. Coca-Cola Co.*, 255 F. 894, 896 (9th Cir. 1919).

35 Humphrey McQueen, *The Essence of Capitalism: The Origins of Our Future* (Montreal: Black Rose Books, 2003), 185.

36 Frederick Allen, *Secret Formula*, 86–87, 123.

37 Humphrey McQueen, *The Essence of Capitalism*, 185; Mark Pendergrast, *For God, Country & Coca-Cola*, 130.

38 *Coca-Cola Co. v. Koke Co. of Am.*, 254 U.S. 143 (1920), Petitioner's Brief, 39, 67, 28.

39 *Coca-Cola Co. v. Koke Co. of Am.*, 254 U.S. 143, 146 (1920).

40 Coca-Cola Company, *Opinions, Orders, Injunctions, and Decrees Relating to Unfair Competition and Infringement of Trade-mark* (Atlanta, 1923, 1939); Coca-Cola Company 1935 Annual Report, 3.

41 David S. Clark, "Adjudication to Administration: A Statistical Analysis of Federal District Courts in the Twentieth Century," *Southern California Law Review* 55 (1981–1982), 69–72; Justice Swayne statement quoted in Morton J. Horwitz, *The Transformation of American Law, 1870–1960: The Crisis of Legal Orthodoxy* (New York: Oxford University Press, 1992), 145. For excellent histories of the American legal system during the nineteenth and early twentieth centuries, see also Lawrence M. Friedman, *A History of American Law* (New York: Simon and Schuster, 1973), and Lawrence M. Friedman, *American Law in the Twentieth Century* (New Haven: Yale University Press, 2002).

3. SUGAR: SATIATING CITIZEN CANE'S SWEET APPETITE

1 M. Lenoir, F. Serre, L. Cantin, S. H. Ahmed, "Intense Sweetness Surpasses Cocaine Reward," *PLoS ONE* 2, no. 8 (August 2007): 1. In a related article on

sugar addiction, researchers at Princeton University concluded that "sugar is noteworthy as a substance that releases opioids and dopamine and thus might be expected to have addictive potential." N. M. Avena, P. Rada, and B. G. Hoebel, "Evidence for Sugar Addiction: Behavioral and Neurochemical Effects of Intermittent, Excessive Sugar Intake," *Neuroscience and Biobehavioral Reviews* 32, no. 1 (2008): 20.

2 Frederick Allen, *Secret Formula*, 104. On the effects of phosphoric acid on sweetness, see Giora Agam, *Industrial Chemicals: Their Characteristics and Development* (Amsterdam: Elsevier, 1994), 54; W. H. Waggaman, "Welcome, Little Fizz Water," *Collier's Weekly* 65, January 17, 1920, 22; B. Taylor, "Acids, Colours, Preservatives, and Other Additives," in *Formulation and Production of Carbonated Soft Drinks*, ed. A. J. Mitchell (Glasgow: Blackie, 1990), 92. In 2006, the Department of Transportation issued a Notice of Probable Violation to Coca-Cola Enterprises Inc. for improperly shipping "hazardous materials—Corrosive Liquids, Acidic, Organic, n.o.s. (citric acid solution), 8, UN 3265, III; and Phosphoric Acid, Liquid, 8, UN 1805, III." United States Department of Transportation, Pipeline and Hazardous Materials Safety Administration (PHMSA), Notice of Probable Violation to Respondent, Coca-Cola Enterprises, Docket #PHMSA-2006-24464, April 1, 2006.

3 Daniel Levy and Andrew T. Young, "'The Real Thing': Nominal Price Rigidity of the Nickel Coke, 1886–1959," *Journal of Money, Credit and Banking* 36, no. 4 (August 2004): 768–769; Letter from Ralph Hayes to Robert Woodruff, October 22, 1951, box 138, folder 2, RWW Papers, MARBL.

4 Anthropologist Sidney Mintz explained the rise of sugar's popularity in *Sweetness and Power: The Place of Sugar in Modern History* (New York: Penguin Books, 1985); Sidney L. Mintz, "Sweet, Salt, and the Language of Love," *MLN* 106, no. 4 (September 1981): 853; Sidney L. Mintz, *Sweetness and Power*, 31; Richard Tucker, *Insatiable Appetite*, 16–17. Other excellent works that examine the cultural history of sugar cultivation and consumption over the longue durée include Elizabeth Abbott's *Sugar: A Bittersweet History* (London; New York: Duckworth Publishers, 2009); Peter Macinnis's *Bittersweet: The Story of Sugar* (St. Leonards, New South Wales: Allen and Unwin, 2002); and J. H. Galloway's *The Sugar Cane Industry: An Historical Geography from Its Origins to 1914* (Cambridge: Cambridge University Press, 1989); on the vertical integration of the American sugar-refining industry in the nineteenth century, see César J. Ayala, *American Sugar Kingdom: The Plantation Economy of the Spanish Caribbean, 1898–1934* (Chapel Hill: University of North Carolina Press, 1999).

5 On slavery and sugar, see David Brion Davis, *Inhuman Bondage: The Rise and Fall of Slavery in the New World* (Oxford: Oxford University Press, 2006). See also Ira Berlin, *Generations of Captivity: A History of African-American Slaves* (Cambridge: Belknap Press of Harvard University Press, 2003); Ira Berlin, *Many Thousands Gone: The First Two Centuries of Slavery in North America* (Cambridge: Belknap Press of Harvard University Press, 1998); W. R. Aykroyd, *Sweet Malefactor: Sugar, Slavery, and Human Society* (London: Heinemann, 1967). On the ecological costs of sugarcane cultivation, see Richard Tucker, *Insatiable Appetite: The United States and the Ecological Degradation of the Tropical World*, 15–63.

6   Sidney Mintz, *Sweetness and Power*, 148, 180.

7   US Department of Agriculture, Economic Statistics and Cooperative Service, *A History of Sugar Marketing Through 1974* (hereinafter USDA, *A History of Sugar Marketing*), Agricultural Economic Report No. 382, prepared by Roy A. Ballinger (Washington, DC: March 1978), 6.

8   César J. Ayala provided an excellent chart of raw versus refined sugar duties from 1789 to 1861 in *American Sugar Kingdom*, 49; "The Sugar Refiners' Trust," *New York Times*, October 13, 1887, 8; César J. Ayala, *American Sugar Kingdom*, 50.

9   Richard Zerbe, "The American Sugar Refinery Company, 1887–1914: The Story of a Monopoly," *Journal of Law and Economics* 12, no. 2 (October 1969): 340; John N. Ingham, *Biographical Dictionary of American Business Leaders*, vol. 2 (Westport, CT: Greenwood Press, 1983), 559; USDA, *A History of Sugar Marketing*, 11.

10   "A Strike for Eight Hours; Havemeyers & Elder Lose Their Firemen and Boilermen," *New York Times*, June 15, 1893, 1.

11   Richard Zerbe, "The American Sugar Refining Company, 1887–1914," 350–351.

12   *People v. North River Sugar Refining Co.*, 24 N.E. 839 (N.Y., 1890); César J. Ayala, *American Sugar Kingdom*, 39; Richard Zerbe, "The American Sugar Refining Company, 1887–1914," 354.

13   Brian Balogh, *A Government out of Sight*, 329–331.

14   The McKinley Tariff, enacted in 1890, removed the duty on imported raw sugar, established a duty of half a cent per pound on all imported refined sugar, and established a 2-cent-per-pound bounty—direct subsidy—for domestic sugar growers (which at this point were still mainly Louisiana cane growers but also included a small cohort of beet farmers in California and other regions of the American West and Midwest). The shift in policy, in part a response to a series of government surpluses that had accumulated over the past couple of years, allowed American Sugar Refining Company to purchase sugar at record low prices. After 1894, when hard economic times forced the government to look for new revenues, Congress would reinstate a small duty on raw sugar, but the protection on US refined sugar would remain. USDA, *A History of Sugar Marketing*, 11; Richard Zerbe, "The American Sugar Refining Company, 1887–1914," 341. As tariff historian Frank William Taussig explained, "With a barrier against foreign competitors such as the tariff of 1890 gave, the profits were enormous." Frank William Taussig, *The Tariff History of the United States* (New York: G. P. Putnam's Sons, 1914), 312.

15   Thomas J. Heston, *Sweet Subsidy*, 48–50; Lippert S. Ellis, *The Tariff on Sugar* (Freeport, IL: Rawleigh Foundation, 1933), 44–46; USDA, *A History of Sugar Marketing*, 12; César J. Ayala, *American Sugar Kingdom*, 37.

16   Bill Albert and Adrian Graves, eds., *The World Sugar Economy in War and Depression, 1914–1940* (London and New York: Routledge, 1988), 1; Thomas J. Heston, *Sweet Subsidy: The Economic and Diplomatic Effects of the U.S. Sugar Acts, 1934–1974* (New York and London: Garland, 1987), 31.

17   Describing the relationship between Revere and the American Sugar Refining Company, historian César Ayala asserted, "The one independent refinery in the United States, the Revere Refinery in Boston, worked harmoniously with the

trust and was, through the brokerage house of Nash, Spaulding, and Company, the largest minority holder of American Sugar Refining Company stock. It cannot be called an independent refinery." César J. Ayala, *American Sugar Kingdom*, 37; Charles Howard Candler, *Asa Griggs Candler* (Atlanta: Emory University 1950), 113. Speaking of Revere's relationship to American, the *New York Times* reported in January of 1892 that the Boston refinery "has been an ally rather than a competitor" of the Sugar Trust. "The Sugar Trust," *New York Times*, January 15, 1892, 4. The 300,000 reflects Coke syrup gallon sales of 76,224 for 1895 and is an extremely conservative estimate. For gallon sales, see Chart of Coca-Cola's Gallon Sales, Grand Consolidated (The Coca-Cola Co. and Its Subsidiaries), undated, box 22, folder 14, Mark Pendergrast Research Files, MARBL.

18 In 1935, an insurance company reporting on Coke's sleek business structure would comment, "As the manufacturing process is very simple, overhead costs are low. Labor is largely unskilled and is a very small cost in relation to sales." Letter from William T. Dorsey to Bernard M. Culiver, September 23, 1938, box 371, folder 13, RWW Papers, MARBL; Frederick Allen, *Secret Formula*, 69. See photo of Coca-Cola employees, 1899, middle insert herein.

19 USDA, *A History of Sugar Marketing*, 9; Richard Tucker, *Insatiable Appetite*, 40–41. Though the Spanish crown officially ceded the Philippines and Puerto Rico to the United States under the Treaty of Paris, it did not allow for Cuba's annexation. Nonetheless, under the Teller Amendment and later the Pratt Amendment, the US government continued to hold significant control over the Caribbean island up through the beginning of the 1930s.

20 For the seminal work on this shift toward an expansionist foreign policy, see Walter LaFeber, *The New Empire: An Interpretation of American Expansion, 1860–1898* (Ithaca: Cornell University Press, 1963).

21 USDA, *A History of Sugar Marketing*, 18; César J. Ayala, *American Sugar Kingdom*, 83–84, 120, 100, 76, 217, 218.

22 Earl Babst, *A Century of Sugar Refining in the United States* (New York: De Vinne Press, 1916), 15–17.

23 Richard Tucker, *Insatiable Appetite*, 41; John N. Ingham, *Biographical Dictionary of American Business Leaders*, 559.

24 "Sugar Position as of March 9, 1928," Sugar Inventory and Commitments Balance Sheet, box 58, folder 5, RWW Papers, MARBL; *Sugar Institute, Inc. v. United States*, 297 U.S. 553 (1936), Transcript of Record, 969; Frederick Allen, *Secret Formula*, 104.

25 USDA, *A History of Sugar Marketing*, 21–22; Frederick Allen, *Secret Formula*, 104; Michael Blanding, *The Coke Machine*, 43; "Making a Soldier of Sugar," internal company memorandum, unknown date, box 58, folder 6, RWW Papers, MARBL.

26 Pendergrast, *For God, Country & Coca-Cola*, 127–128; "Making a Soldier of Sugar," internal company memorandum, box 58, folder 6, RWW Papers, MARBL; Blanding, *The Coke Machine*, 25; Frederick Allen, *Secret Formula*, 90, 104. As Frederick Allen noted, "The episode was a foreshadowing of the strategy that would serve Coca-Cola so well during World War II: Lobby furiously behind the scenes, give

in gracefully when the cause is lost, and be sure to associate the product with the highest national interest." Frederick Allen, *Secret Formula*, 89–90.

27 John E. Dalton, *Sugar: A Case Study of Government Control* (New York: Macmillan, 1937), 59; Daniel Levy and Andrew T. Young, "'The Real Thing,'" 773; Mark Pendergrast, *For God, Country & Coca-Cola*, 137–139, 142.

28 Mark Pendergrast, *For God, Country & Coca-Cola*, 188.

29 "Coca-Cola Co. Amplifies Its '20 Statement," *Atlanta Georgian*, February 24, 1921, cited in Mark Pendergrast, *For God, Country & Coca-Cola*, 139; J. C. Louis and Harvey Z. Yazijian, *The Cola Wars* (New York: Everest House, 1980), 49; Michael Blanding, *The Coke Machine*, 53.

30 For an excellent history of the Hershey Chocolate Company, see Michael D'Antonio, *Hershey: Milton S. Hershey's Extraordinary Life of Wealth, Empire, and Utopian Dreams* (New York: Simon and Schuster, 2006), 130, 174.

31 Ibid., 128–32.

32 Ibid., 160–165.

33 "Seeing Hershey, Cuba, with Mr. M. S. Hershey," *Hershey Press News*, April 12, 1923, 1 (complete copies of these newspapers can be found in the Hershey Community Archives, Hershey Online Collection); Oral History Interview with James E. Bobb, March 22, 2001, 2001OHO1, 11, Hershey Community Archives Oral History Collection, Hershey, PA. On the wartime pressures that spurred Hershey to action, see James D. McMahon Jr., *Built on Chocolate: The Story of the Hershey Chocolate Company* (Santa Monica, CA: General Publishing Group, 1998), 82. It should be noted that in 1899 Warren Candler, Asa Candler's brother, also founded a Methodist school in Cuba that came to be known as Candler College. See www.candlercollege.org.

34 Hershey Chocolate Corporation 1920 Annual Report, 2; "Seeing Hershey, Cuba, with Mr. M. S. Hershey," *Hershey Press News*, April 12, 1923, 1; Michael D'Antonio, *Hershey*, 163, 167–168.

35 Thomas R. Winpenny, "Milton S. Hershey Ventures into Cuban Sugar," *Pennsylvania History* 62, no. 4 (Fall 1995): 492, 494–495.

36 "Seeing Hershey, Cuba, with Mr. M. S. Hershey," *Hershey News Press*, April 12, 1923, 1.

37 *Coca-Cola Bottling Co. of Elizabethtown, Inc. v. Coca-Cola*, 988 F.2d 386 (1993).

38 Address by William E. Robinson, President of the Coca-Cola Company, at a meeting of the New York Society of Security Analysts, January 12, 1956, box 3, folder 5, Mark Pendergrast Research Files, MARBL; Mark Pendergrast, *For God, Country & Coca-Cola*, 197.

39 "Sugar Position as of March 9, 1928," Sugar Inventory and Commitments Balance Sheet, box 58, folder 5, RWW Papers, MARBL. Howard Candler did approve the experimental construction of sugar-refining infrastructure at company syrup plants in the early 1920s, another rare instance of vertical integration. The paper trail is thin, but it seems the goal was to find a way to process raw sugar directly into syrup, using a new purification technique known as the "Norit process." Newspapers reported in 1920, 1921, and 1922 that construction of on-site refineries had begun in Atlanta, Baltimore, and Boston, with other reports suggesting that similar "experimental" expansions were taking place at the company's syrup

factory in Havana, Cuba, but little seems to have come of these projects in the long run. Whatever the case may be, Coke continued to buy its sugar from independently owned refineries in the 1920s. For discussion of Coke's experiments with the Norit process, see the comments of Judge Murray M. Schwartz in the 1986 suit led by Coke bottlers against the Coca-Cola Company: "The 'Norit process,' under development by the company" in the 1920s "produced a 'water-white' syrup directly from raw sugar. The process was experimental . . . and was apparently unsuccessful and never utilized." *Coca-Cola Bottling Co. of Elizabethtown, Inc. v. Coca-Cola Co.*, 654 F. Supp. 1388 (D. Del. 1986); "Coca-Cola to Build in Boston," *Wall Street Journal*, January 6, 1922, 3; "New Sugar Refineries in Operation and Additional Expansion Contemplated," *Chemical and Metallurgical Engineering* 26, no. 4 (January 25, 1922): 182; "Own Sugar Refinery Operated," *American Bottler* 41, no. 4 (May 1921): 14; "Large Scale Sugar Users Seek to Assure Supply," *Facts About Sugar* 10, no. 4 (January 24, 1920): 1.

40 "KO Stock Year-End Market Value Since 1919," box 43, folder 1, Joseph W. Jones Papers, MARBL; Coca-Cola Company Annual Reports, 1922–1929; Mark Pendergrast, *For God, Country & Coca-Cola*, 157, 170; Frederick Allen, *Secret Formula*, 177.

41 Mark Pendergrast, *For God, Country & Coca-Cola*, 159–160.

42 Michael D'Antonio, *Hershey*, 190, 197–198; Oral History Interview with James E. Bobb, March 22, 2001, 2001OHO1, 12, Hershey Community Archives Oral History Collection, Hershey, PA.

43 "Sugar Position as of March 9, 1928," Sugar Inventory and Commitments Balance Sheet, RWW Papers, box 58, folder 5, MARBL; Memorandum of Conversation between Robert W. Woodruff and Milton S. Hershey, February 13, 1929, box 371, folder 13, RWW Papers, MARBL. Thomas R. Winpenny explored the close partnership between Coca-Cola and the Hershey Company during the interwar years in "Corporate Lobbying Was No Match for the Tide of History: Hershey and Coca-Cola Battle the U.S. Sugar Tariff, 1929–1934," *Journal of Lancaster County's Historical Society* 111, no. 3 (Fall/Winter 2009/2010): 114–124. Christina J. Hostetter's master's thesis, "Sugar Allies: How Hershey and Coca-Cola Used Government Contracts and Sugar Exemptions to Elude Sugar Rationing Regulations" (University of Maryland, College Park, 2004), also looked at the effects of this corporate alliance. "Hoover Statement in Sugar Row Urged," *Washington Post*, December 21, 1929, 1; "Shattuck Tells Senators He Never Discussed Sugar Tariff with the President," *New York Times*, December 20, 1929, 1; "Sugar Witness Hotly Scolds Lobby Quizzers," *Chicago Daily Tribune*, January 9, 1930, 3; "Senate to Resume Sugar Lobby Probe," *Washington Post*, January 7, 1930, 2; "Another Lakin Note Brought in Hoover," *New York Times*, December 21, 1929, 4.

44 *Ralph Hayes, 1894–1977*, biographical essay published by the New York Community Trust, undated, 5, available online at http://www.nycommunitytrust.org/Portals/0/Uploads/Documents/BioBrochures/Ralph%20Hayes.pdf.

45 Ralph Hayes to Robert W. Woodruff, April 10, 1952, box 138, folder 2, RWW Papers, MARBL.

46 Letters from Ralph Hayes to Senator Walter F. George, June 1, 1936, and June 4,

1936; Letter from Senator Walter F. George to Ralph Hayes, June 6, 1936, box 58, folder 5, RWW Papers, MARBL.

47 "KO Stock Year-End Market Value Since 1919," box 43, folder 1, Joseph W. Jones Papers, MARBL; Coca-Cola Company Annual Reports, 1928–1938; Mark Pendergrast, *For God, Country & Coca-Cola*, 170, 177.

48 Mark Pendergrast, *For God, Country & Coca-Cola*, 161, 163, 173; Chart of Coca-Cola's Gallon Sales, Grand Consolidated (The Coca-Cola Co. and Its Subsidiaries), undated, box 22, folder 14, Mark Pendergrast Research Files, MARBL.

49 US Department of Agriculture, Bureau of Agricultural Economics, *Sugar During World War II*, War Records Monograph 3, prepared by Roy A. Ballinger, June 1946, 4, 6.

50 Ibid.; "Investor's Guide," *Chicago Daily Tribune*, February 3, 1940.

51 Christina J. Hostetter, "Sugar Allies," 30, 32–33, 38.

52 Letter from Ben Oehlert to Mr. A. A. Acklin, January 19, 1942, box 58, folder 6, RWW Papers, MARBL.

53 "Oehlert Appointed Envoy to Pakistan," *Atlanta Journal*, June, 21, 1967; "Benjamin H. Oehlert, Jr., 75; Former Coca-Cola Executive," *New York Times*, June 5, 1985, B6; Frederick Allen, *Secret Formula*, 249, 250, 252, 255; Mark Pendergrast, *For God, Country & Coca-Cola*, 196–197.

54 Letter from Ben Oehlert to Mr. A. A. Acklin, February 5, 1942, quoted in Mark Pendergrast, *For God, Country & Coca-Cola*, 196; "U.S. Agency Takes Coca-Cola's Sugar," *Washington Post*, February 27, 1942, 26.

55 Ed Forio, "Out of the Crucible," *Coca-Cola Bottler*, December 1945, 15; "U.S. at War: Bedrock Living," *Time*, March 1, 1943.

56 Letter from Benjamin Oehlert to A. S. Nemir, Sugar Division, Food Supply Branch of the Office of Production Management, January 6, 1942, box 58, folder 6, RWW Papers, MARBL; Michael Blanding, *The Coke Machine*, 99; Christina J. Hostetter, "Sugar Allies," 66.

57 Ed Forio, "Out of the Crucible," *Coca-Cola Bottler*, December 1945, 15; Michael Blanding, *The Coke Machine*, 49; Daniel Levy and Andrew T. Young, "'The Real Thing,'" 773; Classified Message from Eisenhower's Headquarters in North Africa, June 29, 1943, box 85, folder 2, RWW Papers, MARBL.

58 Coca-Cola Company 1944 Annual Report, 5.

59 Frederick Allen, *Secret Formula*, 211–213; Mark Pendergrast, *For God, Country & Coca-Cola* (New York: Basic Books, 2013), 178.

60 *Coca-Cola Co. of Canada, Ltd. v. Pepsi-Cola Co. of Canada, Ltd.*, [1938] Ex. C.R. 263 (Ex. Ct.); reversed [1940] S.C.R. 17 (S.C.C.); affirmed [1942] 2 W.W.R. 257 (P.C.).

61 Frederick Allen, *Secret Formula*, 212, 237, 243.

62 Letter from Walter Mack to Chester Bowles, Director of the Office of Price Administration, October 9, 1944, box 927, "Sugar Problems," Records of the Office of Price Administration, Record Group 188, National Archives II, College Park, MD (hereinafter NARA II).

63 Christina J. Hostetter, "Sugar Allies," 110; Coca-Cola Company Annual Reports, 1941–1947; Pepsi-Cola Company Annual Reports, 1941–1947; Chart of Coca-Cola's Gallon Sales, Grand Consolidated (The Coca-Cola Co. and Its Subsidiar-

ies), undated, box 22, folder 14, Mark Pendergrast Research Files, MARBL; Mark Pendergrast, *For God, Country & Coca-Cola*, 187.

64 Oral History Interview with Violet Pierce, April 7, 2012, 2011OH35, 2; Oral History Interview with Samuel Hinkle, February 21, 1991, 91OH1, 8; Oral History Interview with James E. Bobb, May 12, 1981, 2001OH01, March 22, 2001, 11, Hershey Community Archives Oral History Collection, Hershey, PA; James D. McMahon Jr., *Built on Chocolate*, 154; Michael D'Antonio, *Hershey*, 140; "Staples, Percy Alexander; 1883–1956," Biographical Essay, Hershey Community Archives, http://www.hersheyarchives.org/essay/details.aspx?EssayId=35&Rurl=%2Fre-sources%2Fsearch-results.aspx%3FType%3DBrowseEssay.

65 The 600 million figure was calculated from the Chart of Coca-Cola's Gallon Sales, Grand Consolidated (The Coca-Cola Co. and Its Subsidiaries), undated, box 22, folder 14, Mark Pendergrast Research Files, MARBL.

4. COCA LEAF EXTRACT: HIDING THE COCAINE-COLA CONNECTION

1 This chapter builds on the work of Latin American historian Paul Gootenberg, who first discovered the Federal Bureau of Narcotics files prominently featured here. See Paul Gootenberg, *Andean Cocaine: The Making of a Global Drug* (Chapel Hill: University of North Carolina Press, 2008) 233–265; Paul Gootenberg, "Secret Ingredients: The Politics of Coca in US-Peruvian Relations, 1915–65," *Journal of Latin American Studies* 36, no. 2 (May 2004): Paul Gootenberg, "Between Coca and Cocaine: A Century or More of U.S.-Peruvian Drug Paradoxes, 1860–1980" (Washington, DC: Woodrow Wilson Center, 2001); Paul Gootenberg, "Reluctance or Resistance? Constructing Cocaine (Prohibitions) in Peru, 1910–50," in Paul Gootenberg, ed., *Cocaine: Global Histories* (New York: Routledge, 1999); "Apple Remains No. 1 in the BrandZ™ Top 100 Ranking of the Most Valuable Global Brands," *Bloomberg*, May 21, 2013, http://www.bloomberg.com/bb/newsarchive/a7agtQMCemV8.html. Coca-Cola Company 2013 10-K *SEC Report*, 39, 76.

2 For excellent histories of coca cultivation, see Kenneth T. Pomeranz and Steven Topik, eds., *The World That Trade Created: Society, Culture, and the World Economy—1400 to the Present*, 2nd ed. (Armonk, NY: M. E. Sharpe, 2006); Steven Topik, Carlos Marichal, and Zephyr Frank, eds., *From Silver to Cocaine: Latin American Commodity Chains and the Building of the World Economy, 1500–2000* (Durham: Duke University Press, 2006); Angelo Mariani, *Coca and Its Therapeutic Application*, 2nd ed. (New York: J. N. Jaros, 1892).

3 Albert Niemann, "Ueber eine neue organische Base in den Cocablättern," *Archiv der Pharmazie* 153, no. 2 (1860):129–256; Dominic Streatfeild, *Cocaine: An Unauthorized Biography* (New York: Picador, 2001), 55–59.

4 Commenting on the popularity of Vin Mariani in 1885, the *American Druggist* reported, "The marked attention now paid by physicians to coca, cocaine, etc, as therapeutic agents of a very high order would alone justify us in referring our readers to the preparation of Erythroxylon Coca, now so widely and favorably

known as 'Vin Mariani.'" "Erythroxylon Coca," *American Druggist*, July 1885, 39, box 11, folder 1, Mark Pendergrast Research Files, MARBL; Paul Gootenberg, *Andean Cocaine*, 23, 60; Mark Pendergrast, *For God, Country & Coca-Cola*, 21–22.

5   "Coca: Historical Notes," *American Druggist*, May 1886, 87, box 11, folder 1, Mark Pendergrast Research Files, MARBL; Richard Ashley, *Cocaine: Its History, Uses, and Effects* (New York: Warner Books, 1975), 18; Paul Gootenberg, *Cocaine Global Histories*, 22–23; Joseph F. Spillane, *Cocaine: From Medical Marvel to Modern Menace in the United States, 1884–1920* (Baltimore: Johns Hopkins University Press, 2000), 43; "Coca Leaves and Cocaine," *American Druggist*, June 1885, 109, box 11, folder 1, Mark Pendergrast Research Files, MARBL; Mark Pendergrast, *For God, Country & Coca-Cola*, 21.

6   Joseph Spillane, "Making a Modern Drug," in Paul Gootenberg, ed., *Cocaine: Global Histories*, 22: David F. Musto, "Illicit Price of Cocaine in Two Eras: 1908–14 and 1982–89," *Pharmacy in History* 33 (1991): 5; Paul Gootenberg, "Reluctance and Resistance," 50.

7   Paul Gootenberg, *Andean Cocaine*, 62. For a discussion of Peruvian nationalists' contributions to the construction of a cocaine industry in Peru in the late nineteenth century, see chapter 1, "Imagining Coca, Discovering Cocaine, 1850–1890," in *Andean Cocaine*, 15–54.

8   Angelo Mariani, *Coca and Its Therapeutic Application*, 2nd ed. (New York: J. N. Jaros, 1892), 13; W. Golden Mortimer, *Peru: History of Coca, "The Divine Plant of the Incas,"* (New York: J. H. Vail, 1901), 234; Joseph E. Spillane, "Making a Modern Drug," 21.

9   For a discussion of the Frank Robinson formula, see Mark Pendergrast's footnote in *For God, Country & Coca-Cola*, 53. If Robinson's formula is accurate, then a serving of Coca-Cola in 1886 contained 4.3 milligrams of cocaine. (A "bump" for a modern user would likely be at least 30 milligrams.) In 1931, Coke's Legal Department claimed that extract from Javan coca leaves did not produce the same taste as extract produced from Trujillo coca leaves and advised against switching to the non-Peruvian variety. Letter from Harold Hirsch to Robert W. Woodruff, October 21, 1931, box 55, folder 7, RWW Papers, MARBL. Paul Gootenberg noted Coke's dependence on Peruvian coca in "Secret Ingredients": "Peru held a de facto world monopoly in extract-leaf (but not cocaine-grade coca, which by the 1910s spread to tropical colonies like Java and Formosa). Peru could have steeply increased the costs of making Coca-Cola, particularly in a world formally set on limiting coca crops" (246). "Wonderful Coca," *Atlanta Constitution*, June 21, 1885, 8; Coca-Cola Company 1923 Annual Report, 18.

10   Paul Gootenberg, "Reluctance or Resistance?" 48. Michael M. Cohen discussed the racial fears that led to cocaine bans throughout the American South in "Jim Crow's Drug War: Race, Coca Cola, and the Southern Origins of Drug Prohibition," *Southern Cultures* 12, no. 3 (Fall 2006): 55–79; "Cocaine Sniffers: Use of the Drug Increasing Among Negroes of the South," *New York Times*, June 21, 1903, box 11, folder 2, Mark Pendergrast Research Files, MARBL; Mark Pendergrast, *For God, Country & Coca-Cola*, 89.

11   Cocaine, How Sold, H. B. 92-99, No. 61, 1902, box 11, folder 2, Mark Pendergrast Research Files, MARBL.

12 In "Secret Ingredients," Paul Gootenberg discussed in detail Maywood's opera-
    tions as they related to the Coca-Cola Company, but he largely saw the two acting
    as one. As he put it, "in practice," Maywood and Coca-Cola "became indistin-
    guishable" (246). For the history of the professionalization of the American med-
    ical industry, see Paul Starr, *The Social Transformation of American Medicine* (New
    York: Basic Books, 1982). Starr chronicles Progressive attacks on patent medicine
    makers in chapter 3, "The Consolidation of Professional Authority, 1850–1930,"
    127–134. See also Robert Wiebe, "The Fate of the Nation," chapter 4 in *The Search
    for Order, 1877–1920* (New York: Hill and Wang, 1967).

13 For an excellent summary of this history, see chapter 5, "Anticocaine: From Reluc-
    tance to Global Prohibitions, 1910–1950," in Paul Gootenberg, *Andean Cocaine*,
    189–244.

14 Paul Gootenberg, "Secret Ingredients," 255. Schaeffer Alkaloid Works was one of
    many chemical firms bringing coca leaves into the United States at the turn of the
    century. In the late nineteenth century, the federal government permitted small
    businesses like the Coca-Cola Company to import coca leaves directly from South
    American providers, and there were at least five major chemical-processing firms
    importing coca leaves into the United States on a regular basis. In Germany, there
    were roughly fifteen firms engaged in cocaine manufacturing and distribution.
    Paul Gootenberg, *Andean Cocaine*, 109, 121.

15 Paul Gootenberg, "Reluctance or Resistance?" 50. In speaking of state demands
    for regulatory legibility, I am drawing on James Scott, *Seeing Like a State: How
    Certain Schemes to Improve the Human Condition Have Failed* (New Haven: Yale
    University Press, 1998). The story of counternarcotics policy told here confirms
    the findings of other scholars that Progressive Era regulation aided corporate
    consolidation in the early twentieth century. For this literature, see Gabriel Kolko,
    The Triumph of Conservatism; Thomas K. McCraw, *Prophets of Regulation*; Mar-
    tin J. Sklar, *The Corporate Reconstruction of American Capitalism, 1890–1916*; James
    Weinstein, *The Corporate Ideal in the Liberal State, 1900–1918*.

16 Memorandum from Harold Hirsch to R. W. Woodruff, October 21, 1931, box 55,
    folder 7, RWW Papers, MARBL; Paul Gootenberg, "Secret Ingredients," 242.

17 Transcript of Testimony at 1296, *United States v. Forty Barrels and Twenty Kegs of
    Coca-Cola*, 241 U.S. 265 (1916).

18 Mark Pendergrast, *For God, Country & Coca-Cola*, 184; Frederick Allen, *Secret
    Formula*, 194. For statistics on typical coca inventory practices, see Ralph
    Hayes to William J. Hobbs, July 24, 1946, box 55, folder 7, RWW Papers,
    MARBL.

19 Paul Gootenberg, *Andean Cocaine*, 223. Paul Gootenberg, "Secret Ingredients,"
    247–248, 252; Frederick Allen, *Secret Formula*, 193; Undated Memorandum,
    "Preliminary History," Subject Files Related to the Control of Narcotics Traffic,
    1903–1955, box 4, "Coca-Cola Extract," Record Group 59, General Records of the
    Department of State, NARA II.

20 Frederick Allen, *Secret Formula*, 196; W. P. Heath to Harold Hirsch, October 30,
    1931, box 55, folder 7, RWW Papers, MARBL.

21 Paul Gootenberg, *Andean Cocaine*, 203.

22 Ralph Hayes to Robert W. Woodruff, March 19, 1936; Ralph Hayes Memorandum

re: Better Kola Corporation and the Kola Highball Company, March 10, 1936, box 55, folder 7, RWW Papers, MARBL.

23 Ralph Hayes to Robert W. Woodruff, March 19, 1936, and February 18, 1936, box 55, folder 7, RWW Papers, MARBL.

24 The FBN's language comes directly from a letter from George Gaffney, Acting Commissioner of Narcotics in the Federal Bureau of Narcotics to Nolan Murrah, Royal Crown Cola Company, October 20, 1964, Subject Files of the Bureau of Narcotics and Dangerous Drugs, 1916–1970 (hereinafter Bureau of Narcotics), box 64 (old box 20), Record Group 170, Records of the Drug Enforcement Administration, 1915–1946, 1969–1980 (hereinafter RG 170), NARA II; Memorandum from Ralph Hayes, July 9, 1936, box 55, folder 7, RWW Papers, MARBL; Paul Gootenberg, "Secret Ingredients," 255.

25 Coke's Legal Department supported Hayes's efforts to put pressure on Maywood, saying, "This idea is good," in internal correspondence. Ralph Hayes to Robert W. Woodruff, March 19, 1936, box 55, folder 7, RWW Papers, MARBL. In the 1940s, the company issued a brief on company policies to Coke officials in which it stated that the company never "used our volume and power to force unfair advantage or exclusive rights," but in the 1930s, it clearly did just that to preserve exclusive access to Maywood's coca leaf extract. "Outline of Brief on Company Policies," 1939, box 56, folder 9, RWW Papers, MARBL. The quarter-million figure comes from a letter from Harrison Jones to Robert Woodruff providing details about the Maywood contract. In it, Jones stated that the price of Merchandise #5 was set at $1.11 per pound. Considering that the company's annual demand for #5 was over 240,000 pounds, and that processing of "special leaves" required additional fees, this estimate is probably low. Harrison Jones to Robert Woodruff, July 28, 1930, box 55, folder 3, RWW Papers, MARBL.

26 Ralph Hayes to Robert W. Woodruff, March 19, 1936, box 55, folder 7, RWW Papers, MARBL; Confidential Memorandum from Oehlert to Talley, October 17, 1958, box 242, folder 5, RWW Papers, MARBL.

27 Memorandum from Ralph Hayes to John Sibley, March 20, 1937, box 53, folder 5, RWW Papers, MARBL; Mark Pendergrast, *For God, Country & Coca-Cola*, 184.

28 Paul Gootenberg, *Andean Cocaine*, 181.

29 See Paul Gootenberg's discussion of Soldán in *Cocaine: Global Histories*, 52–63; Paul Gootenberg, "Secret Ingredients," 253–254, 258–259; Paul Gootenberg, *Andean Cocaine*, 240.

30 Memorandum from Benjamin Oehlert to W. J. Hobbs, Robert W. Woodruff, Harrison Jones, and Pope F. Brock, February 27, 1948, box 242, folder 4, RWW Papers, MARBL.

31 Letter from Harry Anslinger to Charles B. Dya, Foreign Relations Division of the Office of Political Affairs in New York, January 10, 1951, Bureau of Narcotics, box 63 (old box 19), "Drugs-Beverages, 1947–1959," RG 170, NARA II.

32 Frederick Allen, *Secret Formula*, 195; Memorandum from Benjamin Oehlert to W.J. Hobbs, R. W. Woodruff, Harrison Jones, and Pope F. Brock, February 27, 1948, box 242, folder 4, RWW Papers, MARBL.

33 Memorandum from Benjamin Oehlert to W. J. Hobbs, Robert W. Woodruff,

Harrison Jones, and Pope F. Brock, February 27, 1948, box 242, folder 4, RWW Papers, MARBL.

34 Memorandum from Ralph Hayes to Robert W. Woodruff, April 2, 1937, box 55, folder 7, RWW Papers, MARBL.

35 Ralph Hayes to Clifford Schillinglaw, January 12, 1959, box 138, folder 6, RWW Papers, MARBL.

36 Ralph Hayes to Henry L. Giordano, Commissioner of the Bureau of Narcotics, October 10, 1962, Bureau of Narcotics, box 64 (old box 20), "Drugs-Coca Leaves, University of Hawaii, Project, Coca-Cola-Maywood, October 1962 thru February 1966" (hereinafter Alakea Project), RG Group 170, NARA II; Paul Gootenberg, "Secret Ingredients," 262–264.

37 John T. Maher to Henry L. Giordano, October 19, 1962, Bureau of Narcotics, box 64 (old box 20), "Alakea Project," RG 170, NARA II.

38 Hawaii had just become a state in 1959. Many of the state officials who took part in the development of Coke's coca project certainly had to consider how the project might affect their political careers in a state in which political alliances were yet fragile and unstable. Ralph Hayes to Henry Giordano, October 16, 1962, Bureau of Narcotics, box 64 (old box 20), "Alakea Project," RG 170, NARA II.

39 Memorandum Report of the Bureau of Narcotics, District No. 16, Gen. File Title: Coca Cola Company Project (Hawaii), August 2, 1963, Bureau of Narcotics, box 64 (old box 20), "Alakea Project," RG 170, NARA II; Henry Giordano to Benjamin Oehlert, June 24, 1963, Bureau of Narcotics, box 63 (old box 19), "Alakea Project," RG 170, NARA II.

40 Thomas H. Hamilton to Benjamin Oehlert, December 23, 1963, Bureau of Narcotics, box 64 (old box 20), "Alakea Project," RG 170, NARA II.

41 Benjamin Oehlert to Henry Giordano, January 17, 1964, and Henry Giordano to Benjamin Oehlert, January 31, 1964, Bureau of Narcotics, box 64 (old box 20), "Alakea Project," RG 170, NARA.

42 Ben Oehlert to Thomas H. Hamilton, February 4, 1964, Bureau of Narcotics, box 64 (old box 20), "Alakea Project," RG 170, NARA II.

43 Thomas H. Hamilton to Benjamin Oehlert, February 11, 1964, Bureau of Narcotics, box 64 (old box 20), "Alakea Project," RG 170, NARA II.

44 Benjamin Oehlert to Thomas H. Hamilton, February 11, 1964, Bureau of Narcotics, box 64 (old box 20), "Alakea Project," RG 170, NARA II.

45 Memorandum of Agreement between the University of Hawaii Foundation and Stepan Chemical Company (Maywood Chemical Works Division), Maywood, New Jersey, for a Grant in Aid of a Research Project, signed June 1, 1964, by all parties, Bureau of Narcotics, box 64 (old box 20), "Alakea Project," RG 170, NARA II.

46 Memorandum Report re: Progress of this project by the University of Hawaii, completed by W. F. Tollenger, Narcotic Agent for the FBN, December, 14, 1964, and Memorandum from John Maher to Commissioner Giordano, February 14, 1966, Bureau of Narcotics, box 64 (old box 19), "Alakea Project," RG 170, NARA II.

47 "Acquisition and Disposal of Erythroxylon Coca Plants Materials July 1, 1964, to

June 30, 1965," Bureau of Narcotics, box 64 (old box 20), "Alakea Project," RG 170, NARA II.

48 Freelance journalist Jeremy Bigwood suggested that the first fungal outbreaks began in 1964, but there was very little evidence to confirm exactly when the blight began. Jeremy Bigwood, "Repeating Mistakes of the Past: Another Mycoherbicide Research Bill," report by the Drug Policy Alliance Network (March 2006), 4, http://www.drugpolicy.org/docUploads/Mycoherbicide06.pdf. Bigwood graciously provided me with copies of this report and other Network publications related to mycoherbicides. Paul Gootenberg, "Secret Ingredients," 264.

49 Memorandum of Agreement between the University of Hawaii Foundation and Stepan Chemical Company (Maywood Chemical Works Division), Maywood, New Jersey, for a Grant in Aid of a Research Project, signed June 1, 1964, by all parties, Bureau of Narcotics, box 64 (old box 19), "Alakea Project," RG 170, NARA II.

50 Donald H. Francis (Stepan Chemical Company) to Henry L. Giordano (Commissioner of the Bureau of Narcotics), June 16, 1966; Letter from Donald H. Francis to Henry Anslinger, June 16, 1966, Bureau of Narcotics, Brief Description of Records–0660–Foreign Countries–Mexico–Peru, box 161 (old box 29), "Peru, 1953–1967," RG 170, NARA II; Paul Gootenberg, "Secret Ingredients," 260.

51 "How Coca-Cola Obtains Its Coca," *New York Times*, July 1, 1988, D1; Ralph Hayes to Benjamin Oehlert, August 31, 1964, box 139, folder 2, RWW Papers, MARBL.

52 Hugo Cabieses Cubas, *Commercializing Coca: Possibilities and Proposals*, translated by James Lupton, Catholic Institute for International Relations (CIIR), Narcotics and Development Discussion Paper No. 11 (March 1996), 2.

53 This information comes from interviews I conducted with investigators Jérôme Mangelinckx and Ricardo Soberón Garrido at the Centro de Investagación Drogas y Derechos Humanos (CIDDH) in Lima, Peru, in January of 2012. Mr. Soberón was formerly the head of the Peruvian National Commission for Development and Life Without Drugs (DEVIDA) and had been an aggressive campaigner for coca leaf revalorization initiatives. In part because of his attacks on state policies that limit licit coca leaf production, he was forced to resign from DEVIDA in January of 2012. In 2012, Evo Morales, now president of Bolivia, pledged to ban the sale of Coca-Cola within country borders.

54 This discovery belongs to Mark Pendergrast, who found a conversation between Coke chairman and CEO Robert Goizueta and an advertising executive named John Bergin in which Woodruff stated that New Coke would not contain decocainized coca leaf extract. Mark Pendergrast, *For God, Country & Coca-Cola*, 348. Coke spokesman Randy Donaldson, in an interview with the *New York Times*, refused to comment on whether New Coke contained any coca, "noting that it was company policy not to discuss its product formulas." "How Coca-Cola Obtains Coca," *New York Times*, July 1, 1988, D1.

55 "Formula Woes Coke Furor May Be 'The Real Thing,'" *Los Angeles Times*, June 27, 1985, 1.

5. COCOA WASTE: SYNTHESIZING CAFFEINE IN CHEMICAL LABS

1 Senate Committee on Ways and Means, *Tariff Readjustment—1929. Vol. 1: Schedule 1: Chemical, Oils, and Paints*, 70th Cong., 2nd Sess., January 7–9, 1929, 295–301; "Caffeine," undated document, series 3, box 1, Caffeine (General), Monsanto Company Records; Letter from J. W. Livingston to John F. Queeny, February 4, 1928, series 3, box 1, Caffeine (General), Monsanto Company Records; Plot Plan of Monsanto Chemical Company, Norfolk, Virginia, October 17, 1949, series 2, box 3, USA (Norfolk, Virginia), Monsanto Company Records; General Information about the Norfolk Plant, undated document, series 2, box 3, USA (Sales Contracts), Monsanto Company Records.

2 Dan J. Forrestal, a former Monsanto employee, wrote a history of the chemical company, *Faith, Hope and $5,000: The Story of Monsanto* (New York: Simon and Schuster, 1977); it offers a useful overview of the company's development. "P.S. Just Got Our Special on Monday," undated document, series 3, box 1, Caffeine (General), Monsanto Company Records.

3 Letter from Ralph Hayes to Robert W. Woodruff, May 5, 1954, box 138, folder 3, RWW Papers, MARBL; Coca-Cola Sales Contracts with Coca-Cola Co.—USA, undated document, series 3, box 1, Caffeine (Sales Contracts), Monsanto Company Records; Coca-Cola Company 1934 Annual Report, 5, and 1939 Annual Report, 5.

4 Letter from Robert W. Woodruff to Edgar M. Queeny, September 19, 1942; Letter from Robert W. Woodruff to Edgar M. Queeny, September 3, 1935, box 257, folder 2, RWW Papers, MARBL; Sales of Caffeine to the Coca-Cola Co.—USA, undated document, series 3, box 1, Caffeine (Sales Contract), Monsanto Company Records.

5 Letter from Edgar Queeny to Robert W. Woodruff, June 3, 1935, box 257, folder 2, RWW Papers, MARBL.

6 Letter from Ralph Hayes to Robert W. Woodruff, May 5, 1954, box 138, folder 3; Memorandum from Ralph Hayes to W. J. Hobbs, September 12, 1947, box 49, folder 7, RWW Papers, MARBL.

7 Letter from Ralph Hayes to Robert W. Woodruff, May 5, 1954, box 138, folder 3, RWW Papers, MARBL.

8 Letter from G. Lee Camp, Vice President of Monsanto, to Horace Garner, Purchasing Agent for the Coca-Cola Company, December 5, 1941, series 3, box 1, Caffeine (Sales Contracts), Monsanto Company Records; R. S. Wobus, Monanto's Norfolk Plant Manager, "Norfolk War History," undated document, series 2, box 3, USA (Norfolk, Virginia), Monsanto Company Records; Memorandum from John B. Smiley, Chief of the Beverage and Tobacco Branch of the War Production Board (WPB), to Edward Browning Jr., Assistant Chief Stock Pile and Shipping Branch of the WPB, November 5, 1942, quoted in Murray Carpenter, *Caffeinated*, 98.

9 R. S. Wobus, "Norfolk War History," undated document, series 2, box 3, USA (Norfolk, Virginia), Monsanto Company Records.

10 Letter from Ralph Hayes to Robert W. Woodruff, May 5, 1954, box 138, folder 3, RWW Papers, MARBL; Frederick Allen, *Secret Formula*, 253.

11 Letter from Ralph Hayes to A. A. Acklin, September 16, 1942, box 137, folder 3, RWW Papers, MARBL.

12 Letter from Ralph Hayes to Robert W. Woodruff, May 5, 1954, box 138, folder 3, RWW Papers, MARBL; Mark Pendergrast, *For God, Country & Coca-Cola* (Collier Books, 1994), 469.

13 Ralph Hayes to Robert W. Woodruff, May 5, 1954, box 138, folder 3, RWW Papers, MARBL; "Caffeine," undated Monsanto Company document, series 3, box 1, Caffeine (General), Monsanto Company Records.

14 Coca-Cola Company 1945 Annual Report, 3.

15 Letter from Arthur Acklin to Robert W. Woodruff, April 19, 1945, box 2, folder 4, RWW Papers, MARBL.

16 Company publication written by Braxton Pollard, "NOW-Synthetic Caffeine," undated document, series 3, box 1, Caffeine (General), Monsanto Company Records; "Industrial News," *Chemical Engineering News* 23, no. 21 (1945): 1964–1978; Report on caffeine and theobromine prepared by John Ragsdale, 1945, series 3, box 1, Caffeine (General), Monsanto Company Records.

17 For a detailed history of the Monsanto Company's postwar operations, see Dan J. Forrestal, *Faith, Hope and $5,000: The Story of Monsanto*, 93–107; company publication written by Braxton Pollard, "NOW-Synthetic Caffeine," undated document, series 3, box 1, Caffeine (General), Monsanto Company Records; News Release on Monsanto Synthetic Caffeine Operations, 1945, series 3, box 1, Monsanto Company Records.

18 Memorandum from Ralph Hayes re: "Merchandise No. 3 Through January 1948," February 18, 1948, box 49, folder 7, RWW Papers, MARBL; House of Commons Debate, July 12, 1950, *Hansard's*, 477:1343–1344, http://hansard.millbanksystems.com/commons/1950/jul/12/cocoa-tree-disease.

19 Letter from Ralph Hayes to W. P. Heath, April 12, 1948, box 49, folder 7, RWW Papers, MARBL.

20 Letter dated June 27, 1951, series 3, box 1, Caffeine (General), Monsanto Company Records; William S. Knowles, interview by Michael A. Grayson at St. Louis, Missouri, January 30, 2008, Chemical Heritage Foundation Oral History Transcript 0406 (available by request from the Chemical Heritage Foundation); Letter dated June 27, 1951, series 3, box 1, Caffeine (General), Monsanto Company Records.

21 Memorandum from Ralph Hayes to Daphne Robert, January 10, 1948, box 49, folder 7, RWW Papers, MARBL.

22 Letter from Ralph Hayes to Robert W. Woodruff, January 10, 1962, box 139, folder 2, RWW Papers, MARBL.

23 Ibid.

24 For a description of carbon-dating techniques used to identify synthetic caffeine, see Albert B. Allen (Coca-Cola Export Corporation), "Caffeine Identification: Differentiation of Synthetic and Natural Caffeine," *Agricultural and Food Chemistry* 9, no. 4 (July–August 1961): 294–295, and Angus J. Shingler (Coca-Cola Company) and Jack K. Carlton (Louisiana State University), "Method for the Separation and Determination of Theophyllin, Theobromine, and Caffeine," *Analytical Chemistry* 31, no. 10 (October 1959): 1679–1680.

25 Letter from Ralph Hayes to Robert W. Woodruff, January 10, 1962, box 139, folder

2, RWW Papers, MARBL; "Monsanto Cuts Synthetic Caffeine Price Sharply, Cites Import Pressure," *Wall Street Journal*, December 22, 1958, 32.

26 Letter from Edgar Queeny to Robert W. Woodruff, March 11, 1955, box 257, folder 2, RWW Papers, MARBL.

27 Letter from Robert W. Woodruff to Edgar Queeny, March 19 1955, box 257, folder 3, RWW Papers, MARBL.

28 Letter from Ralph Hayes to Robert W. Woodruff, May 5, 1954, box 138, folder 3, RWW Papers, MARBL.

29 Ibid.

30 Coca-Cola Personnel Report, Coca-Cola Company and Subsidiaries, Number of Employees, January 31, 1945, box 55, folder 5, RWW Papers, MARBL.

PART II: THE COSTS OF EMPIRE, 1950 TO TODAY

1 Coca-Cola Company, "125 Years of Sharing Happiness: A Short History of the Coca-Cola Company" (Richmond, British Columbia: Blanchette Press, 2011), http://www.thecoca-colacompany.com/heritage/pdf/Coca-Cola_125_years_booklet.pdf; "The Sun Never Sets on Coca-Cola," *Time*, May 15, 1950; Chart of Coca-Cola's Gallon Sales, Grand Consolidated (The Coca-Cola Co. and Its Subsidiaries), undated, box 22, folder 14, Pendergrast Research Files, RWW Papers, MARBL.

2 Coca-Cola Company 1950 Annual Report, 7, and 1930 Annual Report, 5.

3 "The Sun Never Sets on Coca-Cola," *Time*, May 15, 1950.

6. WATER FROM ABROAD: SECURING ACCESS TO OVERSEAS OASES

1 Constance Hays explained that Coca-Cola's Foreign Department was in many ways modeled on the US State Department. Constance Hays, *The Real Thing*, 80; "A Brief History of Coca-Cola Overseas," *Coca-Cola Bottler*, April 1959, 181–182.

2 Frederick Allen, *Secret Formula*, 173.

3 "A Brief History of Coca-Cola Overseas," *Coca-Cola Bottler*, April 1959, 182; Mark Pendergrast, *For God, Country & Coca-Cola*, 167.

4 Mark Pendergrast, *For God, Country & Coca-Cola*, 184; Frederick Allen, *Secret Formula*, 199; Letter from William T. Dorsey to Mr. Bernard H. Culver re: The Coca-Cola Co., September 23, 1938, box 371, folder 13, RWW Papers, MARBL.

5 Constance Hays, *The Real Thing*, 81–82; Woodruff quoted in Mark Pendergrast, *For God, Country & Coca-Cola*, 195, 196–197.

6 Classified Message from Eisenhower's Headquarters in North Africa, June 29, 1943, box 85, folder 2, RWW Papers, MARBL; Letter from Lieutenant Colonel John F. Neu to the Quartermaster General, War Department, January 29, 1942; Letter from Brigadier General H. C. Ingles to Board of Economic Warfare, August 14, 1941, Rationing Department, National Office, Food Rationing Division, Office of the Director: General Correspondence Related to Food Rationing, 1942–1945, box 588, Record Group 188, Records of the Office of Price Administration, NARA II. Spe-

cial thanks to Kellen Backer for bringing these OPA files to my attention. His PhD dissertation, "World War II and the Triumph of Industrialized Food" (University of Wisconsin–Madison, 2012), dealt at length with Coke's OPA negotiations.

7   J. C. Louis and Harvey Z. Yazijian, *The Cola Wars*, 57; Mark Pendergrast, *For God, Country, and Coca-Cola*, 198.

8   Classified Message from Eisenhower's Headquarters in North Africa, June 29, 1943, box 85, folder 2, RWW Papers, MARBL; Constance Hays, *The Real Thing*, 81–82.

9   Translated "Desfile" article, "An Interview with James Farley, 'The Right Hand' of Roosevelt," February 21, 1941; Article appearing in "Novedades," México, D. F., "The Ex-President of the Democratic Party Arrives in This Capital," August 10, 1941, box 103, folder 10, RWW Papers, MARBL; "James Farley," biographical sketch, no date, box 104, folder 4, RWW Papers, MARBL.

10 "The Sun Never Sets on Coca-Cola," *Time*, May 15, 1950.

11 Ibid.; Frederick Allen, *Secret Formula*, 312.

12 Paul Austin, Speech to the Association of National Advertisers International, Advertising Workshop Meeting, Hotel Plaza, New York City, April 18, 1963, box 15, folder 8, RWW Papers, MARBL.

13 For the seminal work on the European Recovery Program, see Michael Hogan, *The Marshall Plan: America, Britain, and the Reconstruction of Western Europe, 1947–1952* (Cambridge: Cambridge University Press, 1987, 89.); Senator Arthur H. Vanderberg quoted, 108. See also Hadley Arkes, *Bureaucracy, the Marshall Plan, and the National Interest* (Princeton: Princeton University Press, 1972). Nicolaus Mills, *Winning the Peace: The Marshall Plan and America's Coming of Age as a Superpower* (Hoboken, NJ: John Wiley & Sons, 2008), 5.

14 Letter from Coca-Cola Export Corporation to the Administrator for Economic Cooperation, August 16, 1948, Mission to Greece, Construction Division Subject Files, 1947–1953, box 4, "Industries-Coca-Cola," Records of US Foreign Assistance Agencies, 1948–1961, Record Group 469 (hereinafter RG 469), NARA II.

15 Letter from D. A. Fitzgerald, ECA Director of Food, to John Goodloe, Secretary of the Coca-Cola Company, August 18, 1948, Executive Secretariat, General Correspondence (Name Files), 1948–1954, box 7, "Coca-Cola Export Corp. 1948," RG 469, NARA II.

16 Letter from John C. Dewilde to E. T. Dickinson, August 26, 1948, Executive Secretariat, General Correspondence (Name Files), 1948–1954, box 7, "Coca-Cola Export Corp. 1948," RG 469, NARA II.

17 Letter from Coca-Cola Export Corporation to the Administrator for Economic Cooperation, August 16, 1948, and Memorandum from Harper Sowles to C. L. Terrel, December, 10, 1948, Mission to Greece, Construction Division Subject Files, 1947–1953, box 4, "Industries-Coca-Cola," RG 469, NARA II.

18 House Committee on Foreign Affairs, *Extension of European Recovery Program, Part I*, 81st Cong., 1st Sess., February 8–11, 15–18, 1949, 54, 540. Evidence suggests that the ECA might have shipped some Coca-Cola syrup to European nations under the Marshall Plan, though how much is unclear. In a hearing on foreign aid appropriations in 1949, Massachussetts congressman Richard B. Wigglesworth testified that "a small amount of beverages, I think probably less than $200,000 for all coun-

tries" went to aid countries. When asked whether Coca-Cola syrup was specifically part of that allotment, Wigglesworth commented, "We do not identify those products by brand." House Committee on Foreign Affairs, Subcommittee on Deficiency Appropriations, *Foreign Aid Appropriation Bill for 1949, Part I*, 80th Cong., 2nd Sess., May 3–8, 10, 15, 1948, 730–731. Considering such obfuscation, it is possible Coca-Cola received some aid from ECA. Nevertheless, foreign aid agents clearly resisted Coke's appeals for bottling plant guaranties. In the final calculus, the ECA held that "suggestions for guaranties of expansion of the business of the Coca-Cola Co. in Europe . . . did not seem to be important for recovery." House Committee on Foreign Affairs and Senate Committee on Foreign Relations, *Extension of European Recovery Program, Part 1*, 81st Cong., 1st Sess., February 8–11, 15–18, 1949, 54.

19 Senate Committee on Appropriations, *Economic Cooperation Administration*, 80th Cong., 2nd Sess., May 13, 1948, 2. For more on Hoffman's views of ECA's mission, see Statement by Paul G. Hoffman on European Economy, October 31, 1949, Economic Cooperation Administration File, P. G. Hoffman Papers, Harry S. Truman Library, http://www.trumanlibrary.org/whistlestop/study_collections/marshall/large/index.php; On ECA projects abroad, see Fifth Report to Congress of the Economic Cooperation Administration, for the Period April 3–June 20, 1949 (Washington, DC: USGPO, 1950), 38; Sixth Report to Congress of the Economic Cooperation Administration, for the Quarter Ended September 30, 1949 (Washington, DC: USGPO, 1950), 54–55; Seventh Report to Congress of the Economic Cooperation Administration, for the Quarter Ended December 31, 1949 (Washington, DC: USGPO, 1950), 49.

20 Jordan Tama, "More than Deference: Eisenhower, Congress, and Foreign Policy," paper prepared for Eisenhower and Congress: Lessons for the 21st Century, American University, February 19, 2010, 23; Vernon W. Ruttan, *United States Development Assistance Policy: The Domestic Politics of Foreign Economic Aid* (Baltimore: John Hopkins University, 1996), 71.

21 Letter from G. Anton Burgers to Charles B. Warden, Chief Investment Guaranty Staff, October 11, 1957, ICA US Operations Mission to India, Industry Division Investment Branch, Subject Files, 1953–1960, box 4, "Coca-Cola Company," RG 469, NARA II.

22 Letter from Charles Warden, Chief of Investment Guaranty Staff to G. Anton Burgers, Investment Adviser, US Technical Cooperation Mission to India at the American Embassy, October 28, 1957, ICA US Operations Mission to India, Industry Division Investment Branch, Subject Files, 1953–1960, box 4, "Coca-Cola Company," RG 469, NARA II.

23 "W. J. Hobbs Is Dead at 73; Former Coca-Cola Chief," *New York Times*, July 13, 1977, B21; Frederick Allen, *Secret Formula*, 268–270, 272.

24 Pepsi-Cola Company Annual Reports, 1949–1960; Coca-Cola Company Annual Reports, 1949–1960; "Pepsi Commercial (1950)," http://www.youtube.com/watch?v=MQfikxbS4zE; Frederick Allen, *Secret Formula*, 275, 296–297.

25 Stockholders wrote Woodruff raving about Talley, describing him as "a man who came up through the ranks" and someone who would have a "profound effect on the morale of your entire organization." Letter from James B. Robinson Jr., Chairman of the First National Bank of Atlanta, to Robert W. Woodruff, May 9, 1958, box 307, folder 10, RWW Papers, MARBL; Frederick Allen, *Secret Formula*, 308–

310; "Coca-Cola Current Sales, Net 'Very Good,'" *Wall Street Journal*, March 20, 1962, 31; Coca-Cola Company 1962 Annual Report, 7.

26 Eric Schlosser, *Fast Food Nation: The Dark Side of the All-American Meal* (Boston: Houghton Mifflin, 2001), 19–22, 24.

27 Letter from Henry R. Labouisse, Director of the State Department's Task Force on Foreign Economic Assistance, May 10, 1961, box 309, folder 1, RWW Papers, MARBL; State Department Memorandum sent to Robert W. Woodruff dated May 9, 1961, box 309, folder 1, RWW Papers, MARBL.

28 State Department Memorandum sent to Robert W. Woodruff dated May 9, 1961; Letter from John Sibley to Henry Labouisse, May 19, 1961, box 309, folder 1, RWW Papers, MARBL.

29 Clarence R. Miles to Robert W. Woodruff, September 30, 1963, box 183, folder 1, RWW Papers, MARBL.

30 Paul Austin, "Managing Abundance," speech given at the Economic Club of Detroit, Detroit, MI, November 27, 1967, reprinted in *Vital Speeches of the Day* 34 (February 1, 1968): 245–248.

31 Coca-Cola Company 1962 Annual Report, 9; "J. Paul Austin Dead; Coca-Cola Leader," *New York Times*, December 27, 1985, B10.

32 For a broad history of corporate diversification in the twentieth century, see Alfred Chandler's *Strategy and Structure*.

33 *Refresher*, November 1972, 3; "Coca-Cola Puts 2nd Period Net Up over 11%, Weighs National Bottled-Water Operations," *Wall Street Journal*, July 29, 1971, 6.

34 Coca-Cola Company 1972 Annual Report, 10; "Coca-Cola Co. Seeking Access to Soviet Union, China, and Middle East," *Wall Street Journal*, November 8, 1977, 21.

35 "20 Desalination Plants to Cost Saudis 15 Billion," *New York Times*, May 24, 1977, 51; Mark Pendergrast, *For God, Country & Coca-Cola*, 296; "Clean Environment is Prime Goal of this Subsidiary of the Coca-Cola Company," reprinted from *Refresher* 4, no. 11 (November 1972): 3–4, box 48, folder 6, RWW Papers, MARBL.

36 "Putting the Daring Back in Coke," *New York Times*, March 4, 1984, F1; "Coca-Cola to Sell Aqua-Chem Unit to Paris Company," *Wall Street Journal*, July 15, 1981, 31; "Spritzing New Zest Into Coke," *Industry Week*, November 1, 1982, 47; "Aqua-Chem," Special Supplement to *Coca-Cola Overseas* 23, no.4, undated, box 48, folder 7, RWW Papers, MARBL.

37 Coca-Cola Company 1954 Annual Report, 6, and 1981 Annual Report, 30. For a biography of Goizueta, see business journalist David Greising's *I'd Like the World to Buy a Coke: The Life and Leadership of Roberto Goizueta* (New York: John Wiley and Sons, 1997); Coca-Cola Company News Release, "Goizueta Elected President of the Coca-Cola Company," no date, box 121, folder 6, RWW Papers, MARBL; "The Engineer Who Is Putting New Sparkle into Coke," *Financial Times*, October 1, 1980, 29; Frederick Allen, *Secret Formula*, 376–378, 386–387; Mark Pendergrast, *For God, Country & Coca-Cola*, 328–329.

38 Constance Hays, *The Real Thing*, 35, 52, 175.

39 Ibid., 52–53.

40 Senate Committee on Foreign Relations, *Overseas Private Investment Corporation*, 96th Cong., 2nd Sess., June 11–12, 1980, 200, 205, 229; House Committee

on International Relations, *Extension and Revision of Overseas Private Investment Corporation Programs*, 95th Cong., 1st Sess., June 21, 23, July 19–21, September 8, 12, 16, 1977, 360; Senate Committee on Foreign Relations, *Hearing to Receive Testimony on Overseas Private Investment Corporation Amendments Act of* 1988, S. 2006, 100th Cong., 2nd Sess., July 6, 1988, 14, 27; House Committee on Foreign Affairs, *Reauthorization of the Overseas Private Investment Corporation*, 99th Cong., 1st Sess., June 18, 20, 25, 1985, 601; "Spreading Global Risk to American Taxpayers," *New York Times*, September 20, 1998, BU1.

41 Martin Melosi, *Sanitary City*, 357, 359.

42 "Managing Change—Challenge of the '80s," Remarks by Roberto C. Goizueta to the Georgia Bankers Association, Marketing Conference, February 12, 1981, box 121, folder 7, RWW Papers, MARBL; Letter from Donald Keough to Jerry A. Ross, Vice President of Casey Electric Inc., August 25, 1981, box 56, folder 8, RWW Papers, MARBL.

43 Letter from Donald Keough to Jerry A. Ross, Vice President of Casey Electric Inc., August 25, 1981, box 56, folder 8, RWW Papers, MARBL; *Coca-Cola Bottler*, September 1985, 5.

44 "Ingenuity, Plus Spring Water, Turns Handicap to Build Sales," *Coca-Cola Bottler*, April 1960, 29. In Aberdeen, South Dakota, concerns about the municipal water supply caused "families with babies" to turn "to the Coca-Cola Bottling Company of Aberdeen for their water needs," reported the *Coca-Cola Bottler* in 1961. The plant's water, the *Bottler* explained, "is treated beyond the requirements of most local waterworks and is as pure as pure can be." Citizens in the town were invited "to drop by with jars, buckets and other containers and help themselves." "A Life-Saver for Babies: When City Water Develops Off-Taste, Aberdeen Bottler Comes to Rescue," *Coca-Cola Bottler*, October 1961, 32; Craig E. Colten, *An Unnatural Metropolis: Wresting New Orleans from Nature* (Baton Rouge: Louisiana State University Press, 2006), 130.

45 Coca-Cola Company 1980 Annual Report, 1.

46 Robert Foster, *Coca-Globalization: Following Soft Drinks from New York to New Guinea* (New York: Palgrave Macmillan, 2008), 65; D.L.I. Productions, Canadian Broadcasting Corporation, Télé-Québec, Channel Four (Great Britain), and Microfilms Inc., *The Cola Conquest: A Trilogy*, DVD (Canada: Microfilms Inc., 2004); Mark Pendergrast, *For God, Country & Coca-Cola*, 366; Roger Enrico and Jesse Kornbluth, *The Other Guy Blinked: How Pepsi Won the Cola Wars* (Toronto and New York: Bantam, 1986), 15.

47 Letter from C. A. Shillinglaw to James A. Schroeder, March 10, 1971, box 48, folder 11, RWW Papers, MARBL.

48 *Coca-Cola Bottler*, September 1982, 1; Coca-*Cola Bottler*, December 1982, 2; *Coca-Cola Bottler*, January 1983, 3.

49 Constance Hays, *The Real Thing*, 246.

50 Ibid., 247. As anthropologist Martha Kaplan pointed out, part of what made the Dasani campaign so successful from the start was the fact that company bottlers were "there, available, through the Company's extensive distribution system." Coke's century-long campaign to tap into public utilities all over the world provided it with a global reach that few source-based spring water companies

could compete with. As a result, Aquafina and Dasani became two of the top four water bottle labels by the early 2000s, Dasani controlling 11.3 percent and Aquafina 10 percent of the market by 2004. Martha Kaplan, "Fijian Water in Fiji and New York: Local Politics and a Global Commodity," *Cultural Anthropology* 22, no. 4 (2007): 697; Steve Martinez, "Soft Drink Companies Make Splash in Bottled Water," *Amber Waves* 5 (June 2007): 4.

51 Tony Clarke, *Inside the Bottle: Exposing the Bottled Water Industry* (Ottawa: Canadian Centre for Policy Alternatives, Polaris Institute, 2007), 81.

52 Robert J. Glennon, *Water Follies: Groundwater Pumping and the Fate of America's Fresh Waters* (Washington, DC: Island Press, 2002), 2; Morrison quoted in Peter Gleick, *Bottled and Sold: The Story Behind Our Obsession with Bottled Water* (Washington, DC: Island Press, 2010), 7.

53 Senate Committee on Foreign Relations, *Overseas Private Investment Corporation*, 96th Cong., 2nd Sess., June 11–12, 1980, 200, 205, 229; House Committee on International Relations, *Extension and Revision of Overseas Private Investment Corporation Programs*, 95th Cong., 1st Sess., June 21, 23, July 19–21, September 8, 12, 16, 1977, 360; Senate Committee on Foreign Relations, *Hearing to Receive Testimony on Overseas Private Investment Corporation Amendments Act of* 1988, S. 2006, 100th Cong., 2nd Sess., July 6, 1988, 14, 27; House Committee on Foreign Affairs, *Reauthorization of the Overseas Private Investment Corporation*, 99th Cong., 1st Sess., June 18, 20, 25, 1985, 601; "Spreading Global Risk to American Taxpayers," *New York Times*, September 20, 1998, BU1.

54 Letter from Project Monitoring Coordinator Brenda Simonen-Moreno to the Principal Financial Analyst at the Coca-Cola Company, April 29, 1998 (FOIA Request 2010-00033 with OPIC); Letter from Project Monitoring Coordinator David L. Husband to the Coca-Cola Company, July 7, 1997 (FOIA Request 2010-00033 with OPIC); Letter from OPIC Senior Coordinator James E. Gale to the Coca-Cola Company, July 18, 1996 (FOIA Request 2010-00033 with OPIC); Letter from OPIC Vice President of Insurance Felton M. Johnston to Senior Risk Analyst at the Coca-Cola Company, March 25, 1993 (FOIA Request 2010-00033 with OPIC). OPIC redacted insurance coverage amounts from these files, which they produced pursuant to a Freedom of Information Act request filed by the author in June of 2010. Besides insurance and guaranty amounts, a large amount of other information, including the specifics of how OPIC money was to be used, was also redacted. OPIC claimed that the information was protected because it fell under the category of "trade secrets" or "commercial or financial information obtained from a person that is privileged or confidential"; Carlos Stagliano OPIC Report for Coca-Cola Nigeria Limited Monitoring Trip, November 13, 2009, 2 (FOIA Request 2010-00033 with OPIC). A survey of Coca-Cola Sabco bottling plants in Africa revealed that these enterprises usually employed anywhere from two hundred to seven hundred people. The company makes strong claims that these plants help multiply jobs in other industries, suggesting, for example, that its three plants in Mozambique generate over 10,000 jobs even though the company hires only a few hundred employees. Coca-Cola Sabco Territories website, www.cocacolasabco.com/Territory.aspx/Show/Mozambique.

55 For Isdell's account of his time at Coca-Cola, see Neville Isdell with David Beasley, *Inside Coca-Cola: A CEO's Life Story of Building the World's Most Popular Brand* (New York: St. Martin's Press, 2011), 11–25, 114–119.

56 Ibid., 141.

57 Carlos Stagliano OPIC Report for Coca-Cola Nigeria Limited Monitoring Trip, November 13, 2009, 10–11 (FOIA Request 2010-00033). The report did note that Coke had "plans to implement its 'Green Borehole' program, which involves digging solar energy powered boreholes that will provide free potable water for town residents." This, however, was not a part of the original contract. See Carlos Stagliano's OPIC Report, 5; World Health Organization and UNICEF, *Progress on Sanitation and Drinking-Water, 2010 Update* (Geneva: WHO Press, 2010), 47.

58 "USAID Partners with Coca-Cola, Government to Provide Water Projects in Kano," *USAID Newsletter*, June 2008, 2; "The Coca-Cola Company and USAID Expand Global Water Partnership," USAID Press Release, March 22, 2010; Coca-Cola Company 2012 Water Stewardship and Replenishment Report, 16.

59 Coca-Cola Company 2012 Water Stewardship and Replenishment Report, 16; "Rehabilitating the TextAfrica Water Treatment System," Coca-Cola Press Release, March 18, 2008.

60 Coca-Cola Company 2012 Water Stewardship and Replenishment Report, 12–13, A3–A4.

61 "EKOCENTER Delivers Safe Access to Water and Other Basic Necessities to Communities in Need," Coca-Cola Company website, September 24, 2013, http://www.coca-colacompany.com/ekocenter; "Slingshot Inventor Dean Kamen's Revolutionary Clean Water Machine," Coca-Cola Company website, November 2, 2012, http://www.coca-colacompany.com/stories/slingshot-inventor-dean-kamens-revolutionary-clean-water-machine. "The Coca-Cola Company and USAID Expand Global Water Partnership," USAID Press Release, March 22, 2010, http://www.usaid.gov/news-information/press-releases/coca-cola-company-and-usaid-expand-global-water-partnership.

62 In 2012, Coca-Cola reported that the company, along with its "partners" (presumably NGOs, government agencies, and other businesses), had contributed roughly $49.4 million annually toward international water projects since 2008. Coca-Cola Company 2012 Water Stewardship and Replenishment Report, 1, 16.

63 Carlos Stagliano OPIC Report for Coca-Cola Nigeria Limited Monitoring Trip, November 13, 2009, 11 (FOIA Request 2010-00033 with OPIC).

64 Mark Thomas, *Belching Out the Devil*, 291; June Nash, "Consuming Interests: Water, Rum, and Coca-Cola from Ritual Propitiation to Corporate Expropriation in Highland Chiapas," *Cultural Anthropology* 22, no. 4 (2007): 631.

65 Cameron Houston and Liselotte Johnsson, "Drought? It's Being Given Away," *Age*, November 4, 2006; "Coke Cleared to Pump Extra Water, Court Rules," *Sydney Morning Herald*, October 4, 2008.

66 P. R. Sreemahadevan Pillai, *The Saga of Plachimada* (Mumbai: Vikas Adhyayan Kendra, 2008), 60–62; Michael Blanding, "The Case Against Coke," *Nation*, April 13, 2006; K. N. Nair, Antonyto Paul, and Vineetha Menon, *Water Insecurity, Institutions and Livelihood Dynamics* (Kerala: Center for Development Studies, 2008); Mark Thomas, *Belching Out the Devil*, 189–246. For Coke's denial, see a *Bloomberg.com* interview of Jeff

Seabright, Vice President, Environment and Water Resources at Coca-Cola, published November 25, 2013. Eric Roston, "Why Can I Buy a Coke Without Sugar or Caffeine but Not Water? Dumb Question," http://www.bloomberg.com/news/2013-11-25/why-can-i-buy-a-coke-without-sugar-or-caffeine-but-not-water-dumb-question.html.

67 Despite frequent requests, the bottling company refused to grant me an on-site tour of the facilities. For footage of the Rajasthan conflict, see the documentary *Thirst* by Alan Snitow, Deborah Kaufman, Kenji Yamamoto, and Snitow-Kaufman Productions (Oley, PA: Bullfrog Films, 2005); Nicole Kornberg, "'Good Drinking Water Instead of Coca-Cola': Elaborating Ideas of Development Through the Case of Coca-Cola in India" (Master's Thesis, University of Texas at Austin, 2007), 10, 75–76; Michael Blanding, "The Case Against Coke," *Nation*, April 13, 2006; TERI (The Energy and Resource Institute), *Independent Third Party Assessment of Coca-Cola Facilities in India*, chapter 4A, "Kaladera," Report No. 2006WM21, January 2008, 123–183; TERI, "Executive Summary of the Study on Independent Third Party Assessment of Coca-Cola Facilities in India," Report No. 2006WM21, 2006, 22. As this book went to print in the summer of 2014, community activism in the Indian state of Uttar Pradesh forced the temporary closure of yet another Coca-Cola bottling plant just outside the city of Varanasi. In issuing the order to stop production at the Coke facility, the Uttar Pradesh Pollution Control Board held that Coke was exacerbating water shortages in the region. A national environmental tribunal overturned the injunction just weeks after its issuance, but resistance to reopening the plant remained. "Court Allows Plant to Reopen in Uttar Pradesh," *New York Times*, India Ink Blogs, June 20, 2014, http://india.blogs.nytimes.com/2014/06/20/court-allows-coca-cola-plant-to-reopen-in-uttar-pradesh/.

68 Coca-Cola Company 2012 Sustainability Report, 69; Coca-Cola Company 2012 Water Stewardship and Replenish Report, 6.

69 Coca-Cola Company 2012 Sustainability Report, 76.

70 For the Aqueduct Water Risk Atlas, visit http://insights.wri.org/aqueduct/welcome. The extraction figure is a low estimate, based on 2006 water consumption at the Coke bottling plant in Amman, Jordan, which totaled 309 million liters. Based on unit case sales, it is clear that some plants on this map extract much more water, but precise data is not available. Coca-Cola Içeçek (bottler) Corporate Social Responsibility Report (March 2008–March 2009), 52, 56.

71 See Coca-Cola Company 2012 Water Stewardship and Replenishment Report; Coca-Cola Company and the Nature Conservancy, "Quantifying Replenish Benefits in Community Water Partnership Project" (February 2013), http://assets.coca-cola company.com/2f/cb/e5d2ca1e4c58a38adbe8586d06db/final-quantification-report -water-pdf.pdf.

72 EPA, *Clean Water and Drinking Water Infrastructure Gap Analysis Report* (Washington, DC: USGPO, September 2002), 43.

7. COFFEE BEANS: CAPITALIZING ON THE DECAF BOOM

1 Mark Pendergrast, *Uncommon Grounds*, 110.

2 Prices for green coffee beans were extremely low at this time, and market forces

would have driven growers out of business, ultimately yielding production short-ages, but the Brazilian government intervened to stabilize prices in the early 1900s, fueling an expansion of the coffee industry in the country. Implementing a "valorization" program designed to increase coffee prices, the state borrowed from international lenders to pay for surplus coffee bags, which the government either stockpiled in silos or burned. As historian Richard Tucker explained, the "valorization mechanism encouraged maximum expansion of coffee production by guaranteeing planters a profitable price without fixing any limits to government purchases." To be sure, international prices increased as a result of the subsidy program, but they remained well below the level they had reached in the 1870s. Richard Tucker, *Insatiable Appetite*, 191–192. Tucker catalogued the environmental degradation caused by the expansion of coffee plantations in the late nineteenth and early twentieth centuries in "The Last Drop: The American Coffee Market and the Hill Regions of Latin America," *Insatiable Appetite*, 179–225.

3   "General Foods Corp.," *Wall Street Journal*, July 30, 1931, 6; Display Ad, *Washington Post*, July 25, 1933, 8.

4   "General Foods Cuts Decaffeinated Coffees; Puts Them into 35 to 37 Cent Retail Range," *New York Times*, July 21, 1939, 32. United States Bureau of the Census, *Historical Statistics of the United States: Colonial Times to 1970*, vol. 2 (Washington, DC: USGPO, 1975), 213.

5   Monsanto Sales Survey: Caffeine and Theobromine, August 3, 1944, series 3, box 1, Caffeine (General), Monsanto Company Records; Letter from Ralph Hayes to Robert W. Woodruff, January 15, 1959, box 138, folder 6, RWW Papers, MARBL.

6   General Foods Corporation Annual Reports for 1955–1965.

7   Letter from Ralph Hayes to Robert W. Woodruff, January 15, 1959, box 138, folder 6, RWW Papers, MARBL; Letter from Ralph Hayes to John Stounton, January 12, 1959, box 138, folder 6, RWW Papers, MARBL; Memorandum re: Mdse. #3 in 1957 from Ralph Hayes, January 17, 1958, box 138, folder 5, RWW Papers, MARBL. For an illuminating glimpse into the inner workings of a present-day decaffeination plant, see journalist Murray Carpenter's account of his trip to a Houston-based Maximus Coffee Group plant formerly owned by General Foods (*Caffeinated*, 93–98).

8   Letter from Ralph Hayes to Robert W. Woodruff, January 10, 1962, box 139, folder 2, RWW Papers, MARBL; "Caffeine Prices Slashed by Monsanto Chemical and General Foods," *Wall Street Journal*, July 31, 1957, 18; "Caffeine Prices Slashed; Cheap Imports Blamed," *New York Times*, July 31, 1957, 32; "Monsanto Cuts Synthetic Caffeine Price Sharply, Cites Import Pressure," *Wall Street Journal*, December 22, 1958, 32.

9   Letter from Ralph Hayes to Robert W. Woodruff, January 10, 1962, and Letter from Ralph Hayes to Ira Vandewater, President of R. W. Greef & Co., January 14, 1959, box 138, folder 6, RWW Papers, MARBL.

10 General Foods Corporation 1956 Annual Report, 8–9; General Foods Corporation 1957 Annual Report, 4; Mark Pendergrast, *Uncommon Grounds*, 249–256.

11 Nina Luttinger and Gregory Dicum, *The Coffee Book: Anatomy of an Industry from Crop to the Last Drop* (New York: New Press, 2006), 6; "Cheaper Coffee," *Wall Street Journal*, February 11, 1955, 1; General Foods Corporation 1957 Annual Report, 4; "Coffee Grinds Fuel for the Nation," *USA Today*, April 9, 2013; Gen-

eral Foods Corporation 1961 Annual Report, 6–7; Mark Pendergrast, *Uncommon Grounds*, 216.

12 "Lee Talley Put Fizz Back into Coca-Cola," *Miami News*, November 17, 1963, 12A; Mark Pendergrast, *For God, Country & Coca-Cola*, 272; Frederick Allen, *Secret Formula*, 308–310.

13 "Minute Maid Discussing Merger with Tenco, Coffee Processor," *New York Times*, August 28, 1959, 30; Minute Maid Corporation Prospectus for Coca-Cola shareholders review, February 9, 1960, box 55, folder 8, RWW Papers, MARBL; Mark Pendergrast, *Uncommon Grounds*, 241, 272. For a history of instant coffee, see John M. Talbot, "The Struggle for Control of a Commodity Chain: Instant Coffee from Latin America," *Latin American Research Review* 32, no. 2 (1997): 117–135. "Business Milestones: Minute Maid Holding Merger Talks with Soluble Coffee Maker," *Wall Street Journal*, August 28, 1959, 11; "Coca-Cola Holds Merger Talks with Minute Maid," *Wall Street Journal*, September 9, 1960, 5; Coca-Cola Company 1960 Annual Report, 7, and 1961 Annual Report, 8, 10.

14 Reflecting on Coke's Tenco purchase, longtime coffee industry executive Stuart Daw said, "Coca Cola [*sic*] bought out Tenco, a group of 10 amalgamated instant coffee producers, not because it wanted to enter the coffee business per se, but for the procurement of caffeine." Stuart Daw, "Reflections in a Cup: Caffeine Anyone?" *Canadian Vending and Office Coffee Service Magazine*, http://www.canadianvending.com/content/view/1113; "Coffee Decline—Fewer Drinkers, Fewer Cups," *New York Times*, March 15, 1975, 12; Mark Pendergrast, *Uncommon Grounds*, 302.

15 Letter from Benjamin Oehlert to Lee Talley, July 19, 1961, box 242, folder 5, RWW Papers, MARBL.

16 Letter from Charles W. Duncan Jr. to Lee Talley, May 8, 1964, box 82, folder 8, RWW Papers, MARBL; Coca-Cola Company 1963 Annual Report, 6; "Coca-Cola Says It Plans to Buy Duncan Foods Co.," *Wall Street Journal*, January 28, 1964, 7; Frederick Allen, *Secret Formula*, 359.

17 Report from Ed Aborn, June 21, 1961, box 35, Mark Pendergrast Research Files, MARBL; "Minute Maid Discussing Merger with Tenco, Coffee Processor," *New York Times*, August 28, 1959, 30; "Coca-Cola to Sell Tea, Coffee Unit to Tetley," *Wall Street Journal*, November 18, 1981, 4.

18 Report from Ed Aborn, June 21, 1961, box 35, Mark Pendergrast Research Files, MARBL; "Coca-Cola to Sell Tea, Coffee Unit to Tetley," *Wall Street Journal*, November 18, 1981, 4.

19 General Foods Corporation 1977 Annual Report, 3; "Nestle's Brewing Something New," *New York Times*, October 1, 1971, 66; "Coffee Decline—Fewer Drinkers, Fewer Cups," *New York Times*, March 15, 1975, 12; "Worries Start Bubbling Up over Caffeine in Colas," *Washington Post*, January 11, 1970, B5; "How Dangerous is Caffeine in Cola?" *Los Angeles Times*, January 15, 1970, G18; "The Caffeine," *Washington Post*, February 26, 1986, H12.

20 "Pfizer Buys Citro Chemical Co.," *New York Times*, October 8, 1947, 42; "Pfizer Employee Checks Lab Work," *Groton News* (Groton, CT), July 18, 1970, 13; Memorandum from Ralph Hayes to Daphne Robert, January 10, 1948, box 49, folder 7, RWW Papers, MARBL; Pfizer Inc. 1965 Annual Report, 12; Murray Carpenter, *Caffeinated*, 99–100, 105.

21 Author's conversation with Coca-Cola customer service representative, September 19, 2012.

22 House Committee on Ways and Means, Subcommittee on Trade, *Written Comments on Certain Tariff and Trade Bills, Vol. III*, 100th Cong., 2nd Sess., February 5, 1998, 134; "Pfizer's Chemicals Division Raises Some of Its Prices," *Wall Street Journal*, November 30, 1970, 3; "For Years Industry Soared," *New York Times*, February 24, 1985, 124; Shelina Sharif, "Keeping Up with Caffeine," *Chemical Week*, April 10, 1991, 33; For more on China and the synthetic caffeine industry, see Murray Carpenter, *Caffeinated*, 101–112. Carpenter told of his failed attempt to enter a caffeine-manufacturing plant in the Chinese city of Shijiazhuang, a testament to just how secretive this international trade remained as of 2014.

23 Memorandum from J. Paul Austin to Robert W. Woodruff, April 17, 1973; Memorandum from J. Paul Austin to the Chairman of the Finance Committee, May 4, 1973; Letter from J. Paul Austin to Robert W. Woodruff, May 4, 1973, all in box 49, folder 2, RWW Papers, MARBL; Frederick Allen, *Secret Formula*, 358–359.

24 Senate Committee on Labor and Public Welfare, Subcommittee on Migratory Labor, *Migrant and Seasonal Farmworker Powerlessness, Part 8-C: Who Is Responsible?*, 91st Cong., 2nd Sess., July 24, 1970, 5841–5914; Mark Pendergrast, *For God, Country & Coca-Cola*, 294–295.

25 "Leader of Farm Workers Says Union Faces Life or Death," *New York Times*, September 22, 1973, 34.

26 Memorandum from Paul Austin to R. W. Woodruff, September 19, 1969, box 16, folder 1, RWW Papers, MARBL.

27 Senate Committee on Labor and Public Welfare, Subcommittee on Migratory Labor, *Migrant and Seasonal Farmworker Powerlessness, Part 8-C: Who Is Responsible?* 91st Cong., 2nd Sess., July 24, 1970, 5875–5880.

28 "Corporations: The Candor That Refreshes," *Time*, August 10, 1970; "Life Improves for Florida's Orange Harvesters," *New York Times*, March 19, 1973, 53; Mark Pendergrast, *For God, Country & Coca-Cola*, 294–295.

29 "Coca-Cola Foods' Teasly Focuses Marketing on Minute Maid Juices," *Wall Street Journal*, June 23, 1988, 1. "Coca-Cola Invites Growers to Meet with Farm Workers," *Lakeland Ledger*, April 27, 1994, 1E; "Coca-Cola Sells Off Its Groves," *Miami Herald*, October 30, 1993, 1C; "FPL's Citrus Unit for Sale," *Miami Herald*, June 18, 1998, 1C.

30 For excellent environmental histories of coffee cultivation in Latin America, see Warren Dean's *With Broadax and Firebrand: The Destruction of the Brazilian Atlantic Forest* (Berkeley and Los Angeles: University of California Press, 1997) and Richard Tucker's *Insatiable Appetite*. For a comprehensive understanding of the political economy of coffee growing in Brazil, see Joe Foweraker's *The Struggle for Land: A Political Economy of the Pioneer Frontier in Brazil from 1930 to the Present Day* (Cambridge: Cambridge University Press, 1981). For a global economic perspective, see Steven Topik and William Gervase Clarence-Smith, eds., *The Global Coffee Economy in Africa, Asia, and Latin America, 1500–1989* (Cambridge: Cambridge University Press, 2003); Richard Tucker, *Insatiable Appetite*, 181–184; Warren Dean, *With Broadax and Firebrand*, 188.

31 Warren Dean, *With Broadax and Firebrand*, 220–221, 240; "When They Shout, 'Yanqui, No!'" *New York Times*, January 26, 1964, SM9. On immigrant labor in

Brazil, see Warren Dean's chapter "The Wage Labor Regime" in *Rio Claro: A Brazilian Plantation System, 1820–1920* (Stanford: Stanford University Press, 1976), 156–194. See also Thomas H. Holloway, "The Coffee *Colono* of São Paulo, Brazil: Migration and Mobility, 1880–1930," in *Land and Labour in Latin America: Essays on the Development of Agrarian Capitalism in the Nineteenth and Twentieth Centuries*, ed. Kenneth Duncan and Ian Rutledge with Colin Harding (Cambridge: Cambridge University Press, 1977): 301–322.

32 Richard Tucker, *Insatiable Appetite*, 181; Warren Dean, *With Broadax and Firebrand*, 6, 13–14, 247, 250.

33 Warren Dean, *With Broadax and Firebrand*, 216–218. Jason Clay penned a chapter on soil erosion and other environmental factors associated with monocrop coffee cultivation; see his *World Agriculture and the Environment: A Commodity-by-Commodity Guide to Impacts and Practices* (Washington, DC: Island Press, 2004), 69–91.

34 Richard Tucker, *Insatiable Appetite*, 181, 209–225. On Colombia especially, see Marco Palacios's *Coffee in Colombia, 1850–1970: An Economic, Social and Political History* (Cambridge: Cambridge University Press, 1980).

35 Nina Luttinger and Gregory Dicum, *The Coffee Book*, 55–56. For histories of the Green Revolution, see John Perkins, *Geopolitics and the Green Revolution: Wheat, Genes, and the Cold War* (New York: Oxford University Press, 1997); and Nick Cullather, *The Hungry World: America's Cold War Battle Against Poverty in Asia* (Cambridge: Harvard University Press, 2010).

36 Jason Clay, *World Agriculture and the Environment*, 74, 76; "African/Asian Coffees: Overview—Crossroads for Robustas?" *World Coffee and Tea Journal*, June 1965, 17; Nina Luttinger and Gregory Dicum, *The Coffee Book*, 101; Richard Tucker, *Insatiable Appetite*, 95.

37 "Clear Answers Lacking on Caffeine's Effects," *Los Angeles Times*, October 15, 1972, E6; Bennett Alan Weinberg and Bonnie K. Bealer, *The World of Caffeine: The Science and Culture of the World's Most Popular Drug* (New York: Routledge, 2001), 189.

38 Letter from Lewis Robinson, Manager, Boy Scouts Band, Schenectady Council, to the Department of Agriculture, June 5, 1940; Letter from Eugene Schachner, Correspondent for "The London News Chronicle," to the Bureau of Standards, August 10, 1941; Letter from Mrs. Mabel Flagg of Morningdale, Massachusetts, to Food and Drug Administration, June 26, 1941, box 22, folder 6, Mark Pendergrast Research Files, MARBL (numerous consumer letters can be found in this file); "Labels Required for Soft Drinks," *New York Times*, June 15, 1961, 45.

39 They also made the argument that caffeine deserved special exemption because it was a "flavor" and should be subject to the provisions of the law that allow "flavors" to be listed simply as "flavoring." Letter from Edgar Forio and Benjamin Oehlert to George Larrick, July 21, 1965, box 2, folder 243, RWW Papers, MARBL.

40 Frederick Allen, *Secret Formula*, 329.

41 Ibid.

42 Code of Federal Regulations, Title 21—Food and Drugs (revised January 1, 1967), 297–298.

43 James S. Turner, *The Chemical Feast: The Ralph Nader Study Group Report on Food Protection and the Food and Drug Administration* (New York: Grossman, 1970);

Rachel Carson, *Silent Spring* (Boston: Houghlin Mifflin; Cambridge, MA: Riverside Press, 1962).

44 Memorandum from Benjamin Oehlert to W. J. Hobbs, Robert W. Woodruff, Harrison Jones, and Pope Brock, February 27, 1948, box 242, folder 4, RWW Papers, MARBL.

45 Bennett Alan Weinberg and Bonnie K. Bealer, *The World of Caffeine*, 189–190; Mark Pendergrast, *Uncommon Grounds*, 309.

46 The annual budget for ILSI in the mid–1980s was $3 million. "NIH Official's Role Disputed," *Washington Post*, September 28, 1985, A2; J. A. Treichel, "Good News for Caffeine Consumers?" *Science News* 122, no. 20 (November 13, 1982); "No Need for Coffee Fears, Experts Say," *Chicago Tribune*, November 5, 1982, 12; "No Caffeine-Tumor Link Seen," *New York Times*, October 19, 1982, C7.

47 Matt Clark with Mariana Gosnell, Deborah Witherspoon, and Mary Hager, "Is Caffeine Bad for You?" *Newsweek*, July 19, 1982, 62; "Diet Therapy for Behavior Is Criticized as Premature," *New York Times*, December 4, 1984, C14.

48 "Scientists Question Objectivity of Top NIH Nutrition Official," *Washington Post*, December 24, 1985, A6; "NIH Official's Role Disputed," *Washington Post*, September 28, 1985, A2; "NIH Reassigns Controversial Official," *Washington Post*, April 13, 1986, A5. The institute continued its international conferences into the 1990s and 2000s and published several major works on caffeine consumption and human health. In 2010, it completed a comprehensive review of all the scientific studies relating to caffeine consumption and birth defects, publishing its findings in a well-read journal, *Food and Chemical Toxicology*, in 2010. The report concluded current science did not warrant written warnings. Psychologist Jack E. James claimed that ILSI's 1993 publication *Caffeine, Coffee, and Health* (ed. Silvio Garattini; New York: Raven Press, 1993) fell "short of providing adequate coverage of the available evidence on" the "health implications" of caffeine consumption, adding, "Much of the extant literature is either scantily covered or omitted altogether, including the work of several major research groups (e.g., Shapiro et al. at UCLA, Lane et al. at Duke University, and Smits et al. at the University of Njmegen, The Netherlands)." Jack E. James and Michael Gossop, book review of *Caffeine, Coffee and Health*, *Addiction* 90, no. 1 (January 1995): 134–135. James elaborates on his concerns about ILSI in "Caffeine, Health and Commercial Interests," *Addiction* 89, no. 12 (December 1994): 1595–1599. International Life Sciences Institute (ISLI) North America 2010 Annual Report.

49 As Dan Carpenter has shown in his book *Reputation and Power: Organizational Image and Pharmaceutical Regulation at the FDA* (Princeton: Princeton University Press, 2010), the desire to preserve institutional reputation often took precedence over public health interests, and in the case of caffeine, FDA scientists simply were not willing to take the risk of exposing the agency to public ridicule in light of conflicting evidence about the health costs of caffeine consumption. "Caffeine Quandary Illustrates F.D.A.'s Plight," *New York Times*, January 8, 1980, C1.

50 "The Caffeine," *Washington Post*, February 26, 1986, H12.

51 Ibid.; "A Coffee Drinker's Guide to Decaffeinated Varieties," *New York Times*, August 1, 1984, C1.

52 "Coca-Cola Co. Plans to Test Caffeine-Free Coke Classic," *Wall Street Journal*, October 19, 1989, B7.

53　Heather Landi, "A Challenging Year," *Beverage World* 127, no. 4 (April 15, 2008), S6; Harvey W. Wiley, "The Effects of Caffeine upon the Human Organism," June 1915, box 192, Harvey Washington Wiley Papers, Library of Congress, Washington, DC.

54　"Coke and Nestlé Plan Coffee and Tea Drinks," *New York Times*, November 30, 1990, D5; "Coke Blak Goes Black," BevNet.com, August 31, 2007, http://www.bevnet .com/news/2007/08-31-2007-Blak_coca-cola.asp; "Coke CEO Sees Canned Coffee Growing Despite Recession," *Reuters*, May 28, 2009, http://www.reuters.com/ article/2009/05/28/coke-illy-idUSN2833611620090528. Never in history has caffeine been available in such large supply at so little cost. Huge quantities of this drug can be channeled into consumers' bodies by mass-marketing firms, which raises the question: is all this caffeine good for us? What are the human health costs of this new hypercaffeinated industry? While new studies suggest that, indeed, a cup of coffee a day may keep the doctor away, other research shows that excessive caffeine consumption could be producing troubling problems, especially among young people. Energy drink consumption has been linked to increased hyperactivity among children, and reports of caffeine intoxication (over 5000 in 2007 alone) have been on the rise. Other studies have shown that heavy daily consumption of caffeine can contribute to seizures, stroke, and in some cases even heart attack. "Energy Drinks May Harm Health, Especially for Children," *Time*, February 14, 2011; Chad J. Reissig, Eric C. Strain, and Roland R. Griffiths, "Caffeinated Energy Drinks—A Growing Problem," *Drug and Alcohol Dependence* 99 (January 1, 2009): 1–10; Sara M. Seifert, Judith L. Schaechter, Eugene R. Hershorin, and Steven E. Lipshultz, "Health Effects of Energy Drinks on Children, Adolescents, and Young Adults," *Pediatrics* 127, no. 3 (March 1, 2011): 511–528; N. Gunja and J. A. Brown, "Energy Drinks: Health Risks and Toxicity," *Medical Journal of Australia* 196, no. 1 (January 16, 2012): 46–49.

55　Muhtar Kent, Statement for Rio+20, July 18, 2012, published by the Avoided Deforestation Partners, https://www.youtube.com/watch?v=h548OnhSyuc.

56　Coca-Cola Company website, Product Descriptions: Coffee, http://www.thecoca -colacompany.com/brands/coffee.html.

8. GLASS, ALUMINUM, PLASTIC:
SELLING CURBSIDE RECYCLING TO AMERICA

1　A version of this chapter was published in the Autumn 2012 issue of Harvard Business School's *Business History Review.*

2　Few scholars, whether focusing on Progressive Era enterprises, agribusinesses of the 1930s, or high-tech industries of the Cold War, have treated the construction of public waste-management systems as an essential government intervention that aided big-business growth in the latter half of the twentieth century. Corporate giants that had first emerged in the Progressive Era produced large amounts of packaging refuse by midcentury, causing consumers to question the prudence of supporting an economy dependent on centralized distributors using one-way packaging. Developing public infrastructure that would help megafirms mollify these fears was critical to the future solvency of some of the most profitable business enterprises the world had ever seen. For excellent works on the development of curbside recycling programs, see Frank Ackerman, *Why Do We Recycle: Markets, Values, and Public Policy* (Washington, DC: Island Press, 1997); Martin Melosi, *Garbage in the Cities: Refuse, Reform, and the Environment: 1880–1980* (College Station: Texas A&M University Press, 1981); Martin Melosi, *The Sanitary City: Urban Infrastructure in America from Colonial Times to the Present* (Baltimore: Johns Hopkins University Press, 2000); Heather Rogers, *Gone Tomorrow: The Hidden Life of Garbage* (New York: New Press, 2005); Elizabeth Royte, *Garbage Land: On the Secret Trail of Trash* (New York: Little, Brown, 2005); Louis Blumberg and Robert Gottlieb, *War on Waste: Can America Win Its Battle with Garbage?* (Washington, DC: Island Press, 1989); Carl A. Zimring, *Cash for Your Trash: Scrap Recycling in America* (New Brunswick: Rutgers University Press, 2005). For an international perspective on beverage-container recycling and an excellent discussion of the sociocultural construction of reverse vending machines (RVMs), see Finn Arne Jørgensen, *Making a Green Machine: The Infrastructure of Beverage Container Recycling* (New Brunswick: Rutgers University Press, 2011).

3 "Deposit System," *Southern Carbonator and Bottler*, November 1905, 10; "Bulletin of the Coca-Cola Bottlers' Association," *Coca-Cola Bottler*, April 1929, 33–35.

4 The forty-to-fifty figure reflects return rates for some bottles in the 1960s as calculated by the Investment Research Department of Laidlaw and Company in an investment report for the Coca-Cola Company, "Follow-Up Report No. 6 to Basic Report Dated October, 1963," August 1965, box 57, folder 1, RWW Papers, MARBL; United States Resource Conservation Committee, *Committee Findings and Staff Papers on National Beverage Container Deposits* (Washington, DC: Resource Conservation Committee, 1979), 75, 76, 84; William K. Shiremanm, Frank Sweeney, et al., *The CalPIRG-ELS Study Group Report on Can and Bottle Bills* (hereinafter *Can and Bottle Bills*) (Stanford, CA: Stanford Environmental Law Society, 1981), 5.

5 Constance Hays, *The Real Thing*, 11; United States Office of Technology Assessment, *Materials and Energy from Municipal Waste: Resource Recovery and Recycling from Municipal Solid Waste* (Washington, DC: USGPO, 1979), 189.

6 William K. Shireman, Frank Sweeney et al., *Can and Bottle Bills*, 4; American Can Company, *A History of Packaged Beer and Its Market in the United States* (New York: American Can Co., 1969), 7; Maureen Ogle, *Ambitious Brew: The Story of American Beer* (Orlando: Harcourt, 2006), 183–185, 213, 216; A. M. McGahan, "The Emergence of the National Brewing Oligopoly: Competition in the American Market, 1933–1958," *Business History Review* 65, no. 2 (Summer 1991): 230.

7 American Can Company, *A History of Packaged Beer*, 29.

8 "Soft Drinks: Will the Cans Take Over?" *Business Week*, January 1954, 47; Shireman et al., *Can and Bottle Bills*, 9; "Canned Soda Pop," *Wall Street Journal*, September 24, 1953, box 292, folder 10, RWW Papers, MARBL. A. M. McGahan, "The Emergence of the National Brewing Oligopoly," 230, 247–248.

9 "Soft Drinks: Will the Cans Take Over?" *Business Week*, January 30, 1954; William K. Shireman et al., *Can and Bottle Bills*, 9; John Stuart, "C&C Super Corp. to Open Third Plant Next Month to Can Soft Drinks in Chicago," *New York Times*, April 25, 1954, F1; "Canned Soda Pop," *Wall Street Journal*, September 24, 1953, box 292, folder 10, RWW Papers, MARBL.

10 "Now! Your Favorite Soft Drinks in Cans!" *Daily Mirror*, June 10, 1953, 19, box 292, folder 10, RWW Papers, MARBL.

11 "C&C Super Corp. to Open Third Plant Next Month to Can Soft Drinks in Chicago," *New York Times*, April 25, 1954, F1.

12 H. B. Nicholson, "The Fabulous Frontier," Speech for the American Bottlers of Carbonated Beverages, November 11, 1953, box 58, folder 1, RWW Papers, MARBL; "The Overseas Story," *Coca-Cola Overseas*, June 1948, 5; United States Office of Technology Assessment, *Materials and Energy from Municipal Waste: Resource Recovery and Recycling from Municipal Solid Waste* (Washington, DC: USGPO, 1979), 189.

13 Constance Hays, *The Real Thing*, xii.

14 "Coca-Cola in Cans for the Far East," *Coca-Cola Bottler*, April 1955, 28; "Sales of Canned Soft Drinks Soar," *Coca-Cola Bottler*, July 1965, 25–27; "Aluminum Aftermath," *Wall Street Journal*, November 22, 1965, 2.

15 Senate Committee on Commerce, Science, and Transportation, *Reuse and Recycling Act of* 1979, 96th Cong., 2nd Sess., March 3, 1980, 58; Senate Subcommittee for Consumers, Committee on Commerce, Science, and Transportation, *Beverage Container Reuse and Recycling Act of* 1977, 95th Cong., 1st Sess., January 25, 26, 27, 1978, 158.

16 Senate Subcommittee on Environment, Committee on Commerce, *Solid Waste Management Act of* 1972, 92nd Cong., 2nd Sess., March 6, 10, 13, 1972, 35; Senate Subcommittee on Environment, *Nonreturnable Beverage Container Prohibition Act*, 93rd Cong., 2nd Sess., May 6, 7, 1974, 95, 108; Heather Rogers, *Gone Tomorrow*, 136–37.

17 Senate Subcommittee on Environment, *Nonreturnable Beverage Container Prohibition Act*, 108; Constance Hays, *The Real Thing*, 11, 182.

18 The soft drink industry consistently claimed that consumers forced the beverage companies to adopt one-way containers. It was a bottom-up process, Coke and its industry allies argued. Consumers living in the automobile age had more mobility than ever before and wanted the convenience of not having to return packaging to retail outlets. While such claims were in part true, left unsaid were the business forces that shaped America's throwaway culture. One-way containers helped soft drink businesses achieve economies of scale in their bottling industries, reducing costs associated with collecting and processing returnables. Convenience packaging, in other words, was as much a product of consumer demand as it was an industry solution to a distribution dilemma. For excellent works that explore both business and consumer forces that shaped America's throwaway culture, see Susan Strasser, *Waste and Want: A Social History of Trash* (New York: Metropolitan Books, 1999); Susan Strasser, *Satisfaction Guaranteed: The Making of the American Mass Market* (New York: Pantheon Books, 1989); "Throwaway Society," in Ted Steinberg's *Down to Earth: Nature's Role in American History* (New York: Oxford University Press, 2002): 226–239; Susan Strasser, "'The Convenience Is Out of This World': The Garbage Disposer and American Consumer Culture," in *Getting and Spending: European and American Consumer Societies in the Twentieth Century*, ed. Susan Strasser, Charles McGovern, and Matthias Judt (Cambridge: Cambridge University Press, 1998): 263–280.

19 This interpretation of the rise of the modern environmental movement draws heavily on Samuel P. Hays's *Beauty, Health, and Permanence: Environmental Politics in the United States* (Cambridge: Cambridge University Press, 1987).

20 "Beer Bottle Plan Offered by Delegate," *Washington Post*, March 17, 1953, 26.

21 In 1961, John Atlee Kouwenhoven published *The Beer Can by the Highway: Essays on What's American About America* (Garden City, NY: Doubleday, 1961), a testament to public concern about the aesthetic costs associated with one-way container waste; Andre J. Rouleau, administrator of Vermont Beverage Container Law, "Vermont Deposit Law and Recycling," presented at Vermont Solid Waste Summit, November 8, 1985, 2, available online from P2 InfoHouse, www.p2pays.org/ref/24/23636.pdf.

22 "Heads New Anti-Litter Group," *New York Times*, October 14, 1954, 31; Elizabeth Royte, *Garbage Land*, 184; Martin Melosi, *Garbage in the Cities*, 225–26; Heather Rogers, *Gone Tomorrow*, 141–146.

23 Anthropologist Caroline W. Lee has shown that even Progressive Era businesses engaged in astroturfing. See "The Roots of Astroturfing," *Contexts* 9, no. 1 (Winter 2010): 73–75. Nevertheless, KAB took these tactics to another level. The large-scale anti-litter campaigns it mobilized would provide a model for similar highly organized national corporate campaigns of the late twentieth century.

24 "Litter Increased in Crowded Cities," *New York Times*, December 7, 1954, 40.

25 "Keep America Beautiful Ad 1960s," http://www.youtube.com/watch?v=AQtlRfg LdsQ&videos=OP4RmRuVjmA.

26 Ginger Strand, "The Crying Indian: How an Environmental Icon Helped Sell Cans—and Sell Out Environmentalism," *Orion Nature Quarterly*, November/December 2008, 24; Finis Dunaway, "Gas Masks, Pogo, and the Ecological Indian: Earth Day and the Visual Politics of American Environmentalism," *American Quarterly* 60, no. 1 (March 2008): 67–99; Elizabeth Royte, *Garbage Land*, 184.

27 Martin Melosi, *Garbage in the Cities*, 170; *Beverage Industry* 87 (June 1996): 26, reproduced at http://memory.loc.gov/ammem/ccmphtml/indsthst.html; Letter from Paul Austin to Robert W. Woodruff, November 28, 1969, box 16, folder 1, RWW Papers.

28 Paul Austin, "Environmental Renewal or Oblivion . . . Quo Vadis?" Speech given to the Georgia Bankers Association, Atlanta, Georgia, April 16, 1970, reprinted in *Vital Speeches of the Day* 36, no. 15 (March 15, 1970): 471–472, 475.

29 Ibid., 474.

30 "Litter Bits," *NSDA Bulletin*, January–February 1968, 6.

31 *American Soft Drink Journal*, July 1967, 34; "Litter Letter Future Doubtful," *NSDA Bulletin*, April 26, 1968, 5.

32 "Keep America Beautiful Ad 1960s," KAB commercial, http://www.youtube.com/watch?v=AQtlRfgLdsQ&videos=OP4RmRuVjmA; "The Crying Indian," KAB commercial, http://www.youtube.com/watch?v=j7OHG7tHrNM. See also Ginger Strand, "The Crying Indian"; "After the 'Crying Indian,' Keep America Beautiful Starts a New Campaign," *New York Times*, July 17, 2013, B5.

33 "Earth Week: April 19–26," *Speckled Bird*, April 20, 1970, 3; "Scope," *Soft Drinks* (formerly *National Bottlers' Gazette*), May 1970; "Coca-Cola's Confrontation," *Business Week*, May 2, 1970, 22.

34 Letter from Paul Austin to Robert W. Woodruff, November 28, 1969, box 16, folder 1, RWW Papers, MARBL.

35 "'Bend a Little' and 'Keep America Beautiful,'" featured on Coca-Cola's company

blog, Coca-Cola Conversations, edited by archivists Ted Ryan and Phil Mooney, http://www.coca-colaconversations.com/2009/04/bend-a-little-and-keep-america -beautiful.html.

36 Mark Pendergrast, *For God, Country & Coca-Cola*, 295; Display Ad, *New York Times*, April 22, 1970, 33.

37 For an excellent survey of American advertising and youth culture in the twen- tieth century, see Lisa Jacobson, *Raising Consumers: Children and the American Mass Market in the Early Twentieth Century* (New York: Columbia University Press, 2004); Phil Mooney, "Man in His Environment Ecology Kit," Coca-Cola Conver- sations company blog, http://www.coca-colaconversations.com/2009/04/man-in- his-environment-ecology-kit.html.

38 For a detailed history of the Oregon battle, see Brent Walth, "No Deposit, No Return: Richard Chambers, Tom McCall, and the Oregon Bottle Bill," *Oregon His- torical Quarterly* 95, no. 3 (Fall 1994): 278–299.

39 Stanford Environmental Law Society, *Disposing of Non-Returnables: A Guide to Minimum Deposit Legislation* (Stanford, CA: Stanford Environmental Law Society, 1975), 17.

40 Lewis Gould, *Lady Bird Johnson and the Environment* (Lawrence: University Press of Kansas, 1988). See also Lewis Gould, ed., *Lady Bird Johnson: Our Environmental First Lady* (Lawrence: University Press of Kansas, 1988); Martin Melosi, *Garbage in the Cities*, 198, 200–201.

41 House Subcommittee on Public Health and Welfare, Committee on Interstate and Foreign Commerce, *Prohibit Certain No-Deposit, No-Return Containers*, 91st Cong., 2nd Sess., September 18, 1970, 53.

42 Ibid., 46; Senate Subcommittee on Environment, *Solid Waste Management Act of 1972*, 79.

43 Senate Subcommittee on Science, Technology, and Space, Committee on Com- merce, Science, and Transportation, *Materials Policy*, 95th Cong., 1st Sess., July 14, 19, 1977, 62.

44 Heather Rogers, *Gone Tomorrow*, 150; "Yonkers Studies a No-Return Ban," *New York Times*, September 9, 1971, 59.

45 Heather Rogers, *Gone Tomorrow*, 166, 172.

46 Carl A. Zimring, *Cash for Your Trash*, 160; Finn Arne Jørgensen, *Making a Green Machine*, 29–31.

47 Heather Rogers, *Gone Tomorrow*, 140.

48 Meeting minutes from the State Association Conference, National Soft Drink Association, November 10, 1970, 12, American Beverage Association (ABA) Infor- mation Center, Washington, DC.

49 "Advertising: Reynolds in an Ecology Drive," *New York Times*, April 13, 1971, 63; Display Ad, *New York Times*, February 9, 1971, 25; Senate Subcommittee on Envi- ronment, *Solid Waste Management Act of 1972*, 81.

50 Martin Melosi, *Garbage in the Cities*, 221; "Recycling Efforts Faltering on L. I.," *New York Times*, February 13, 1972, A1.

51 "Waste Recycling Effort Found to Lag," *New York Times*, May 7, 1972, 1; "A Guide to Recycling," *Washington Post*, April 13, 1978, VA1.

52 "Waste Recycling Effort Found to Lag," *New York Times*, May 7, 1972, 1, 57; Senate Subcommittee on Environment, *Solid Waste Management Act of 1972*, 26.

53 House Subcommittee on Public Health and Welfare, Committee on Interstate and Foreign Commerce, *Prohibit Certain No-Deposit, No-Return Containers*, 91st Cong., 2nd Sess., September 18, 1970, 39; Elizabeth Royte, *Garbage Land*, 127.

54 Senate Subcommittee on Environment, *Solid Waste Management Act of 1972*, 35.

55 Senate Subcommittee for Consumer, Committee on Commerce, Science, and Transportation, *Beverage Container Recycling and Reuse*, 95th Cong., 2nd Sess., January 25, 26, 27, 1978, 203.

56 Robert G. Hunt and William E. Franklin, "LCA—How It Came About: Personal Reflections on the Origin and the Development of LCA in the USA," *International Journal of Life Cycle Assessment* 1, no. 1 (March 1996): 4.

57 Ibid.

58 E-mail to author, February 8, 2010.

59 William K. Shireman et al., *Can and Bottle Bills*, 5; EPA, *Resource and Environmental Profile Analysis of Nine Beverage Container Alternatives* (Washington, DC: USGPO, 1974), 1–8; United States Office of Technology Assessment, *Materials and Energy from Municipal Waste*, 190.

60 Robert G. Hunt and William E. Franklin, "LCA—How It Came About," 4; Mark Duda and Jane S. Shaw, "Life Cycle Assessment," *Society* 35, no. 1 (November 1997): 38–39.

61 Phone Interview with Robert Hunt, Franklin Associates Ltd., February 9, 2010. Speaking of Coke's secrecy, Hunt added, "Coke was not forthcoming to us exactly why they were doing" the 1969 study.

62 "Coca-Cola Plastic Bottle Undergoes Test Selling in 3 New England Cities," *Wall Street Journal*, March 24, 1970, 23; Robert G. Hunt and William E. Franklin, "LCA—How It Came About," 4; Food and Drug Administration, *Final Environmental Impact Statement: Plastic Bottles for Carbonated Beverages and Beer* (Washington, DC: USGPO, September 1976), 45.

63 "Coca-Cola Trying a Plastic Bottle," *New York Times*, June 4, 1975, 65; Food and Drug Administration, *Final Environmental Impact Statement: Plastic Bottles for Carbonated Beverages and Beer*, 23; "Monsanto to Expand Plastic Bottle Output, Has Accord to Supply Coca-Cola Bottlers," *Wall Street Journal*, October 15, 1973, 13; "Coca-Cola Trying a Plastic Bottle," *New York Times*, June 4, 1975, 65.

64 "Suffolk Prepares to Battle a Bottle," *New York Times*, December 5, 1976, 442.

65 "Technology: The Dispute over Plastic Bottles," *New York Times*, April 13, 1977, 79; Letter from Paul Austin to Woodruff, February 15, 1977, box 16, folder 5, RWW Papers, MARBL; "Monsanto to Expand Plastic Bottle Output, Has Accord to Supply Coca-Cola Bottlers," *Wall Street Journal*, October 15, 1973, 13; "A Market Thirst, Never Quenched," *New York Times*, April 9, 1978, F1; *Coca-Cola Bottler*, January 1984, 9; Coca-Cola Company 1978 Annual Report, 6, 8.

66 "Garbage Crisis: After Landfills, What?" *New York Times*, April 2, 1978; "Suburbs Facing a Tough Fight over Sites for Garbage Dumps," *Chicago Tribune*, August 9, 1979, N2; "End Is Nearer for Kane Landfill," *Chicago Tribune*, July 2, 1989, C1. On the birth of the environmental justice movement, see Eileen Maura McGurty,

"From NIMBY to Civil Rights: The Origins of the Environmental Justice Movement," in *Environmental History and the American South: A Reader*, ed. Paul Sutter and Christopher J. Manganiello (Athens: University of Georgia Press, 2009); and Robert Bullard, *Dumping in Dixie: Race, Class, and Environmental Quality* (Boulder, CO: Westview Press, 1990). For works on the emergence of the modern environmental movement, see Samuel P. Hays, *Beauty, Health, and Permanence: Environmental Politics in the United States, 1955–1985* (Cambridge: Cambridge University Press, 1987); Ted Steinberg, "Shades of Green," chapter 15 in *Down to Earth: Nature's Role in American History* (New York: Oxford University Press, 2002), 239–261; Adam Rome, *The Bulldozer in the Countryside: Suburban Sprawl and the Rise of American Environmentalism* (Cambridge: Cambridge University Press, 2001). According to Heather Rogers, one study showed that roadside litter in Oregon decreased by 35 percent in the wake of the new deposit law. Heather Rogers, *Gone Tomorrow*, 147.

67 Senate Committee on Commerce, Science, and Transportation, *Reuse and Recycling Act of 1979*, 68.

68 Finn Arne Jørgensen, *Making a Green Machine*, 89.

69 Heather Rogers, *Gone Tomorrow*, 154.

70 "Bottle Bill Foes' Recycling Claim Disputed," *Washington Post*, October 25, 1987, B7; Senate Committee on Energy and Natural Resources, *Recycling*, 102nd Cong., 2nd Sess., September 17, 1992, 160; House Subcommittee on Transportation and Hazardous Materials, Committee on Energy and Commerce, *Recycling of Municipal Solid Waste*, 101st Cong., 2nd Sess., July 12, 13, 1989, 256. For a thorough analysis of the DC bottle bill debate, see Joy A. Clay, "The D.C. Bottle Bill Initiative: A Casualty of the Reagan Era," *Environmental Review* 13, no. 2 (Summer 1989): 17–31.

71 L. L. Gaines and A. M. Wolsky, "Resource Conservation Through Beverage Container Recycling," *Conservation and Recycling* 6, no. 1/2 (1983): 11–14.

72 Bruce van Voorst and Rhea Schoenthal, "The Recycling Bottleneck," *Time*, September 14, 1992; Carl A. Zimring, *Cash for Your Trash*, 134; Debi Kimball, *Recycling in America: A Reference Handbook* (Santa Barbara, CA: ABC-CLIO, 1992), 23–24.

73 Elizabeth Royte, *Garbage Land*, 14; "Who Foots the Bill for Recycling," *New York Times*, April 25, 1993, F5; David H. Folz, "Municipal Recycling Performance: A Public Sector Environmental Success Story," *Public Administration Review* 59, no. 4 (July–August 1999): 343; David H. Folz, Robert A. Bohm, Jean H. Peretz, and Bruce E. Tonn, "Analysis of National Solid Waste Recycling Programs and Development of Solid Waste Recycling Cost Dunctions: Summary Statistics for Data Set No. 1," Research into Economic Factors Influencing Decisions in Environmental Decision Making, prepared under US EPA Cooperative Agreement CR822614-01 (July 1999), 10; Daniel H. Loughlin and Morton A Barlaz, "Policies for Strengthening Markets for Recyclables: A Worldwide Perspective," *Critical Reviews in Environmental Science and Technology* 36, no. 4 (2006): 290; EPA, *Municipal Solid Waste Generation, Recycling, and Disposal in the United States: Facts and Figures for 2012* (Washington, DC: USGPO, 2013).

74 I spoke with Container Recycling Institute executive director Susan Collins about calculating a figure for taxpayer commitment to curbside recycling. She ventured a very rough estimate—perhaps $2.5 billion annually in 2013 for single-family households—but said there simply is no agency or database that catalogs these

nationwide costs effectively. E-mail to author, December 17, 2013. For over two decades, Collins worked with municipalities in California to help them develop solid-waste management and recycling systems.

75 Heather Rogers, *Gone Tomorrow*, 176; "Can or Bottle, Bill Wants Makers to Pay for Recycling," *New York Times*, July 11, 2002; Government Accountability Office (GAO), *Recycling: Additional Efforts Could Increase Municipal Recycling*, December 2003, 11; EPA, *Municipal Solid Waste in the United States: 2009 Facts and Figures* (Washington, DC: USGPO, 2010), 52; National Association for PET Container Recycling (NAPCOR), 2011 *Report on Postconsumer PET Container Recycling Activity: Final Report*, http://www.napcor.com/pdf/NAPCOR_2011RateReport.pdf. The 55 percent aluminum recycling rate comes from the Container Recycling Institute. A detailed explanation of the institute's calculations can be found here: http://www .container-recycling.org/index.php/calculating-aluminum-can-recycling-rate. The 29 percent PET recycling rate reported by industry does not take into account the large quantity of recycled PET that cannot be resold because of contamination. Subtracting this waste PET generated during recycling from the total PET available for resale yields a reclamation rate closer to 21 percent. Letter from Susan Collins, Executive Director of the Container Recycling Institute, to Hope Pilsbury, Office of Resource Conservation and Recovery, Environmental Protection Agency, September 30, 2011, provided to the author by Susan Collins. For the number of bottles and cans landfilled each year, see http://www.container-recycling.org.

76 Coca-Cola Enterprises 2009 Corporate Responsibility and Sustainability Report, 36, 40; "Coca-Cola Says S.C. Recycling Joint Venture to Be Restructured," *Atlanta Journal-Constitution*, April 20, 2011; "Part of Waste Problem Is Now Part of Solution," *New York Times*, April 22, 2012; Michael Blanding, *The Coke Machine*, 138.

77 EPA, *Municipal Solid Waste Generation, Recycling, and Disposal in the United States: Facts and Figures for 2012* (Washington, DC: USGPO, 2013), 7.

9. HIGH-FRUCTOSE CORN SYRUP:
STORING SWEETENERS IN STOMACH SILOS

1 After CFCs were banned, Coke switched to refrigeration systems that emitted hydrofluorocarbons (HFCs), which later proved to be a potent greenhouse gas. Since 2000, Coke has committed itself to replacing all HFC-emitting units with new refrigerators that do not emit greenhouse gases; Coca-Cola has also begun to invest in hybrid heavy-duty trucks, and in 2012 the company could boast the "largest hybrid electric fleet" in the world. Still, hybrids represented less than 1 percent of all trucks in the Coca-Cola system, 700 out of 200,000. See the Coca-Cola Company 2010/2011 Sustainability Report, 18.

2 USDA Economic Research Service, Food Availability Data System, Beverages Data Set, Update August 20, 2012, http://www.ers.usda.gov/data-products/food -availability-(per-capita)-data-system.aspx#2793.

3 "'Freer Market' for Sugar Urged by Industrial Users," *New York Times*, February 22, 1974, 43; Letter from Ovid Davis to Paul Austin, June 6, 1974, box 70, folder 10, RWW Papers, MARBL.

4 "World Approaching Sugar Shortage," *Washington Post*, February 27, 1974, A14; "Butz Sugar Sale Plan Killed After Lobby Bid," *New York Times*, May 20, 1974, A1.

5 Betty Fussell, *The Story of Corn* (New York: Knopf, 1992), 273; "The Wet Millers of Corn," *Washington Post*, June 11, 1981, A1.

6 Michael Pollan, *The Omnivore's Dilemma: A Natural History of Four Meals* (New York: Penguin Books, 2006), 49; Willard W. Cochrane, *Development of American Agriculture: A Historical Analysis* (Minneapolis: University of Minnesota Press, 1979; 1993), 140–143. Citations are to the 1993 edition.

7 On the Agricultural Adjustment Act's effects on agriculture in the American South and how it encouraged the growth of agribusiness, see Pete Daniel, *Breaking the Land*, 63–183; Julie Guthman, *Weighing In: Obesity, Food Justice, and the Limits of Capitalism* (Berkeley and Los Angeles: University of California Press, 2011), 120.

8 Arturo Warman, *Corn and Capitalism: How a Botanical Bastard Grew to Global Dominance*, trans. Nancy L. Westrate (Chapel Hill: University of North Carolina Press, 2003), 189. See also Sarah Phillips, *The Price of Plenty: From Farm to Food Politics in Postwar America* (Oxford: Oxford University Press, forthcoming).

9 In *The Omnivore's Dilemma: A Natural History of Four Meals*, food journalist Michael Pollan described the transformative power of Butz's seemingly innocuous policy initiative: "The change from loans to direct payments hardly seemed momentous—either way, the government pledges to make sure the farmer receives some target price for a bushel of corn when prices are weak. But in fact paying farmers directly for the shortfall in the price of corn was revolutionary, as its proponents surely must have understood. They had removed the floor under the price of grain. Instead of keeping corn out of a falling market, as the old loan programs and federal granary had done, the new subsidies encouraged farmers to sell their corn at any price, since the government would make up the difference" (52). Butz comment quoted in David B. Danbom, *Born in the Country: A History of Rural America* (Baltimore: Johns Hopkins University Press, 1995), 255.

10 "US Monthly Average Corn Price Received for the 1970–1980 Calendar Years," University of Illinois at Urbana-Champaign farmdoc database, http://farmdoc .illinois.edu/manage/uspricehistory/excel/uscorn.xls.

11 "Coke OKs Corn Sugar in Non-Colas," *Chicago Tribune*, July 1, 1978, H6.

12 "Fructose Makers Say 'How Sweet It Is,' as Sweetener Wins Major Acceptance," *Wall Street Journal*, August 3, 1978, 10; "Coke OKs Corn Sugar in Non-Colas," *Chicago Tribune*, July 1, 1978, H6; "Commodities: Sugar Bill Called Aid to Fructose," *New York Times*, November 2, 1981, D4.

13 "Case of the Sugar Papers," *Chicago Tribune*, July 10, 1978, 10; Michael Pollan, *The Omnivore's Dilemma*, 105.

14 McDonald's Corporation 1996 Annual Report, 3; Eric Schlosser, *Fast Food Nation*, 54; Michael Blanding, *The Coke Machine*, 67, 68.

15 *The Bankers' Magazine and Statistical Register* 41 (New York: Homans, 1886–1887), 655; USDA Agriculture Factbook 2001–2002, 20.

16 United States Census Bureau, Urban and Rural Populations, Table 4, Population: 1790–1990, http://www.census.gov/population/www/censusdata/files/table-4.pdf;

David B. Danbom, *Born in the Country*, 212; Jack Temple Kirby, *Rural Worlds Lost*, 60–69.

17 Bureau of Labor Statistics, Employment by Major Industry Sector, 1994, 2004, and projected 2014, http://www.bls.gov/opub/ted/2005/dec/wk3/art01.htm; United States Census Bureau, "Commuting in the United States: 2009—American Consumer Survey Reports," September 2011, 3–4; United Bureau of Labor Statistics, Spotlight on Statistics: Sports and Exercise, May 2008, 2. http://www.bls.gov/spotlight/2008/sports/pdf/sports_bls_spotlight.pdf.

18 House Committee on Agriculture, *Compilation of Responses to Farm Bill Feedback Questionnaire*, 111th Cong., 2nd Sess., September 2010, 279.

19 Betty Fussell, *The Story of Corn*, 159; United States Department of Agriculture, "Feed Grains: Background for 1995 Farm Legislation," Agricultural Economic Report No. AER714, prepared by William Lin, Peter Riley, and Sam Evans, April 1995, 53.

20 K. M. Flegal, M. D. Carroll, C. L. Ogden, and L. R. Curtin, "Prevalence and Trends in Obesity Among US Adults, 1999–2008," *Journal of the American Medical Association* 303, no. 3 (January 20, 2010): 235–241; K. M. Flegal, M. D. Carroll, R. J. Kuczmarski, and C. L. Johnson, "Overweight and Obesity in the United States: Prevalence and Trends, 1960–1994," *International Journal of Obesity* 22, no. 1 (January 1998): 39–47; Michael Blanding, *The Coke Machine*, 78. Interestingly, Julie Guthman has shown in her book *Weighing In* that the biology of obesity may not be as simple as we once thought. In a provocative chapter on chemicals in America's food supply, she argued that certain pesticides and food additives might have disrupted digestive tract regulatory mechanisms, preventing people from properly recognizing carbohydrate intake (101–115).

21 K. M. Flegal, M. D. Carroll, B. K. Kit, and C. L. Ogden, "Prevalence and Trends in Obesity Among US Adults, 1999–2010," *Journal of the American Medical Association* 307, no. 5 (February 1, 2012): 491–497; C. L. Ogden, M. M. Lamb, M. D. Carroll, and K. M. Flegal, "Obesity and Socioeconomic Status in Adults: United States, 2005–2008," *National Center for Health Statistics Data Brief* 50 (December 2010). On obesogenic environments, see B. G. Swinburn and F. Raza, "Dissecting Obesogenic Environments: The Development and Application of a Framework for Identifying and Prioritizing Environmental Interventions for Obesity," *Preventative Medicine* 29 (December 1999): 563–570; and J. O. Hill and J. C. Peters, "Environmental Contributions to the Obesity Epidemic," *Science* 280, no. 5368 (May 1998): 1371–1374. Julie Guthman aptly noted that obesogenic environments should be seen as a symptom of an inequitable economy rather than the chief causal factor of obesity in low-income communities. As she argued, creating food hubs and farmers' markets in impoverished regions of the country will not fix the obesity problem if we fail to address wage disparities and the deep roots of poverty in America. See Julie Guthman, *Weighing In*, 66–90.

22 Centers for Disease Control and Prevention, "Percentage of Civilian, Noninstitutionalized Population with Diagnosed Diabetes by Age, United States, 1980–2008," posted October 15, 2010, www.cdc.gov/diabetes/statistics/prev/national/figbyage.htm; Michael Blanding, *The Coke Machine*, 81.

23 Eric A. Finkelstein, Justin G. Trogdon, Joel W. Cohen, and William Dietz,

"Annual Medical Spending Attributable to Obesity: Payer-and-Service Specific Estimates," *Health Affairs* 28, no. 5 (September 2009): w822.

24 USDA Economic Research Service, Food Availability Data System, Beverages Data Set, Update August 20, 2012, http://www.ers.usda.gov/data-products/food-availability-(per-capita)-data-system.aspx#2793; Centers for Disease Control, Research to Practice Series No. 3, September 2006, http://www.cdc.gov/nccdphp/dnpa/nutrition/pdf/r2p_sweetened_beverages.pdf; Caroline M. Apovian, "Sugar-Sweetened Soft Drinks, Obesity, and Type 2 Diabetes," *Journal of the American Medical Association* 292, no. 8 (August 25, 2004): 978; H. K. Choi and G. Curhan, "Soft Drinks, Fructose Consumption, and the Risk of Gout in Men: Prospective Cohort Study," *British Medical Journal* 336, no. 7639 (February 9, 2008): 309; Mark Bittman, "Soda: A Sin We Sip Instead of Smoke?" *New York Times*, February 12, 2010, WK1. Coke scholar Michael Blanding explained the connection between Coca-Cola and obesity thus: "At the same time that America's obesity rates doubled, so has Americans' soda consumption; between 1970 and 1980, it accounted for nearly half the increase in calories in the average diet." Michael Blanding, *The Coke Machine*, 79.

25 "Diet Coke Reflects Changes in Market and the Industry," *New York Times*, August 23, 1982, D4.

26 Memorandum to the Directors of Coca-Cola, October 20, 1969, box 16, folder 1, RWW Papers, MARBL. In 1969 and early 1970s, studies hypothesizing a link between cyclamate consumption and cancer were inconclusive. See M. W. Wagner, "Cyclamate Acceptance," *Science* 26, no. 3939 (1970): 1605. In a recent study published in the *Annals of Oncology*, scientists concluded that "epidemiological studies in humans did not find the bladder cancer-inducing effects of saccharin and cyclamate that had been reported from animal studies in rats." W. R. Weihrauch and V. Diehl, "Artificial Sweeteners—Do They Bear a Carcinogenic Risk?" *Annals of Oncology* 15, no. 10 (October 2004): 1460–1465.

27 Senate Select Committee on Nutrition and Human Needs, *Hearing on Nutrition and Human Needs, Part 13C: Nutrition and Private Industry*, 90th Cong., 2d Sess., July 30, 1969, 4609.

28 "Cyclamates and the Try for Reimbursement," *Washington Post*, September 22, 1972, A26; "Bill to Provide Relief from Cyclamate Losses Expected to be Introduced by Sen. Griffin of Michigan," *NSDA Bulletin*, July 1970, 6; "Decision on FDA Petition Not Due Until 1975, FDA Says," *NSDA Bulletin*, March 1974, 2; Beatrice Trum Hunter, *The Sweetener Trap and How to Avoid It: The Power and Politics of Sweeteners and Their Impact on Your Health* (Laguna Beach, CA: Basic Health Publications, 2008), 372.

29 "Calorie Council Sparks Protest Against Saccharin Ban," *Chicago Tribune*, March 15, 1977, C9; Calorie Control Council Ad copied in Carolyn de la Peña's *Empty Pleasures: The Story of Artificial Sweeteners from Saccharin to Splenda* (Chapel Hill: University of North Carolina Press, 2010), 171.

30 In *Empty Pleasures*, Carolyn de la Peña provided an illustrative look into the Calorie Control Council anti-ban campaign, showing how the organization effectively motivated constituencies of influential politicians to act in favor of a government moratorium (170–175). Explaining Coke's level of involvement in CCC politicking, the *New York Times* reported in 1978, "Coca-Cola is fighting hard against the pro-

posed [saccharin] ban, and is the largest single contributor to the Calorie Control Council, the chief lobbyist against the ban." "A Market Thirst Never Quenched," *New York Times*, April 9, 1978, F4.

31 Coke decided to use 100 percent aspartame in its diet beverages in 1984. "Coke Sweetener," *New York Times*, November 30, 1984, D4; "The Bittersweet Mystery Behind Aspartame," *Chicago Tribune*, June 26, 1983, N1. *Oshana v. Coca-Cola Co.*, 472 F.3d 506 (7th Cir. 2006). Saccharin was only removed from the Department of Health and Human Services list of potential carcinogens in 2000, twenty-three years after the FDA moved to ban the product in 1977.

32 Carolyn de la Peña, *Empty Pleasures*, 11, 180–181, 216. Diet drinks represented just 24 percent of the soft drink market in 2003. Carbonated beverages with caloric sweeteners remained by far the industry leader. USDA Economic Research Service, Food Availability Data System, Beverages Data Set, Update August 20, 2012, http://www.ers.usda.gov/data-products/food-availability-(per-capita)-data-system.aspx#2793.

33 S. E. Swithers and T. L. Davidson, "A Role for Sweet Taste: Calorie Predictive Relations in Energy Regulation by Rats," *Journal of Behavioral Neuroscience* 122, no. 1 (February 2008): 161–173; Mark Hyman, "How Diet Soda Makes You Fat (and Other Food and Diet Industry Secrets)," *Huffington Post*, March 7, 2013, http://www.huffingtonpost.com/dr-mark-hyman/diet-soda-health_b_2698494. html. For a study that suggested caution in linking diet drink consumption with obesity, see R. D. Mattes and B. M. Popkin, "Nonnutritive Sweetener Consumption in Humans: Effects on Appetite and Food Intake and Their Putative Mechanisms," *American Journal of Clinical Nutrition* 89 (2009): 1–14.

34 USDA Economic Research Service, Carbonated Beverages Per Capita Availability Spreadsheet (2003), http://www.ers.usda.gov/datafiles/Food_Availability_Per_Capita_Data_System/Food_Availability/beverage.xls.

35 "Get Slim with Higher Taxes," *New York Times*, December 15, 1994, A29; "Americans, Obesity and Eating Habits," *New York Times*, January 29, 1995, CN3.

36 Michael F. Jacobson and Kelly D. Brownell, "Small Taxes on Soft Drinks and Snack Foods to Promote Health," *American Journal of Public Health* 90, no. 6 (June 2000): 854–857; K. D. Brownell and D. Yach, "The Battle of the Bulge," *Foreign Policy* (November/December 2005): 26–27.

37 "Soft-Drink Industry Is Fighting Back over New Taxes," *New York Times*, March 24, 1993, A12; "Pop People Say This Levy Makes Soft Drinks a Bit Hard to Swallow," *Wall Street Journal*, December 11, 1992, B1; "'Snack Tax' Repeal on Way to Governor," *Baltimore Sun*, April 2, 1996.

38 Michael F. Jacobson, *Liquid Candy: How Soft Drinks Are Harming Americans' Health* (Washington, DC: Center for Science in the Public Interest, 1998); "Extra Soft Drink Is Cited as Major Factor in Obesity," *New York Times*, February 16, 2001, A12; Michael Blanding, *The Coke Machine*, 79–80, 85; R. D. Mattes and D. P. DiMeglio, "Liquid Versus Solid Carbohydrates: Effects on Food Intake and Body Weight," *International Journal of Obesity* 24, no. 6 (2000): 794–800.

39 "A Soda Ban, L.A. Style," *Los Angeles Times*, June 21, 2012; Robert Foster, *Coca-Globalization*, 216; Michael Blanding, *The Coke Machine*, 103–104.

40 Quoted in Neville Isdell, *Inside Coca-Cola*, 162.

41 Constance Hays, *The Real Thing*, 155–156. Throughout the 2000s, CCE continued to accumulate debts to the point that incoming revenue barely covered the cost of servicing interest owed on outstanding loans. Year after year, the Coca-Cola Company funneled cash toward CCE's struggling operations. In the spring of 2008, the Coca-Cola Company reported that it faced a 23 percent reduction in quarterly profits in large part because of CCE expenses. In an attempt to further insulate itself from the megabottler's financial liabilities, Coca-Cola reduced its ownership stake in the bottler to just 35 percent by December of 2007. Constance Hays, *The Real Thing*, 157; "Biggest Bottler of Coke Plans to Increase Prices," *New York Times*, July 18, 2008, C3; Coca-Cola Company 2008 SEC 10-K Report, 5. In 2006, CCE was one of the biggest money losers of the year, posting a $1.2 billion loss in that year alone.

42 Neville Isdell, *Inside Coca-Cola*, 1, 162–163; Constance Hays, *The Real Thing*, 313.

43 Robert Foster, *Coca-Globalization*, 212–214. See also Michael Blanding's chapter "The Battle for Schools," *The Coke Machine*, 89–117.

44 Coca-Cola Company, "Our Position on Obesity: Including Well-Being Facts," July 2012, 8–9; "Big Food's Health Education," *San Francisco Chronicle*, September 7, 2005.

45 "Fat Tax for Lean Times," *New York Times*, April 3, 2005, CY11; "In a Fat War, Albany Isn't Eating What It Preaches," *New York Times*, June 19, 2003, B5.

46 "Striking Back at the Food Police," *New York Times*, June 12, 2005; "Girth of a Nation," *New York Times*, July 4, 2005, A13.

47 Michael Pollan, "The (Agri)Cultural Contradictions of Obesity," *New York Times*, October 12, 2003, SM41.

48 Ibid.; Michael Pollan, "You Are What You Grow," *New York Times Magazine*, April 22, 2007.

49 Neville Isdell, *Inside Coca-Cola*, 183, 201; School bans may have contributed to a significant reduction in soft drink consumption among schoolchildren. Studies have shown that caloric soft drink consumption among youth aged two to nineteen declined in the first decade of the 2000s. See Brian K. Kit, Tala H. I. Fakhouri, Sohyun Park, Samara Joy Nielsen, and Cynthia L. Ogden, "Trends in Sugar-Sweetened Beverage Consumption Among Youth and Adults in the United States, 1999–2010," *American Journal of Clinical Nutrition* 98, no. 1 (July 2013): 180–188. Some believe this reduction in consumption has affected obesity rates. See "Obesity Dropped 43% Among Young Children in Decade," *New York Times*, February 26, 2014, A1.

50 Scott Drenkard, *Overreaching on Obesity: Governments Consider New Taxes on Soda and Candy*, Tax Foundation Special Report No. 196 (October 31, 2011), http://taxfoundation.org/article/overreaching-obesity-governments-consider-new-taxes-soda-and-candy; Jason M. Fletcher, David Frisvold, and Nathan Tefft, "Can Soft Drink Taxes Reduce Population Weight," *Contemporary Economic Policy* (2009), 3.

51 Michael Pollan, "You Are What You Grow," *New York Times Magazine*, April 22, 2007; Interview with Mayor Bloomberg, *MSNBC*, May 31, 2012.

52 Monologue by Jon Stewart, *The Daily Show*, aired on Comedy Central May 31, 2013; "60% Oppose Bloomberg's Soda Ban, Poll Finds," *New York Times*, August 22, 2012, A19; "Soda Ban Backlash: Mike Bloomberg's Plan Takes Supersized P.R. Hit," *Village*

Voice, July 6, 2012; "NYC Defends Soda Ban; Foes Call It Illegal," *UPI.com* (United Press International), January 24, 2013, http://www.upi.com/Top_News/US/2013/01/24/NYC-defends-soda-ban-foes-call-it-illegal/UPI-26561359016200/; "No Local Toast for New York's Soda Ban," *U-T San Diego*, August 6, 2012, http://www.utsandiego.com/news/2012/Aug/06/no-local-toast-for-bloombergs-soda-ban/.

53 "Soda Makers Begin Their Push Against New York Ban," *New York Times*, July 2, 2012, A10; "'Nanny Bloomberg' Ad in New York Times Targets N.Y. Mayor's Anti-Soda Crusade," *Huffington Post*, June 4, 2012, http://www.huffingtonpost.com/2012/06/04/nanny-bloomberg-ad-in-new_n_1568037.html.

54 *New York Statewide Coalition of Hispanic Chambers of Commerce v. New York City Department of Health and Mental Hygiene* WL 1343607, 2013 N. Y. Slip Op. 30609 (U) (Trial Order) (N. Y. Sup. Mar. 11, 2013); "Minority Groups and Bottlers Team Up in Battles over Soda," *New York Times*, March 13, 2013, A1; "Judge Cans Soda Ban," *Wall Street Journal*, March 12, 2013, A19.

55 "How Big Soda Co-Opted the NAACP and Hispanic Federation," *Huffington Post*, January 25, 2013, www.huffingtonpost.com/nancy-huehnergarth/minorities_soda_lobby_b_2541121.html; "When Jim Crow Drank Coke," *New York Times*, January 29, 2013, A23.

56 "NYC Soda Ban Rejected: Judge Strikes Down Limit on Large Sugary Drinks as 'Arbitrary, Capricious,'" *Huffington Post*, March 11, 2013, http://www.huffingtonpost.com/2013/03/11/nyc-soda-ban-dismissed-judge-large-sugary-drinks_n_2854563.html; Michael Moss, *Salt Sugar Fat: How the Food Giants Hooked Us* (New York: Random House, 2013), 99; "At 7-Eleven, the Big Gulps Elude a Ban by the City," *New York Times*, June 7, 2012, A20.

57 *New York Statewide Coalition of Hispanic Chambers of Commerce v. New York City Department of Health and Mental Hygiene*, No. 653584/12, WL 1343607, 2013 N.Y. Slip Op. 30609 (U) (Trial Order) (N.Y. Sup. Mar. 11, 2013). Leave to appeal was granted by the Court of Appeals, *New York Statewide Coalition of Hispanic Chambers of Commerce v. New York City Department of Health and Mental Hygiene*, 22 N.Y.3d 853976 N.Y.S.2d447 (Table), 2013 WL 5658229, 2013 N.Y. Slip Op. 88505 (U) (N.Y. Oct. 17, 2013).

58 K. D. Brownell and T. R. Frieden, "Ounces of Prevention—The Public Policy Case for Taxes on Sugared Beverages," *New England Journal of Medicine* 360, no. 18 (April 30, 2009): 1805; "Elasticity: Big Price Increases Cause Coke Volume to Plummet," *Beverage Digest*, November 21, 2008, 3–4.

59 "Poll: Most Oppose Tax on Junk Food," *CBS News*, January 7, 2010, http://www.cbsnews.com/news/poll-most-oppose-tax-on-junk-food.

60 Michael Pollan, "You Are What You Grow," *New York Times Magazine*, April 22, 2007.

61 For an excellent summary of these trends, see Michael Pollan, *The Omnivore's Dilemma*, 32–56.

62 Office of Management and Budget, Fiscal Year 2013, Cuts, Consolidations, and Savings: Budget of the U.S. Government, available online at http://www.whitehouse.gov/sites/default/files/omb/budget/fy2013/assets/ccs.pdf; "Obama Reiterates Call for Farm Subsidy Cuts," *Reuters.com*, February 13, 2012, http://www.reuters.com/article/2012/02/13/us-usa-budget-farm-idUSTRE81C18R20120213; "House Approves Farm Bill, Ending a 2-Year Impasse," *New York Times*, January 30, 2014, A14; "5

Things the Farm Bill Will Mean for You," *CNN Politics*, February 4, 2014, http://www.cnn.com/2014/02/04/politics/farm-bill/. For examples of citizen petitions for Farm Bill reform, see House Committee on Agriculture, *Compilation of Responses to Farm Bill Feedback Questionnaire*, 111th Cong., 2nd Sess., September 2010.

63 "U.S. Farmers Plant Largest Corn Crop in 63 Years," USDA, National Agricultural Statistics Service (NASS) Press Release, June 29, 2007; Michael Pollan, *The Omnivore's Dilemma*, 32–56. See also the documentary by Ian Cheney, Curt Ellis, and Aaron Woolf, *King Corn* (New York: Docurama Films, distributed by New Video, 2008).

64 Oxfam International, "Sugar Rush: Land Rights and the Supply Chains of the Biggest Food and Beverage Companies," Oxfam Briefing Note, October 2, 2013, 5, 7–8; "Will Coca-Cola Do the Right Thing in Cambodia," *Kansas City Star*, December 6, 2013; Peter Singer, "The Trouble with Big Sugar," *Slate*, November 24, 2013; "Coke, Pressed by Oxfam, Pledges Zero Tolerance for Land Grabs in Sugar Supply Chain," *Washington Post*, November 8, 2013.

65 "Industry Awakens to Threat of Climate Change," *New York Times*, January 24, 2014, A1.

66 Muhtar Kent, GBCHealth Conference Keynote Address, Roosevelt Hotel, New York, New York, May 14, 2012.

67 Coca-Cola Company 2013 SEC 10-K Report, 42, 44, and 2012 SEC 10-K Report, 5.

68 "Diet Coke May Be the New #2, but U.S. Soda Market Is Declining," *Fortune*, March 22, 2011; "The Most Popular Sodas in the World," *Huffington Post*, February 23, 2012, http://www.huffingtonpost.com/2012/02/23/top-soda-brands_n_1297205 .html#s719889&title=1_Coke_CocaCola.

69 Coca-Cola Company 2012 SEC 10-K Report, 48.

EPILOGUE: SUSTAINING COKE'S FUTURE?

1 For an excellent history of Apple and its visionary cofounder Steve Jobs, see Walter Isaacson, *Steve Jobs* (New York: Simon and Schuster, 2011), 361. Julie Froud, Sukhdev Johal, Adam Leaver, and Karel Williams, "Apple Business Model: Financialization Across the Pacific," Centre for Research on Socio-Cultural Change (CRESC) Working Paper No. 111, University of Manchester Business School, April 2012, 8, 20–21, 22.

2 Google Inc., 2010 SEC 10-K Report, 3.

3 On the decline of the U.S. steel industry, see Paul A. Tiffany, *The Decline of American Steel: How Management, Labor, and Government Went Wrong* (New York: Oxford University Press, 1988); Paul A. Tiffany, "The Roots of Decline: Business-Government Relations in the American Steel Industry, 1945–1960," *Journal of Economic History* 44, no. 2 (June 1984): 407–419; and Kenneth Warren, *Big Steel: The First Century of the United States Steel Corporation*, 1901–2001 (Pittsburgh: University of Pittsburgh Press, 2001). For General Motors, see Maryann Keller, *Rude Awakening: The Rise, Fall, and Struggle for Recovery of General Motors* (New York: William Morrow, 1989).

4 "Coca-Cola Enterprises' Bad News About Profit Makes a Soft Landing on Bottler's

Stock Price," *Wall Street Journal*, September 1, 1989, C2; "Coca-Cola Enterprises' Reorganization Gets Mixed Views on Debt," *Wall Street Journal*, January 23, 1992, C12; "Earnings Down 80% at Big Coke Bottler," *New York Times*, October 18, 2001, C5; "Global 500 Money Losers," http://money.cnn.com/galleries/2007/fortune/0707/gallery.global500_losers.fortune/6.html; "Coke Plans Return to Franchise Model in North America," *New York Times*, December 12, 2013; "When Will Coca-Cola Sell its Rebuilt Botlers? CEO Muhtar Kent Explains," *DailyFinance.com*, February 10, 2011, http://www.dailyfinance.com/2011/02/10/will-coca-cola-sell-its-bottlers-ceo-muhtar-kent-explains.

5 Coca-Cola Enterprises 2006 Corporate Responsibility and Sustainability Report, 4; "Coca-Cola's CEO Muhtar Kent Sees a World of Opportunity," excerpts from Muhtar Kent's speech, May 19, 2010, http://www.economicclub.org/doc_repo/Kent_Transcript%20JF%20Revision.pdf; Coca-Cola Company 2013 SEC 10-K Report.

6 Eric A. Finkelstein, Justin G. Trogdon, Joel W. Cohen, and William Dietz, "Annual Medical Spending Attributable to Obesity: Payer-and-Service Specific Estimates," *Health Affairs* 28, no. 5 (September 2009): w822; Daniel Hoornweng and Perinaz Bhada-Tata, *What a Waste: A Global Review of Solid Waste Management*, World Bank Urban Development Series, Knowledge Papers No. 15, March 2012, vii.

Bibliography

MANUSCRIPTS AND ARCHIVES

American Beverage Association Information Library, Washington, DC (access granted to author by ABA representative)

Atlanta History Center
>   Arthur and LaFayette Montgomery Papers, 1911–1961, MS 164
>   Joseph and Sinclair Jacobs Papers, MS 222

Bondurant Mixson & Elmore (BME), LLP. Case files for *Coca-Cola Bottling Company of Elizabethtown, Inc., et. al. v. The Coca-Cola Company*, 988 F.2d 386 (1993) (access to nonprivileged documents granted to author by firm)

East Carolina University, East Carolina Manuscript Collection, J. Y. Joyner Library, Greenville, NC
>   James L. Fleming Papers, MS 437

Emory University, Manuscript, Archives, and Rare Book Library, Atlanta, GA
>   Asa Griggs Candler Papers, 1821–1951, MS 1
>   Charles Howard Candler Papers, 1878–1957, MS 3
>   Coca-Cola Collection, 1912–1990, MS 620
>   Frederick Allen Papers, MS 850
>   Joseph W. Jones Papers, 1912–2005 (Bulk 1947–2003), MS 1003
>   Mark Pendergrast Research Files, MS 741
>   Robert Winship Woodruff Papers, 1819–1996 (Bulk 1924–1986), MS 10
>   John A. Sibley Papers, ca. 1920–1989, MS 437

Digital National Security Archive, George Washington University, Accessible online here: http://nsarchive.chadwyck.com/home.do

Kissinger Telephone Conversations Collection, 1969–1977

Peru: Human Rights, Drugs, and Democracy Collection, 1980–2000

Harry S. Truman Presidential Library, Independence, MO

P. G. Hoffman Papers, accessible online here: http://www.trumanlibrary.org/
whistlestop/study_collections/marshall/large/index.php

Hershey Community Archives, Hershey, PA

Hershey Press News Digital Collection, www.hersheyarchives.org/collection-
research/

Oral History Collection

Paul Wallace Manuscript Collection, 1700–1974

Library of Congress (LOC), Washington, DC

Harvey Washington Wiley Papers, MS 45690

James Farley Papers, MS 20263

National Agricultural Library, Beltsville, MD

USDA History Collection, MS 182

National Archives II, College Park, MD

Record Group 16, Records of the Office of the Secretary of Agriculture, 1794–
ca. 2003

Record Group 59, General Records of the Department of State, 1789–2002

Record Group 170, Records of the Drug Enforcement Administration, 1915–
1946, 1969–1980

Record Group 188, Records of the Office of Price Administration

Record Group 469, Records of US Foreign Assistance Agencies, 1948–1961

National Archives, Southeast Region, Morrow, GA

Record Group 21, Records of United States District Courts

Washington University, St. Louis, MO, University Archives, Department of Special
Collections

Monsanto Company Records, MS 006

Virginia Historical Society, Richmond, Virginia

Records of the Central Coca-Cola Bottling Company Inc., 1906–2003, MSS
3C332aFA2

INTERVIEWS EXECUTED BY AUTHOR

Blanding, Michael. Author of *The Coke Machine*. May 11, 2010.

Bijoy, C. R. Environmental and social activist in Coimbatore, Tamil Nadu, India.
November 17, 2010.

Camino, Alejandro. Director of the Museo de Plantas Sagradas, Mágicas y Medici-
nales, Cuzco, Peru. January 20, 2012.

Chirinos Nuñez, Humberto. Director of the Programa de Monitoreo de Cultivos Ilí-
citos, United Nations Office on Drugs and Crime (UNODC), Lima, Peru. With
assistance from Lorenzo Vallejos Mazzini, project coordinator at UNODC. January 16, 2012.

Esty, Daniel. Coca-Cola Environmental Advisory Board member. May 28, 2010.

Hunt, Bob. Franklin Associates scientist. February 9, 2010.

Mangelinckx, Jérôme. Investigator for Centro de Investigación Drogas y Derechos Humanos (CIDDH), Lima, Peru. January 17, 2012.

Paull, Robert. Professor and chair of the Department of Tropical Plant and Soil Sciences at the University of Hawaii at Manoa. September 11, 2009.

Rathore, Manohar S. Director of the Centre for Environment and Development Studies, Jaipur (CEDSJ), in Jaipur, Rajasthan, India. November 21, 2010.

Soberón Garrido, Ricardo. Former director of the National Commission for Development and Life Without Drugs (DEVIDA), Lima, Peru. January 17, 2012.

Vermeer, Dan. Former head of Coca-Cola's Global Water Initiative. September 24, 2010.

FREEDOM OF INFORMATION ACT (FOIA) RESPONSES

FOIA Request 2010-000033 filed with the Overseas Private Investment Corporation (OPIC). Response received November 17, 2010.

FOIA Request 2010-4539 filed with the Department of Health and Human Services. Response received July 19, 2010 (no documents produced).

FOIA Request F-00191-10 filed with United States Agency for International Development. Response received January 12, 2010.

FOIA Request CRRIF 11-344 filed with the United States Department of Commerce. Response received March 19, 2012.

FOIA Request C7548 filed with the United States Department of State on June 7, 2010. Response received November 24, 2010.

FOIA Request HQ-FOI-01378-10 filed with the United States Environmental Protection Agency. Response received July 22, 2010.

CORPORATE PUBLICATIONS, PRESENTATIONS, AND TRADE JOURNALS

American Druggist and Pharmaceutical Record

American Soft Drink Journal

Aqueduct Water Risk Atlas. World Resource Institute. Data produced by Coca-Cola. http://insights.wri.org/aqueduct/welcome.

Beverage Daily

Beverage Industry

Beverage World

Brown, Paul (Water Technologies Director, Coca-Cola). "Our Commitment to the Environment." Presentation given to Coca-Cola Employees in San Jose, Costa Rica, September 24, 2009.

Coca-Cola Bottler

Coca-Cola Company 10-K Securities and Exchange Commission Reports

Coca-Cola Company 2007/2008 Sustainability Review

Coca-Cola Company 2010 Replenish Report

Coca-Cola Company 2010/2011 Sustainability Report

Coca-Cola Company 2012 Global Response Initiative Report

Coca-Cola Company 2012 Sustainability Report

Coca-Cola Company 2012 Water Stewardship and Replenishment Report

Coca-Cola Company 2012/2013 Global Reporting Initiative

Coca-Cola Company. "125 Years of Sharing Happiness: A Short History of the Coca-Cola Company." Richmond, British Columbia: Blanchette Press, 2011. http://www.thecoca-colacompany.com/heritage/pdf/Coca-Cola_125_years_booklet.pdf.

Coca-Cola Company and the Nature Conservancy. "Product Water Footprint Assessments: Practical Application in Corporate Water Stewardship." September 2010.

Coca-Cola Company and the Nature Conservancy. "Quantifying Replenish Benefits in Community Water Partnership Project." February 2013. http://assets.coca-colacompany.com/2f/cb/e5d2ca1e4c58a38adbe8586d06db/final-quanitification-report-water-pdf.pdf.

Coca-Cola Company: An Illustrated Profile of a Worldwide Company. Atlanta: Coca-Cola Company, 1974.

Coca-Cola Company Annual Reports to Stockholders, 1922–2011

Coca-Cola Company. "Our Position on Obesity: Including Well-Being Facts." July 2012.

Coca-Cola Company Press Releases

Coca-Cola Company Public Relations Department. *Chronological History of the Coca-Cola Company.* Atlanta: Coca-Cola Company, 1971.

Coca-Cola Company. Water Footprint Sustainability Assessment (Europe). August 2011. Available online via http://www.coca-colacompany.com/stories/community-water-programs.

Coca-Cola Conversations. Coca-Cola's company blog, edited by archivists Ted Ryan and Phil Mooney. www.coca-colaconversations.com.

Coca-Cola Enterprises 2006 Corporate Responsibility and Sustainability Report

Coca-Cola Enterprises 2009 Corporate Responsibility and Sustainability Report

Coca-Cola Hellenic (bottler) 2011 Corporate Social Responsibility Report

Coca-Cola Içeçek (bottler) Corporate Social Responsibility Report (March 2008–March 2009)

Coca-Cola Overseas

Coffee and Tea (trade journal)

General Foods Annual Reports to Stockholders, 1929–1984

Kent, Muhtar. GBCHealth Conference Keynote Address. Roosevelt Hotel, New York, New York. May 14, 2012.

———. Statement for Rio+20, July 18, 2012. Published by the Avoided Deforestation Partners. https://www.youtube.com/watch?v=h548OnhSyuc.

Monsanto Chemical Company Annual Reports to Stockholders, 1933–1958

McDonald's Corporation Annual Reports to Stockholders, 1996

National Bottlers' Gazette

National Carbonator and Bottler

NSDA Bulletin (National Soft Drink Association)

Pfizer Inc. Annual Reports to Stockholders, 1960–1970

The Refresher

The Southern Carbonator and Bottler
World Coffee and Tea (trade journal)

NEWSPAPERS, MAGAZINES, AND NEWSLETTERS

Atlanta Constitution
Atlanta Journal
Atlanta Journal-Constitution
Charlotte Observer
Chemical Week
Chicago Daily Tribune
Cincinnati Lancet-Clinic
Collville Examiner (Collville, Washington)
Columbus Daily Enquirer (Columbus, Georgia)
Daily Herald (Biloxi, Mississippi)
Daily Oklahoman (Oklahoma City, Oklahoma)
Dallas Morning News
Emory Wheel (Emory University)
Fortune
Groton News (Groton, Connecticut)
Hershey Press News
Lakeland Ledger (Lakeland, Florida)
Los Angeles Times
Macon Telegraph (Macon, Georgia)
Miami Herald (Miami, Florida)
Miami News (Miami, Florida)
Montgomery Advertiser (Montgomery, Alabama)
New York Times
New York Times Magazine
OPIC Highlights
OPIC News
Reuters
Salt Lake Tribune
San Francisco Chronicle
Spokane Press
Sydney Morning Herald
Time
Times-Picayune (New Orleans, Louisiana)
USAID Newsletter
U-T San Diego (daily newspaper)
Village Voice
Wall Street Journal
Washington Post

COURT CASES

Coca-Cola Bottling Co. v. Coca-Cola Co., 269 F. 796 (D. Del. 1920).

Coca-Cola Bottling Co. of Elizabethtown, Inc. v. Coca-Cola Co., 654 F. Supp. 1388 (D. Del. 1986).

Coca-Cola Bottling Co. of Elizabethtown, Inc. v. Coca-Cola Co., 988 F.2d 386 (1993).

Coca-Cola Co. v. Koke Co. of Am., 254 U.S. 143 (1920).

Coca-Cola Co. of Canada, Ltd. v. Pepsi-Cola Co. of Canada, Ltd., [1938] Ex. C.R. 263 (Ex. Ct.); reversed [1940] S.C.R. 17 (S.C.C.); affirmed [1942] 2 W.W.R. 257 (P.C.).

Coca-Cola Co. v. Koke Co. of Am., 235 F. 408 (D. Ariz. 1916).

Coca-Cola Company, *Opinions, Orders, Injunctions, and Decrees Relating to Unfair Competition and Infringement of Trade-mark.* Atlanta, 1923, 1939.

Koke Co. of Am. v. Coca-Cola Co., 255 F. 894 (9th Cir. 1919).

New York Statewide Coalition of Hispanic Chambers of Commerce v. New York City Department of Health and Mental Hygiene, 22 N.Y.3d 853976 N.Y.S.2d447 (Table), 2013 WL 5658229, 2013 N.Y. Slip Op. 88505 (U) (N.Y. Oct. 17, 2013).

New York Statewide Coalition of Hispanic Chambers of Commerce v. New York City Department of Health and Mental Hygiene No. 653584/12, 2013 WL 1343607, 2013 N.Y. Slip Op. 30609 (U) (Trial Order) (N.Y. Sup. Mar. 11, 2013).

Oshana v. Coca-Cola Co., 472 F.3d 506 (7th Cir. 2006).

People v. North River Sugar Refining Co., 24 N.E. 839 (N.Y., 1890).

Sugar Institute, Inc. v. United States 297 U.S. 553 (1936).

United States v. Forty Barrels and Twenty Kegs of Coca-Cola, 191 F. 431 (E.D. Tenn. 1911).

United States v. Forty Barrels and Twenty Kegs of Coca-Cola, 241 U.S. 265 (1916).

PUBLISHED SOURCES, ACADEMIC PAPERS, AND MEDIA

Abaka, Edmund. *"Kola Is God's Gift": Agricultural Production, Export Initiatives, and the Kola Industry of Asante and the Gold Coast c. 1820–1950.* Athens: Ohio University Press, 2005.

Abbott, Elizabeth. *Sugar: A Bittersweet History.* London and New York: Duckworth Publishers, 2009.

Ackerman, Frank. *Why Do We Recycle: Markets, Values, and Public Policy.* Washington, DC: Island Press, 1997.

Agam, Giora. *Industrial Chemicals: Their Characteristics and Development.* Amsterdam: Elsevier, 1994.

Albert, Bill, and Adrian Graves, eds. *The World Sugar Economy in War and Depression, 1914–1940.* London and New York: Routledge, 1988.

Allen, Albert B. "Caffeine Identification. Differentiation of Synthetic and Natural Caffeine." *Agricultural and Food Chemistry* 9, no. 4 (July–August 1961): 294–295.

Allen, Frederick. *Secret Formula: How Brilliant Marketing and Relentless Salesmanship Made Coca-Cola the Best-Known Product in the World.* New York: HarperBusiness, 1994.

American Can Company. *A History of Packaged Beer and Its Market in the United States.* New York: American Can Co., 1969.

Anderson, Oscar E., Jr. *The Health of a Nation: Harvey W. Wiley and the Fight for Pure Food.* Chicago: University of Chicago Press, 1958.

Apovian, Caroline M. "Sugar-Sweetened Soft Drinks, Obesity, and Type 2 Diabetes." *Journal of the American Medical Association* 292, no. 8 (August 25, 2004): 978–979.

Arkes, Hadley. *Bureaucracy, the Marshall Plan, and the National Interest.* Princeton: Princeton University Press, 1972.

Ashley, Richard. *Cocaine: Its History, Uses and Effects.* New York: Warner Books, 1975.

Austin, Paul. "Managing Abundance." *Vital Speeches of the Day* 34 (February 1, 1968): 245–248.

Avena, N. M., P. Rada, B. G. Hoebel. "Evidence for Sugar Addiction: Behavioral and Neurochemical Effects of Intermittent, Excessive Sugar Intake." *Neuroscience and Biobehavioral Reviews* 32, no. 1 (2008): 20–39.

Ayala, César J. *American Sugar Kingdom: The Plantation Economy of the Spanish Caribbean, 1898–1934.* Chapel Hill: University of North Carolina Press, 1999.

Ayers, Edward L. *The Promise of the New South: Life After Reconstruction.* New York: Oxford University Press, 1992.

Aykroyd, W. R. *Sweet Malefactor: Sugar, Slavery, and Human Society.* London: Heinemann, 1967.

Babst, Earl. *A Century of Sugar Refining in the United States.* New York: De Vinne Press, 1916.

Balogh, Brian. *A Government out of Sight: The Mystery of National Authority in Nineteenth-Century America.* Cambridge: Cambridge University Press, 2009.

The Bankers' Magazine and Statistical Register. Vol. 41. New York: Homans Publishing Company, 1886–1887.

Barlow, Maude. *Blue Covenant: The Global Water Crisis and the Coming Battle for the Right to Water.* Toronto: McClelland and Stewart, 2007.

Barlow, Maude, and Tony Clarke. *Blue Gold: The Fight to Stop the Corporate Theft of the World's Water.* New York: New Press, 2002.

Barnet, Richard J., and Ronald E. Müller. *Global Reach: The Power of the Multinational Corporations.* New York: Simon and Schuster, 1974.

Berlin, Ira. *Generations of Captivity: A History of African-American Slaves.* Cambridge: Belknap Press of Harvard University Press, 2003.

Bigwood, Jeremy. "Repeating Mistakes of the Past: Another Mycoherbicide Research Bill." A report by the Drug Policy Alliance Network (March 2006). http://www.drugpolicy.org/docUploads/Mycoherbicide06.pdf.

Blake, Nelson Manfred. *Water for the Cities: A History of the Urban Water Supply Problem in the United States.* Syracuse, NY: Syracuse University Press, 1956.

Blanding, Michael. "The Case Against Coke." *Nation*, April 13, 2006.

———. *The Coke Machine: The Dirty Truth Behind the World's Favorite Soft Drink.* New York: Avery, 2010.

Blumberg, Louis, and Robert Gottlieb. *War on Waste: Can America Win Its Battle with Garbage?* Washington, DC: Island Press, 1989.

Brandt, Allan. *The Cigarette Century: The Rise, Fall, and Deadly Persistence of the Product That Defined America*. New York: Basic Books, 2007.

Brownell, K. D. and D. Yach. "The Battle of the Bulge." *Foreign Policy* (November/December 2005): 26–27.

Bullard, Robert. *Dumping in Dixie: Race, Class, and Environmental Quality*. Boulder, CO: Westview Press, 1990.

Campbell, William T. *Big Beverage*. Atlanta: Tupper and Love, 1952.

Candler, Charles Howard. *Asa Griggs Candler*. Atlanta: Emory University, 1950.

Carpenter, Dan. *Reputation and Power: Organizational Image and Pharmaceutical Regulation at the FDA*. Princeton: Princeton University Press, 2010.

Carpenter, Murray. *Caffeinated: How Our Daily Habit Helps, Hurts, and Hooks Us*. New York: Hudson Street Press, 2014.

Carson, Rachel. *Silent Spring*. Boston: Houghlin Mifflin; Cambridge, MA: Riverside Press, 1962.

Centers for Disease Control, Research to Practice Series, no. 3. September 2006. http://www.cdc.gov/nccdphp/dnpa/nutrition/pdf/r2p_sweetend_beverages.pdf.

Chandler, Alfred. "The Beginnings of 'Big Business' in American Industry." *Business History Review* 33, no. 1 (Spring 1959): 1–31.

———. "Development, Diversification, and Decentralization." In *Postwar Economic Trends in the United States*, ed. Ralph E. Freeman. New York: Harper and Brothers, 1960.

———. *Scale and Scope: The Dynamics of Industrial Capitalism*. Cambridge: Belknap Press of Harvard University Press, 1990.

———. *Strategy and Structure: Chapters in the History of the Industrial Enterprise*. Cambridge: MIT Press, 1962.

———. *The Visible Hand: The Managerial Revolution in American Business*. Cambridge: Belknap Press of Harvard University Press, 1977.

Cheney, Ian, Curt Ellis, and Aaron Woolf. *King Corn*. DVD. New York: Docurama Films, distributed by New Video, 2008.

Choi, H. K., and G. Curhan. "Soft Drinks, Fructose Consumption, and the Risk of Gout in Men: Prospective Cohort Study." *British Medical Journal* 336, no. 7639 (February 9, 2008): 309–312.

Clairmonte, Frederick, and John Cavanagh. *Merchants of Drink: Transnational Control of World Beverages*. Penang, Malaysia: Third World Network, 1988.

Clapp, Brian William. *An Environmental History of Britain Since the Industrial Revolution*. London: Longman, 1994.

Clark, David S. "Adjudication to Administration: A Statistical Analysis of Federal District Courts in the Twentieth Century." *Southern California Law Review* 55 (1981–1982): 65–152.

Clark, Eric. *The Want Makers: The World of Advertising—How They Make You Buy*. London: Hodder and Stoughton, 1998; New York: Viking, 1989.

Clarke, Tony. *Inside the Bottle: Exposing the Bottled Water Industry*. Ottawa: Canadian Centre for Policy Alternatives, Polaris Institute, 2007.

Clay, Jason. *World Agriculture and the Environment: A Commodity-by-Commodity Guide to Impacts and Practices*. Washington, DC: Island Press, 2004.

Clay, Joy A. "The D.C. Bottle Bill Initiative: A Casualty of the Reagan Era." *Environmental Review* 13, no. 2 (Summer 1989): 17–31.

"Clean Water Infrastructure: A Variety of Issues Need to Be Considered When Designing a Clean Water Trust Fund." US Government Accountability Office, May 2009.

Coase, Ronald E. "Accounting and the Theory of the Firm." *Journal of Accounting and Economics* 12 (1990): 3–13.

———. "The Nature of the Firm," *Economica* 4, no. 16 (November 1937): 386–405.

Cohen, Benjamin R. "Analysis as Border Patrol: Chemists Along the Boundary Between Pure Food and Real Adulteration." *Endeavour* 35, no. 2–3 (June–September 2011): 66–73.

Cohen, Michael M. "Jim Crow's Drug War: Race, Coca Cola, and the Southern Origins of Drug Prohibition." *Southern Cultures* 12, no. 3 (Fall 2006): 55–79.

Colton, Craig E. *An Unnatural Metropolis: Wresting New Orleans from Nature.* Baton Rouge: Louisiana State University Press, 2006.

Coke's First Hundred Years. Sheperdsville, KY: Keller International Publishing Corporation, 1986.

Collective Testimony of the Benefit and Virtue of the Famous French Tonic Vin Mariani. New York: Mariani, 1910.

Coons, George H. "The Sugar Beet: Product of Science." *Scientific Monthly* 68, no. 3 (March 1949): 149–164.

Cronon, William. *Nature's Metropolis: Chicago and the Great West.* New York: Norton, 1991.

Crosby, Alfred W. *Ecological Imperialism: The Biological Expansion of Europe, 900–1900.* Cambridge: Cambridge University Press, 2004.

Cullather, Nick. *The Hungry World: America's Cold War Battle Against Poverty in Asia.* Cambridge: Harvard University Press, 2010.

Dalton, John E. *Sugar: A Case Study of Government Control.* New York: Macmillan, 1937.

Danbom, David B. *Born in the Country: A History of Rural America.* Baltimore: Johns Hopkins University Press, 1995.

Daniel, Pete. *Breaking the Land: The Transformation of Cotton, Tobacco, and Rice Cultures Since 1880.* Urbana: University of Illinois Press, 1985.

D'Antonio, Michael. *Hershey: Milton S. Hershey's Extraordinary Life of Wealth, Empire, and Utopian Dreams.* New York: Simon and Schuster, 2006.

Davis, David Brion. *Inhuman Bondage: The Rise and Fall of Slavery in the New World.* Oxford: Oxford University Press, 2006.

Daw, Stuart. "Reflections in a Cup: Caffeine Anyone?" *Canadian Vending and Office Coffee Service Magazine.* http://www.canadianvending.com/content/view/1113.

Dean, Warren. *Rio Claro: A Brazilian Plantation System, 1820–1920.* Stanford: Stanford University Press, 1976.

———. *With Broadax and Firebrand: The Destruction of the Brazilian Atlantic Forest.* Berkeley and Los Angeles: University of California Press, 1997.

de la Peña, Carolyn. *Empty Pleasures: The Story of Artificial Sweeteners from Saccharin to Splenda.* Chapel Hill: University of North Carolina Press, 2010.

Desrochers, Pierre. "How Did the Invisible Hand Handle Industrial Waste? By-product Development Before the Modern Environmental Era." *Enterprise and Society* 8, no. 2 (June 2007): 348–374.

————. "Industrial Ecology and the Rediscovery of Inter-Firm Recycling Linkages: Some Historical Perspective and Policy Implications." *Industrial and Corporate Change* 11, no. 5 (November 2002): 1031–1057.

DeWitt, Patricia J. B. "A Brief History of Tea: The Rise and Fall of the Tea Importation Act." Third Year Writing Requirement, Harvard Law School, 2000.

Diamond, Jared. *Guns, Germs, and Steel.* New York: Norton, 1998.

Dietz, Lawrence. *Soda Pop: The History, Advertising, Art, and Memorabilia of Soft Drinks.* New York: Simon and Schuster, 1973.

D. L. I. Productions, Canadian Broadcasting Corporation, Télé-Québec, Channel Four (Great Britain), and Microfilms Inc. *The Cola Conquest: A Trilogy.* DVD. Canada: Microfilms Inc., 2004.

Doane, Seth. "Battling Obesity in America." *CBS News,* posted January 7, 2010. http://www.cbsnews.com/stories/2010/01/07/eveningnews/main6069163.shtml?tag =contentMain;contentBody.

Donovan, Tristan. *Fizz: How Soda Shook Up the World.* Chicago: Chicago Review Press, 2014.

Drenkard, Scott. *Overreaching on Obesity: Governments Consider New Taxes on Soda and Candy.* Tax Foundation Special Report No. 196. October 31, 2011. http://taxfoundation.org/article/overreaching-obesity-governments-consider-new-taxes-soda-and-candy.

"Dr. Louis Schaeffer." *American Perfumer and Essential Oil Review* 7, no. 10 (December 1912): 246.

Duda, Mark, and Jane S. Shaw. "Life Cycle Assessment." *Society* 35, no. 1 (November 1997): 38–43.

Dufty, William. *Sugar Blues.* Radnor, PA: Chitton Books Co., 1978.

Dunaway, Finis. "Gas Masks, Pogo, and the Ecological Indian: Earth Day and the Visual Politics of American Environmentalism." *American Quarterly* 60, no. 1 (March 2008), 67–99.

Duncan, Kenneth, and Ian Rutledge with Colin Harding, eds. *Land and Labour in Latin America: Essays on the Development of Agrarian Capitalism in the Nineteenth and Twentieth Centuries.* Cambridge: Cambridge University Press, 1977.

Einhorn, Robin L. *Property Rules: Political Economy in Chicago, 1833–1872.* Chicago: University of Chicago Press, 1991.

Elliott, Charles. *A Biography of the "Boss": Robert Winship Woodruff.* Robert W. Woodruff Estate, 1979.

Ellis, John, and Stuart Galishoff. "Atlanta's Water Supply, 1865–1918." *Maryland Historian* 8 (Spring 1977): 5–22.

Ellis, Lippert S. *The Tariff on Sugar.* Freeport, IL: Rawleigh Foundation, 1933.

Enrico, Roger, with Jesse Kornbluth. *The Other Guy Blinked: How Pepsi Won the Cola Wars.* Toronto and New York: Bantam, 1986.

Ettinger, Steven. *Twinkie, Deconstructed: My Journey to Discover How the Ingredients in Processed Foods Are Grown, Mined (Yes, Mined), and Manipulated into What America Eats.* New York: Hudson Street Press, 2007.

Finkelstein, Eric A., Justin G. Trogdon, Joel W. Cohen, and William Dietz. "Annual

Medical Spending Attributable to Obesity: Payer-and-Service Specific Estimates." *Health Affairs* 28, no. 5 (September 2009): w822–w831.

Fischer-Kowalski, Marina. "Society's Metabolism: The Intellectual History of Materials Flow Analysis, Part I: 1860–1970." *Journal of Industrial Ecology* 2, no. 1 (Winter 1998): 61–78.

Flegal, K. M., M. D. Carroll, C. L. Ogden, and L. R. Curtin. "Prevalence and Trends in Obesity Among US Adults, 1999–2008," *Journal of the American Medical Association* 303, no. 3 (January 20, 2010): 235–241.

Flegal, K. M., M. D. Carroll, R. J. Kuczmarski, and C. L. Johnson. "Overweight and Obesity in the United States: Prevalence and Trends, 1960–1994." *International Journal of Obesity* 22, no. 1 (January 1998): 39–47.

Fletcher, Jason M., David Frisvold, and Nathan Tefft. "Can Soft Drink Taxes Reduce Population Weight?" *Contemporary Economic Policy* 28, no. 1 (January 2010): 23–35.

Food and Drug Administration. *Final Environmental Impact Statement: Plastic Bottles for Carbonated Beverages and Beer.* Washington, DC: USGPO, September 1976.

Foweraker, Joe. *The Struggle for Land: A Political Economy of the Pioneer Frontier in Brazil from 1930 to the Present Day.* Cambridge: Cambridge University Press, 1981.

Folz, David H. "Municipal Recycling Performance: A Public Sector Environmental Success Story." *Public Administration Review* 59, no. 4 (July–August 1999): 336–345.

Forrestal, Dan J. *Faith, Hope and $5,000: The Story of Monsanto.* New York: Simon and Schuster, 1977.

Foster, Robert. *Coca-Globalization: Following Soft Drinks from New York to New Guinea.* New York: Palgrave Macmillan, 2008.

Freud, Sigmund. *Cocaine Papers.* Ed. Robert Byck. New York: Stonehill, 1974.

Friedman, Lawrence M. *American Law in the Twentieth Century.* New Haven: Yale University Press, 2002.

———. *A History of American Law.* New York: Simon and Schuster, 1973.

Froud, Julie, Sukhdev Johal, Adam Leaver, and Karel Williams. "Apple Business Model: Financialization Across the Pacific." Centre for Research on Socio-Cultural Change (CRESC) Working Paper No. 111, University of Manchester Business School (April 2012).

Frundt, Henry J. *Refreshing Pauses: Coca-Cola and Human Rights in Guatemala.* New York: Praeger, 1987.

Fussell, Betty. *The Story of Corn.* New York: Knopf, 1992.

Galambos, Louis. "Global Perspectives on Modern Business." *Business History Review* 71, no. 2 (Summer 1997): 287–290.

Galambos, Louis, and Joseph Pratt. *The Rise of the Corporate Commonwealth: U.S. Business and Public Policy in the Twentieth Century.* New York: Basic Books, 1988.

Galloway, J. H. *The Sugar Cane Industry: An Historical Geography from its Origins to 1914.* Cambridge: Cambridge University Press, 1989.

Garrett, Franklin. *Atlanta and Environs: A Chronicle of Its People and Events.* 2 vols. New York: Lewis Historical Publishing, 1954.

Garattini, Silvio, ed. *Caffeine, Coffee, and Health.* New York: Raven Press, 1993.

Girard, Richard. "Coca-Cola Company: Inside the Real Thing." Polaris Institute Corporate Profile. August 2005. http://www.polarisinstitute.org/files/Coke%20profile%20August%2018.pdf.

Gleick, Peter. *Bottled and Sold: The Story Behind Our Obsession with Bottled Water.* Washington, DC: Island Press, 2010.

Glennon, Robert J. *Water Follies: Groundwater Pumping and the Fate of America's Fresh Waters.* Washington, DC: Island Press, 2002.

Gootenberg, Paul. *Andean Cocaine: The Making of a Global Drug.* Chapel Hill: University of North Carolina Press, 2008.

————."Between Coca and Cocaine: A Century or More of U.S.-Peruvian Drug Paradoxes, 1860–1980." Washington, DC: Woodrow Wilson Center, 2001.

————. "Reluctance or Resistance?: Constructing Cocaine (Prohibitions) in Peru, 1910–50." In *Cocaine: Global Histories,* ed. Paul Gootenberg. New York: Routledge, 1999.

————. "Secret Ingredients: The Politics of Coca in US-Peruvian Relations, 1915–65." *Journal of Latin American Studies* 36, no. 2 (May 2004): 233–265.

Gorman, Hugh S. "Efficiency, Environmental Quality, and Oil Field Brines: The Success and Failure of Pollution Control by Self-Regulation." *Business History Review* 73, no. 4 (Winter 1999): 601–640.

Gould, Lewis, ed. *Lady Bird Johnson: Our Environmental First Lady.* Lawrence: University Press of Kansas, 1999.

————. *Lady Bird Johnson and the Environment.* Lawrence: University Press of Kansas, 1988.

Greising, David. *I'd Like the World to Buy a Coke: The Life and Leadership of Roberto Goizueta.* New York: John Wiley and Sons, 1997.

Gunja, N., and J. A. Brown. "Energy Drinks: Health Risks and Toxicity." *Medical Journal of Australia* 196, no. 1 (January 16, 2012): 46–49.

Hacker, Jacob. *The Divided Welfare State: The Battle over Public and Private Social Benefits in the United States.* Cambridge: Cambridge University Press, 2002.

Hamilton, Shane. *Trucking Country: The Road to America's Wal-Mart Economy.* Princeton: Princeton University Press, 2008.

Hausman, William J. "U.S. Business History at the End of the Twentieth Century." In *Business History Around the World,* ed. Franco Amatori and Geoffrey Jones, 83–110. Cambridge: Cambridge University Press, 2003.

Hays, Constance L. *The Real Thing: Truth and Power at the Coca-Cola Company.* New York: Random House, 2004.

Hays, Samuel P. in collaboration with Barbara D. Hays. *Beauty, Health, and Permanence: Environmental Politics in the United States, 1955–1985.* Cambridge: Cambridge University Press, 1987.

Heston, Thomas J. *Sweet Subsidy: The Economic and Diplomatic Effects of the U.S. Sugar Acts, 1934–1974.* New York and London: Garland, 1987.

Hogan, Michael. *A Cross of Iron: Harry S. Truman and the Origins of the National Security State, 1945–1954.* Cambridge: Cambridge University Press, 1998.

————. *The Marshall Plan: America, Britain, and the Reconstruction of Western Europe, 1947–1952.* Cambridge: Cambridge University Press, 1987.

Hollander, Gail M. *Raising Cane in the 'Glades: The Global Sugar Trade and the Transformation of Florida.* Chicago: University of Chicago Press, 2008.

Horwitz, Morton J. *The Transformation of American Law, 1870–1960: The Crisis of Legal Orthodoxy.* New York: Oxford University Press, 1992.

Howard, Christopher. *The Hidden Welfare State: Tax Expenditures and Social Policy in the United States.* Princeton: Princeton University Press, 1997.

Hostetter, Christina J. "Sugar Allies: How Hershey and Coca-Cola Used Government Contracts and Sugar Exemptions to Elude Sugar Rationing Regulations." Master's thesis, University of Maryland, College Park, 2004.

Hunter, Beatrice Trum. *The Sweetener Trap and How to Avoid It: The Power and Politics of Sweeteners and Their Impact on Your Health.* Laguna Beach, CA: Basic Health Publications, 2008.

Hunt, Robert G., and William E. Franklin. "LCA—How It Came About: Personal Reflections on the Origin and the Development of LCA in the USA." *International Journal of Life Cycle Assessment* 1, no. 1 (March 1996): 4–7.

Hyman, Louis. *Debtor Nation: The History of America in Red Ink.* Princeton: Princeton University Press, 2011.

———. "Rethinking the Postwar Corporation: Management, Monopolies, and Markets." In *What's Good for Business: Business and American Politics Since World War II,* ed. Kim Phillips-Fein and Julian E. Zelizer, 195–211. Oxford: Oxford University Press, 2012.

Ingham, John N. *Biographical Dictionary of American Business Leaders.* Vol. 2. Westport, CT: Greenwood Press, 1983.

Isaacson, Walter. *Steve Jobs.* New York: Simon and Schuster, 2011.

Isdell, Neville, with David Beasley. *Inside Coca-Cola: A CEO's Life Story of Building the World's Most Popular Brand.* New York: St. Martin's Press, 2011.

Jacobson, Lisa. *Raising Consumers: Children and the American Mass Market in the Early Twentieth Century.* New York: Columbia University Press, 2004.

Jacobson, Michael F. *Liquid Candy: How Soft Drinks Are Harming Americans' Health.* Washington, DC: Center for Science in the Public Interest, 1998.

Jacobson, Michael F., and Ted Nixon. Interviews by Allison Aubrey, "Coca-Cola Modifies Caramel Color to Avoid Cancer Warning Label." *Morning Edition,* NPR, March 7, 2012.

James, Jack E. and Michael Gossop. Book review of *Caffeine, Coffee, and Health. Addiction* 90, no. 1 (January 1995), 134–135.

———. "Caffeine, Health and Commercial Interests," *Addiction* 89, no. 12 (December 1994): 1595–1599.

Jørgensen, Finn Arne. *Making a Green Machine: The Infrastructure of Beverage Container Recycling.* New Brunswick: Rutgers University Press, 2011.

Kahn, E. J., Jr. *The Big Drink: The Story of Coca-Cola.* New York: Random House, 1960.

Kaminski, Edward S. *Maywood: The Borough, the Railroad, and the Station.* Charleston, SC: Arcadia Publishing, 2010.

Kaplan, Martha. "Fijian Water in Fiji and New York: Local Politics and a Global Commodity." *Cultural Anthropology* 22, no. 4 (2007): 685–706.

Kauffman, George B. "Pharmacology of Caffeine." *Merck's Archives of Materia Medica and Drug Therapy* 3, no. 10 (October 1901): 393–395.

Keller, Maryann. *Rude Awakening: The Rise, Fall, and Struggle for Recovery of General Motors.* New York: William Morrow, 1989.

Kimball, Debi. *Recycling in America: A Reference Handbook.* Santa Barbara, CA: ABC-CLIO, 1992.

King, Monroe Martin. "Dr. John S. Pemberton: Originator of Coca-Cola." *Pharmacy in History* 29, no. 2 (1987): 85–89.

Kirby, Jack Temple. *Rural Worlds Lost: The American South, 1920–1960.* Baton Rouge: Louisiana State University, 1987.

Knowles, William S. Transcript of an interview conducted by Michael A. Grayson at St. Louis, Missouri, January, 30, 2008. Chemical Heritage Foundation Oral History Transcript 0406 (available by request from the Chemical Heritage Foundation).

Kolko, Gabriel. *The Triumph of Conservatism: A Reinterpretation of American History, 1900–1916.* New York: Free Press of Glencoe, 1963.

Kornberg, Nicole. "'Good Drinking Water Instead of Coca-Cola': Elaborating Ideas of Development Through the Case of Coca-Cola in India." Master's thesis, University of Texas at Austin, 2007.

Kouwenhoven, John Atlee. *The Beer Can by the Highway: Essays on What's American About America.* Garden City, NY: Doubleday, 1961.

Kramek, Niva, and Lydia Loh. *The History of Philadelphia's Water Supply and Sanitation System: Lessons in Sustainability for Developing Urban Water Systems.* Philadelphia: Philadelphia Global Water Initiative, June 2007.

Krippner, Greta R. *Capitalizing on Crisis: The Political Origins of the Rise of Finance.* Cambridge: Harvard University Press, 2011.

LaFeber, Walter. *The New Empire: An Interpretation of American Expansion, 1860–1898.* Ithaca: Cornell University Press, 1963.

Langlois, Richard N. "The Vanishing Hand: The Changing Dynamics of Industrial Capitalism." *Industrial and Corporate Change* 12, no. 2 (2003): 351–385.

Lazonick, William. "The Financialization of the U.S. Coporation: What Has Been Lost, and How It Can Be Regained." *Seattle University Law Review* 36 (2013): 857–909.

Lears, Jackson. *Rebirth of a Nation: The Making of Modern America, 1877–1920.* New York: HarperCollins, 2009.

Lee, Caroline. "The Roots of Astroturfing." *Contexts* 9, no. 1 (Winter 2010): 73–75.

Lenoir, M., F. Serre, L. Cantin, and S. H. Ahmed. "Intense Sweetness Surpasses Cocaine Reward." *PLoS ONE* 2, no. 8 (August 2007): 1–10.

Levy, Daniel, and Andrew T. Young. "'The Real Thing': Nominal Price Rigidity of the Nickel Coke, 1886–1959." *Journal of Money, Credit and Banking* 36, no. 4 (August 2004): 765–799.

Lipsett, Charles. *Industrial Wastes and Salvage: Conservation and Utilization.* New York: Atlas, 1963.

Loughlin, Daniel H., and Morton A. Barlaz. "Policies for Strengthening Markets for Recyclables: A Worldwide Perspective." *Critical Reviews in Environmental Science and Technology* 36, no. 4 (2006): 287–326.

Louis, J. C., and Harvey Z. Yazijian. *The Cola Wars*. New York: Everest House, 1980.

Macinnis, Peter. *Bittersweet: The Story of Sugar*. St. Leonards, New South Wales: Allen and Unwin, 2002.

Madhok, Anoop. "Reassessing the Fundamentals and Beyond: Ronald Coase, The Transaction Cost and Resource-Based Theories of the Firm and the Institutional Structure of Production." *Strategic Management Journal* 23, no. 6 (June 2002): 535–550.

Mariani, Angelo. *Coca and Its Therapeutic Applications*. 1886; 2nd ed. New York: J. N. Jaros, 1892.

Marsh, Barbara. *A Corporate Tragedy: The Agony of International Harvester Company*. Garden City, NY: Doubleday, 1985.

Martinez, Steve. "Soft Drink Companies Make Splash in Bottled Water." *Amber Waves* 5 (June 2007): 4.

Mattes, R. D., and D. P. DiMeglio. "Liquid Versus Solid Carbohydrates: Effects on Food Intake and Body Weight." *International Journal of Obesity* 24, no. 6 (2000), 794–800.

McCraw, Thomas K. *Prophets of Regulation: Charles Francis Adams, Louis D. Brandeis, James M. Landis, Alfred E. Kahn*. Cambridge: Belknap Press of Harvard University Press, 1984.

———, ed. *The Essential Alfred Chandler: Essays Toward a Historical Theory of Big Business*. Boston: Harvard Business School Press, 1988.

McGahan, A. M. "The Emergence of the National Brewing Oligopoly: Competition in the American Market, 1933–1958." *Business History Review* 65, no. 2 (Summer 1991): 229–284.

McGurty, Eileen Maura. "From NIMBY to Civil Rights: The Origins of the Environmental Justice Movement." In *Environmental History and the American South: A Reader*, ed. Paul Sutter and Christopher J. Manganiello, 372–399. Athens: University of Georgia, 2009.

McMahon, James D., Jr. *Built on Chocolate: The Story of the Hershey Chocolate Company*. Santa Monica, CA: General Publishing Group, 1998.

McQueen, Humphrey. *The Essence of Capitalism: The Origins of Our Future*. Montreal: Black Rose Books, 2003.

Mekonnen, M. M., and A. Y. Hoekstra (UNESCO, Institute for Water Health). *National Water Footprint Accounts: The Green, Blue and Grey Water Footprint of Production and Consumption*. Value of Water Research Report no. 50, UNESCO Institute for Water Health, 2011. Available online via http://www.waterfootprint.org/?page=files/Publications.

Melosi, Martin. *Garbage in the Cities: Refuse, Reform, and the Environment*. College Station, Texas: Texas A&M University Press, 1981.

———. *The Sanitary City: Urban Infrastructure in America from Colonial Times to the Present*. Baltimore: Johns Hopkins University Press, 2000.

———. "Waste Management: The Cleaning of America." *Environment* 23, no. 8 (October 1981): 6–13; 41–44.

Mills, Nicolaus. *Winning the Peace: The Marshall Plan and America's Coming of Age as a Superpower*. Hoboken, NJ: John Wiley & Sons, 2008.

Mintz, Sidney. *Sweetness and Power: The Place of Sugar in Modern History.* New York: Penguin Books, 1985.

———. "Sweet, Salt, and the Language of Love." *MLN* 106, no. 4 (September 1981): 852–860.

Mitchell, A. J., ed. *Formulation and Production of Carbonated Soft Drinks.* Glasgow: Blackie, 1990.

Mortimer, W. Golden. *Peru: History of Coca, "The Divine Plant" of the Incas.* New York: J. H. Vail, 1901.

Moss, Michael. *Salt Sugar Fat: How the Food Giants Hooked Us.* New York: Random House, 2013.

Musto, David F. "Illicit Price of Cocaine in Two Eras: 1908–14 and 1982–89." *Pharmacy in History* 33 (1991): 3–10.

Nair, K. N., Antonyto Paul, and Vineetha Menon. *Water Insecurity, Institutions and Livelihood Dynamics.* Kerala: Center for Development Studies, 2008.

National Association for PET Container Recycling (NAPCOR). *2011 Report on Post-consumer PET Container Recycling Activity: Final Report.* http://www.napcor.com/pdf/NAPCOR_2011RateReport.pdf.

Nash, June. "Consuming Interests: Water, Rum, and Coca-Cola from Ritual Propitiation to Corporate Expropriation in Highland Chiapas." *Cultural Anthropology* 22, no. 4 (2007): 621–639.

Niemann, Albert. "Ueber eine neue organische Base in den Cocablättern." *Archiv der Pharmazie* 153, no. 2 (1860): 129–256.

Novak, William J. "The Myth of the 'Weak' American State." *American Historical Review* 113, no. 3 (June 2008): 752–772.

Ogden, C. L., M. M. Lamb, M. D. Carroll, and K. M. Flegal. "Obesity and Socioeconomic Status in Adults: United States, 2005–2008." *National Center for Health Statistics Data Brief* 50 (December 2010).

Ogle, Maureen. *Ambitious Brew: The Story of American Beer.* Orlando: Harcourt, 2006.

———. "Water Supply, Waste Disposal, and the Culture of Privatism in the Mid-Nineteenth-Century American City." *Journal of Urban History* 25 (1999): 321–47.

Oliver, Thomas. *The Real Coke, the Real Story.* New York: Random House, 1986.

Osleeb, Jeffrey P., and Robert G. Cromley. "The Location of Plants of the Uniform Delivered Price Manufacturer: A Case Study of Coca-Cola Ltd." *Economic Geography* 54, no. 1 (January 1978): 40–52.

Ott, Julia. *When Wall Street Met Main Street: The Quest for an Investors' Democracy.* Cambridge: Harvard University Press, 2011.

Palacios, Marco. *Coffee in Colombia, 1850–1970: An Economic, Social and Political History.* Cambridge: Cambridge University Press, 1980.

Pendergrast, Mark. *For God, Country & Coca-Cola: The Definitive History of the Great American Soft Drink and the Company That Makes It.* New York: Maxwell McMillan, 1993; New York: Scribner, 1993; New York, Basic Books, 2013. Citations are to the 1993 edition.

———. *Uncommon Grounds: The History of Coffee and How It Transformed Our World.* New York: Basic Books, 1999.

Centers for Disease Control and Prevention. "Percentage of Civilian, Noninstitutionalized

Population with Diagnosed Diabetes by Age, United States, 1980–2008." Posted October 15, 2010. www.cdc.gov/diabetes/statistics/prev/national/figbyage.htm.

Perkins, John. *Geopolitics and the Green Revolution: Wheat, Genes, and the Cold War.* New York: Oxford University Press, 1997.

Perry, George Powell. *Wealth from Waste; or, Gathering Up the Fragments.* New York: F. H. Revell, 1908.

Pillai, P. R. Sreemahadevan. *The Saga of Plachimada.* Mumbai: Vikas Adhyayan Kendra, 2008.

Pollan, Michael. *The Omnivore's Dilemma: A Natural History of Four Meals.* New York: Penguin Books, 2006.

Pomeranz, Kenneth T., and Steven Topik, eds. *The World That Trade Created: Society, Culture, and the World Economy—1400 to the Present.* 2nd ed. Armonk, NY: M. E. Sharpe, 2006.

Powledge, Fred. *Water: The Nature, Uses, and Future of Our Most Precious and Abused Resource.* New York: Farrar, Straus and Giroux, 1982.

Ralph Hayes, 1894–1977. Biographical essay published by the New York Community Trust. Undated. http://www.nycommunitytrust.org/Portals/0/Uploads/Documents/Bio Brochures/Ralph%20Hayes.pdf.

Rawson, Michael. "The Nature of Water: Reform and the Antebellum Crusade for Municipal Water in Boston." *Environmental History* 9, no. 3 (July 2004): 411–445.

Reisner, Marc. *Cadillac Desert: The American West and Its Disappearing Water.* New York: Viking, 1986.

Reissig, Chad J., Eric C. Strain, and Roland R. Griffiths. "Caffeinated Energy Drinks—A Growing Problem." *Drug Alcohol Dependency* 99 (January 1, 2009): 1–10.

Restivo, Sal, ed. *Science, Technology, and Society: An Encyclopedia.* New York: Oxford University Press, 2005.

Riley, John J. *A History of the American Soft Drink Industry.* New York: Arno, 1958; rpt. New York: Ayer, 1972.

Rogers, Heather. *Gone Tomorrow: The Hidden Life of Garbage.* New York: The New Press, 2005.

Rome, Adam. *The Bulldozer in the Countryside: Suburban Sprawl and the Rise of American Environmentalism.* Cambridge: Cambridge University Press, 2001.

Rosen, Christine Meisner, and Christopher Sellers. "The Nature of the Firm: Towards an Ecocultural History of Business." *Business History Review* 73, no. 4 (Winter 1999): 577–600.

Rosen, Christine Meisner. "Industrial Ecology and the Greening of Business History." *Business and Economic History* 26, no. 1 (Fall 1997): 123–137.

Rouleau, Andre J. "Vermont Deposit Law and Recycling." Presented at Vermont Solid Waste Summit, November 8, 1985. Available online from P2 InfoHouse, www .p2pays.org/ref/24/23636.pdf.

Royte, Elizabeth. *Bottlemania: How Water Went on Sale and Why We Bought It.* New York: Bloomsbury, 2008.

———. *Garbage Land: On the Secret Trail of Trash.* New York: Little, Brown, 2005.

Ruttan, Vernon W. *United States Development Assistance Policy: The Domestic Politics of Foreign Economic Aid.* Baltimore: John Hopkins University Press, 1996.

Scott, James. *Seeing like a State: How Certain Schemes to Improve the Human Condition Have Failed.* New Haven: Yale University Press, 1998.

Schlosser, Eric. *Fast Food Nation: The Dark Side of the All-American Meal.* Boston: Houghton Mifflin, 2001.

Schulman, Bruce J. *From Cotton Belt to Sunbelt: Federal Policy, Economic Development, and the Transformation of the South, 1938–1980.* New York: Oxford University Press, 1991.

Scranton, Philip. *Endless Novelty: Specialty Production and American Industrialization, 1865–1925.* Princeton: Princeton University Press, 1997.

Seifert, Sara M., Judith L. Schaechter, Eugene R. Hershorin, and Steven E. Lipshultz. "Health Effects of Energy Drinks on Children, Adolescents, and Young Adults." *Pediatrics* 127, no. 3 (March 1, 2011): 511–528.

Shah, Sonia. "Coke in Your Faucet?" *Progressive* 65, no. 5 (August, 2001): 28–30.

Shingler, Angus J., and Jack K. Carlton. "Method for the Separation and Determination of Theophyllin, Theobromine, and Caffeine." *Analytical Chemistry* 31, no. 10 (October 1959): 1679–1680.

Shireman, William K., Frank Sweeney, et al. *The CalPIRG-ELS Study Group Report on Can and Bottle Bills.* Stanford, CA: Stanford Environmental Law Society, 1981.

Sklar, Martin J. *The Corporate Reconstruction of American Capitalism, 1890–1916.* Cambridge: Cambridge University Press, 1988.

Slade, Giles. *Made to Break: Technology and Obsolescence in America.* Cambridge: Harvard University Press, 2006.

Snitow, Alan, Deborah Kaufman, Kenji Yamamoto, and Snitow-Kaufman Productions. *Thirst.* DVD. Oley, PA: Bullfrog Films, 2005.

Snitow, Alan, and Deborah Kaufman with Michael Fox. *Thirst: Fighting the Corporate Theft of Our Water.* San Francisco: John Wiley and Sons, 2007.

Soluri, John. *Banana Cultures: Agriculture, Consumption, and Environmental Change in Honduras and the United States.* Austin: University of Texas Press, 2005.

Sparrow, James T. *Warfare State: World War II Americans and the Age of Big Government.* Oxford: Oxford University Press, 2011.

Spillane, Joseph F. *Cocaine: From Medical Marvel to Modern Menace in the United States, 1884–1920.* Baltimore: Johns Hopkins University Press, 2000.

Spooner, Henry J. *Wealth from Waste: Elimination of Waste a World Problem.* London: G. Routledge and Sons, 1918.

Stanford Environmental Law Society. *Disposing of Non-Returnables: A Guide to Minimum Deposit Legislation.* Stanford: Stanford Environmental Law Society, 1975.

Starr, Paul. *The Social Transformation of American Medicine.* New York: Basic Books, 1982.

Steinberg, Ted. *Down to Earth: Nature's Role in American History.* New York: Oxford University Press, 2002.

———. *Nature Incorporated: Industrialization and the Waters of New England.* Cambridge: Cambridge University Press, 1991.

Strand, Ginger. "The Crying Indian: How an Environmental Icon Helped Sell Cans—and Sell Out Environmentalism." *Orion Nature Quarterly* 27, no. 6 (November/December 2008): 20–27.

Strasser, Susan. *Satisfaction Guaranteed: The Making of the American Mass Market.* New York: Pantheon Books, 1989.

————. *Waste and Want: A Social History of Trash*. New York: Metropolitan Books, 1999.

Strasser, Susan, Charles McGovern, and Matthias Judt, eds. *Getting and Spending: European and American Consumer Societies in the Twentieth Century*. Cambridge: Cambridge University Press, 1998.

Talbot, John M. "The Struggle for Control of a Commodity Chain: Instant Coffee from Latin America." *Latin American Research Review* 32, no. 2 (1997): 117–135.

Tama, Jordan. "More than Deference: Eisenhower, Congress, and Foreign Policy." Paper prepared for "Eisenhower and Congress: Lessons for the 21st Century," American University, February 19, 2010.

Tarr, Joel. "The Evolution of the Urban Infrastructure in the Nineteenth and Twentieth Centuries." In *Perspectives on Urban Infrastructure*, ed. Royce Hanson, 4–66. Washington, DC: National Academy Press, 1984.

Tarr, Joel, and Gabriel Dupuy, eds. *Technology and the Rise of the Networked City in Europe and America*. Philadelphia: Temple University Press, 1988.

Tarr, Joel A., and Patrick Gurian. "The First Federal Drinking Water Quality Standards and Their Evolution: A History from 1914 to 1974." In *Improving Regulation: Cases in Environment, Health, and Safety*, ed. Paul S. Fischbeck and R. Scott Farrow, 43–69. Washington, DC: Resources for the Future, 2001.

Taussig, Frank William. *The Tariff History of the United States*. New York: G. P. Putnam's Sons, 1914.

Taylor, Norman. *Plant Drugs That Changed the World*. London: George Allen and Unwin, 1966.

TERI (The Energy and Resources Institute), New Delhi, India. "Executive Summary of the Study on Independent Third Party Assessment of Coca-Cola Facilities in India." Report No. 2006WM21, 2006.

————. *Independent Third Party Assessment of Coca-Cola Facilities in India*. Report No. 2006WM21, January 2008.

Treichel, J. A. "Good News for Caffeine Consumers?" *Science News* 122, no. 20 (November 13, 1982): 311.

Thomas, Mark. *Belching Out the Devil: Global Adventures with Coca-Cola*. New York: Nation Books, 2008.

Tiffany, Paul A. *The Decline of American Steel: How Management, Labor, and Government Went Wrong*. New York: Oxford University Press, 1988.

————. "The Roots of Decline: Business-Government Relations in the American Steel Industry, 1945–1960." *Journal of Economic History* 44, no. 2 (June 1984): 407–419.

Topik, Steven. "Historicizing Commodity Chains: Five Hundred Years of the Global Coffee Commodity Chain." In *Frontiers of Commodity Chain Research*, ed. Jennifer Blair. Stanford: Stanford University Press, 2009.

Topik, Steven, Carlos Marichal, and Zephyr Frank, eds. *From Silver to Cocaine: Latin American Commodity Chains and the Building of the World Economy, 1500–2000*. Durham: Duke University Press, 2006.

Topik, Steven, and William Gervase Clarence-Smith, eds. *The Global Coffee Economy in Africa, Asia, and Latin America, 1500–1989*. Cambridge: Cambridge University Press, 2003.

Tracy, Campbell. *The Politics of Despair: Power and Resistance in the Tobacco Wars.* Lexington: University Press of Kentucky, 1993.

Tucker, Richard. *Insatiable Appetite: The United States and the Ecological Degradation of the Tropical World.* Berkeley: University of California Press, 2000.

Turner, James S. *The Chemical Feast: The Ralph Nader Study Group Report on Food Protection and the Food and Drug Administration.* New York: Grossman, 1970.

United Nations International Narcotics Control Board. *Effectiveness of the International Drug Control Treaties: Supplement to the Report of the International Narcotics Control Board for 1994.* New York: United Nations, 1995.

United States Bureau of the Census. *Commuting in the United States: 2009—American Consumer Survey Reports.* September 2011.

———. *Historical Statistics of the United States: Colonial Times to 1970.* Vol. 2. Washington, DC: USGPO, 1975.

———. Urban and Rural Populations, Table 4, Population: 1790–1990. http://www .census.gov/population/www/censusdata/files/table-4.pdf.

United States Bureau of Labor Statistics. Employment by Major Industry Sector, 1994, 2004, and projected 2014. http://www.bls.gov/opub/ted/2005/dec/wk3/ art01.htm.

——— Spotlight on Statistics: Sports and Exercise. May 2008. http://www.bls.gov/ spotlight/2008/sports/pdf/sports_bls_spotlight.pdf.

United States Congress. House. Committee on Agriculture. *Compilation of Responses to Farm Bill Feedback Questionnaire,* 111th Cong. 2nd Sess., September 2010.

———. House. Committee on Banking and Currency. *Rationing and Price Control of Sugar.* 80th Cong., 1st Sess., March, 6, 7, 10, 11, and 12, 1947.

———. House. Committee on Energy and Commerce. Subcommittee on Transportation and Hazardous Materials, *Recycling of Municipal Solid Waste.* 101st Cong., 2nd Sess., July 12, 13, 1989.

———. House. Committee on Foreign Affairs. *Reauthorization of the Overseas Private Investment Corporation.* 99th Cong., 1st Sess., June 18, 20, 25, 1985.

———. House. Committee on Foreign Affairs; Senate. Committee on Foreign Affairs, *Extension of European Recovery Program, Part 1.* 81st Cong., 1st Sess., Feb. 8–11, 15–18, 1949.

———. House. Committee on Foreign Affairs. Subcommittee on Deficiency Appropriations, *Foreign Aid Appropriation Bill for 1949, Part I.* 80th Cong., 2nd Sess., May 3–8, 10, 15, 1948, 730–731.

———. House Committee on International Relations. *Extension and Revision of Overseas Private Investment Corporation Programs.* 95th Cong., 1st Sess., June 21, 23, July 19–21, September 8, 12, 16, 1977.

———. House. Committee on Interstate and Foreign Commerce. Subcommittee on Public Health and Welfare, *Prohibit Certain No-Deposit, No-Return Containers,* 91st Cong., 2nd Sess., September 18, 1970.

———. House. Committee on Ways and Means. Subcommittee on Trade. *Written Comments on Certain Tariff and Trade Bills, Volume III.* 100th Cong., 2nd Sess., February 5, 1998.

————. House. Committee on Ways and Means. *Tariff Hearings, 1896–97, Vol.* 1. 54th Cong., 2nd Sess., December 28, 30, 31, 1896, and January 4, 5, 8, 9, 11, 1897.

————. Senate. Committee on Appropriations. *Economic Cooperation Administration.* 80th Cong., 2nd Sess., May 13, 1948.

————. Senate. Committee on Commerce, Science, and Transportation. *Reuse and Recycling Act of 1979.* 96th Cong., 2nd Sess., March 3, 1980.

————. Senate. Committee on Commerce, Science, and Transportation. Subcommittee for Consumers. *Beverage Container Reuse and Recycling Act of 1977.* 95th Cong., 1st Sess., January, 25, 26, 27, 1978.

————. Senate. Committee on Commerce, Science, and Transportation. Subcommittee on Science, Technology, and Space. *Materials Policy.* 95th Cong., 1st Sess., July 14, 19, 1977.

————. Senate. Committee on Commerce. Subcommittee on Environment. *Nonreturnable Beverage Container Prohibition Act.* 93rd Cong., 2nd Sess., May 6, 7, 1974.

————. Senate. Committee on Commerce. Subcommittee on Environment. *Solid Waste Management Act of 1972.* 92nd Cong., 2nd Sess., March 6, 10, 13, 1972.

————. Senate. Committee on Energy and Natural Resources. *Recycling.* 102nd Cong., 2nd Sess., September 17, 1992.

————. Senate. Committee on Finance. *Schedule A: Duties on Chemicals, Oils, and Paints.* 62nd Cong., 2nd Sess., March 14, 15, 19–22, 1912.

————. Senate. Committee on Finance. *Tariff Act of 1921, Vol. 2. Schedule 1: Chemicals, Oils, and Paints; Schedule 2: Earths, Earthenware, and Glassware.* 67th Cong., 2nd Sess., 1921.

————. Senate. Committee on Foreign Relations. *Hearing to Receive Testimony on Overseas Private Investment Corporation Amendments Act of 1988, S. 2006.* 100th Cong., 2nd Sess., July 6, 1988, 14, 27.

————. Senate. Committee on Foreign Relations. *Overseas Private Investment Corporation,* 96th Cong., 2nd Sess., June 11–12, 1980.

————. Senate. Committee on Labor and Public Welfare. Subcommittee on Migratory Labor. *Migrant and Seasonal Farmworker Powerlessness, Part 8-C: Who Is Responsible?* 91st Cong., 2nd Sess., July 24, 1970.

————. Senate. Committee on Ways and Means. *Tariff Readjustment—1929. Vol. 1: Schedule 1: Chemical, Oils, and Paints.* 70th Cong., 2nd Sess., January 7–9, 1929.

————. Senate. Select Committee on Nutrition and Human Needs. *Hearing on Nutrition and Human Needs, Part 13C: Nutrition and Private Industry.* 90th Cong., 2nd Sess., July 30, 1969.

United States Department of Agriculture. Agriculture Factbook 2001–2002. Washington, DC, 2003. http://www.usda.gov/factbook/chapter2.pdf.

United States Department of Agriculture. Bureau of Agricultural Economics. *Sugar During World War II.* War Records Monograph 3, prepared by Roy A. Ballinger (June 1946).

————. Economic Research Service. Carbonated Beverages Per Capita Availability Spreadsheet. 2003.

————. Economic Research Service. Food Availability Data System, Beverages Data

Set. Update August 20, 2012. http://www.ers.usda.gov/data-products/food
-availability-(per-capita)-data-system.aspx#2793.

———. Economic Statistics and Cooperative Service. *A History of Sugar Marketing Through 1974.* Agricultural Economic Report No. 382, prepared by Roy A. Ballinger. Washington, DC, March 1978.

———. "Feed Grains: Background for 1995 Farm Legislation." Agricultural Economic Report No. AER714, prepared by William Lin, Peter Riley, and Sam Evans (April 1995).

——— *Trends in the United States Sugar Industry: Production Processing Marketing.* Washington, DC: USGPO, 1958.

Fifth Report to Congress of the Economic Cooperation Administration, for the Period April 3–June 20, 1949. Washington, DC: USGPO, 1950.

Sixth Report to Congress of the Economic Cooperation Administration, for the Quarter Ended September 30, 1949. Washington, DC: USGPO, 1950.

Seventh Report to Congress of the Economic Cooperation Administration, for the Quarter Ended December 31, 1949. Washington, DC: USGPO, 1950.

United States Department of Transportation. Pipeline and Hazardous Materials Safety Administration (PHMSA). Notice of Probable Violation to Respondent, Coca-Cola Enterprises. Docket #PHMSA-2006-24464, April 1, 2006.

United States Environmental Protection Agency (EPA). *Clean Water and Drinking Water Infrastructure Gap Analysis Report.* Washington, DC: USGPO, September 2002.

———. *Municipal Solid Waste Generation, Recycling, and Disposal in the United States: Facts and Figures for 2012.* Washington, DC: USGPO, 2013.

———. *Municipal Solid Waste in the United States: 2009 Facts and Figures.* Washington, DC: USGPO, 2010.

———. *Resource and Environmental Profile Analysis of Nine Beverage Container Alternatives.* Washington, DC: USGPO, 1974.

United States Government Accountability Office (GAO). *Recycling: Additional Efforts Could Increase Municipal Recycling.* Washington, DC: GAO, 2006.

United States Government Printing Office. *Summary of Tariff Information.* Prepared for the Use of the Committee on Ways and Means, United States House of Representatives. Washington, DC: USGPO, 1920.

United States Office of Management and Budget. Fiscal Year 2013, Cuts, Consolidations, and Savings: Budget of the U.S. Government. http://www.whitehouse.gov/sites/default/files/omb/budget/fy2013/assets/ccs.pdf.

United States Office of Technology Assessment. *Materials and Energy from Municipal Waste: Resource Recovery and Recycling from Municipal Solid Waste.* Washington, DC: USGPO, 1979.

United States Resource Conservation Committee. *Committee Findings and Staff Papers on National Beverage Container Deposits.* Washington, DC: Resource Conservation Committee, 1979.

Veblen, Thorstein. *The Theory of the Leisure Class.* New York: Modern Library, 1934.

Vogt, Paul Leroy. *The Sugar Refining Industry in the United States: Its Development and Present Condition.* Philadelphia: University of Pennsylvania, 1908.

Waggaman, W. H. "Welcome, Little Fizz Water." *Collier's Weekly* 65 (January 17, 1920): 8, 22, 41.

Wagner, M. W. "Cyclamate Acceptance." *Science* 26, no. 3939 (1970): 1605.

Walth, Brent. "No Deposit, No Return: Richard Chambers, Tom McCall, and the Oregon Bottle Bill." *Oregon Historical Quarterly* 95, no. 3 (Fall 1994): 278–299.

"War Burdens of Water-Works in the United States." *American City* 19 (September 1918): 193–194.

Warman, Arturo. *Corn and Capitalism: How a Botanical Bastard Grew to Global Dominance.* Trans. Nancy L. Westrate. Chapel Hill: University of North Carolina Press, 2003.

Warren, Kenneth. *Big Steel: The First Century of the United States Steel Corporation, 1901–2001.* Pittsburgh: University of Pittsburgh Press, 2001.

Watters, Pat. *Coca-Cola: An Illustrated History.* Garden City, NY: Doubleday, 1978.

Weihrauch, W. R., and V. Diehl. "Artificial Sweeteners—Do They Bear a Carcinogenic Risk?" *Annals of Oncology* 15, no. 10 (October 2004): 1460–1465.

Wells, Bert (Chemist, Chemical Control Department, Coca-Cola Company). "Traveling Laboratory Control of Bottlers' Operation." *Journal of the American Waterworks Association* 34, no. 7 (July 1942): 1035–1041.

Weinberg, Bennett Alan, and Bonnie K. Bealer. *The World of Caffeine: The Science and Culture of the World's Most Popular Drug.* New York: Routledge, 2001.

Weinstein, James. *The Corporate Ideal in the Liberal State, 1900–1918.* Boston: Beacon Press, 1968.

Weirick, Ray F. "The Park and Boulevard System of Kansas City, Mo." *American City* 3 (November 1910): 211–218.

White, Richard. *Railroaded: The Transcontinentals and the Making of Modern America.* New York: Norton, 2011.

Wiebe, Robert. *The Search for Order, 1877–1920.* New York: Hill and Wang, 1967.

Wiley, Harvey W. *The History of a Crime Against the Food Law.* 1929; New York: Arno Press, 1976.

Williamson, Oliver E. "Strategizing, Economizing, and Economic Organization." *Strategic Management Journal* 12 (Winter Special Issue, 1991): 75–94.

———. "Transaction-Cost Economics: The Governance of Contractual Relations." *Journal of Law and Economics* 22, no. 2 (October 1979): 233–261.

Winpenny, Thomas R. "Corporate Lobbying Was No Match for the Tide of History: Hershey and Coca-Cola Battle the U.S. Sugar Tariff, 1929–1934." *Journal of Lancaster County's Historical Society* 111, no. 3 (Fall/Winter 2009/2010): 114–124.

———. "Milton S. Hershey Ventures into Cuban Sugar." *Pennsylvania History* 62, no. 4 (Fall 1995): 491–502.

Worster, Donald. *Rivers of Empire: Water, Aridity, and the Growth of the American West.* 1985; Oxford: Oxford University Press, 1992.

Young, James Harvey. *Pure Food: Securing the Federal Food and Drugs Acts of 1906.* Princeton: Princeton University Press, 1989.

———. "Three Atlanta Pharmacists." *Pharmacy in History* 31, no.1 (1989): 16–22.

———. "Three Southern Food and Drug Cases." *Journal of Southern History* 49 (February 1983): 3–36.

Young, Kenneth R. "Environmental and Social Consequences of Coca/Cocaine in Peru: Policy Alternatives and a Research Agenda." In *Dangerous Harvest: Plants and the Transformation of Indigenous Landscapes*, ed. Michael K. Steinberg, Joseph J. Hobbs, and Kent Mathewson, 153–166. Oxford: Oxford University Press, 2004.

Zerbe, Richard. "The American Sugar Refinery Company, 1887–1914: The Story of a Monopoly." *Journal of Law and Economics* 12, no. 2 (October 1969): 339–375.

Zimring, Carl A. *Cash for Your Trash: Scrap Recycling in America*. New Brunswick: Rutgers University Press, 2005.

Zorn, Dirk, Frank Dobbin, Julian Dierkes, and Man-Shan Kwok. "Managing Investors: How Finance Markets Reshaped the American Firm," in *The Sociology of Financial Markets*, ed. Karen Knorr-Letina and Alex Preda. New York: Oxford University Press, 2009.

Illustration Credits

Georgia Military Academy cadet officers, 1908. *Courtesy Robert W. Woodruff Papers, Manuscript, Archives, and Rare Book Library, Emory University.*

Vin Mariani advertisement, 1894. *Courtesy Bridgeman Art Gallery.*

Pemberton Wine of Coca advertisement, 1885. *Courtesy* Atlanta Journal-Constitution.

Employees of the Coca-Cola Company in Atlanta, Georgia, January 1899. *Courtesy Corbis.*

Coca-Cola syrup truck, Atlanta, Georgia, 1911. *Courtesy Asa Griggs Candler Papers, Manuscript, Archives, and Rare Book Library, Emory University.*

Coca-Cola bottling plant, North Carolina, date unknown. *Courtesy Corbis.*

Jawbone Siphon, Los Angeles Aqueduct. *Courtesy Milstein Division of United States History, Local History & Genealogy, The New York Public Library, Astor, Lenox and Tilden Foundations.*

Milton Hershey and Robert W. Woodruff, 1924. *Courtesy Robert W. Woodruff Papers, Manuscript, Archives, and Rare Book Library, Emory University.*

Ox carts unloading Hershey's sugarcane harvest onto railroad cars in Cuba, ca. 1924–1945. *Courtesy Hershey Community Archives, Hershey, PA.*

Monsanto caffeine plant in Norfolk, Virginia, 1948. *Monsanto Company Records, 1901-2008, University Archives, Department of Special Collections, Washington University Libraries.*

Protest at Plachimada plant, 2006. *Courtesy Sho Kasuga.*

Closed Plachimada bottling plant, 2010. *Taken by author.*

Men harvesting coca leaves near Quillabamba, Peru. *Courtesy Gustavo Gilabert/CORBIS SABA.*

SodaStream Unbottle the World Day, 2012. *Courtesy Getty Images/Donald Bowers.*

Fight against soda ban in New York, 2012. *Courtesy AP Photo/Kathy Willens*

Index